The
SEA CAPTAIN'S WIFE

Also by Martha Hodes

White Women, Black Men:
Illicit Sex in the Nineteenth-Century South

Sex, Love, Race:
Crossing Boundaries in North American History (editor)

The

SEA CAPTAIN'S WIFE

*A True Story of Love, Race, and War
in the Nineteenth Century*

MARTHA HODES

W. W. Norton & Company
New York   London

Since the copyright page cannot legibly accommodate all the credits,
pages 367–69 constitute an extension of the copyright page.

Copyright © 2006 by Martha Hodes

All rights reserved
Printed in the United States of America
First Edition

For information about permission to reproduce selections from this book,
write to Permissions, W. W. Norton & Company, Inc.,
500 Fifth Avenue, New York, NY 10110

Manufacturing by R. R. Donnelley, Bloomsburg Division
Book design by Rhea Braunstein
Production manager: Julia Druskin

Library of Congress Cataloging-in-Publication Data

Hodes, Martha Elizabeth.
The sea captain's wife : a true story of love, race, and war in the nineteenth
century / Martha Hodes. — 1st ed.
p. cm.
Includes bibliographical references and index.
ISBN-13: 978-0-393-05266-4 (hardcover)
ISBN-10: 0-393-05266-4 (hardcover)
1. Connolly, Eunice Richardson Stone, 1831–1877. 2. Women—United
States—Biography. 3. Women—United States—History—19th century—
Sources. 4. United States—History—19th century—Sources. I. Title.
HQ1413.C66 H63 2006
306.84'6097309034—dc22
2006015574

W. W. Norton & Company, Inc.
500 Fifth Avenue, New York, N.Y. 10110
www.wwnorton.com

W. W. Norton & Company Ltd.
Castle House, 75/76 Wells Street, London W1T 3QT

1 2 3 4 5 6 7 8 9 0

For Bruce, as ever

For Ryn and Tal, my sisters

and in loving memory of
Jane Allerton Cushman, 1938–2002

CONTENTS

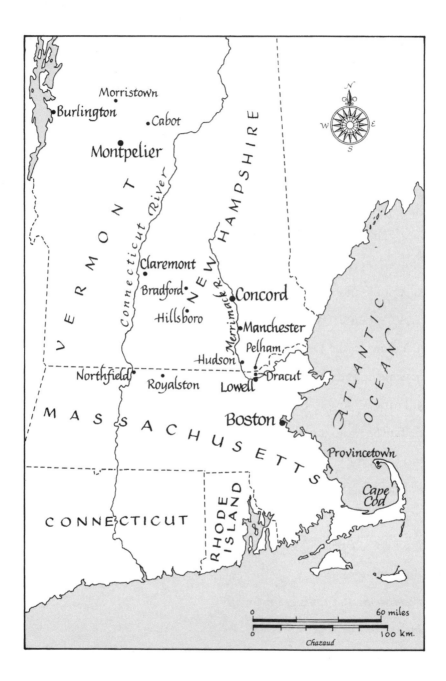

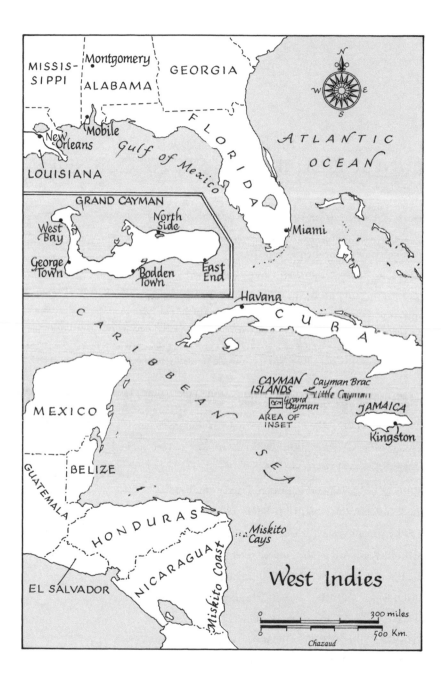

THE FAMILY OF
EUNICE RICHARDSON STONE CONNOLLY

Eunice's parents and their families

LUTHER RICHARDSON SR.: Eunice's father

LOIS (WRIGHT) RICHARDSON DAVIS: Eunice's mother

BRADLEY DAVIS: Lois (Wright) Richardson Davis's second husband

ADDIE DAVIS: Bradley Davis's daughter

MARTHA (WRIGHT) JOHNSON: Lois (Wright) Richardson Davis's sister

Eunice's siblings and their spouses

ANN (RICHARDSON) PUTNAM MCCOY: Eunice's sister

DAVID MCCOY: Ann (Richardson) Putnam McCoy's second husband

HARRIET (RICHARDSON) HARVEY ("HATTIE"): Eunice's sister

IRA HARVEY: Harriet (Richardson) Harvey's husband

JANE (RICHARDSON) LULL: Eunice's sister

WESLEY LULL: Jane (Richardson) Lull's husband

ADELIA RICHARDSON: Eunice's sister

ELLEN (RICHARDSON) MERRILL: Eunice's sister

DUDLEY D. MERRILL: Ellen (Richardson) Merrill's husband

LUTHER L. RICHARDSON JR.: Eunice's brother

CHARLES HENRY RICHARDSON ("HENRY"): Eunice's brother

CLARA (PRAY) RICHARDSON: Charles Henry Richardson's wife

Eunice's first husband and family

WILLIAM C. STONE: Eunice's husband

CLARENCE STONE: Eunice and William Stone's son

CLARA STONE: Eunice and William Stone's daughter

MELISSA (STONE) RANKIN: William Stone's sister

MOSES RANKIN: Melissa (Stone) Rankin's husband

MARGARET (STONE) RUSSELL: William Stone's sister

ALONZO RUSSELL: Margaret (Stone) Russell's husband

ALBERT RUSSELL: Margaret and Alonzo Russell's son

MARY RUSSELL: Albert Russell's wife

Eunice's second husband and family

WILLIAM SMILEY CONNOLLY ("SMILEY"): Eunice's husband

LOUISA CHARLOTTA CONNOLLY: Eunice and William Smiley Connolly's daughter

CARAMIEL CONNOLLY: Eunice and William Smiley Connolly's daughter

JOHN JARRETT CONOLLY: William Smiley Connolly's father

THOMAS DIGHTON CONOLLY ("DIGHTON"): William Smiley Connolly's half brother

JOSEPH GAMALIEL CONNOLLY ("GAMALIEL"): William Smiley Connolly's son

JOHN CORNELIUS CONNOLLY ("CORNELIUS"): William Smiley Connolly's son

THOMAS JARRETT CONNOLLY ("JARRETT"): William Smiley Connolly's son

THREE NOTES TO THE READER

I have rendered Eunice's words in italic type, and without quotation marks, in an effort to integrate her perspective more seamlessly into the story.

With the exception of minimal changes for the sake of readability, I have retained original spelling, punctuation, and grammar in all quotations from the family's letters.

Eunice's second husband spelled his last name "Connolly," whereas other family members rendered the name as "Conolly." Occasionally, people writing about Eunice and Smiley used one *n*; I have changed this for the sake of uniformity. Different descendants use different spellings.

The
SEA CAPTAIN'S WIFE

1
A STORY AND A HISTORY

I'm Nobody! Who are you?
Are you—Nobody—Too?
—Emily Dickinson

idwinter 1881, Ellen Merrill received a letter. It came from the West Indies, written by a man Ellen didn't know, and the news was bad. That was clear from the second sentence, in which the stranger spoke of "the late Mr. and Mrs. Connolly." When Ellen reached the end of the letter, she read it again, and then again, before she took out a sheet of paper. "My Dear Brother," she wrote to Henry Richardson, "I have at last succeeded in learning the fate of Mrs. Connolly and family." She asked Henry to impart the news to their mother and to their sister Ann McCoy. As Ellen signed off, she thought about dangerous weather. "We had a Storm here last week which blowd the tide in and nearly washed us away for three days." She posted the letter from Mississippi to Massachusetts.

THE HURRICANE that swirled off the Miskito Cays of Central America in September 1877 took the life of an American woman named Eunice Connolly. Eunice was an ordinary woman who led an extraordinary life by making momentous decisions within a world that offered her few choices. Eunice Richardson Stone Connolly was born white and working class in New England in 1831. She married a fellow New Englander who took her to the South and fought for the Confederacy in the Civil War, while Eunice's two brothers fought for the Union. After the war, Eunice married a well-to-do man of color and went to live in a settlement of former slaves on the British Caribbean island of Grand Cayman. This book tells her story.

I discovered Eunice in a box full of letters. Loving and hostile, revealing and mundane, the Lois Wright Richardson Davis Papers, preserved at Duke University in Durham, North Carolina, span the 1850s to the 1880s. Archivists named the collection for Eunice's mother because much of the correspondence flowed to her. Of the five hundred family letters saved from the trash heap or the fireplace, Eunice wrote about a hundred of them. Others were composed by her mother, sisters, brothers, brothers-in-law, children, second husband, and a few miscellaneous relatives and acquaintances. From all that Eunice wrote, it's clear that she received at least as many letters in return, yet the family papers contain fewer than ten pieces of correspondence addressed to her. Most of Eunice's mail was left behind somewhere, thrown out, or deliberately destroyed.

I first met Eunice in the course of researching relationships between white women and black men in the nineteenth century, but at the time I was concerned exclusively with the history of the South. Years later, with a dissertation finished and a book published, I decided to go back to Duke and look again. There were many more letters than I had remembered, hundreds more, in that brimming box, the words evenly spaced or crowded onto mostly white and cream-colored pages, the black ink long ago faded to brown. I had forgotten just how faded and hard to decipher some of Eunice's letters were, but seeing them again renewed my sense of her presence: the paper she had creased and folded, the ink she had blown dry. I transcribed forty-one letters onto my laptop that first day, and that wasn't even one folder's worth. Eunice's sister Ellen had just moved to Alabama when I had to leave. I returned later that summer, staying until Eunice, alone and poor, began to worry about the approaching New Hampshire winter of 1863. I visited again in December and stayed until Eunice's sister Ellen imparted the terrible news to their brother Henry in 1881.

Poring over the collection, I understood how unusual it was that these letters had been preserved. The middle and upper classes wrote to one another voluminously in the era before telephones became commonplace. With a ready supply of paper and ink, men and women closed deals, courted lovers, debated politics, and charted travels. Ordinary folks wrote letters too—especially in New England, where literacy rates were high—but less frequently kept their mail. Poorer families like Eunice's moved often, from one cramped set of rooms to the next, scratched on cheap paper with inferior ink, and seldom imagined their daily rounds to be of interest to anyone else. But Eunice's brother Henry, who became a successful businessman in the Appleton Mills of Lowell, Massachusetts, after the Civil War, cared about family history. He carried wartime mail back to New England, then harbored the family papers and passed them down, until the bundles of envelopes came into the possession of a great-granddaughter. One day, almost a century after Eunice's death, a gentleman knocked at her door. The young mother had fallen on hard times and called a collector who bid on valuables from old New England families. That day, she traded the letters for cash. Soon she regretted the sale, but the documents had swiftly changed hands and already proved untraceable. Twenty-five years later, I was able to tell Eunice's great-grandniece that the letters rested in the Rare Book, Manuscript, and Special Collections Library of Duke University. Purchased for their value to Civil War researchers, the Davis Papers are today preserved in optimal conditions of temperature and light, neatly arranged in that single sturdy archival box.

To write Eunice's story, I followed her from New England to the Deep South and across the Caribbean Sea, searching for clues to her daily life and changing sensibilities in the different places where she lived. Like hundreds of thousands of working-class women in the nineteenth century, Eunice rarely appears in formal historical records beyond the most commonplace documents: a birth certificate, a marriage registration, a census listing. I gleaned everything I could from vital records, city directories, and village maps, then pieced together context from town records, newspaper reports, and regimental histories. The writings of others who worked in northern mills, who visited the South from New England, or who traveled to the Caribbean in the nineteenth century shed further light, as did nineteenth-century novels about race and romantic love. Studying the Civil War, labor history, the history of women and gender, and African American and African Caribbean history also filled in the contours of Eunice's life. Finally, and unexpectedly, conversations with descendants contributed to the unfolding of Eunice's story and enriched the search for meaning within that story.

THE WORLD CHANGED enormously over the course of Eunice's life, offering her occasion to ponder the grand themes of American history: class and opportunity, faith and religious practice, slavery and freedom, politics and war, racism and equality. As the cotton mills of industrial capitalism grew denser along the riverbanks of New England in the years just after Eunice was born, the residents of rural hamlets boarded steam-powered railroad cars to visit once-remote cities. President Andrew Jackson neared the height of his popularity during those years, riding the crest of an expanding democracy that nonetheless excluded white women and all African Americans. The Protestant religious revivals of the Second Great Awakening held out spiritual equality to those who lived on the margins, inspiring both righteous and self-righteous Americans to think hard about problems like poverty and immigration. Most especially in 1831, the year of Eunice's birth, the problem of slavery loomed in the nation's consciousness. On January 1, a radical white Bostonian named William Lloyd Garrison published the first issue of the *Liberator*, echoing the call of black abolitionists for the immediate emancipation of slaves in the southern states, thereby fueling a growing debate in the young nation. That summer, a Virginia slave led the most successful and alarming uprising the South had ever known, killing fifty-five white people and citing the Bible as justification. That autumn, Nat Turner was executed. Eunice was born in December.

When Eunice toiled in the New England mills or labored as a servant, the details of her life echoed those of many other women in the nineteenth century. Her story is conventional too, in that she strived for the stability of marriage and ultimately found great comfort in the domestic sphere. But Eunice also realized her visions of happiness in a way that cast her far from conformity. In its barest outlines, hers is a story of a woman who descended into poverty and then climbed out. What makes Eunice's version of that tale unusual is that she was a white woman who rescued herself from destitution by marrying across the color line.

Eunice's story and the choices she made expose the complexities of racial classification across geographical borders. Her family traced their lineage back to England and France, but as Eunice worked in the mills and labored as a servant, she came precariously close to the degraded status of impoverished Irish and black women. Later, when she married a "man of color" (that was the phrase invoked at the time), she found out that reputation also counted in a person's racial status and that for women, whiteness depended upon specific ideas about purity. Then, when Eunice took up residence on a West Indian island, she realized that labels like "white," "black," "mulatto," and "colored" carried different meanings in different places. Eunice's story illuminates the complexities of racism too: Her unusual experiences make clear just how mercurial racial categories could be in the nineteenth century, but her life also proves just how much power those mercurial markers could exert to confine—or transform—a person's life. In her voyages from New England to the Deep South to the British Caribbean, Eunice also made a journey from the life of an impoverished white woman in the United States to the life of an elite woman of color in the West Indies.

To GIVE READERS a sense of Eunice's voice, each chapter that follows, save the final two, opens with a single letter that she composed. A great deal was at stake in the production of a letter in Eunice's day. In mid-nineteenth-century New England, a young man could board newly inaugurated rail lines to find work elsewhere for a season or forever, a bride could follow her new husband aboard a steamship sailing for the South, a father could take advantage of increasingly well-surfaced routes to scout out land far to the west. Where dirt roads, passable only in dry weather, had once kept communities fairly insular, the transportation revolution put great distances between loved ones. In a world that permitted the fast and efficient separation of people, writing a letter often became the sole means of maintaining intimacy. But writing a letter was also a formidable enterprise. For working-class people like Eunice and her family, the endeavor of sending a single piece of communication brought both frustration and satisfaction.

To begin with, time for literary production was brief. *I cant rock the cradle and write too*, Eunice warned. Or as her mother sighed, though each passing day brought the resolve to write the next, "when tomorrow came it brought its work and cares," leaving not an extra hour. The Sabbath was the most common day to repay epistolary debts, and one Sunday Eunice owed letters to her mother *and Henry and Ann and Williams folks and some of my aquaintances*, while on another, she had before her *seven unanswered letters*. With her sons in the Union Army, Eunice's mother wrote "evry sabbath," first to Luther, then to Henry, "in turn." Indeed, the Civil War years became a historical moment in which families and friends wrote unprecedented numbers of letters—to and from the battlefield but also to and from those on the home front who lived too far apart for daily or weekly get-togethers.

Before pen could be set to paper, supplies had to be gathered. For wageworkers, paper itself constituted a luxury, and space on each sheet became precious. *Dont think because I send you my refuse paper that it is any lack of respect to you*, Eunice made clear to her mother, *but I had rather send it to you than to strangers, for you know the circumstances*. As soldiers in the Union Army, Henry and Luther sent messages on whatever stock came their way: stationery distributed by northern charities, "a leaf from an old account Book," even Confederate notepaper. Ordinarily a letter ended only when the blank page ran out ("well I have about finished my paper so must close"); by the same token, filling only part of a sheet demanded an explanation (*It is a shame to waste so much paper, but I have no more sence or nonsence*). More commonly, margins and corners came crammed with messages. Sometimes Eunice resorted to crosshatching. She first filled the page, then turned the paper ninety degrees and wrote across the lines just set down. Once, in a pinch, she turned the paper upside down and filled the spaces in between each line.

Pens were always superior to pencils, though never a guarantee of flowing narration. One day, Eunice tried out a variety of implements in an effort to *find one I can write decent with but guess I shall not succeed*, she lamented, while soldier Henry rejected the steel pen his mother sent from the home front, reasoning that it was "too coarse pointed." Ink, homemade from powder mixed with water, shaken and strained, could turn equally fickle, with blotting and spilling a constant threat. From the barracks, Luther confessed that "one of the boys tipped over my ink and I have not got mutch left." Eunice's trials with a bottle of dark liquid were exacerbated one New England day when her tenement mate's young son *came in and turned my ink over into my lap and all over the side of my dress*. With the vessel nearly emptied, Eunice's vexation rose, then turned to wrath when the boy's mother shrugged off the mishap with *it aint as if your clothes were nice ones*. A crestfallen Eunice had dressed in a *delaine shirt that I think every thing of*, and the cruel remark *provoked me more than all the rest*, she wrote, as she tried for an hour to get the stains out. After all that, the final ingredients were envelopes, wax and gum for sealing, and postage. At mid-century, the writer paid three cents for a half ounce. *It costs a little every letter you know*, Eunice reminded her correspondents.

Every letter left unwritten for want of an hour, a candle, a sheet, or a pen edged Eunice's family closer to silence and invisibility, for only with time and supplies at the ready could one compose a record of a day or a week, of a successful or failed endeavor, an important opinion, a pressing sentiment. Yet the very act of writing could prove discouraging for those of little schooling. Eunice's insis-

Because paper was scarce in the Cayman Islands, Eunice turned this page upside down and wrote in between each line. Bearing the dateline "March 7, 1870, East End, Grand Cayman," the letter begins, "My own dear Mother, It is with great satisfaction that I address you now."

tence on calling the contents of her letters *nonsence* echoes a common refrain of female self-effacement in the nineteenth century (Lois sometimes characterized her own attempts as "insipid"), but Eunice also cared about the literary quality of her letters. *She writes very pretty indeed*, she once commented wistfully of a family friend. *I like her style of writing.*

In happier times, Eunice produced more skillful prose, but bitterness diminished her mastery over composition, and agitation bred the poorest grammar; that was when the *ain't*s crept in. Even in their most careful narrations, Eunice and her family employed far from perfect English, and abundant misspellings are matched by a dearth of punctuation. All too brief intervals of idle time were an added obstacle to fluent prose, not to mention fine handwriting. As Eunice's stepsister, Addie Davis, summed it up, "excuse this miserably written epistle for I have scratched it off as fast as I could." No doubt seated by meager candlelight, Eunice's aunt Martha requested simply, "do excus my writing it is evening." Of course even the most learned have been known to decry the unsatisfactory nature of words on paper. *O Mother there are so many things I want to say to you, but how can I?* Eunice wondered, echoing countless letter writers across time. *If I could see you I could talk so you would understand me better.*

Writing was more arduous for some family members than others, and brother Luther's letters proved the worst, with the sloppiest handwriting, most convoluted phrasing, and relentlessly creative spelling. But since Luther tended to write out words just as he pronounced them, his pages drop clues about the family's manner of speaking. Although Eunice wrote about doing the *washing*, she probably pronounced it the way Luther spelled it, "worshing." From Luther, we know that a watch was a "worch," citizens were "citersons," and someone who agreed with his "polerticks" was a

"Simperthiser." He even spelled "was" as "wors." Eunice's spelling improved upon Luther's, but every so often she gave away her pronunciation too, as when she wrote of *surporting* her children. She probably delivered the words "at all" as "a-tall" (rendered by Luther as "atall"), just as she would *try afinish* her work and her son, Clarence, went "a Fishing." All the sisters nearly always wrote "prehaps" for "perhaps," and that too may have reflected their articulation. All in all, such imperfections inadvertently breathe sound into the family's written record.

As for the content of the letters, all writers are influenced by what they read, and working-class men and women in Eunice's day consumed popular fiction in the form of dime novels and serialized stories marked by sentimentality and sensationalism. Henry's wartime letters make clear that soldiers in camp devoured whatever came their way (he requested "story papers" to "help to pass off the long nights when I am on guard"), but the women in Eunice's family hardly ever mentioned the act of reading, beyond the Bible. It's hard to imagine when they would have found the time, but Sundays after church and railway journeys with sleeping children might present moments of opportunity.

One Sunday evening, sister Hattie had been reading before she sat down to write to her mother, and the letter she produced faithfully imitated the pages in which she had just immersed herself. "A Lonely Hour," Hattie entitled the letter, as if composing a story herself. Glancing at the foot-high February snow, she thought of her traveling husband and crossed out the words "for he has gone with a horse & sleigh," replacing them with "& it seems to add to the lonliness of the hour." She guided her readers into "the family sitting room of a large old fashioned house," introducing them to two people singing hymns at the piano, a purring white cat, and popcorn crackling on the stove. "Hark! the outer door opens who can be coming this stormy day," she continued, as the minister arrived to join in the music making. After that, Hattie resumed more ordinary narration, and although no other letter in the Davis Papers mimics popular fiction so self-consciously, scattered words and turns of phrases across the decades likely echo contemporary literary material.

Handbooks for letter writers counseled Hattie and the others to invoke the language of conversation instead, insisting that correspondence was akin to "talking on paper," if a bit more "carefully and elegantly." Books like *How to Write: A Pocket Manual of Composition and Letter-Writing*, published at midcentury, were directed toward the middle classes, and even if Eunice and her family had skimmed such pages, they would soon have found the rules impossible to follow (choose "the best white letter paper" and leave "a broad margin on the left-hand side"). Quality and margins aside, however, few of the letters in the Davis Papers would pass muster, since spelling and punctuation mattered a great deal, the misuse of capital letters constituted a severe "blemish," and underlinings or writing in between lines were simply "objectionable." Moreover, content and mood were to be carefully controlled; those who wrote to family members were to give "warm affections their natural expression in words," a directive that assumed such affections existed or could be easily fabricated. It was "best, generally, to refrain from writing when in a gloomy or desponding state of mind," one manual instructed, for a letter should be "a storehouse of bright and happy thoughts." Fortunately Eunice and her family ignored those kinds of imperatives, leaving sadness, anger, anxiety, and foul moods unconcealed in their correspondence, at least some of the time.

Forthright as the family could be, letters are nonetheless peculiar historical documents that must also be read for what is evaded or unspoken. People's lives, and the ways in which they remember and

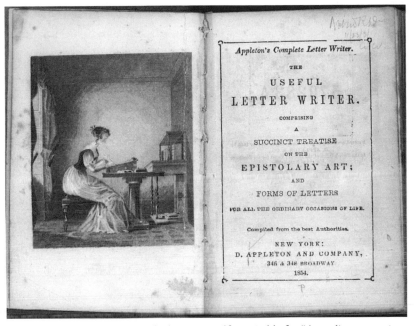

This 1854 letter-writing manual advertises itself as suitable for "the ordinary occasions of life," but the accompanying illustration of a well-dressed lady and her elegant stationery does not represent the experience of working-class correspondents like Eunice and her family.

record those lives, can never be perfect reflections of one another. The act of recounting always involves the selection of observations, the editing of emotions, even the omission of entire experiences. By choosing which episodes to dwell upon and which sentiments to impart, Eunice continually crafted a particular account of her life. Sometimes, after recording her innermost thoughts, she would destroy the evidence—maybe her words didn't ring true upon rereading, or maybe their accuracy struck her as overly indulgent. *I write you a good many letters that I dont send*, she once admitted to her mother. *When I feel lonesome and bad as if I must see you, I set down and write, then the next day burn them up*. If Eunice sometimes incinerated an evening's chronicles, other times she hoped the recipient would consign her pages to the oven, like when she imagined meddlesome relatives *poking over* a recent letter and instructed her mother to *burn it up*. Although Lois disregarded those wishes, it's likely that others faithfully carried out similar orders.

Time stolen, supplies gathered, sentences composed: After that, an unreliable postal service could render all such efforts in vain. Whereas the well-off could place their envelopes in the hands of traveling merchants or touring acquaintances for personal delivery, families like the Richardsons had few such connections. For everything it took to ready a letter for the post office, it might never arrive. As Eunice's grandfather wrote from Massachusetts to New Hampshire, "This day received a letter from you . . . wherein you say that you have repeatedly written to me, but I have never received a single line from you." During the Civil War, communications sent north were apt to be unsealed by Confederate authorities and relegated to the dead letter office. *I have written so many times since I have heard from you,* Eunice appealed from the South to New England, *but I presume you do not get them, or if you do and answear them, I never recieve yours.*

Waiting only fostered anxiety. "Have you herd from the boys or Eunice lately?" sister Ann inquired of their mother. "I want to hear so, I dont know what to do." Lack of word could mean anything, from bad weather to death. "Dear Sister," Aunt Martha wrote to Lois with greater frankness, "I received your letter in due time, very glad to know that you are living." Even those whose survival was imperiled on the battlefield worried about relatives at home. "Another Mail has just come in and not one word for me from any one," Henry cried from the war. "What in the world does it mean, are you all sick or dead?" Once, when Ellen received a letter after a very long interval, she "spoiled several sheets of paper with tears in the attempt to answer." Even a promptly delivered letter might end up lost, since house-to-house delivery came only after the Civil War and only to big cities. Indeed, writers often signed family correspondence with their last names in order to increase the odds of their efforts landing in the right hands (as Ellen discovered in Manchester, there was "another girl here by my name and she takes all my letters").

When anxiety ran its course, ire rushed in. Finding mail at the post office contributed substantially to a person's contentment, and Eunice consumed valuable paper and ink if she believed that fact forgotten. *All this long, long time I have waited, and watched for a letter from you, but I have waited in vain,* she declared from down south. *Put yourselves far away from home and friends, in conflicting times like these*—the word "friends" in nineteenth-century parlance referred to family members as well as to close acquaintances—*and see how dear, and how cheering a message from the distant loved ones at home would be.* Steamships that brought mail to Union soldiers were greeted with a similar swirl of emotions. "There never has been such a wide awake time," Luther wrote from Mississippi, "as there wors larst night when the mail came in." Yet too often there followed the same betrayed expectations. "It is provoking to keep writing and waiting for the mail to come in so you can hear from home," Henry scolded, "and then when the mail comes in have every other man in the Company get letters and papers while we have to stand around looking on and asking what the news is."

Part of the problem was that working people moved around so often, from one tenement to the next, from one job and one town to another. "How is Mother this winter & where does she live," Ann queried Henry. Or as Henry told his mother, "I would write to Eunice but I dont know where to direct a letter for her." Unknown whereabouts inevitably meant belated tidings. When Eunice's aunt offered news of a death two years' past, she explained, "we could not write you because we did not know where you was." When one of Eunice's sisters died of tuberculosis, another sister was at a loss to tell the dispatch office where to go. "I knew you had moved and did not know where," she later informed their mother. When letters did arrive, they were often shared commodities. One method was to copy over the lines ("I will write it word for word as she has rote it"); another simply to enclose the pages (Clarence *recieved a letter from Henry last week. Mother got it first and sent it to him*) or to orchestrate its forwarding (*You may send this letter to Ann if you have a chance for I shall not write particularly to her now*). From the West Indies, where postal service was most undependable, Eunice explained that a single long letter *must answer for you and Ann & Harriet & Henry and all that want to hear from me.*

Letters, like visits, did not always bring dispersed family members closer together. A piece of correspondence took so long to arrive, it took so long to answer, and return mail could be so slow that the wounds of misinterpretation had weeks or months to fester. *If you see Ann tell her that if I said any thing in any of my letters that displeased her to over look it,* Eunice once directed. Sometimes it was easier just to take back the outbursts of an honest moment. After Henry had proclaimed his feelings hurt, he ordered his mother to burn the pages "and forget the contents." Alternatively, a perfectly clear assertion might spark disagreement and conflict, even if correspondents didn't necessarily challenge one another directly; for Eunice's mother the Emancipation Proclamation was "hailed with joy," whereas Henry disdained the "accursed Abolitionists." And what did Eunice make of Henry's sarcastic boasting toward the end of the war that he had hired "a nigger—beg your pardon—a colored citizen of African descent" to shine his shoes and sword? As a one-sided conversation, a letter always posed risks. Where relationships were forced to thrive in ink, tension always lurked.

As nineteenth-century Americans journeyed from village to city, across state borders, regions, and oceans, letters both retraced their paths and trailed after them. Ideally, supplies were handy, time cooperated, and good news traveled swiftly in both directions. In reality, the stationery might be handsome, but the news bad, or the news might be happy, but the letter so belated as to have already precipitated terrible dread. Nonetheless, the ability to communicate across great expanses was often an endeavor that sustained families in the face of rapidly changing communities. "It gives me new courage evry time you write," Eunice's mother told one of her sons in the Union Army. Or as Martha reassured her sister Lois, "What a comfort that we can write to each other, and how the distance has been shortened between us." Eunice too expressed such happiness. *I recieved your kind letter Thursday Evening*, she wrote to her mother one winter day during the war. *I was very glad to hear from you.* It had been so long, she added, *that it began to worry me to know what so long a silence could mean.* Eunice didn't intend to dilute her appreciation; rather, her words alluded to the well-understood brittleness of everyday life.

The fragility of life and the hardships that precipitated that fragility constitute a theme running through the family's correspondence, apparent in their constant efforts to find work, stay warm, or visit one another across distances that today seem small. Following the birth of her daughter Clara in 1862, Eunice wrote, *If nothing happens I shall go down stairs next Sunday.* And about her new baby, *If nothing happens she will be large enough to help me some time to pay for all the sacrifices I have to make.* Those three words, "if nothing happens," oft repeated in the letters, point to a sense of pervasive peril in the lives of struggling people in the nineteenth century.

Indeed, countless mundane activities merited reflections on the proximity of disaster. On knitting a pair of stockings, Eunice wrote, *I shall get them done if nothing happens*; on making a dress, *shall try to finish it to day if nothing happens*; on determining holiday plans, *if nothing happens I shall be with you*. Other times, the hazards of human existence were noted with yet greater candidness. When Eunice contemplated a visit back north from the Deep South, she planned to travel, she wrote, *if I live till another summer*. Even the most prosaic circumstances might prompt reflections on one's demise. When Eunice asked her mother to save an old black hat for her, she added that she would wear it for another winter, *if I live*. Over and over, Eunice's ink leaked that conventional phrase of nineteenth-century correspondence. On her son, Clarence: *He has got to get used to disapointments in life if he lives*. On where to reside: *I can spend the Winter with you, if I live*. And then, doubting that decision: *I dont know yet what I shall do if I live*.

THE DAVIS PAPERS seemed so promising at first, yet like so many historical documents thick with words, they proved also, in many ways, resolutely mute. In each phase of Eunice's life, it turned out, one pivotal question remained unanswerable in any definitive way. How did she judge the Irish immigrants who worked alongside her in the New England mills? What opinions did she formulate about slavery when she lived in the Deep South? What did it mean to her that her husband fought for the South during the Civil War? How did she make sense of race in the British Caribbean? Eunice's letters never expounded, in any concerted manner, upon any of those issues. As for the details of her life, the greatest mystery remains where and how she met the West Indian man whom she married after the Civil War, for the historical sources are entirely unyielding on that point.

A Richardson family descendant labeled this photograph "Gm. Davis?/63?," but the woman is too young to be grandmother Lois Davis, and the archivist at Duke University relabeled the photograph "Eunice Stone? ca. 1863" (the middle-parted hairstyle, plain calico dress, and band collar fastened with a brooch date the photograph to the 1860s). Either an ornate frame was placed in front of the subject, or the tintype photograph was placed inside a decorative mat.

Before I left Duke University after transcribing the last letters in the collection, I looked again at one of the photographs. Sometime in the past, someone had written on the back, "Gm Davis?/63." Whichever descendant believed this to be a likeness of Grandmother Davis, the archivist understood that the woman was too young to be Eunice's mother, Lois Davis, in 1863, and so added in pencil, "Eunice Stone? ca. 1863." Taken in a professional studio on Merrimack Street in Lowell, Massachusetts, the vignette or gem portrait (likely a tintype, resilient and cheap to produce in multiple copies) displays a woman with dark hair parted in the middle and wearing a band collar fastened at the throat with a brooch. The long exposure time of early photography required one to sit immobile, so that the camera appears to have caught Eunice in a blank stare. Or maybe she simply wished to guard her thoughts and emotions before the lens.

Indeed, not once did Eunice—or anyone in the family—imagine that a scholar in a university library would study her letters or reconstruct her travels more than a century after her death, much less that readers would find her words and thoughts printed in a book. In the course of researching Eunice's life, I therefore came to understand that secrets of circumstance and sentiment are as important to Eunice's story as everything revealed in the historical documents. Eunice told her own story in the letters she wrote, her voice growing bolder across the years of hardship and loss. Then, from the West Indies, she narrated her life with newfound confidence, even as others hoped that her scandalous actions would be erased from the record and forgotten in family history. Although I set out to learn as much as I possibly could about Eunice, I also wanted to respect the archival record that she and her family helped to create, including all that they intentionally omitted or purged, for the consequences of those actions are also part of Eunice's story. Although at times I have extrapolated beyond the most literal evidence of the letters, I have invented nothing; instead, I invoke words like "perhaps," "maybe," and "probably" where it is impossible to know precisely what came to pass or how people felt. In place of fiction, I offer the craft of history, assisted by the art of speculation.

I open the text of each chapter that follows, again save the last two, with a brief act of historical imagination, conjuring Eunice's surroundings when she lived in the towns and villages of northern New England, the southern city where she was sojourning when the Civil War broke out, and the remote Caribbean island where she ultimately found a measure of happiness. Historical actors know more about their own lives than those who write about them ever can, yet historians often grasp more about the context and meaning of those lives than can the actors themselves. Because I have fashioned out of Eunice's life and letters a significance beyond her own vision, I can claim only that this is the story of Eunice Connolly as I have understood and distilled it. In the pages that follow, I have tried always to be faithful to Eunice's presentation of experience, even as I have discerned a deeper historical significance for her life.

14/1 Manchester April 15 /60

Dear Brother

I recieved
your letter Wednesday evening which
was the Night before Fast. I am much
obliged to you for being so prompt in
answering my letter. you seem to
to be having a good time and enjoying
yourself generally I think. well I
am glad of it I like to have young people
be young people. I want very much to
see you if I could leave I think I
would come to your place and make
you a visit. but I dont know as
I can at present. are you boarding in
a boarding house or a private family.

2
A CARPENTER'S WIFE

Manchester, New Hampshire, April 15, 1860

Dear Brother

I recieved your letter Wednesday Evening which was the Night before Last. I am much obliged to you for being so prompt in answering my letter. You seem to be having a good time and enjoying yourself generally I think. Well I am glad of it. I like to have <u>young people be young people</u>. *I want very much to see you if I could leave. I think I would come to your place and make you a visit, but I dont know as I can at present. Are you boarding in a boarding house or a private family. I hope you are steady and keep good Company. You spoke of going to a Ball. Do you dance? Well we must enjoy life as we go along. Do not carry dancing to an excess so it will be an injury to you. What I mean is do not indulge in such things when you work hard to undermine your health. Now you will laugh Luther, but I have lived a few more years than you have and seen the ways of the world more. I am anxious that you should be some body in the world. If a Sisters prayers and anxiety would accomplish it then you will be. But that will not do it with out an effort on your part. I should like to know about your work. Is it any like weaving in a Cotton Mill? O how I wish you was up here to work, how pleasant it would be. Would'nt it? By the way do you make the aquaintance of any of the young Ladies? I have told the girls where I board about my*

Brother till they are all dying to see you. One black eyed damsel sitting here wants to know if I am writing to my Brother. I told her I was. O she says give my love to him so here it is "accept the love of Miss S. J. Smith." Now what have you to say in return. You can surly thank her if you can not send your love. By the way I have promised you to this same girl, no harm done I hope. Oh well fun is fun and you know I am as full of fun as an Egg is full of Meat. Do you go to Church any? If so where do you go to what denomination? It rained last Sabbath so I did not go and to day has been very cold and windy and I have not been out of the house all day. I thought by the way you wrote that you did not intend to stay long where you are. What do you think of doing? Let me know if you do change your situation please, and what you are doing. Write again soon, you do not know how much real pleasure it gives me to recieve a letter from you. How I do want to see you. Write all about your self when you write and do not neglect to write to me. What is the use Luther of a Brother & Sister living so near as we do and know so little of each other, and only think of it, only hear from each other once or twice in a year. It is ridiculous I think. Write as soon as convenient or I shall be giving you a Certain Lecture. Accept this from a loving Sister to a much loved Brother.

E. L. Stone

To conjure Eunice's life in Manchester, New Hampshire, in the 1850s, look to the remnants of the Amoskeag Manufacturing Company that dominated her landscape. Today, viewed from afar, the buildings retain their impressive stature, standing attentively in red-brick rows evenly punctuated by windows, chimneys, and dormers. Take a closer look, though, and you can see the covered windows and hollow bell tower of the mills and the peeling paint and cracked cement of the workers' tenements where Eunice once boarded. After the Civil War, laborers at the Amoskeag (pronounced A´-mos-kag) spun sixty million miles of yarn a year, and by the turn of the twentieth century the Amoskeag was the largest textile manufacturer in the world. But the corporation shut down during the Depression, and Interstate 93 later razed many of the city's historic structures, with so-called urban renewal bringing vacant expanses in their wake. Revitalization is just now beginning to brighten the edges of Manchester, with the recently opened Millyard Museum earnestly guiding visitors to imagine the past.

Eunice moved to Manchester with her family during part of its first great construction boom, and to a newcomer the city appeared "a magnificent specimen of the enterprise and skill of the New England people," as one early gazetteer put it. Any traces of the house where Eunice's mother lived at 18 Hanover Street have since been buried in the handsome brick and sandstone buildings of the Harrington-Smith Block dating from the 1880s, but Eunice surely walked through Concord Square and cast her glance upon the Gothic Revival City Hall at Elm and Hanover streets. If there were days, as the autumn air crackled or winter gave in to spring, when the pealing factory bells seemed to hearken uplift and advancement, Eunice's years in Manchester yielded more uncertainty than assurance and much more disappointment than promise.

Eunice's life began unremarkably, no different from the lives of thousands of other New Englanders in the nineteenth century. It was the national crisis of slavery and the outbreak of the Civil War that prompted her to make decisions that ultimately cast her as an extraordinary woman. Of course, even as slavery began to fracture the nation in the 1850s, Eunice couldn't foresee the whole of what was to come. For one thing, the world around her was transforming in so many ways that it was hard to separate the different forces of change. For another, the Richardson family's own set of fractures at mid-century sometimes obscured national affairs.

EUNICE LOUENSA RICHARDSON was a Yankee. Born white and free in New England to New England parents in 1831, she could trace her ancestors back to colonial America. Hard work and the hope of upward mobility animate the family's story, though wealth found no place among the leaves of their genealogy. Eunice came to the city of Manchester from the tiny western Massachusetts town of North-field, near the New Hampshire border, where her mother had been born in 1805. The meadows and fertile plains just east of the Connecticut River had attracted white settlers in the early seven-teenth century, Lois Wright's ancestors among them. The ancestors of Luther Richardson, Eunice's father, had settled in Massachusetts in the 1600s too. His father had ventured north to Vermont, where Luther was born in 1804, but eventually returned the family to his native Royalston, Massachusetts, about fifteen miles east of North-field. In 1826, Lois Wright wed Luther Richardson.

All of Lois and Luther's children were born in the farming village of Northfield. Ann arrived in 1828, followed by Harriet (called Hattie). Less than two years later, Eunice was born. Then came Jane and Adelia, both of whom would die young, Adelia at fifteen, Jane at twenty-three. Ellen was the last of the sisters, ten years younger than Ann. After that came the first son, Luther junior, and two years later, in 1843, the last child, Charles Henry (called Henry). Among the siblings, Eunice grew up to be the most expressive of her emotions, whereas Ellen worked hardest at pushing her feelings away. Ann, the eldest, turned out to be the most serious, and Luther junior by far the most carefree—or the most irresponsible; if anyone in the family distrusted the promise of American upward mobility, it was he. Hattie and Henry, by contrast, grew up to be the strong-willed and judgmental ones, and it was they who were to climb the farthest out of poverty. Eunice too eventually climbed out of poverty, though not by following any predictable path.

Over the course of Eunice's girlhood, the Richardson family directly experienced the most significant effect of all the changes going on around them: Men's traditional authority began to erode. Luther Richardson Sr. had brought few resources to his marriage. New England fathers who passed property to their male heirs divided and subdivided plots of land, until a son, or a pair of brothers, or a whole generation inherited meager parcels or nothing at all. Some of the empty-handed learned a trade; some claimed land farther north or out west; others struck out for the cities. Luther Richardson worked in a sawmill, hoping eventually to acquire arable acres, but as he became a father himself in the late 1820s, the very nature of rural life had already changed with surprising rapidity.

New England villages in the 1830s and 1840s balanced on the brink of disruption. During Eunice's childhood, her mother cleaned, cooked, baked, planted vegetables, sewed, mended, cared for the children, and taught her daughters all those skills. Farmers planted hay, rye, oats, hops, and corn; families raised farm animals, tended fruit orchards, and traded with one another in town. During the walk to school or in the course of daily errands, young Eunice passed artisans' workshops and small manufactories, where men and boys made barrels and bricks, shoes and saddles, cabinets and nails, plows and wagons. At the sawmill, men cut trees into lumber; at the gristmill, they ground grain into flour. Northfield residents (all claimed exclusive English descent and Congregationalist roots) gathered at the post office or village store; women quilted at one another's homes; men drank together at the tavern. Neighbors took care of each other, but they also meddled, gossiped, argued, and slandered. Meanwhile the weekly horse-drawn stagecoach to and from Boston brought into town new items, which villagers exchanged for their surplus livestock, tanned leather, or distilled liquor. As she grew up, Eunice saw cash assume a more prominent place in local dealings. Unlike barter, money worked to the advantage of storekeepers, who could purchase more goods to sell at a profit.

Luther Richardson Sr. owned only a scant patch of land in Northfield, and his wife and daughters probably contributed to the family's livelihood by way of outwork; spinning finished yarn into cloth on handlooms at home was the earliest form of wage earning for Yankee women. Lois and the older daughters probably also supplemented Luther senior's unsteady cash wages by making and selling butter and cheese or braiding straw hats. Luther often went away to find work, then remained absent for extended periods of time ("you was deprived of a Father almost in your infancy," Lois wrote to her son Henry, born in 1843). Families in the rural North welcomed the beginnings of industrial capitalism—paved roads and railroad stations, markets to trade farm products, and stores that sold them ready-made goods—but they also experienced the breaking apart of once-insular communities. Husbands and sons left villages; wives and daughters stayed behind or followed the men to mill towns to join a newly industrial workforce. Some women found unforeseen independence, others greater hardship, and sometimes one came with the other.

By the mid-1840s, Luther Richardson owned only a single cow—he had lost even his negligible parcel of land—and in 1845 he packed up his family and took them to Manchester. Some of the rural folk who struck out for mill towns like Manchester or Lowell painted a bright picture. Factory work offered ready money, and operatives toiled as few as thirteen hours a day, with Sundays off. That compared favorably with a farm family's daily dawn-to-dusk exertions, and even more favorably when compared with living off dwindling crops and pastures.

As New Englanders moved from farm to factory, whole families left the countryside to find wagework, and the shift from used-up homestead to expanding city held the assurance of a fresh beginning. A skilled artisan who displayed steady habits might enter the merchant class, and if he climbed from worker to employer, his daughter had a better chance of finding a husband within those ranks. A woman who departed the family farm for a stint in the textile mills likewise welcomed both wages and autonomy. Indeed, without enough land, households became increasingly dependent upon the labor and wages of women and girls, and this newfound measure of female independence threatened family patriarchs. Then, in the city, families became part of a labor system that favored women and children for millwork, further challenging the power of men like Luther senior. Those challenges, in countryside and city alike, could easily precipitate a family's breakup, since a landless man had fewer economic roots to sever. Railroads made it possible to travel greater distances from home, and industrialization made it easier for semiskilled or unskilled men to find work anywhere.

Lois's explanation for the uprooting no doubt echoed that of another New England woman who wrote of "the hard times to get aliving off the farm" for such a "large famely." But labor and ambition came coupled with the persistent reality of economic descent for most who turned their backs on worn-out farmland to face the expanding urban centers of industrialism. A newly capitalist economy by its very nature favored the few, leaving many permanently landless and struggling to survive on low wages or desperate to find work at all. The Richardsons were no exception. Even as they faltered, though, Eunice and her family interpreted their own circum-

stances—the hopes they harbored and the decisions they reached—
in light of the mythology of economic opportunity for all. To be
sure, they never plunged into the ranks of the poorest of the poor.
The men didn't dig canals or work on the docks, the children never
picked rags or swept cinders, nor did the women resort to prostitution or the almshouse. Yet the first tensions between aspiration and
reality became manifest for them within Manchester's city limits,
and for a long time afterward Eunice's aspirations were checked by
disappointment and loss.

ON THE BANKS of the Merrimack River, the roar of the Amoskeag
Falls echoed for miles—Henry David Thoreau wrote that the cas-
cades "foamed and fumed as purely, and boomed as savagely and
impressively, as a mountain torrent." That forcefully flowing water
allowed wage earners to change raw cotton into finished fabric in
astounding quantities, and New England entrepreneurs built the
nation's industry in cloth out of waterfalls and capital, looms and
labor. Across the ocean, Manchester, England, already claimed title
as the world's largest textile center. The power loom was invented
there in the eighteenth century, and in 1810 American visionaries
appropriated that city's name for their own riverside settlement in
New Hampshire, at the time (as one resident recalled) "hardly more
than a worthless sandbank."

　　While Thomas Jefferson exalted the independent farmer, picturing
a nation void of the poverty that accompanied British industrialization, American captains of industry deftly twisted the Jeffersonian
dream to their own ends, extolling the factory that transformed pastoral landscapes into productive terrain. In 1831, the year of Eunice's
birth, a coterie of Boston businessmen took over canal companies in
Manchester, purchased ample acreage, acquired water rights, incorpo-

The roaring Amoskeag Falls transformed Manchester, New Hampshire, from sand-bank to mill town in the early nineteenth century.

rated themselves as the Amoskeag Manufacturing Company, and pro-ceeded to construct a city around their enterprise.

Along the east bank of the Merrimack stretched the buildings of the millyard, its bell towers situated to rise within view of pedestri-ans on any street. Manchester's magnates knew that farmers kept time by the sun and the seasons; audible chimes would be necessary to orient new arrivals from the countryside to the unvaried, year-round tempo of factory labor. Time, after all, was more and more interchangeable with money, as hours and minutes were counted, saved, and spent.

Marching uphill, set perpendicular to the factory structures, came rows of long red-brick boardinghouses for the workers, fash-ioned in conservative Greek Revival style. Their design was elegant, stepped to accommodate the sloping land, with paired chimneys, gabled dormers, and raking eaves. Wooden privy sheds lined the back of every block, with each spacious yard enclosed by a picket fence and stone posts. Mapping status onto the land, hilltops were reserved for the houses and well-tended gardens of the overseers. In the streets beyond, the company carved out public squares, auctioned off plots, and donated property for churches. At midcentury, with a population of nearly fourteen thousand, Manchester was the largest city in New Hampshire, and the young women who wrote home to their farm families described their new surroundings as "clean" and "prety." All in all, the earliest arrivals saw an orderly and snugly enclosed townscape.

Ticking, drillings, sheetings, shirtings, denims, and flannels: Girls and women produced these coarse goods from bales of cotton planted and harvested by slaves down south. At the Exhibition of the Works of Industry of All Nations, held at the London World's Fair in 1851, Manchester, New Hampshire, took home first prize for cotton fabrics. The volume of the city's textile production was surpassed in New England only by Lowell, down the curving Merrimack River in Massachusetts. The builders of Manchester had copied Lowell's urban planning, then watched their accomplishment become a model for the future. Workers in Manchester's woolen mills turned out delaine and cashmere, while in the machine shop, men and boys made equipment for the mills, as well as locomotives and fire engines for export overseas. Later they turned out Springfield muskets for the Union Army.

Eunice turned fourteen in 1845, the year the family moved to Manchester, and it's not unlikely that she went straight into the mills, seeking to replace the lost wages of her father. By that time, the Amoskeag dominated the city, and labor itself had become a commodity that workers sold and factory owners bought. Now girls and women entered the ranks of wage earners in substantial numbers for the first time. They also petitioned and went on strike, demanding better pay and conditions, likening themselves to southern slaves. "We have to labor from thirteen to fourteen hours per day," one Manchester agitator asserted, "before the sound of the bell, like the slavedriver's whip hurries us to our work, there to toil like the slave himself." One laborers' resolution plainly matched "Corporation Tyranny" to "Southern Slavery," and operatives spoke of bondage across the nation, proclaiming that "Slave-driverism at the South and Overseerism at the North is one and the same thing."

Then, on a hopeful autumn day in 1849, Eunice became the wife of William C. Stone, a carpenter. Like most New England women, Eunice married within her own station. Her father worked in a sawmill; the men on her mother's side were farmers, carpenters, shoemakers, or hired laborers. A few ventured west to the prairies or dug for gold in California. Like Eunice's mother, their wives struggled to match low wages to high prices. For Yankee daughters, marriage represented a means of betterment, and mill girls tended to imagine future husbands rescuing them from the spinning or weaving room. ("Now soon you'll see me married / And settled with a man," one popular ditty taunted. "Then I'll say to all you factory girls / Come and see me when you can.") William Stone had traveled south and east to Manchester from Claremont, another New Hampshire mill town. Maybe he crossed paths with Eunice's father at the sawmill and understood how keenly and immediately one of Luther's daughters needed a husband. Or maybe Eunice and William met at church. The Stones were Congregationalists and Universalists; the Richardsons were Congregationalists, though Eunice found herself drawn to Universalism. In any case, if Eunice was working in the mill that year, she quit, since wifehood was meant to make female wages unnecessary.

When one young woman in the Amoskeag mills mentioned a beau in a letter home, the return mail arrived thick with inquiries. "Is he industrious?" her country relatives wanted to know. "Is he economical? Does he save his wages?" Eunice surely had to answer similar queries about William, for matrimony defined an economic relationship as much as anything else. According to Christian doctrine and Anglo-American law alike, a wife enjoyed the privilege of dependence upon her husband: She served, he provided and protected. If romance mattered to Eunice and William, there is no record of it. Eunice was lucky to be marrying an artisan rather than a factory worker, and on that October day when she transferred her identity from daughter to wife, she imagined herself en route to the security and respectability of a comfortable domestic life. But William Stone, like Luther Richardson Sr. had trouble fulfilling his part of the bargain. The couple would at first board with Eunice's parents, while William worked as a wheelwright. Eunice was seventeen years old when she became a carpenter's wife, and her marriage to William became the part of her story marked first by expectation, then by blighted hope.

TWO YEARS LATER, Eunice's father left her mother for good. It was to be the first in a sequence of separations that the Richardsons—and Eunice in particular—were to endure. Luther senior had brought his family to the city, but his shadowy presence at home in Manchester in the late 1840s explains why Eunice married at a younger than usual age, why her sisters Hattie and Jane married during those same years, and why sister Ellen also married at seventeen, likely without their father's permission or even his attendance. In 1851, Luther probably left to find work once again and this time never came back. Abandonment was hard on those left behind, not only because neighbors alternately pitied and gossiped but also because without a man's resources, working-class families suffered yet more. It wasn't so much that Lois had to find employment (she already took in boarders and probably sewed for cash) as that men drew better pay, and so desertion brought a woman and her children closer to poverty in an economy where survival was newly dependent upon wages. When Luther deserted, he and Lois had been married for twenty-five years, and she was devastated.

Practically speaking, Lois needed her husband, and soon after Luther senior left for the last time, she hired a lawyer, who located him working at a sawmill in a nearby town—and married to a woman who had several children. For Lois, humiliation mixed with distress. Luther had been her "young hearts first Love," she mourned in an original poem, a meditation on romance and disillusion that mimicked the sentimental verses found in contemporary periodicals. "None no thine goodness Like the Fragrant mint," Lois wept, waxing nostalgic for bygone kindnesses, even as her beloved "sought the dark haunts of vice." How could it be, she asked, reverting to prose, that "a dear and once loved husband must be led the downward dissipated road to licenciousness, and to compleet the work of distruction on himself and family, to take to himself a fallen prostitute"—that term defined any woman judged to be immoral—"and have the sin of Bigamy upon his head?" Eunice, the young bride, watched her mother fret over her "orphans"—meaning the fatherless Luther junior and Henry, now ten and eight years old—and lament her own status as "tenfold worse than widowed."

The swirling gossip maligned Lois, maybe for driving away her husband or just for choosing a wayward man in the first place. "We have no hardness towards you nor do I believe what has been said," Lois's mother-in-law assured her from Royalston. "If I could write any thing about Luther to comfort your heart," Lois's sister up in Northfield offered, "how gladly would I do it, but I cannot." When Luther's new wife died in 1855, "in a shocking condition," "filthy & decomposed," neighbors intervened to take away the children, and then Luther married yet again "to one of the same family to live in the same filthy way," according to Lois's sister. Such a description pointedly combined dirt with vice, and Luther's wicked ways reflected poorly, if unfairly, on Lois and the children.

In the years after the desertion, the family took comfort in one another's steady company. Following the birth of their son, Clarence, in 1852, Eunice and William moved to Mast Road in the western part of Manchester, first living on their own, then boarding with William's employer, the sash manufacturer Mr. Wallace. Lois and the boys rented a tenement on Hanover Street—a "tenement" referred simply to a rented house, and Lois thought hers "beautifull" and "conveinant." Hattie lived on Hanover Street too, with her husband, Ira Harvey, a shoemaker and sawyer, and after Ellen married Dudley Merrill (he too was a carpenter), the couple took up residence on the same road as Eunice and William. Sister Ann, already widowed by the early 1850s, also lived in Manchester. Only sister Jane had moved away, joining her husband's family up in Claremont.

Soon, though, the family experienced another separation. Lois needed a man's wages, and at fifty years old she had her pick among widowed suitors in need of a woman to keep house. ("If you and i ware both Suted i should like to make a wife of you," wrote a fellow who didn't get his way.) When Lois settled on Bradley Davis in the mid-1850s, she was likely taken most by the security of his shoemaking skills. He came with children in tow and took Lois and her own boys (now fourteen and twelve) to Dracut, Massachusetts, just across the river from Lowell. At first, that didn't seem so far away, since Manchester and Lowell, those two model cities on the Merrimack, thirty-five miles apart, were so well connected. By mid-century, nine rail lines converged in Manchester, and the cars, powered by wood-burning locomotive engines, covered fifteen or twenty miles in an hour. Manchester's gleaming new train station, near Canal and Granite streets, linked arriving cars with countless transfers between rail and stagecoach, but for a working-class family, a visit nevertheless felt out of reach. "I thought of coming down to see you this summer," Ellen told her mother from Manchester in 1857, until unforeseen expenses forced her, she explained, to "stay at home and save my coppers." Travel plans thwarted by lack of money: That refrain was to echo through family correspondence across the decades.

Back in Manchester, the sisters visited one another frequently. *Ira and Harriet & Ella & Ann & Charley have been over to day and staid to supper*, Eunice recorded one time, naming her sisters and their children; *Ira and Harriet rode over after meeting and we all went up to Duds new house*, she wrote another day. They celebrated Christmas at one abode, New Year's at another. Straitened circumstances meant little time or means for more public social gatherings like sewing circles, church suppers, or temperance meetings, and in the face of a vanished father and an absent mother, living near one another eased the loneliness of hard times. Meanwhile, though, the arduousness of communication fostered new tensions. "We are all very sorry that Henry has forgotten us so quick," the ever-critical Hattie bristled from Manchester, writing to her brother Luther in Dracut. "We dont heare from him no more than if there was no such boy." Ellen, closest in age to the brothers, found herself especially downcast. "If they knew how lonesome I am sometimes and how ofn I think of them they would send me a word now and then," she sniffed.

The first letter from Eunice to be found in the family papers illuminates the troubles of an unraveling family. The occasion was the death of sister Jane from tuberculosis in 1856, only five years after the loss of sister Adelia from the same illness, and relaying the news proved a cumbersome process. Someone in Claremont had sent word to Eunice, who was *very sorry*, she wrote to Henry, *that Mother did not get a dispatch*; the messenger had required an exact address, which no one knew. Difficult too was the prospect of capturing feelings on paper. "Mother you wanted me to write about Janes death but I canot write half," Ann decided. Only in person could she tell "more of her sufferings than pen can write." Eunice, on the other hand, sat down, she told Henry, *with a heavy heart and aching head*, dipping her pen to write the *sad news* that *Dear Sister Jane is no more*. The family had *lost one of the best and most affectionate of sisters*, and Eunice felt sure that Jane was *an Angel in heaven*.

Truth was, Eunice's words papered over less pleasant sentiments. Jane had insisted to her sisters that her husband, Wesley Lull, provided a good home, but Hattie had visited, only to find Jane "keeping house in an unfinished chamber" with only "two or three old cracked plates that was Lulls Mothers." Distance had strained Jane's relations with the family, and the bitterness heightened when the news of Lois's remarriage reached her through other sources. "Dear Mother if you will permit me to adress you thus," she greeted Lois. "If not I will say my Dear Mrs. Davis for I under stand that this is your title altho you have neglected me so and never so much as dropped me so much as one word." Gossipers, Jane worried, would "say that they gess my folks dont care much a boute me, and I know they dont." As for her brothers and sisters, "give my love to them," she directed, "and ask them if they knew that they had a sister Jane."

Such rancor lends a different meaning to Eunice's *heavy heart* and *aching head* about her *best and most affectionate* sister. Ellen proved more circumspect when she commented that Jane "has left this world of trouble and I think she is happy in another." For now, Eunice rewrote a bit of family history in the face of com-

Eunice lived in Manchester, New Hampshire, when this photograph of Elm Street, the city's main thoroughfare, was taken around 1858. Shops carried a seemingly endless variety of wares, especially in the eyes of newcomers from the countryside.

pounded losses from desertion, departure, and, again, death. Only later, when times got harder, did Eunice no longer attempt to seal away hostility and sorrow.

CHANGE FELT relentless in an industrializing city, and as the Richardsons suffered new dislocations, they tended to frame their losses as individual and personal, unable to discern the larger economic and cultural forces conspiring to break the family apart. Factories and timekeeping transformed the contours of labor, railroads brought enticing merchandise to new neighborhood shops, and crowds of migrants and immigrants arrived from the countryside and overseas. Families like the Richardsons were caught in the midst of these revolutions, trying to make sense of where they stood and who they would become.

"The city has changed a sight since you was here especially Elm and Hanover St.," Hattie wrote to Henry in 1856, and in that remark lay a world of meaning. Elm Street was Manchester's main thoroughfare, its shady blocks running north-south, parallel to the Merrimack River, with a mile's worth of elm trees planted by order of Amoskeag stockholders. To the west, company housing spread down to the water; to the east, downtown streets formed a grid. By the early 1850s, gas lamps lit up intersections until nearly midnight. Elm Street's wood and brick buildings offered residents an awesome variety of wares: confections and jewelry, handkerchiefs and hosiery. "Anyone can get anything they want if they have the money to buy with," marveled one beholder, and Hattie's commentary on change probably referred in part to such abundance. A Manchester minister asked his congregation how a young female factory worker could pass the "brilliantly illuminated show windows" filled with "ten thousand nameless necessaries and elegancies" and resist the amusements and adornments, the fortune-teller and dram seller.

Surely Hattie noticed all this, but the history of Manchester gives yet greater resonance to her plaint. For change came too in the form of strangers, specifically Irish immigrants, whose presence ultimately altered the status of struggling Yankee women like Eunice. At midcentury, the majority of Manchester residents were New England natives. They came from rural New Hampshire, from Massachusetts, Vermont, and Maine. Smaller numbers departed from Canada, England, and Scotland, and already about 10 percent of the population had sailed from Ireland. Families escaping the potato famine had flooded into Boston in the 1840s, and Irish railroad workers soon followed the freshly laid tracks north to Manchester. Irish girls and women came to find work in the mills, the city's first Roman Catholic church was under construction by 1850, and native-born Americans reacted with violence. In the summer of 1854, Manchester residents led a riot on Irish neighborhoods, but the newcomers remained undeterred. And even when

New Englanders called for stricter naturalization laws, they understood the need for an immigrant workforce in a rapidly industrializing world. By 1860, a fifth of Manchester's residents were Irish.

These same changes recast New England's political alliances, and it's not hard to figure out how the men in Eunice's family voted. New Hampshire had been a Democratic bastion before the 1850s, with the party finding its support among farmers who worked the state's rocky soil. Andrew Jackson's democratic ideas appealed as well to unskilled laborers, bringing together common white men against the inequities of rising capitalist privilege. Not surprisingly, Irish immigrants joined the Democrats too. But right around the time that the Richardson family moved to the city, the Democratic Party began to lose its grip in New Hampshire. Even with sizable worker and immigrant populations, mill towns like Manchester came to be dominated by the interests of the rising middle classes, the factory owners and businessmen who turned down Jacksonian Democracy to side with the commercial-minded Whig Party.

The Richardson brothers and brothers-in-law doubtless supported the Whigs too, despite their own precarious positions. By clinging to crafts like carpentry and shoemaking, they defined themselves less as laborers and more as artisans. They were white, native-born American men who, along with their womenfolk, believed deeply in the Protestant work ethic and the attendant promise of upward mobility. That was why the family left Northfield for Manchester, why the daughters married skilled laborers, and why the boys—especially Henry—looked ahead to greater fortunes.

Then, at mid-century, a festering controversy in the young nation became an explosive political question with immense implications for families like the Richardsons. If Irish Catholic immigrants had so recently seemed a threatening presence in northern cities, slave labor in the South now loomed as more menacing still. In the

1850s, proslavery politics came to dominate the Democratic Party, alienating a majority of its northern constituents. Northern Whigs were faltering too, and by 1854, when Congress voted to permit the extension of slavery into the west, that party collapsed for good. Antislavery, anti-Catholic politics jolted the upstart "Know-Nothing" Party to sudden success—denunciations of "rum, Romanism, and slavery" won them brief control in New Hampshire. But when they too equivocated on slavery, opportunity ripened for the recently created Republican Party. Into their ranks flowed northerners who put anti-Catholic sentiment second to the urgent containment of slavery.

It was not so much that white northerners were morally opposed to slavery—only a minority joined African Americans in that stance—as that Republicans spoke squarely to families like the Richardsons when they championed equality of opportunity and the conviction that all people must be free to sell their labor on an open market in order to move up in the world. Slavery, the party argued, debased the dignity of workers by cheapening work itself. In the North, proclaimed a popular Republican orator in 1860, "commerce and industry," "progress and enterprise" were duly fostered by "making the laborer intelligent, respectable, and aspiring." As white southerners sought to spread slavery west into the nation's new territories and states, northerners became increasingly adamant in support of "free soil, free labor, and free men." That was the newly minted slogan of the Republican Party, and while Hattie Richardson denounced the Irish immigrants of Manchester, the sectional conflict over slavery reached fever pitch across the nation.

Within these spirals of change, Eunice's visions of domesticity were about to be derailed. In the spring of 1857, as she prepared to plant an orchard on a plot of land that William had purchased in West Manchester (no doubt a small one), twenty-five-year-old Eunice pictured her husband as a landowning artisan providing a permanent home for his family. With husband and home would also come the respectability and community status available to white and native-born New England women of the middling classes. As it turned out, however, the national Panic of 1857 was already upon them. *I dont know wheather we shall build this summer or not*, Eunice now deliberated. *Some times we think we will and then we dont know what to do about it*. Men's work became more unsteady, then altogether scarce. "Business is very dull here and times are hard," Hattie reported of Manchester and the Amoskeag. "Part of the mills are stopping here and it makes help more plenty than work." William had been employed in a box shop with Ellen's husband, Dudley Merrill, but both men were laid off in the downturn. Next, William earned the unreliable wages of a day laborer—temporary jobs here and there—and was in and out of the shop again, while Eunice tried dressmaking for extra money. With enough resources, any white man and his family could head west, and William and Dudley no doubt talked over that route. *There will be some way I suppose*, Eunice held out, as the Republican press continued to insist on the inevitable rewards of diligence and frugality. Eunice and her family wanted very much to see the world the same way.

Eunice's *some way* was forecast by her sister Ellen. Dudley Merrill had been making progress on building a house, *a neat cozy little place* near the Stones. But Dudley's health was suffering, and that year's unusual cold meant he couldn't work for weeks at a time. The winter of 1857 began early, enduring thirty-two snowstorms and unprecedented numbers of below-zero days and nights. If Dudley stayed in New England, the doctor warned, "he never will see the trees leave out again." While others gazed west from New England, the Merrills looked south to warmer climes. Migrants often chose destinations where kin had ventured before, and Dudley had a brother in Alabama. If Ellen and Dudley had professed the virtues of northern free labor as recently as the election of 1856, they were now swayed by news from the South depicting good fortune for white people in a slave society. Pressing on toward economic opportunity cost the Merrills more than their Republican principles, for soon another dispersal would rend the family. By September, Ellen, Dudley, and baby Sumner had gone, to the faraway city of Mobile on the Gulf of Mexico.

For everyone else, the autumn of 1857 proved worse than the summer and winter before. *William does not have work much of the time in the Shop*, Eunice worried. *I hardly know how we shall get along if he is out of work this winter.* As chilly weather approached again, Eunice had no news to write, *only hard times and no work.* Hopes for a home of her own receded, as the Stones forfeited their newly acquired land, boarded in one place, then rented another. *I dont know but we shall break up house keeping and board out this summer*, Eunice reported one March day in 1858. "Housekeeping": In colonial America, the word had been nearly synonymous with marriage, part of an understood bargain in which the groom provided land and a home for the bride, who set up the couple's new household. For working-class folks by the mid-nineteenth century, though, the phrase "going to housekeeping" signified merely living in a residence of one's own, even a rented tenement. For the moment, Eunice and five-year-old Clarence imposed on sister Hattie or stayed with William's folks up in Claremont, but Eunice's continued summoning of that phrase over the years betrayed her yearnings for a secure home.

A chorus of possibilities and doubts now laced Eunice's letters. *We think some of going to house keeping this fall but I dont know certain as we shall*, she wrote in September. Hattie and Ira had built themselves a cottage in Bradford, north of the city, and time at their *country home* improved Eunice's health, *but still I feel as if Manchester was home after all*, she sighed. Lois too found herself moving far too frequently, as shoe factories cut into the business of independent cobblers like her new husband, making ever-cheaper rental quarters necessary. "I feel sometimes as tho I had no abiding place on earth," she wrote, in words that could be Eunice's own in years to come.

Young men in search of work floundered too, and these years were equally hard on Eunice's brothers, both under twenty in the late 1850s. In industrializing New England, an ambitious boy, white and native born, would set out to find a "place"—that meant a steady job—much preferable to the transient day labor accepted by Irish immigrant men and boys, but such positions were in short supply. Nor did the brothers have a father to follow into a trade or to rely upon during a troublesome passage. Luther junior worked in Dracut, then moved to Manchester and eventually entered the mills, working in the Amoskeag's repair shop or on the watch force, but the wages were poor. As for Henry, he found temporary work in and around Manchester—farm chores, a milk route, helping out in a sawmill—then found a job in Lowell for the winter, hoping for improvement when the ground thawed. Soon Henry secured a place in a decent-paying machine shop, and in the end, his life bore out the complacent conviction, so sternly disseminated by New England's Protestant and Yankee middle classes, that prosperity followed diligence. Looking back, the whole family could safely attribute Henry's wealth to his boyhood ambition, despite an impoverished and fatherless childhood. Luther junior, never as motivated, was never as lucky either.

Meanwhile the Richardson sisters preoccupied themselves with fears of social descent. Within unpredictable cycles of boom and bust, it became the obligation of women to shore up their families by urging righteousness upon the men. Simply put, virtue was crucial to the climb upward. *Luther*, Eunice wrote to her brother, *I think you need no other warning than our own father and the ship-*

wreck it has made of our once happy family. Keep the right company, the women insisted. Steer clear of gambling, tobacco, and liquor, they scolded. Temperance was a favorite Republican cause, and although Protestants equated habitual drunkenness with Catholic immigrants, Yankee women knew that Irishmen were not the only sinners—in fact, alcohol had likely played a role in Luther senior's downfall. *I hope you will be steady and upright in every thing,* Eunice exhorted the undependable Luther junior, reminding him of *the hearts that will bleed if you are any other way.* "Success in life depends much on the early formation of your habits," Hattie told Henry, grooming him for a lifetime of "virtue & good behavior." Ann put in: "You are both good boys and if you do not get into bad company I hope you will be good Men." Their mother added her own imperatives. "Be prudent and save your hard earnings," she cautioned, recalling how their father's behavior had ravaged the family. Virtue offered one ticket out of destitution, education another. "By all means learn to write," was Hattie's message. "Practice evenings and sundays and every time you have an oportunity." *I hope you will try and learn as much as you can while you have a chance of going to school,* Eunice preached. The women's advice and admonitions were relentless, directing the boys upward in order to ensure that they need never desert future wives and children or precipitate a *shipwreck* like the one Luther senior caused in his *once happy family.*

Accordingly, Eunice saw to it that her own son attended school as often as possible. Clarence was *round with his Book in his hand almost all the time,* she reported proudly. Indeed, Eunice and William Stone meant to make their son's life better than their own. Eunice wanted so much to spare Clarence the hardships of her fatherless brothers, but the Stones' circumstances proved complicated. Two years after the Merrills had headed to Mobile, William was forced to give up his search for work in New

England. November 1859 was a dangerous time to contemplate a move from North to South. Only a month earlier, John Brown, together with his black and white abolitionist compatriots, had raided the federal arsenal at Harpers Ferry, Virginia, in an attack on slavery that riveted the nation. Across the South, whites raged against antislavery audacity; up north, especially in New England, abolitionist messages grew ever more impassioned: The blood of enslaved human beings flowed "on the cotton, and sugar, and rice fields," thundered a New Hampshire minister. In order to remain within the ranks of skilled labor and still hoping to acquire land and a permanent home, Eunice's husband would now join the Merrills in Alabama.

Eunice and Clarence stayed behind for the time being, Eunice trying hard to renew optimism in the face of yet another separation. *I am lonesome and miss William very much indeed, but I get along very well,* she insisted. In another letter, she signed herself an *Alabama widow,* partly in jest, partly pushing away thoughts of her father's desertion. Anyway, the Merrills were planning to remain in Mobile only long enough to save for a farm back north, and Eunice imagined the same scenario for herself. She had been married a decade when William traveled south to shore up his crumbling fortunes, and the couple would spend hardly any more of their lives together—and not a single day of it in Eunice's beloved New England.

EUNICE'S SIGNATURE, rendered as "E. L. Stone," in a ledger of Amoskeag employees, serves as evidence of her dire predicament following William's departure. If her father's failures had prompted Eunice to find work at the Amoskeag fifteen years earlier, the catalyst this time was a faraway husband trying his luck at an admittedly uncertain venture. Eunice had no relatives who could lend interim support, nowhere even to reside without imposing upon other hard-pressed

Eunice worked in the mills of the Amoskeag Manufacturing Company in Manchester, New Hampshire, just before she left New England for the Deep South and just prior to the outbreak of the Civil War. The bell tower, seen in the distance, was visible and audible from all city streets, thereby keeping time for the factory workers.

family members. Providing wages, room, and board, the mills seemed the only answer.

Eunice entered the mills on March 21, 1860, an unusually warm day for early New England springtime. She was to share a bedroom with four or five other girls and women at No. 119 Amoskeag Company, one among the rows of workers' tenements just off Canal Street, with common rooms on the first floor and small sleeping chambers above (one worker described her quarters as "my little attic"). Boardinghouse mattresses were hard, and the rooms cold ("I have had to spread my clothes and shawl on the bed to keep warm," another conceded). Meals consisted of baked fish, fish soup, and fish hash, beans, biscuits, and cheese. Worst of all, children couldn't be accommodated, forcing Eunice to withstand still another fracturing of the family. Clarence, now seven years old, boarded with the widow Mehitable Quimby over in West Manchester. Although the Amoskeag Company liked to fashion itself as a surrogate family, it didn't feel that way to Eunice as she lived apart from her husband and son, while her son lived apart from both his parents.

That same March day in 1860, eleven other girls and women registered at the mill. Eight were Yankees, one hailed from New York, two from Ireland. They were among more than sixty-two thousand females working in the water-powered mills of New England that year, nearly five thousand of them in Manchester, and they were part of an ongoing shift that could scarcely be discerned in a single day's roster. During the 1830s, nearly all millworkers had been young native-born white women recruited from farm families, sojourning to riverbank cities like Manchester and Lowell in order to earn extra money prior to marriage.

Then, as waves of Irish families disembarked in Boston beginning in the 1840s, the workforce changed. "When we needed domestic servants in our towns and cities, and spademen to construct our canals and railroads," a native-born American man observed in 1858, "Ireland furnished the full supply." As industrial expansion kept pace, mill agents enlisted this new labor too, for Irish families were poor and willing to work for lower wages than Yankees. Irish girls and women pre-

On the day she entered the Amoskeag mills, Eunice signed this employee register. "L.W. 5" (under a column labeled "Room") probably refers to "lower weaving room #5"; the ditto marks in the next column indicate Manchester, New Hampshire, as her place of residence; and "119 AC" indicates that she would be living at No. 119 Amoskeag Company, a corporation boardinghouse. The last set of ditto marks indicates the date, March 21, 1860.

ferred the mills to domestic service, just as the men and boys were satisfied to refuse hard outdoor labor if the factories had room for them. The same years also brought new opportunities for better-off Yankee women, who began to take teaching positions or move west with their fathers and husbands. The first generation of Yankee operatives, those who worked only until marriage, measured themselves against women like Eunice. More fortunate Yankee daughters called their struggling sisters "low class New England girls," lumping the poorer American-born women together with Irish immigrants and blaming them all for decreasing factory wages.

If Eunice had worked in the mills before, she now noticed how the expansion of the textile industry fostered worsening conditions. Though Yankee women from better-off families were quick to blame falling wages, speedups, and stretch-outs on the presence of the poorer employees, there were other forces at work. With technological innovation and mill owners' swelling attention to mass production for maximum profit, the 1850s witnessed the debasement of all women's labor in the mills. Yet even as workers went on strike to protest exploitation, Eunice clung to the idea of climbing up and out.

Families like the Richardsons and the Stones, who found themselves slipping down the slope of industrial capitalism, began in the 1850s to emphasize their identity as free and white. As the slavery question took center stage across the nation, native-born Protestant workers likened themselves less often to faraway southern bondspeople and began instead to measure themselves favorably against the foreign-born Irish Catholics in their midst. If Eunice didn't record her sentiments about the growing Irish population around her, sister Hattie showed no such reserve. "I think Manchester has altered a good deal," Hattie reported of the city's landscape, amplifying her earlier grievance. "It seems to me the morals of the place are much corrupted," she complained, explaining that "the Streets in the center of the City seem filthy and mostly inhabited by Irish." In the face of too much "cursing, drunkness, and fighting," Hattie railed on, "the American families all seem to have moved to the outskirts of the city." The "low Irish," on the other hand, "have increased fast and remain in the old tenements while our people have erected new buildings and taken themselves out from amongst them, leaving rather a rough set." Other Yankees agreed. One factory official ordered native-born and immigrant workers segregated both in living quarters and on the shop floor since large numbers of Irish workers would "disgust the American operatives." As if to back him up, one Lowell millworker wrote disdainfully about "the forainers" and "zealous catholicks" before she flounced out of a dormitory with too many Irish roomers, hoping to find a place with "more Americans."

To be American born and of English descent was a mark of moral superiority that came with an exclusive claim to opportunity, or so hoped women like Hattie Harvey. But Hattie's insistence on her family's nationality ("our people") likely stemmed from the fact that her kin too closely resembled the harsh stereotypes of Irish immigrant families. For one thing, their father deserted his wife and children. For another, the Irishwomen so disdained by Hattie worked in the Amoskeag mills, if not alongside her sister Eunice in the weaving and dressing rooms, then nearby in the carding and spinning rooms. Working in the mills, boarding out her son, living far from a husband who had left to find work, Eunice found her circumstances had become increasingly difficult to distinguish from derogatory images of Irish immigrant women. Indeed, the problem of Luther senior only made Hattie more determined to differentiate herself and her sisters from the downtrodden Irish. "Your Father has ben dead nearly 2 years," Lois informed her sons in the spring of 1860. She offered no explanation, likely omitting from the record that Luther senior had died of drink. That excursion into vice, and the poverty that resulted, only exacerbated the whole family's strained reputation.

Manchester laborers produced more than a million yards of cloth each week in 1860, and by the time Eunice joined the workforce at the Amoskeag that year, about a quarter of all the city's millworkers were foreign born. Three-quarters of those were Irish, and tensions continued to escalate across the Northeast. The first naturalization law in the United States, enacted in 1790, extended citizenship to all "free white persons" in the new nation. Beginning with the Irish influx in the 1840s, the unexamined inclusiveness of that phrasing began to unsettle white Americans of British descent. As the concept of the "Anglo-Saxon" gained popularity, racial theorists ranked various nationalities. "Celts," for example, were white, but they might also be savages. As pseudoscientific racism found a popular audience, white Americans parsed other white people into various subcategories, only some of which they considered fit for citizenship. In this scheme, Irish Catholics—unlike people of African descent—were eligible, but native-born Americans hardly welcomed them as equals. Beginning in the 1850s, Anglo-Americans pointed to the Celtic physique as proof of innate inferiority and immutable difference. Irish people were depicted as slothful and sensual, brutish and coarse, dark-skinned, diseased, four-legged, low-browed, and wild.

These kinds of images overlapped with racist depictions of Africans and African Americans, with political cartoons apt to draw Irish people as more simian than human. One prominent New Yorker described Irishmen as bearing "prehensile paws" and likened the mourning of Irishwomen to "wailing as a score of daylight Banshees." A Congregational minister in Boston referred to Irish and Negroes (along with Indians and Mexicans) as "savage, barbarous, half-civilized" populations, and according to one Manchester newspaper in 1858, the Irish were "the offals of Europe, as little qualified to go to the ballot box as the veriest Hottentot."

In 1850, the census taker for Manchester listed one Elias Haskall living in the almshouse; his place of birth was recorded as Ireland, his color as black. A faint parenthetical jotting in another hand reads, "Error no doubt," but on the bottom of the page, the clerk who totaled the numbers added the comment, "Irish 'nigger!'" Certainly the marshal may have recorded the wrong birthplace or the wrong skin color, or maybe Haskall was born in Ireland of African descent. More probably, though, the enumerator considered this poverty-stricken Irishman no better than a black person. One Anglo-American described "the black tint of skin" in "Celtic physiognomy," and a New Hampshire newspaper called the Irish, "next to Slavery, the most dangerous and demoralizing element in our national economy," naming each one "a misfortune and curse to the country." Eunice's brother Henry later wrote home from the Civil War to express his exasperation with drilling a squad of "what we call 'wild Irishmen.'"

If working-class Yankee women like Eunice and her sisters relied on their nationality to distinguish themselves, they also relied on race. The city of Manchester contained a tiny black population of diverse origins, which had arrived from Massachusetts and Vermont, Nova Scotia and Virginia, the West Indies, England, and Spain. Native-born white men filled the ranks of merchants, physicians, bakers, blacksmiths, carpenters, and shoemakers, whereas men of African descent found no such opportunities despite Republican affirmations of equal chance. "The blacks in New England are despised and frowned down," one preacher sermonized, "not admitted to the steamboat, the omnibus, to the school-houses in Boston, or even to the meeting-house with white men; not often allowed to work in company with the whites; and so they are kept in poverty." Barred from so many occupations, including work in the mills, black men with any resources claimed the niche of barbering, passing the skills from father to son, master to apprentice. The fanciest shops served rich white gentlemen, and some Manchester barbers did well enough that their wives and daughters stayed home. But if black women needed to contribute to a family's livelihood, they found little choice beyond domestic service.

The positions of servant, washerwoman, and cook were reserved in the Northeast for Irish girls and women or for African American daughters and wives, and in this way the lives of Irish and black women intersected. (Eunice's aunt hired an "Irish girl" to help around the house, and as another Yankee wrote from Maine, "My colored girl has gone and I am without a servant.") Too many of Eunice's coworkers were Irish, but at least she didn't have to resort to cleaning other people's houses alongside Irish and black women—at least not yet.

With William scouting out the possibilities down south, Eunice spent her workdays weaving in the mills of New Hampshire. Although some facets of textile production required skill (the steps included picking, carding, drawing, spinning, winding, warping, dressing, and weaving), nearly all the work undertaken by women was repetitive, consisting principally of tending machines that accomplished the actual tasks. Weaving had always been the most highly skilled and best paid of textile factory work, and in 1860 it was still common for literate Yankee women to be assigned that task, while Irishwomen performed the lower-paying jobs of carding and spinning. As a weaver, Eunice spent her days in a cavernous space filled with rows of perhaps two hundred power looms, each worker tending several machines under the watchful eye of an overseer perched upon an elevated platform. "We go into work quarter before six in the morning," wrote another Yankee woman at the Amoskeag, "then stay until quarter of seven" in the evening. For more than sixty hours each week (including Saturdays) Eunice remained inside the factory, where operatives likened the sound of the machines to "the thunder of Niagara." As one worker told her family, "if I could only write what I think of while I am to work you would have a nice long letter but when I sit down to write I cant think of a thing." In short, the labor was mind-numbing.

When Eunice signed her name in the Amoskeag ledger on that March day in 1860, she also consented to a set of regulations spelled out in the volume's opening leaves. Employees were "not to be absent from their work without consent"; overseers must make sure that laborers were "in their places" and (in accordance with the visible bell towers) "keep a correct account of their time and work." Church attendance was mandatory. Unmarried girls and women were subject to further instruction from their families about "being a good girl" and saving "both Health & Money." Such a setting felt doubly oppressive to Eunice, a wife and mother in her late twenties, with no use for paternalist authority in the guise of corporate benevolence. Amoskeag employees customarily signed on for a year; Eunice stayed a little over two months.

Eunice laughed with her coworkers, but shop floor companionship mingled with hostilities. Sometimes it was petty, like the worker who carefully compared bonnets, noting that none was "better looking than mine." Other times it was more pronounced, like the operative who wrote home about the snobby "uper *crust*," the unmarried country girls who looked down upon those who entered the mills to ward off poverty. Whether or not Eunice participated in such conversations, her days were dull and her evenings lonely. *How many times I have wished you was up here so I could have some one to go round with and have a good time*, she sighed to brother Luther. *I want to ride horseback*, she declared one time, with a certain whimsy. *Do you know how?* She called on Clarence as often as possible, but if the overseer was short of help, visits to her son had to wait.

If Eunice had worked in the mills when her family arrived in Manchester in the 1840s, the promises of wifehood permitted her to leave. Fifteen years later, Eunice continued to draw upon the enduring mythology that portrayed marriage as the savior of factory girls, bringing a measure of levity to her companions (presumably Yankees too). *I have told the girls where I board about my Brother till they are all dying to see you*, she teased Luther. One *black eyed damsel* even offered her love, and Eunice later threatened to produce a photograph of the handsome boy, *just for fun you know*. Even as Eunice played along that marriage would deliver a working girl from factory to homestead, her own life disproved that deceptive scenario. Now she earned wages of her own, and like Luther Richardson Sr. before him, William Stone saw his authority as patriarch and provider eroding.

THE AMOSKEAG CLOTH that passed through Eunice's hands had originated as cotton planted and picked by enslaved men, women, and children in the South, shipped from southern ports like the place where Eunice's husband now lived. If the small number of black people in Manchester did not infringe upon the day-to-day lives of native-born whites (unlike the supposedly fast-increasing Irish), the fate and meaning of African Americans in the South now mattered deeply to national politics. As early as 1851, Manchester's lyceum had hosted a heated debate about slavery in which white men were begged to resume gentlemanly behavior, and through the decade the slavery question simmered, then boiled over. A few weeks before Eunice entered the mills, Abraham Lincoln had come to the city. Campaigning for the 1860 Republican presidential nomination, the Illinois politician spoke about abolition with a "force of argument that must have had a marked effect on every candid listener," according to one reporter. Though Lincoln's appearance was announced on short notice, Manchester's opera house overflowed, frequent applause interrupted his words, and the crowd departed more determined than ever "to resist the aggressions of the Slave Power to the last."

Lincoln also visited the Amoskeag mills, escorted by a young male worker. As the story came to be told, the Republican candidate shook the astonished laborer's hand, proclaiming that "'the hand of honest toil is never too grimy for Abe Lincoln to clasp.'" Here was free labor ideology at its most compelling, glorifying white working-men and women while erasing the exploitation inherent in their daily endeavors. If the men in Eunice's family earned low pay for unsteady work, if Eunice had no choice but to contribute wages, they were still free: free, unlike slaves, to sell their skills to the highest bidder on the labor market, no matter how low that bidder might send their pay plunging.

Eunice entered the mills just as tensions between North and South became most combustible. Northern white opposition to slavery continued to stem less from moral concerns about racial oppression than from fears about the degradation of free labor—more accurately termed wage labor. The fact too was that whites who railed against slavery dreaded not only competition from enslaved workers in the new territories and states of the West but also the intrusion of African Americans (whether slave or free) into their own workplaces (whether out west or back east). "I would preserve to free white labor a fair country," Pennsylvania Congressman David Wilmot declared in the late 1840s, "a rich inheritance, where the sons of toil, of my own race and own color, can live without the disgrace which association with negro slavery brings upon free labor." Association with "negro slavery" was degrading, but toiling alongside free black people was no better.

Manchester Republicans took up the cry in 1860. "You are a community of laborers," one newspaper proclaimed, without "*gen-*

tlemen who by virtue of their gentility can live in idleness." That kind of contrast between northern workers and southern slaveholders sidestepped the wealth and power of New England's factory owners, and as sectional hostilities mounted, antislavery sentiment more thoroughly obscured the conflicts between boss and employee within the borders of the industrializing North. Workers at the Amoskeag continued to strike for a ten-hour day, yet their own claims to slave status dissipated in these years. Such a comparison, one female mill operative wrote pointedly, "detracts from the dignity of the laborer." An 1860 editorial likewise appealed to "diligent" workers, lauded the "busy hum of toil heard so incessantly" in the New England air, and celebrated the chiming bells that summoned workers to the factory floor. When word of Lincoln's nomination reached Manchester in May, a jubilant demonstration ensued, complete with fireworks and banners. "Liberty and Union," read one; "Liberty, Hope of the World," proclaimed another. More and more, New Englanders distinguished their world from that of the slave South, and it was these kinds of ideals that rekindled Eunice's hopes to leave poverty behind.

Slavery was the crucial issue, but Lincoln's equivocation on racial equality only earned him wider support among white northerners. To be sure, New England had its share of radical white people, those who sided with African Americans in moral opposition to slavery, and Eunice must have noticed that they called meetings in Manchester in 1860. Abolitionism had become a formidable movement three decades earlier, but the state was slow to take up the cause. In 1835, three young black men traveled from New York City to attend a school established by abolitionists in the town of Canaan, New Hampshire. "Fourteen black boys with books in their hands set the entire Granite State crazy!" recalled the minister Alexander Crummell, for whites "could not endure what they called a 'Nigger School' on the soil of New Hampshire." Local rumors equated abolitionism with "*colored gentlemen* walking arm in arm with what ought to be *respectable white females*," prompting the town to pass a resolution swearing that "the close intimacy that exists between some of the colored boys and white females" would soon bring "an amalgamation of blood." Imagining tiny Canaan "overrun with negroes from the South," citizens employed teams of oxen to pull the school from its foundations and drop the building into a swamp. A mob drove the young scholars (Crummell was one of them) out of town. That same year, a New Hampshire radical wrote a letter to an abolitionist newspaper, boldly encouraging "amalgamation" and citing the scriptures' affirmation of a single human race. Much more representative was the Concord newspaper that described abolitionist women as hoping to "take up with 'niggers.'" Years later, after Eunice had made a decision entirely unimaginable to her in 1860, white people whispered the same kinds of words about her.

IT IS EASY to trace an unwavering line from the sectional clashes of the 1850s to the outbreak of a civil war in the spring of 1861. Warnings can be uncovered even farther back, as when a southern senator announced during the Missouri crisis in 1820 that northern determination to interfere with slavery would result in "a brother's sword crimsoned with a brother's blood." A divided nation seemed imminent even as long ago as 1787, when white southern leaders asserted that they would "sooner risk the Constitution" than abridge their right to import slaves. Conflicts over the Declaration of Independence offer hints in hindsight too. "If it is debated, whether their slaves are their property," a southern delegate threatened in 1776, "there is an end of the confederation."

If that progression appears to predict inevitable war, it didn't necessarily seem that way, even in the late 1850s. If William Stone thought about the nation's future before he left New Hampshire for Alabama, he might have discerned only a series of compromises that sealed off any possibility of disunion. Or perhaps he saw Alabama and the cotton South not as the enemy of New Hampshire and the North but rather as the provider of raw material for the textile mills that saved his wife from impoverishment. To be sure, when William joined Ellen and Dudley Merrill in Mobile in the autumn of 1859, there had already been guerrilla fighting over slavery in Kansas in 1854, as well as the recent uprising at Harpers Ferry. As John Brown walked to the gallows in 1859, he handed one of his jailers a note asserting that "the crimes of this *guilty land will* never be purged *away* but with Blood." Black and white abolitionists mourned Brown, but many northern whites also branded him a failed fanatic. Fair to say, then, that nothing told Eunice or her husband in any convincing way that northern New England and the Gulf South were about to cleave into warring states.

Or maybe, in the face of opportunity and the seeming promise of prosperity, it was just as well to ignore the warning signals. Maybe it didn't much matter since any war would be brief and the North triumphant anyway. William wrote from Mobile every week—was *doing well* and *likes it there very much*, Eunice echoed—and when he sent a gold locket with his picture inside (the ornament and photography session attested nicely to her husband's resources), she marveled at his healthy looks. That booming city in the Deep South seemed to offer, at last, a path away from economic uncertainty. Concretely, Mobile offered Eunice a way out of the oppressive conditions of the Amoskeag's weaving room and separation from her young son. Eunice had witnessed her father, one sister, and her husband unyoke themselves from the family's Manchester core, and now it was her turn. In June 1860, Eunice walked out of the mill.

Eunice and Clarence had to wait for an escort, for such a long and arduous journey wasn't to be made without a man's company. Come autumn, Eunice sorted through her meager possessions and packed presents for the Merrill children. Saying good-bye to everyone entailed traveling first from Manchester to William's relations up in Claremont, then to Dracut, and then fitting in a visit to her now-remarried sister Ann in Hudson, New Hampshire, along the way. *I dont see how we can all get to your place unless we come in the cars Tuesday night as I shall have a Trunk*, she fretted to her mother. The prospect of reunion with the Merrills and glimmers of a brighter future tempered the sadness of saying good-bye to New England.

In September, almost a year after John Brown's uprising had roiled the United States, Dudley Merrill arrived from Alabama. *I am going back with him if nothing happens*, Eunice wrote, resorting to the language of portending peril. In November, New Hampshire and the North voted Lincoln to the presidency, and the city of Manchester celebrated, while southern states pondered secession from the Union. By then Eunice and Clarence were gone, into the slave South on the brink of Civil War.

Mobile Alabama April 29th 1861......

Dear Mother:

It has been so long since we have heard from you. but I suppose it is not much use to expect letters now as times are, I have written so many times since I have heard from you. but I presume you do not get them if you do and answer them I never recieve the yours, I wrote to you and Ann both a short time since and I said then I should write no more till I heard from some of you. but I have repented, Mrs Ridley, a lady from Maine that I have become aquainted with here is going home. she will start tomorrow. and has kindly offered to take letters for me with her and mail them after she gets into the United States, so you will be pretty sure of getting this. I do so much want to go with her. but cannot now, I feel bad to have her go, we have become, very much attached to each other. she is the

3

YANKEE IN THE DEEP SOUTH

Mobile, Alabama, April 29, 1861

Dear Mother:

It has been so long since we have heard from you, but I suppose it is not much use to expect letters now as times are. I have written so many times since I have heard from you, but I preseume you do not get them or if you do and answear them I never recieve yours. I wrote to you and Ann both a short time since and I said then I should write no more till I heard from some of you, but I have repented. Mrs Ridley, a Lady from Maine that I have become aquainted with here is going home. She will start tomorrow, and has kindly offered to take letters from me with her and Mail them after she gets into the <u>United States</u>, so you will be pretty sure of getting this. I do so much want to go with her, but cannot now. I feel bad to have her go, we have become very much atached to each other. She is the only one here that I am any aquainted with, for to be plain I do not like the folks here as well as at home. They are so different. We are all pretty well. Times are pretty hard here and I suppose they are every where now. How I do want to hear from home and know where Henry is. I do not expect he is at home. I want to know too how your health is, and how you are get-ting along this Spring, and I want to know so many things, but do not expect to till this War is over. What a dreadful thing war is. I have been homesick ever since it came up. I suppose you hear all kinds of stories there *the same as we do here. Now I am with the North, all though I have to keep it to my self, but still I do not think it is right to push coercion for it will be useless, there never will be a union of feeling any more, if the North does whip the South. I never saw so much determination in my life as is here exhibited every day, and there is but one side of the question here all are agreed upon one thing, if there chance to be one that differs in thought from the rest woe unto him if he mentions it. Well I did not think of discussing the war question when I began, but nothing else is talked of here, and in fact there is nothing else to talk of. That is the business as well as the topic of the day. If the time ever comes that we can get a letter back and forth I hope you will write. Good night from Eunice*

*I*n a quiet neighborhood west of downtown, you can find the dwelling where Eunice lived when she first reached Mobile. The area was mostly rural and residential then, though growing fast. Grander homes dotted the streets, and some of the Creole-style cottages boasted gabled roofs and full-length porches, but the houses of working people were smaller and unadorned. Dudley Merrill worked in a sash and blind factory on Shell Road at Hallett Street, fashioning frames and shutters for windows and doors, and the Merrills lived in a house on the northwest corner of the same intersection. That was where William Stone stayed when he arrived in Alabama in 1859 and where Eunice and Clarence unpacked their bags in the autumn of 1860. Today part of a neighborhood of modest houses, the building has been altered and divided into apartments, but a guidebook describes it as a sash maker's residence built about 1870, noting that "This Creole cottage possibly dates earlier as the home of tenants who worked in a sash factory located on this corner in 1858." That would have been William Stone and Dudley Merrill. These were the corners that Eunice crossed and recrossed as she sought to make her home in the Deep South.

Eunice and William Stone boarded with Eunice's sister and brother-in-law Ellen and Dudley Merrill in this house at the corner of Shell and Hallett streets in Mobile, Alabama, in 1860. The sash factory where William and Dudley worked stood on another corner of the same intersection.

When Eunice traveled from Northfield to Manchester in the 1840s, she had entered a world of streetlights, factories, and immigrants. When she left Manchester for Mobile in 1860, she found a setting shockingly different from either the rural villages or the mill cities of the North. Modern-day tourism divides the city of Mobile between Confederate commemoration and African American history, and Eunice knew something of each realm during the time she lived there. She might have walked past what is now the stately Oakleigh House residence, today presented as a museum reminiscent of "Old Mobile" when "Cotton was King," or she may have come upon the community of Africatown, named for the passengers of an illegal slave ship that arrived around the same time she did. Closer to the center of town, Eunice likely strolled through Bienville Square in what is now the Dauphin Street Historic District, taking in the Italianate and Greek Revival firehouses and the imposing Roman Catholic cathedral.

Eunice had gone to work in the Manchester mills because her husband couldn't provide for his family, but when she followed William to the South, she found no reprieve from day-to-day uncertainties. The move separated her from her mother and siblings at the outbreak of the most tumultuous national event of the century, but the coming of the Civil War also forced Eunice to think hard about what mattered most for her own future and that of her child. For the first time—now living in a world of male transience, coupled with the possibility of greater female self-sufficiency—she would occupy her mind with troubling choices. It was at this moment that Eunice made the first unconventional decision of her life.

EUNICE'S SISTER Ellen was eighteen years old when she boarded the steamship *Alabamia* with her husband, Dudley, and their baby in 1857. *We hear from Nellie quite often*, Eunice reported after the Merrills left New England, using her sister's nickname. *She writes quite favourably of her new home.* "We are safe and sound in the sunny south and I think I shall like it very much," Ellen elaborated, lingering over descriptions of green leaves and robins in wintertime. "I have ben out to day and seen roses and pinks and all other kinds of garden flowers in blossom," Dudley marveled. "What do you think of that for the third day of January?" But the family back north remained unimpressed. *Would to God they might come home this spring*, Eunice pined, echoing the wishes of everyone else. Eunice could tell too that her absent sister was homesick. "You hope I am contented," Ellen wrote evenly. "I some times cast a thought behind but I do not alow myself to dwell upon it." Within the familiar tensions of written communication came confessions of loneliness. "You do not know how close I watch the ofice for a letter from some of my folks and how lonesome I feel when I get none," Ellen admitted to brother Luther, begging him to "fill the sheet with something."

Three years after the Merrills left New England and almost a year after William's departure, Eunice and Clarence followed. From Manchester, the train brought them to Boston, then to New York City, where they progressed from depot to port, to board the steamship *Star of the South* bound for Savannah, where the Georgia Central Railroad connected them to Macon. They switched for Columbus, again for Montgomery, then boarded another boat before landing in Mobile. Perhaps Eunice was thinking of life back on a New England farm when, shipboard, she reassured her mother (and herself) with the imperative to *keep up good courage*, insisting that *it will all end well*. If Eunice ever reread that letter, she would have mourned those unrealized dreams.

Mobile was a flourishing city in the 1850s, but wealth could be elusive in the South too. William Stone and Dudley Merrill had failed to thrive as artisans in industrializing New England. Fear of economic descent at home, and the promise of prosperity elsewhere, brought them to a region where white men's riches depended upon slavery. Just as New Englanders moved west in the early decades of the nineteenth century to claim land in places like Indiana and Wisconsin, so white southerners from the eastern seaboard—at the same time, and on the same quest—headed west to Alabama and Mississippi, bringing their slaves with them. All these migrants remained northerners and southerners respectively, but Eunice and her family traversed two regional boundaries in pursuit of a better life. Not only did they travel from east to west, but they also crossed the border from north to south and precisely at the moment of escalating sectional hostilities.

Approaching the Mobile waterfront, Eunice surveyed a scene

dominated by cotton. Amoskeag workers transformed thirty million pounds of white fiber into cloth in 1860 alone, and that raw substance was unmistakably the lifeblood of Eunice's new southern home. On converging waterways and railroad lines, the cotton planted and picked by Alabama slaves headed north to the mills of New England and across the Atlantic Ocean to British factories. "The great business of the town," observed the landscape designer Frederick Law Olmsted, "is the transfer of cotton," and anyone glancing toward Mobile's wharves understood what he meant. Visitors described the comings and goings of vessels piled high with "small mountains of Cotton," and when it rained, the city's gutters bore "waifs and strays of cotton to the river" until the river itself was "studded and flecked with cotton-drift floating about on its surface." Mobile merchants, it seemed to one traveler, "buy cotton, sell cotton, think cotton, eat cotton, drink cotton, and dream cotton."

Cotton sustained the city's well-to-do white people, but artisans like William Stone and Dudley Merrill stood outside the arena of plantations and ports. As carpenters, they were white workingmen in a society that equated manual labor with black slaves—Dudley's brother only rented the sash and blind factory from the wealthy James H. Daughdrill, who owned thirty-one slaves. *Any one on the street could tell you where Mr Daughdrill lived,* Eunice soon found. *He is a business man and well known any where in Mobile.* An expanding urban landscape should have offered plenty of construction work, as cotton merchants, slave dealers, and land speculators moved their families into town houses and mansions. When the Panic of 1857 hit the South, though, Mobile suffered, and when Dudley sawed off the end of a finger, it set the Merrills back some more. Trouble was, if industrialization made it hard for artisans to earn a living in the North, free black workers and slaves for hire could drive down the wages of white workers in southern cities, precisely the reason why the northern Republican Party condemned slavery as a threat to free white people. "Dear me it costes me as much for boots as it ever did and I go bare footed half the time," Ellen lamented. But bust had turned to boom by the time William arrived in 1859; "Business is good and money is plenty," Dudley could finally report. At the end of the year, he had earned a thousand dollars, and Alice Merrill was born a native Alabamian. The new decade commenced well for Ellen's family, and William Stone hoped to catch up.

From the day Eunice arrived, she wanted mail. *Write all about every thing*, she directed. *Now if some of you dont write pretty soon, I shall think you dont want to hear from me*, she let slip, wondering if her departure had precipitated any ill will. Her own most newsworthy topic was the southern sun, at least that first autumn. *It is such beautiful weather here that it does not seem possible that you can be having cold weather at home*, she bragged. *The little birds sing most beautifuly*. After New England's unforgiving soil, Eunice took pride in her luxurious harvest of garden vegetables and the profusion of flowers. *Such a sight of roses as I have got you never did see*, she went on. *You might pick a bushel basket full and they would never be missed*. Her early impressions blend with those of other northern newcomers to Mobile, like Frederick Law Olmsted (soon to design New York City's Central Park), who waxed eloquent about the magnolias and live oak, the pears, figs, bananas, and flower blossoms, whose mingled aroma "scents the whole air." To those from colder climates, the weather brought special delight. "The air is like summer," wrote a woman from Maine one January, while a European traveler rhapsodized about downtown Mobile, where "the most beautiful young orange-trees, covered with fruit, shine in the sun, and the sun, that beautiful, beneficent southern sun, shines here all day long!"

Unfamiliar yet familiar: for at the same time, Eunice couldn't help detecting some reminders of home. Olmsted likened parts of Mobile to "a thriving New England village," observing that the fanciest hotel was "kept by Boston men, with Irish servants." Indeed, there was no dearth of New England natives among prominent traders and investors, and even on their own less opulent street, the Stones and Merrills were hardly the lone Yankees. Their next-door neighbor was a Jewish schoolteacher from New Hampshire, nearby residents hailed from Maine and Canada, an Alabama-born doctor had taken a Massachusetts bride, and a Georgia woman's husband was a printer from Pennsylvania. Well-to-do Mobilians were even known to summer in Boston.

Still, Eunice noticed right away that the city was *not so clean here as it is at home*, concurring with Olmsted, who pronounced the business district "dirty, and noisy." As for Ellen, she didn't miss frostbite but found the mosquitoes unbearable. And in so many ways, cosmopolitan and international Mobile was startlingly different from home. The city's French and Spanish population dated to the colonial era, and newcomers continued to arrive, not just from the North but also from Europe. "English, French, Spanish and Italian spoken by the attendants of this Establishment," advertised the proprietor of a downtown drugstore, while a variety store sold French, German, Spanish, and Italian newspapers. A European visitor noted the facility with which Mobile's elite spoke French and Spanish, while another expressed surprise that a slave knew Spanish as well as her mistress.

The very street names—Dauphin, St. Louis, La Fayette, Bayou, Joachim—told of French and Spanish, rather than English, history. Within her own neighborhood, Eunice could have made the acquaintance of a cabinetmaker from France and a dyer from Russia. Walking west on Shell Road, she would have encountered slave-owning Europeans, while down on the docks, men from Britain, France,

Sardinia, Sweden, and Finland streamed from a sailor's boarding-house. (When the war came, Mobilians gathered into an array of "for-eign" companies to defend the Confederacy, including English, Irish, Scots, French, Spanish, and German.) Of course it wasn't only the foreigners who seemed strange to Eunice. A New England teacher thought her American neighbors in the South spoke "very queerly," with their refrains of "I reckon," "mighty good," and "right smart." No doubt Eunice agreed.

COTTON, WINTER FLOWERS, outsiders, and southern accents: All these appeared different to Eunice, but nothing felt so different from New England as the workings of slavery and race. Most of all, it was the numbers. New Hampshire and Massachusetts both calculated their populations as 99 percent white in 1860, whereas nearly a third of Mobile's residents were people of African descent. Although southern slavery was largely a rural institution, Mobile slaves worked as cotton pressers, servants, and cooks, and the city was home to about eight hundred "free people of color," as they were called in the Gulf South, almost 10 percent of the black population. As in the North, enslaved and free women of color washed and ironed, and free men of color in Mobile, just as in Manchester, took up barbering. But the men were equally likely to be boatmen, brick-layers, plasterers, blacksmiths, and butchers. They practiced carpentry too, even if the all-white Mobile Carpentry and Joiners' Mutual Benefit Society tried to exclude them from the trade. What was more, free families of color owned property, and some even owned slaves.

Prominent Mobile physician and white supremacist Josiah Nott had recently introduced the idea of polygenesis to American racism, contending that white people and black people were two separate species whose hybrid offspring would die off, but the population of Nott's own city revealed a more complicated reality. If Eunice haggled over prices at the downtown market, she found herself in the midst of a place (as one traveler described it) "crowded with negroes, mulattoes, quadroons, and mestizos of all sorts, Spanish, Italian, and French, speaking their own tongues, or a quaint lingua franca." When the United States acquired Mobile in 1819 (that was the year Alabama became a state), the city was already home to a community of free people of color descended from French and Spanish colonists. Their "quaint" tongue was a Creole dialect; in the Gulf South, the term "Creole" originally referred to people of French or Spanish descent born in the Americas, but the word eventually came to include people of African ancestry. These men and women held themselves apart from the city's other Negro residents, taking pride in their wealth and education, French and Spanish surnames, Catholic faith, and lighter complexions. They had enjoyed the rights of citizenship under French and Spanish rule, but American planters found them a threat to the prospering institution of slavery and cracked down on all people of African descent, no matter their status. By 1859, free Negroes in Mobile were required to register with municipal authorities and obey a ten o'clock curfew.

Most of Eunice's neighbors near Shell and Hallett were white, but one was a woman of color named Cleste Chastang who claimed sixteen hundred dollars' worth of property. Under French and Spanish governance, enslaved women in Mobile could attain freedom for themselves and their children by forming liaisons with white men, and among the best known of such families were the offspring of Jean Chastang and (as noted in his will) his "beloved friend and companion, Louison, a free negro woman." Eunice's near neighbors were Chastang descendants—how odd that a mulatto woman owned so much while Eunice's husband, a white man, owned nothing at all! But New England had failed the Stones, at least for now, and Eunice was as yet reluctant to speak ill of

Mobile's racial order, for it was here, in the Deep South, that the family was meant to attain a comfortable life. In the meantime, the previously mentioned visitor from Maine noted that "poor blacks meet me at every turn," then added, in words that might have been Eunice's own, "I have many thoughts which perhaps had better remain unwritten."

Maybe Eunice quietly agreed with another New England woman who, disgusted to find that a Mobile lady used "a waiting maid *3 years old!*" wondered how any "Northern mother could bring up a child in the region of slavedom." Turning the pages of local newspapers, Eunice couldn't have missed advertisements for the sale of Negroes, while the downtown market exhibited groups of men or even—in fact, especially—young "mulatto" females, available for purchase. Like other white New Englanders, Eunice was undoubtedly struck by the variety of skin colors in her midst. Sailing out of Mobile, a Rhode Island woman recorded that "the sailors are as black as coal, and the Cook is three or four shades blacker," while the steward was "a mulatto, and quite good looking." Another northern sojourner in Mobile found "many more mulattoes and quadroons here than negroes," noting that a Sunday promenade revealed "very good looking yellow girls and boys." Yet when Eunice wrote home, she offered nary an opinion, not even a description, of these unusual spectacles, keeping any misgivings to herself or pushing them to the far corners of her mind.

White visitors to Mobile were also known to slip in as voyeurs at black church services. "The negroes are beautiful singers," wrote a young woman from Massachusetts. "It was a real treat to hear them sing their hymns." The woman from Maine meanwhile "stole out alone to attend the meeting of the colored people," perceiving deep earnestness in their prayers for freedom. Whether or not Eunice dropped in to listen to the sacred music of southern African

Americans, her Universalist faith remained strong in Mobile and provides a clue to her sentiments about slavery. Eunice had made the shift from Congregationalism when she married William Stone; now, from Mobile, she wrote to her brother Henry asking him to *subject* Universalism *to the closest study*, insisting that *the more I studied, the plainer it came to me.*

From Mobile, Eunice asked her family to send along the *Christian Freeman and Family Visiter*, a Universalist newspaper out of Boston that advocated a conservative course of gradual emancipation. New England Universalists were not radical abolitionists, though the denomination, like most northern churches, condemned slavery by the 1850s. A "Prayer for the Slave" in Eunice's hymnbook urged her to "Hear the bondman's anguished cry!" and a sermon in the *Christian Freeman* pronounced slavery to be against the "principles of Universalism." By 1861, the paper plainly equated slavery with barbarism. Southern Universalists, on the other hand, did not mix their liberal theology with antislavery politics. The *Universalist Herald* out of Montgomery thundered that "in Massachusetts, the hot bed of Abolitionism, human beings are left to *perish to death* in the midst of those whining fanatics who have *so much sympathy* for the poor fat negroes," a view that cast wage labor as worse than slave labor.

Universalism formed part of a profound cultural shift toward the democratization of Protestant Christianity that began after the American Revolution, and Eunice's interest developed around the late 1840s, at the denomination's high point. Rejecting the wrathful and inaccessible God of Calvinism, along with the rigid conviction that only the elect few would be saved, Methodists and free will Baptists had already begun to preach the availability of salvation to all converts.

In the newly competitive market for congregants, these denominations directed their egalitarian appeals to common folk, including the working classes of the North, collectively offering an array of theological choices to families like the Richardsons. Universalists competed too, but they differed from other anti-Calvinists, not only because they invoked human reason as a route to the divine but also because their faith guaranteed salvation to all—with or without conversion—a liberal theology that did not sit well with more traditional evangelical believers, Henry included. Universalists suffered extreme condemnation by more orthodox Protestants (in 1832 one New Hampshire newspaper equated them with "Atheists and other *libertines*"), and although they moved closer to mainstream Protestantism by the 1850s, conceding some form of divine punishment prior to salvation, they always remained suspect for their heretical rationalism.

The Richardson siblings' early training held that *any one that was a universalist was not fit to live,* Eunice recalled, and indeed, Henry had already denounced his sister's quest *so bitterly.* The fact was, a doctrine of universal salvation appalled people like Henry, who wanted earthly sins to be paid for in the afterlife. "Eat, drink and be merry, O drunkard, and adulterer, and gambler, and thief," a Manchester minister proclaimed sarcastically in an anti-Universalist sermon, "for to-morrow ye go to heaven." Where was the justice in a man like Henry's own father (a drunkard and adulterer, after all) entering heaven alongside the pious wife and children he had abandoned? For Henry, Universalism only fostered immorality and welcomed transgressors. Their theological disagreement constituted the first serious rift between Eunice and Henry.

Despite Henry's disapproval, Eunice found in Universalism a faith that answered her deepest yearnings for religious meaning and spiritual empowerment. She might have read the indictment of "Calvinistic hell with its writhing inmates" in the Universalist *Ladies' Repository* or pondered the idea that love, not fear, was "the soul of religion." Perhaps Eunice found appeasement in a Universalist poem entitled "I Love This World," in which the author expounded upon each raindrop and blade of grass ("I love it most in saddened hours," goes one line). Eunice almost certainly read Hosea Ballou's famous *A Treatise on Atonement*, published in New Hampshire in 1805, which promised to "prove the doctrine of *universal holiness and happiness*," perhaps lingering over the words "Man's *main* object, in all he does, is *happiness*." Another convert could have been describing Eunice's spiritual journey when she exulted that she was "happy in a brighter outlook than I knew in my youth" and "happy, above all, that I have reached the unshaken conviction that death is but an incident in a life that will never end, and that I shall survive when my body ceases to live." Eunice longed for home and stability in this life; by embracing the optimism of Universalism, she found a faith that prophesied a blessed ending to an increasingly disappointing sojourn on earth.

In Mobile, Eunice took solace in her faith (*I have been reading in my Bible and I find so much there*), but it also amplified her homesickness. Universalists, like evangelicals, had found a following in northern factory towns, and the Manchester church had been remodeled in 1850 to seat more than a thousand congregants. New Hampshire was home to forty-two Universalist churches in 1860, and more than a hundred thrived in Massachusetts. Though the denomination had a small membership in Mobile in the 1840s, by the time Eunice arrived, Universalists maintained only two churches in all of Alabama, neither one in Mobile, and an Alabama Universalist (who included "all men, black and white," in his theology of redemption) found himself "the object of attack." Following William to the South had meant the privation of New England and of family; to these losses, Eunice now added her church.

Ellen was homesick too, but she also found herself impressed with the institution of slavery. "I wish you could see how independent folks are here," she wrote admiringly of southern whites. "The niggers have to do the trotting," she explicated. "The butcher comes and blows his horn and the negro girl goes and gets the meat," or "the milk man comes and rings his bell, the nigger runs and gets her milk." Ellen believed too that "the niggers dont have to work near so hard as the NH factory girls do," a misconception that grew from familiarity with factory life and willful ignorance of the tribulations of legal enslavement.

But Ellen's assertions also echoed a vicious precept of the most extreme proslavery convictions that developed in the South in the late 1850s, just when free labor ideology was sweeping through the North and the Merrills crossed the border. The well-known southern apologist George Fitzhugh brazenly reasoned that the northern laborer was "more of a slave than the negro, because he works longer and harder for less allowance than the slave." And when Ellen complained that she served as her "owne negro so I get my owne milk," she was as good as professing her desire for a household slave of her own and a wish to join the ranks of white ladies who (as one European traveler to Mobile noticed) "cling to the fact, that they cannot do without slaves." In their quest for upward mobility, Ellen and Dudley defended black bondage, discerning in that system a chance for their own elevation. Land and slaves stood as the twin pillars of wealth in the South, and the Merrills hoped to acquire both. After a while, that vision held for them an appeal unmatched by the dream of returning to a New England farm.

INTO THIS SWIRL, by turns like and unlike New England, stepped Eunice, still hoping to realize her own precious vision of a hardworking husband who could provide his family with a respectable home. The Stones had been boarding with the Merrills, but by the end of 1860, when Eunice turned twenty-nine, they moved into their own newly built house and *commenced housekeeping* in Mobile. Clarence, now eight years old, was going to school, learning *Reading, Spelling, Arithmatic, and Geography*, Eunice recounted proudly, and at Christmas, Eunice and William were able to wrap up candy, crackers, nuts, and twenty-five cents for the boy. Another sign of promise came in improving health. "We are all well and growing fat," Ellen wrote. Because girth indicated abundance, the family invoked that quality as a synonym for well-being, and Eunice too reported that she looked nothing like her gaunt New England self. *If I keep on I dont know but I shall be as fat as you are*, she told her mother. *Should'nt I look pretty if I did?*

But the new home, the holiday gifts, and the welcomed weight masked problems to come, for although William had grown stronger upon arrival, he suddenly reacted with a bad case of the chills (*paying Yankee Tax* is how Eunice described it). Maybe it was a delayed round of acclimation, or maybe William had contracted an epidemic disease like yellow fever. Either way, he was unable to work, and prices were high. *O how I should like one Apron full of your good apples*, Eunice sighed to her mother. *We dont get many when Apples are Eight dollars a barrel.* Eggs sometimes cost *seventy five cents a dosen*, and butter, cabbage, meat, lard, and tea were equally exorbitant (a dollar a pound for tea!). When Eunice asked her sister Ann to send her cured pork from her New Hampshire pig, the request betrayed William's defeat. Eunice had hoped to be the one helping Ann, *but William has been sick most all the time since I came out here*, she revealed. With words written at the end of 1860, Eunice gave away her ongoing struggles: *Poor folks cant indulge much.* Mobile wasn't, just now, turning out to be the venue of fortune she had anticipated, and the distance from loved ones added another layer of unhappiness.

There was work for women in Mobile, cleaning hotel rooms or

washing clothes, had Eunice wanted it. Irish families fleeing the
famine arrived in southern cities too, and when immigrant girls and
women took work as maids and laundresses, they displaced African
Americans, the same as Irish men and boys who cleaned streets or
worked on the docks. Irish and German immigrants also served
alongside black people—Deep South employers would "advertise at
the same time for Negroes on hire, and for Irish laborers," an English
visitor discovered, even though that forced an awkward blurring of
hierarchies. "Southerners do not know exactly how to address servants
of their own color," another newcomer realized. African Americans
noticed too, as when one black worker called out to another performing menial labor, " 'you is turned Irishman, is 'ou?' "

Southern whites held inconsistent opinions: Some spoke of the
Irish "as a sort of race of demigods, by negro comparison," whereas
others thought the Irish "almost as degraded a class of beings as the
negroes are here" and were willing to pay more to hire slaves than to
employ the "commonest, stupidest Irish domestic drudges at the
North." Northern transplants added their own brand of nativism
and racism to the mix, with one Massachusetts man wondering why
guests at Mobile's grand hotels "should be waited upon by
unwashed and insolent Irishmen or Germans" when "good-looking
black boys" had been "born expressly to serve tables." More broadly,
Irish laborers and African Americans lived in the same poor Mobile
neighborhoods, working the same jobs and drinking at the same
taverns. (Ironically, when an Irishwoman and a black man were
arrested for illicit intimacy, a white Mobilian pronounced it "one of
those disgusting charges that is deemed goodly and fashionable in
Boston and other places in the North.") Intertwined Irish and black
lives also fostered mutual contempt; their mutual "insolence" and
"hatred," noted the aforementioned English visitor, "are precisely in
proportion to the resemblance between them."

Aspiring white folks like the Stones and Merrills kept their distance from immigrants and blacks, hoping to join the ranks of well-to-do white people, even as they labored in the same realm as some free blacks and found themselves surprisingly worse off than many of Mobile's Creoles. The Stones were struggling, but Eunice didn't wish to work among the Irish again, or maybe William wouldn't hear of it, given the especially stark proximity of Irish and black workers in Mobile. Since that situation too closely resembled Eunice's degrading stint alongside Irish workers in the Manchester mills, it would have been too much an admission of failure, too soon. As for Eunice, as long as she remained poor, she would rather have been back home. *How I should like to run in and see you and chat a while*, she confided to her mother one dark December hour in 1860. *It has been a dreadful lonesome day here, it has rained hard all day and rains now, it is nothing but Mud and splash.* Torn between husband and home, she tried to hold out a strand of hope for a steadier future. When a New England neighbor prepared to return North, Eunice cheered herself by castigating his lack of ambition. *He dont try to do any thing and is going to give it up after spending his money to get here with*, she averred, exposing William's reluctance to head home with nothing to show for his southern enterprise. *I think he is very foolish and have told him so*, Eunice announced, trying to conceal her envy. Then, with springtime, came the war.

LUTHER HAD WRITTEN to the folks in Mobile about "the John Brown excitement" in 1859, but Dudley dismissed the entire ordeal. "I have not heard it mentioned in a month," he insisted. "People here have something else to do." Maybe Dudley worried more than he let on, or maybe he only skimmed the damning language of the local newspapers ("Down with these infamous Southern men with Northern principle," blazed the *Mobile Register*, "who are even worse than the rankest abolitionists in the land"). Still, the Merrills couldn't have ignored the fact that after Harpers Ferry, the Alabama legislature called for a convention to deliberate secession from the United States of America should Abraham Lincoln reach the White House.

Soon after Lincoln won the presidential election of 1860, Eunice composed a letter to her youngest brother. *Now henry,* she told him, *you had better write, for prehaps the first thing you will know we shall be out of the Union. You know that is the talk now, dont you?* The talk it was indeed. As a port town with a commercial middle class, Mobile had nourished the business-minded Whig Party in the 1840s, but a movement toward "southern rights"—meaning the right to own slaves—put northern-born merchants and politicians at odds with their southern-born neighbors by the 1850s. Though many white residents urged simultaneous southern rights and loyalty to the Union (one Mobile mayor was a Connecticut Whig who defended slavery, though not secession), any moderate consensus swiftly lost ground by late 1860. Secession from the United States was a hard call for white Mobilians, since departure from the Union would disrupt the city's all-important cotton trade. After Lincoln's victory, however, support for that course mounted rapidly. Through the rainy southern winter, Eunice uneasily read the local editorials pressing for moderation, even as white Mobilians mounted anti-Union parades, complete with fireworks and enthusiastic gun salutes.

Rain kept up through the new year, permitting Eunice to console herself by imagining the harsh New England climate. *I suppose where the bright, glad sunshine then lay, so warm, and genial, the cold snows of winter are now piled,* she mused as 1861 dawned. *And where the little birds made sweet music all the day in the beautiful shade trees, the wintery winds moan and sigh through their leafless branches.* But war, much more than the poetry of weather, occupied Eunice's thoughts. "The city was one blaze of light from the illuminations, scarcely a window in the whole city that was not lit," recalled a white woman just after South Carolina seceded in December 1860. "Speeches were made, processions paraded the streets with banners flying and drums beating," the woman remembered, "and in fact everything was done to prove that Mobile, at least, approved of what South Carolina had done." *How is it Henry, if war is declared? Are you coming out here to fight us?* Eunice queried her brother in January, including herself as a southerner before she could know the magnitude of the war. *I just want to know, that is all.*

Five days later, following the actions of Mississippi and Florida, Alabama voted itself out of the Union. When delegates met in Montgomery to create the Confederate States of America, newly elected President Jefferson Davis referred to "our late associates, the Northern States," announcing, "It is joyous, in the midst of perilous times, to look around upon a people united in heart." Georgia, Louisiana, and Texas departed next. Trying to persuade Kentucky to secede, an Alabama official proclaimed that Lincoln's election portended all the horrors of West Indian emancipation, including "amalgamation" and the handing over of "wives and daughters to pollution and violation to gratify the lust of half-civilized Africans." Eunice couldn't have imagined at that moment that either the West Indies or the curse of "amalgamation" would bear directly upon her life less than a decade later.

For now, great apprehension colored Eunice's imaginings of the nation's fate. *I hardly think there will be any fighting for a while, we was expecting it every day, but it does not seem so much like it now, although as I said before we do not know what Mr L. will do,* she wrote in March 1861. *But it seems to me, he will see the utter uselessness of sending an army to the South,* she went on, *if the attempt is made it will involve the country into all the horrors of a civil war which when once commenced no one can tell or even think when, or where, or how it will end.* Her last thought on the subject for that day: *There would be such suffering and horrors as are no where to be found in the history of any war before. It is dreadful to think of, at least it is so to my mind.*

It was around this time that Eunice stopped making an effort to conceal her discontent, for these alarming circumstances left little room for cloaked emotions. Though none of the family's letters from New England to Alabama survive, the pages that Eunice posted from Mobile illuminate the news to which she responded. She still tried for humor—*So Henry thinks I am mad does he? because he is coming to fight me?* she wrote to their mother (invoking not insanity but anger). *My Dear Brother do you not know your Sister better than to think she would be mad at an idolised Brother and all on account of a little pleasant railery on his part.* Henry's teasing, casting Eunice as a Confederate sympathizer, was *recieved all in good part, and many laughs have we all indulged in on account of it,* Eunice assured her northern family, but she was only making the best of living in enemy territory. And so Eunice now punctuated her narratives with unadorned unhappiness: William still suffered his *sick spells*; Clarence was in poor health too and missed the North. *I was homesick the other day,* she wrote, *and William came in and catched me crying. He said if I felt so bad as that I might go home in June, but I shall not but mean to if I live till another summer.* As the nation went to war, Eunice's very survival seemed at stake.

Eunice knew that the ever-upright Henry would enlist in the Union Army, and so he did, as soon as the Confederates fired on Fort Sumter on April 12, 1861, and President Lincoln called up seventy-five thousand troops from state militias for three months of service. *And the brave young soldier boy, where is my darling Brother, in these times of Mighty Commotion?* Eunice wondered. She soon learned that although Luther stayed home, Henry departed with the Sixth Regiment of the Massachusetts Volunteer Infantry, the first regiment in the nation to heed Lincoln's call to arms. It was a band of young, largely working-class men and boys, who were greeted by thousands of cheering Yankees as they made their way to Boston, then to New York and Philadelphia, en route to the capital. "The men are all in good spirits, some writing some singing others danseing smoking, &c," seventeen-year-old Henry recounted to his mother from New York City, heading South. "I am glad I came." War loomed as an adventure to these lads; in their collective imagination, the fighting would be brief, their homecoming heroic.

As Virginia, Arkansas, Tennessee, and North Carolina joined the Confederacy, Eunice imagined being *at home on a good farm*, now openly mourning her foiled plans for a happy domestic life. *Times are very hard here, and no prospect of thier being any better at present*, she declared. To be sure, life could be deceptively ordinary for white civilians in Mobile, as families went to work and attended church, and children kept on at school. Still, the needs of the Confederate Army, as well as an immediate federal blockade of the city's port, brought shortages and steadily rising prices (a pound of butter cost fifty cents at the start of war, five dollars three years later). Lack of wood, oil, and candles meant colder nights and darker evenings, and a dearth of fabric soon forced women to sew from homespun scraps.

To these familiar struggles, Eunice added one more worry. With continuing *poor spells* (he was *not very well and never is*), not only was William incapable of lifting his family out of encroaching poverty, but he might not survive at all, thereby heightening Eunice's fears of loss, as she recalled her father's desertion and death. Now Eunice suffered sick spells and headaches too, and any earlier longings for New England seemed of an entirely different order compared with this: wondering how long the war would last, knowing that Henry was heading to the front, only dimly imagining when she might see her mother again.

Waiting for mail now brought anxiety as never before. *Put your-selves far away from home and friends, in conflicting times like these and see how dear, and how cheering a message from the distant loved ones at home would be,* Eunice wrote to the North just days after the firing on Sumter. Pleading that just a few lines would do, she threatened to write only this time, *but not again,* until an answer came. Even under wartime conditions and living across official enemy lines, Eunice wondered if the absence of mail indicated her family's uncaring attitude. *Prehaps you do not know what it is to be thousands of miles from home and friends,* she elaborated to her sister Ann, *and how anxiously the coming of the Mail from home is looked for, and how bitter the disapointment when time after time, you pres-ent yourself, and ask, with beating heart, (sure of getting a letter this time,) "Is there any thing for me"? and recieve the same answer times without number, "Nothing," till you almost wish to yourself there was no such word as nothing.*

Eunice was now more an out-of-place Yankee in the Deep South than ever, for her Union loyalty made life in Mobile yet more strained. *I am with the North,* she spelled out firmly, *all though I have to keep it to my self.* War was the only subject discussed, and there was *but one side of the question,* she explained. Should anyone disagree, *woe unto him if he mentions it.* Support for secession had never been unanimous in the city, but opponents now found them-selves thoroughly silenced. Nor could Eunice count on the New England natives around her. "The separation is final and forever," wrote a Massachusetts man in his Alabama diary, "and no terms of reconciliation that could possibly be proposed by our enemies can change the decree." The animosity was everywhere palpable. A British traveler in the company of white Mobilians found that "not

one of them had a word but of hate and execration for the North."
City aldermen even voted to rename the streets commemorating the
original colonies of the North: New Hampshire was rechristened
Augusta, Massachusetts renamed Charleston, Vermont became Texas,
and Maine, Palmetto.

White southerners did not confine their hostility to sentiment
alone. "Party feeling ran so high," recalled a Mobilian whose
European father sympathized with the North, "that mobs threatened the occupants of any house that did not present candle-lit
front window panes" as proof of Confederate temperament. The
previously mentioned Alabama Universalist, also an abolitionist,
found that Union supporters were not only "socially ostracised" and
"branded as traitors" but also subject to violence. A leading businessman and slaveowner who had arrived from Massachusetts
decades earlier was arrested for loyalty to the Union, and accounts
of local wartime violence can be found in tracts published by anti-
slavery reformers who gathered their information from southern
newspapers. "An Exile from Alabama" recounted the banishment of
Yankees who professed even the faintest reservations about slavery.
A Massachusetts teacher told of his escape from "mob law in
Northern Alabama," where the judge proclaimed, "You came from
Boston, and that is proof enough against you!" Nor were women
exempt; one who hailed from New England listened as her southern
hosts spoke of lynching northern ladies and exhorted one another
"'to shovel Boston out into the Atlantic.'"

Those who had lived in the South for only a short time, or who
did not own slaves, were at greatest risk, and because white southerners who challenged Confederate convictions were also subject to
harm, few allies stepped forward. As one northerner in the South put
it, "Secessionists became more and more intolerant, and Unionists
less and less able to give expression to their sentiments." Mere weeks

after the fall of Fort Sumter, Eunice found herself a woman dispossessed, living, she wrote home, in *a foreign land and a hostile nation.*

"EVERYTHING IS WAR," Lois wrote from Massachusetts to her son Henry. "There is nothing else talked of, nothing else read or preached or sung," and a few weeks later: "we eate it drink it and then dream about it." As the parents of one Amoskeag worker communicated, more prosaically, "there is little thought of but Niggers and little talked of but secession." When Eunice envisioned home, she knew that times were hard there too. The war had started during a cold, wet New England spring, and economic straits only inflamed family conflicts. Although Lowell men had left for the army in great numbers (an impressive 15 percent of the voting population volunteered), work in the city was hard to find for those who stayed behind. Without replenished supplies of cotton, the mills remained idle or shut down altogether, prompting many young newcomers to return to their parents' farms.

Lois was used to working for wages, probably by taking in sewing, but wartime curtailed those opportunities. "Evry one does their own work so I git little to do and have nothing for doing it," she grumbled. "Business dead, provisions verry scarce and high," she added perfunctorily. Before joining the army, Henry had worked as an apprentice machinist in the Lowell mills, where part of his paltry pay always went to his mother. But Luther junior, twenty years old and working as a teamster, proved a poor substitute for his younger brother's responsible habits and a disturbing reminder of his father's unsteady ways. "I suppose he thinks he sprung up like a mushroom and never had aney mother," Lois fumed. What a contrast it all was with last year's Fourth of July, when "Ann Eunice Luther and Henry and two grand children were with me," she grieved. Now sister Hattie boarded the schoolteacher for extra money, with her husband, Ira, hoping to find work for a year or a month. Ann had moved to Pelham, New Hampshire, remarried to a widower and butcher with a brood of his own, keeping her busy enough to preclude visits either down to Dracut or up to Manchester. And Lois's new husband offered little by way of consolation. "You know what Mr Davis is to talk with," she groaned.

Patriotism helped moderate personal forebodings by channeling emotion into national righteousness, as the war offered northern women the opportunity to discuss politics in public. With the publication of *Uncle Tom's Cabin* in 1852, Harriet Beecher Stowe had implored white women to devote themselves to the crusade against slavery as a moral, and a particularly female, calling. Middle-class women now produced essays, editorials, and novels that proclaimed slavery a sin and advocated the virtue of sacrifice, and those with hours to spare entered relief work and nursing. Although these activists appealed to universal womanhood, their entreaties were not directed toward the working classes, people like Lois and Ann and Hattie, who possessed neither the time nor the resources to take up such causes. Yet the meaning of war and the fate of the nation mattered to poor women no less, even if their civic sentiments were confined to family correspondence. "The emotion I felt for thos stars and stripes and the love of my country in this hour of perril tells me not to be selfish," Lois expounded amid her worries for Henry. It was all for "a glorious cause," and the North would "succede in putting down Rebelion that has ben so long striveing to trample our glorious flag in the dust."

Religious fervor also allayed anxiety, as piety mixed easily with public spirit. For American Protestants, the war could not be understood apart from the sovereignty and providence of God, for God acted within the world, they believed, fostering good, responding to human action and prayer, yet permitting evil when necessary.

Northern statesmen and ministers alike proclaimed the Union cause as God's will—black ministers emphasized the destruction of slavery—while families crowded into churches, seeking comfort in Christian ideals of sacrifice. "I hope God will prosper him and alow him to return safe to his friends once more," Hattie appealed, thinking of Henry, and echoing thousands of women who sent brothers, husbands, and sons into battle.

Divine will and protection, ungrateful hearts struggling for gratitude: These were the topics that emptied women's ink bottles when the fighting commenced. "I know you have the Same God to protect you there that you had hear," Ann assured Henry, and herself. Union troops stood *a small chance of ever returning home again,* Eunice wrote in an attempt to prepare herself for loss, but, she reflected, *there is one who knows what is before us all.* Indeed, wartime spiritual invocations permitted the Richardson women to rekindle their roles as the moral guardians of men. "I prey that you will avoid all viccous habits which sometimes ocur in a soldiers life," Lois sermonized to her son. When news came that the men of the Sixth Massachusetts consumed a pint of whiskey a day, she wrote a lecture on temptation and honor ("Now Henry," it began). Hattie meanwhile reminded her brother sternly that he must be prepared to "give an account of your short life"—before God, she meant, should he die on the battlefield.

In small ways, the family arranged for death. Lois reminded Henry always to keep his name and address about him, "with a request to be sent home if you should fall." Along with those up in New England, Eunice surely read the news of her brother's first taste of combat. When the Sixth Massachusetts reached the city of Baltimore, they were met by Rebel white mobs flinging stones, bricks, and gunshots. As Baltimore's black men and women came to the defense of the Union soldiers, Confederate sympathizers called

When the Sixth Massachusetts traveled from Boston to Washington, D.C., in April 1861, Eunice's brother Charles Henry Richardson was caught in the Baltimore riot, in which some of the city's white residents assaulted Union soldiers.

Henry and his comrades "white niggers" and "nigger thieves." Such vilifications made a deep impression upon the young men who had volunteered to fight for their country. Henry, for one, had gone to war to preserve the Union but also, in the resonating words of Pennsylvania Congressman David Wilmot, to "preserve to free white labor a fair country, a rich inheritance," where white men could live "without the disgrace which association with negro slavery brings upon free labor." Henry and most of his fellow soldiers were not fighting for the rights of African Americans, yet at the very start of their military service, their enemies disturbingly blurred the lines between white Union soldiers and black people.

Among the four casualties in Baltimore, counted as the first of the Civil War, two were Lowell factory workers. "We did not know but you had fallen," Lois shuddered. "O it was a week of suspence," with Ann "almost foolish for two or three days." The family tracked the regiment through each newspaper and every rumor, and it was no time to spare emotion. "Dear and never forgote brother," Luther wrote to the front, signing off, "with the love of your Efecernate Brother." Letters suddenly took on an unprecedented intensity of meaning for the Richardsons, as for families everywhere. "It gives me new courage evry time you write," Lois told her son. "You dont know how impatient we are for a letter and if it does not come it makes us almost sick," for she wondered if each envelope might "be the last."

Northerners forecast a victorious skirmish ("I do not think that this trouble will last a great while," Henry surmised), and confidence ran high as the Sixth Massachusetts arrived with great fanfare in Washington, D.C., and was quartered in the chambers of the U.S. Senate before moving out to camp. The soldiers, Henry made clear in his near-daily missives home, were "ready for marching or fighting," though the latter would definitely be preferable. Lois worried, though, as she reported that white southerners "calculate one of their men to whip three yankeys," pressing her son, "Henry how do you feel about it, does your heart fail you?" But she knew what he would say, that he would "fight for the dear old flag" to the end, and that was exactly what Henry was fighting for. To defend and sustain the legacies of the Founding Fathers, the Declaration of Independence, the American Revolution, and the United States Constitution: That was what made the war so compelling to young white men like Henry Richardson. Of course the nation's original statesmen, the historic documents they created, and their Revolutionary War had not ultimately challenged the institution of racial slavery. Two generations later, most white northerners cared about freedom for enslaved Americans only if it proved necessary to preserve the Union.

That summer came the Confederate victory at the First Battle of Bull Run, in Virginia, and the dip in northern morale was palpable for Yankees who had expected a quick war. "It was not more than half as bad as was reported," Henry refuted, brushing off the unsettling news. "Our men are in good spirits." Yet for all his bravado, Henry longed for letters. "It makes me feel home sick sometimes," he admitted, "to see all of the boys getting money and packages from home daily and I get none." In camp, the men passed around northern newspapers that came through the mail and sang songs about war and family ("When Johnny Comes Marching Home" and "Auld Lang Syne" were two favorites). They prayed and found God anew, played chess, checkers, and leapfrog, raced with wheelbarrows, and pulled pranks. They drank whiskey, gambled with cards and dice, told obscene jokes, and read the Bible. Around the fire, the boys and men talked about home and about women, about the enemy, Lincoln, God, and slavery. They wrote letters and reread the ones they had received.

Camp life proved rough, more often than not crowded and dirty, with a dozen or more men sharing a fabric tent. By day, the sun burned down; by night, the smoke of campfires stung. Meager or stale rations could hardly satisfy a soldier's appetite; the staple was hardtack, flour and water crackers that turned out tough as nails, whether boiled, fried, or dunked in coffee. Otherwise a meal was likely to be boiled salt pork, dried potatoes, baked beans, or foraged fruit. "We are used worse than dogs," Henry confided, before asking if Luther could send him a gold dollar. "I will pay it to you if I live," he promised in words that made the customary language of peril more real than ever.

The Union defeat at Bull Run in July 1861 was hard on the northern home front too. "I wish I could learn to be contented," Lois wrote, "but that is not a plant of earthly origin." Accordingly,

Eunice's brothers, Luther I. Richardson, left, and Charles Henry Richardson, posed for these photographs while serving as soldiers in the Union Army.

the women's own lofty altruism came tempered with fervent wishes for Henry's return. Practical queries too interrupted their fulsome rhetoric. Could the family send food or money? What about pen and ink, postage stamps, or a particular newspaper? Henry had signed up for three months, but even that seemed too long. "It dont appear to me that I can bear up under such weight of anxiety," Lois wept after learning from the papers that her son had reenlisted. His interim visit home would be brief, but when the Lowell band left town to escort the regiment back, Lois was "in exstacy" at the thought of reunion.

Eunice learned only later that Luther had joined up too, likely owing to a lack of employment anywhere else. "Can we spare them both?" Hattie wondered, before resigning herself. "Well Mother we are not alone in the affliction, thousands of hearts are sorrowing with

separation from husbands sons & brothers." At least the war permitted Eunice and her female relatives to transform the departure of
men into a comforting story of national sacrifice.

DUDLEY MERRILL and William Stone joined the Confederate Army
almost right away. Dudley served in Captain Charles P. Gage's
Battery of the Alabama light artillery, a company of Mobilians set to
defend the city through the winter—early recruits had practiced firing upon enemy vessels, imagining Abe Lincoln as their target,
"with his heart somewhere near the bull's eye." Dudley later fought
in the Battle of Shiloh in April 1862, before obtaining a medical
discharge that summer. William enlisted in the Confederate Guards
of the Twenty-fourth Alabama infantry, Company I, stationed at
Fort Morgan in Mobile Bay, but his regiment moved around too,
taking part in Mississippi skirmishes and fighting at the Battle of
Stones River in Murfreesboro, Tennessee, in late 1862. Soon thereafter, William would fall sick and convalesce in an Atlanta hospital.

But before any of that, the shocking news of Confederate enlistment reached the New England family, slipped in at the end of a May
1861 letter that Ellen filled with as much other news as she could
muster. Ellen's celebration of slavery had caused her little agitation in
the past, but the outbreak of war stirred a painful ambivalence into
her southern loyalties. "I feel very well contented if I do not think
about home," she wrote to Lois now, "but if I try to write, and think
about Mother Brothers and Sisters it makes me very uneasy." After
that confession, she talked about how much she wanted to see everyone and to meet Ann's new husband, assuring the family that she
would make a visit were it not for the war. Next she related news of
the children (Alice was talking, Sumner growing big) and bragged
about Dudley. "As long as my husband lives I shall have every thing
he can procure for my comfort," she spelled out, in words that Eunice

couldn't truthfully have echoed. Only then came the startling words: "D. & Stone have both joined a military company." And immediately, her signoff: "Excuse haste, this from Ellen Merrill."

That final fragment of information spread as quickly as possible, prompting various explanations up north. Most important, soldier Henry had to be informed, and at first the New England relatives fastened upon the notion that William and Dudley had been coerced into Confederate service, "forced in I suppose to save their lives," as Lois phrased it. In this narrative, Henry was fighting not against, but rather for, his brothers-in-law, to "help them to maintain their rights." Only an afterthought betrayed a shadow of suspicion. "I regret they ever went there," Lois added. "If they had foreseen this dreadful war probably they never would." Hattie alone accounted for the possibility of volition. "I suppose Will and Dud will fight as hard against the *Union* as Henry will for it," she concluded in a letter to Luther. To Henry, she repeated the idea that the men had been coerced but added crucial information from a more detailed letter received from Mobile. "I dont know what their sentiments are," she mused, "but Ellen wrote in her last that she thought the south was right and she hoped they would be victorious."

Ellen had decided, after all, to side with the Confederacy, or maybe it was just simplest to go along with her husband. "It is sad to think that we have Brother arayed against Brother in the fatal conflict," Hattie told Henry. Although she invoked an oft-repeated metaphor for the divided nation ("brother against brother"), the words also described the family's very real experience. Henry's response was clipped. "I was sorry to here that Dudly and William had joined the southern army," he wrote home. "I hope that I shall never meet them on the battle field."

Families divided by the Civil War faced the dilemma of reconciling love and fealty with profoundly different visions of the nation's future.

Most divided families resided in Maryland, Delaware, Kentucky, and Missouri, the four border slave states that never seceded from the Union. New England and the Deep South were more unusual mapping points, but the Richardsons were not entirely alone, and relatives coped in various ways. Some attempted to accommodate opposing views, like the Boston man who wrote to kin in Georgia, calling anti-slavery sentiments "folly & madcap" and so much "blasphemous belchings." Some evaded politics in favor of emotion, like the Vermont mother who wrote with "tenderness and affection" to her Confederate son, whereas others mixed sentiment with partisanship; "I don't much expect to see any of you again on earth," wrote a Louisiana man to his parents in Vermont in 1861, adding, "Whatever you do dont side with that Black Republican Party." Still others openly professed both familial and regional loyalties. "I boast myself Rebel, sing Dixie, shout Southern Rights," proclaimed a Louisiana woman, but of a Union-supporting sibling, she affirmed, "he is always my dear, dear Brother, and tortures should not make me change my opinion." A few acknowledged the awkward bind more openly. "What a remarkable position are we in, we cannot wish for our own success in the solemn strife about to take place without desiring the discomfiture of those near and dear to us," sighed a Yankee mother to her Confederate daughter. Nor was outright hostility unknown. "If I should meet any of my relatives on the battle field in Lincolns army," proclaimed a Vermonter turned Georgian, "they will there be considered as my enemies and treated as such."

Tensions simmered too among the four New Englanders in Alabama. Eunice had written a "long letter," since lost, but in Lois's recounting, she was feeling "verry bad" and wanted more than anything to return north. The recollections of another New England woman in the Deep South in 1860 are suggestive. "I was an alien— in a different country," this woman remembered. "I was completely overwhelmed with my sense of loneliness & isolation & want of sympathy." Eunice felt the same way. *To be plain*, she wrote just after the war began, *I do not like the folks here as well as at home. They are so different.* But Eunice's political sentiments also represented a measure of resolve and autonomy new to a woman who had always taken her husband's path as her own. William had disappointed his wife as patriarch and provider. Now Eunice charted her own course in the newly important realm of national politics.

On the other side stood Ellen and her "real secession letter," as Hattie described it. That letter has not survived either, but the source of Ellen's Confederate posture can be discerned from her circumstances. True, the Merrills had originally envisioned saving money in the South to buy a farm back north, but by the time the war came, Dudley was a landowning artisan in Mobile (he and Ellen had recently purchased acreage across from the sash factory and were soon to resell at a profit). If Ellen deferred to her husband, she also appreciated her status as a white woman in the slave South. Her three years in Mobile, the friends she had made, and the upward mobility she enjoyed permitted her to feel at home there. In short, opportunity had panned out for Ellen in a way that it hadn't for Eunice. Now the Richardson sisters in the South stood on opposite sides of the Civil War.

Something else had come to pass in the Merrills' lives that further explained the sisters' divergence: Ellen now had black household help. The Merrills couldn't afford to purchase a slave, but Dudley either employed a free woman of color or hired out someone else's bondwoman. *You will think poor Ellen has a hard time with two children to wait upon*, Eunice reported, betraying a mixture of disapproval and envy. *No she does not*, she corrected, for Ellen had *a black girl to do every thing*, a servant who undertook *all the work* and *all the care of the children*. That situation, more than anything else, demonstrated to Ellen the benefits of being a white woman in the South, for she at last possessed the independence she had coveted just a few years before. Back then, she had been her "owne negro"; now she moved closer to becoming a lady who couldn't manage without domestic help. Her sentiments, and Dudley's too, were well captured by a Vermont man who, like the Merrills, had moved to the Deep South in the late 1850s. "Could you be here with it and understand the connexion between master and servant you would not be an abolitionist," he wrote to a brother in New England. "We have no option in the matter but to fight and fight to a man for the homes of the sunny south." Elementary school textbooks would soon teach Ellen's children, and Eunice's son, that slavery was God's will, and if Ellen read wartime popular literature, she met fictional faithful slaves who hated the Yankees just as much as their masters did.

The Merrills had practical reasons for siding with the Confederacy, but William Stone's motivation as a still-struggling laborer is less clear, and not a single letter he wrote can be found in the family papers. Maybe William enlisted simply because he had no work and the local army offered steady pay, or maybe he joined in an attempt to smooth the way for his own advancement in Mobile when the war ended. Perhaps he felt pressure from white neighbors, and in fact, Lois and the sisters may have been telling more than a soothing story about coercion into the Confederate military. "The meshes of their cursed net were around me," wrote a New Yorker who had been conducting business in the Deep South at the outbreak of fighting, "and thus I *volunteered!*" Another northern-born man, who made his fortune raising sheep in Texas, told of being "forced into the ranks of the Rebel army," adding, "I honestly believe that I would have lost my life, notwithstanding my professed loyalty to the Confederacy and careful suppression of my real feelings and sentiments." On the other hand, the Richardsons' narrative of intimidation may have been nothing more than wishful thinking. "The whole tenor of your letter seems to be a question whether or not I was 'impressed into the Confederate Service,'" wrote a southern soldier to a brother in a northern regiment; no, the former New Englander announced, he had enlisted, "proud of the appelation, as you would term it, Rebell Soldier, and not sorry as you would think."

Antagonism between husband and wife, and between brothers-in-law, isn't difficult to envision: William yielding to the Confederacy against staunchly Unionist Eunice, Dudley eagerly convincing Ellen to support his decision, successful Dudley against unsuccessful William. Maybe it was most traumatic for Ellen, standing between a Confederate husband and a Union sister, so distressed at times that she refused to write to New England at all. *She has no news*, Eunice had reported of her sister, after the election of Lincoln, *only she wants to go home, and that is not news to any of you, so she has nothing to write*. Ellen wanted to visit New England, but her traitorous politics must also have pained Eunice, only fanning resentment of her sister's capable husband and the Merrills' greater luck. In any case, Eunice kept her envy to herself, and that "real secession letter" was the last anyone in New England heard from the Merrills until the war ended four years later.

Perhaps Eunice wondered, in those early days of war, where her own allegiances would have lain if William had climbed as far upward as Dudley. Had her own husband fared better in the South, perhaps she would have been tempted to take on a black servant of her own and then found it equally difficult to turn against a society that offered her such status. In the meantime, mail arrived in New England that first wartime spring, through a Mobile neighbor returning north. Postmarked from Portsmouth, New Hampshire, a letter imparted the news that (as Lois repeated to Henry) "communication is now cut off from the south." All correspondence would henceforth be read by authorities (letters could run only a single page and relay only family matters), and most ended up in the dead letter office anyway. *I do so much want to go with her,* Eunice wrote of the traveling neighbor, *but cannot now,* yet her words implied that she would find a way home before too long. She signed off as *the absent E.L.S.,* and after that there are no more letters from Eunice while she lived in Alabama. Now the New England relatives remained in "dark suspence" about those who had crossed the Mason-Dixon line.

EUNICE HAD BEEN the last of the family to head south, and she was the first to leave. To return north while her husband fought for the Confederacy and her sister's family stayed in Mobile: This was the first unconventional decision that Eunice made, and it did not come without pain. The departure of men was a familiar occurrence within the Richardson circle, whether for ill or good. Eunice's father had deserted. Her husband had gone away, hoping to forge a better life before sending for his wife and child. Henry had gone to war, then Luther. Now, contrary to customary patterns of leave-taking, Eunice and her young son set off on their own. The Stones could only imagine a time when William might return home, albeit without the all-important farm that the sojourn to Mobile had been meant to yield. The separation was geographical but also in some measure a statement of Eunice's political convictions, against the actions of her husband.

A little over a year after bidding farewell to New England, Eunice and Clarence made the journey back north. Eunice was seven months pregnant when they crossed enemy lines, leaving husband and father in the enemy camp. She probably needed to obtain a pass to travel between the Confederacy and the Union, convincing authorities that she was neither spy nor traitor. With travel so arduous, Eunice was clearly determined, for she was willing to risk going into labor and even losing the baby along the way. Maybe she knew it would be impossible to support two children without the help of extended family; with two children of her own, Ellen couldn't help much, and by the autumn of 1861 plenty of white women and children in Mobile were hungry and sick, going without bread or medicine. Maybe Eunice couldn't bear the thought of Clarence and the new baby being raised in the South should she die in childbirth in Mobile. Maybe traveling now would be easier than traveling with a newborn. Maybe another neighbor was heading north, and Eunice leaped at the chance for an escort. Perhaps Eunice believed that if she and Clarence didn't start out now, they would never make it back home. Even so, Eunice knew that the family up north could offer only so much assistance. With her husband fighting for the South, there would be no Union benefits as a soldier's wife, nor would Confederate benefits reach her up north. Still, she wanted to go, and so she did, in December 1861.

From the accounts of others, it is safe to assume that the excursion was "dreadful—slow trains, dirty cars, stopping for hours in the night, in a cold, cheerless station." The party likely traveled over water as well, adding seasickness to fatigue. Wintertime made the voyage yet more formidable, with snow mounting and ice slickening with every advancing northern mile. Luther was "veary glad to here that Eunice had got home," he later wrote, "but was Sory that she had so mutch troble." Eunice and Clarence would again be living in New England without William, but truth be told, William had never proved much help anyway. If Eunice was going to be poor, she would rather be poor at home, close to her mother and sisters, even without a husband.

, Claremont March 29th 1867
Half past nine evening,

[864]

Dear Mother

I am getting so anxious to
hear from you again, it has
been a good while since you wrote
me, It is over a month since
you wrote me to be ready to
come to Lowell when I was sent
for, I do not see why the boys
do not come home! I am afraid
they will not come. Have you
heard from them yet? I thought
to be sure you would write me as
soon as you heard from them
I keep working and waiting to

4
SERVANT AND WASHERWOMAN

Claremont, New Hampshire, March 29, 1864

Half past nine evening.

Dear Mother

I am getting so anxious to hear from you again. It has been a good while since you wrote me. It is over a month since you wrote me to be ready to come to Lowell when I was sent for. I do not see why the boys do not come home! I am afraid they will not come. Have you heard from them yet? I thought to be sure you would write me as soon as you heard from them—I keep working and waiting to hear from you. I think every week, well I shall hear this week sure. I dont know but I shall work myself to death this Spring, every thing is so high you know and nobody to do any thing but myself. I am afriad if the boys come home that I can not come down to stay long. It will certainly be more difficult for me to make a long stop than it would a month ago but no one is to blame for that of course but I dont see why they do not come or write, do you? Do you want to know what I am doing this Spring? working at my trade— washing. Last week I did three washings and two ironings besides my own washing ironing and house work, week before I did three washings and one ironing besides my own and cut a dress and went out one day all day, doing a little of every thing. Yesterday I did a large washing besides mine. Today I have been away, went at seven oclock this morn-

ing and did not get home till after seven to night, then I had my days house work to do and am tired enough, as I be every night. But what is the use of troubling you with it, it will do no good of course, but I like to tell some body once in the will when I feel bad. We were all invited up to the old Gentlemans to a sugaring but I of course could not go. Mr Russells folks went and took Clarence & Clara with them, that was as well as if I had gone, to me at least. Do write me whether you have heard from the boys or not, and be sure to if you here. I am afraid some thing has happened to them. I believe I am getting rather nervous this spring any way. Write soon wont you.

good night

E. L. Stone

It is now fifteen minutes to ten.

*A*long with the summit of Vermont's Mount Ascutney to the west, the churches and mill buildings of Claremont, New Hampshire, today can only hint at Eunice's surroundings in the 1860s. The Universalist church on Broad Street (now a conference center) stood in her day, as did Trinity Church at Broad and Chapel, First Congregational at Pleasant and Pine, and the Baptist church at Main and Central, although some of their edifices have since been remodeled. Noteworthy buildings of the Downtown Historic District went up after Eunice left, but you can still glimpse the ghosts of her world in the Lower Village Historic District. Back then, workers ground grain into flour at the Sugar River Mill on Main Street (now housing for senior citizens), while others turned out cotton and woolen goods within the Federal-style brick facades of the Monadnock Mills lining Water Street (many now vacant). Efforts at revitalization and historic preservation are moving slowly in Claremont.

Although the once-thriving New England village and its surroundings hills were described by an 1859 visitor as "an enchanting
scene," the years Eunice spent there were far from enchanting.
Eunice chose to settle in Claremont, one among a string of towns
lining the Connecticut River, because it was home to her husband's
kin. Claremont cemeteries harbor Stone family graves back to the
eighteenth century, and William's sister and brother-in-law Margaret
and Alonzo Russell can be found in local Universalist church records.
The Russells' house is labeled on a map printed in 1860, and their
son, Albert, is named in town histories as one of the first to enter the
Confederate capital of Richmond, Virginia, when it fell to the Union
in 1865. During the Civil War, Eunice and her children lived along
Washington Street on the east side of town; the street still exists, but
any remnants of the family's immediate surroundings have been
swallowed by the suburban strip of Route 11/103.

Life back in Manchester had been punctuated by hopes of a
brighter future, and the Stones' foray to Mobile at least briefly held
out the possibility of improvement. But during the years that
Eunice lived in Claremont, her fears of poverty and loss were fully
realized, plunging her to the brink of desperation. As her world
shattered during the years of wartime adversity and loss, she came to
express her sorrow and anger with increasing candor. To conjure
Eunice's life in Claremont, you can walk the streets or search the
archives, but you can also try to imagine a depth of unhappiness
that led her to contemplate suicide.

EUNICE'S DOWNWARD spiral resulted in part from her decision to
leave the South without her husband. If she had acted as an independent woman at that moment, she now found herself in the distinctly troubling role of a dependent and imposing daughter-in-law.

Lois volunteered to shelter Eunice and Clarence upon their return to New England, as did sister Ann (in a borrowed southernism, Eunice wrote of *the offer that you all had made me of a home*), but Eunice's mother was getting too old to take in another family, and Ann already ran a large household of her own. For now, Eunice chose to burden her husband's relatives. Along with William's sister and brother-in-law Margaret and Alonzo Russell, another sister, Melissa Stone, lived in Claremont, and the widowed father Stone lived just south of town up on Bible Hill.

Eunice had last written from Alabama to New England in May 1861, less than a month after the war began. A single sentence in her first letter from Claremont, composed in late December of the same year, indicates the gravity of her decision to leave Mobile: *Margarett says it was all right that I should do as I did, or I never could have kept up.* By *kept up*, Eunice likely referred to both emotions and economics, and now she grasped at small comforts, tempering an unpredictable future with the consolation of familiarity. *I have a little good news to write*, she reported. *My Trunk has come. I was glad to see it. There was but little in it, but what there was, was of value to me.* Comfort came as well from the kindness of her in-laws. William's folks did everything to make her feel at home, she marveled, and Melissa Stone had never seen anyone "so thankfull for enny thing as Eunice & Clarence seam to be, to think they are once more in New England with there friends." In Claremont, Eunice found *a rest of body and mind* that she hadn't known at all in Mobile, and she found too a sympathetic and loving friend in Melissa.

Yet the troubles that strained Eunice's cautious contentment were twofold and intertwined: the fate of her husband and impending impoverishment. *If it was not for such a feeling of dependence that I now have, and my friends in the South were safe, I could enjoy myself some,* she explained. Fear of dependence upon others and unrelieved hardship were to be the central themes of Eunice's Civil War letters, with all possibility for betterment pinned on William's homecoming.

Part of the problem was the new baby. On a blustering cold February morning not two months past her return, Eunice called in the neighborhood midwife and gave birth to a daughter. In the days afterward, Eunice wondered if baby Clara suffered from sore eyes because her mother had *cried so much* during pregnancy. "Eunis says what would William say if he could see his little girl?" Melissa disclosed. Clara increased the economic strain, but she also provided a measure of cheer. *I believe I must brag a little about my baby,* Eunice wrote of the infant's laugh. *She has not said Mother, or grand mother, yet, but we expect every day when she will,* she added in jest (followed by the characteristic dismissal, *well, nonsense aside*). Still, each exultation (*every day she does something new*) renewed the anguish (*How many times in a day do I wish her Father could see her*). Eunice had been homesick in Mobile, but she unexpectedly found herself terribly lonely back in New England too.

Patriotism sustained American women on both sides of the war, at least at first, but for Eunice, the whole question of loyalty was vexed, with her Confederate husband cast as the enemy of her Union brothers and with Luther's enlistment further diminishing the whole family's peace of mind. Both brothers now belonged to the Twenty-sixth Massachusetts, a three-year regiment under the command of General Benjamin Butler. They had departed Lowell for the Gulf South just before Eunice's return from Mobile; after a stint on Ship Island off the coast of Mississippi, the men were to occupy the fallen city of New Orleans and fight in the Shenandoah Valley of Virginia. *So many times every day and night does imagination bear me on its rapid wing to you,* Eunice wrote to Henry and

Luther, as she envisioned the boys on their *lonely rounds of Gaurd duty.* The pride Eunice felt for her soldier brothers compounded the family's confusion over William. The Stones no doubt reiterated the story of coercion into the southern army, both to themselves and to others, even as Claremont neighbors teasingly dubbed newborn Clara *little Secesh Contraband.*

With President Lincoln's call to arms, Claremont's public hall had hosted overflowing crowds, and enormous throngs bade good-bye to Union volunteers. Patriotic songs, fervent prayers, and stirring speeches animated the village, while a town meeting unanimously resolved that the "one vital question" was that of sustaining the government of the United States. The national problem of slavery was not absent from these kinds of events in Claremont: A considerable audience turned out for an antislavery lecture, and a local newspaper pronounced the war to be between "the interests of Freedom and Slavery."

Just like elsewhere in the North, such pronouncements stemmed more from economic concerns than moral convictions. "The harsh sound of Slavery I dispise and utterly abhor," one Claremont man wrote to his son, "and let us use every effort and proper means in our power to prevent its broader spread in our goodly land." Slavery was abhorrent, but what mattered most was not its eradication but the danger of its expansion into western territories, since slaves interfered with the paid labor of free white people. Nor were these New Englanders hesitant to express their prejudices. When Claremont editors denounced "unreasoning hatred of the negro," they also described black people as grateful for removal from "heathen, degraded and brutish" Africa; another newspaper called a radical antislavery congressman (a white man, of course) a "dirty, wooly-headed negro." Like the men in Claremont, and like his brother,

Henry, Luther Richardson went to war to fight for the Union and free labor, not against black slavery.

With the boys garrisoned in Mississippi and Louisiana, and William at first stationed in Mobile, it didn't seem out of the question that the men would meet up. *I do hope William will fall into their hands yet*, is how Eunice envisioned such an encounter. The most promising scenario had William deserting to the Union as the Twenty-sixth Massachusetts entered Mobile (Melissa embellished the script with "I do hope it will be so he can get away from the rebels. If our men could take him prisoner he could come home to his family"). But Eunice's letters also betrayed *many misgivings* about such a turn of events, along with a sense that her own politics clashed with her husband's. *I feel as if it might be by this time William has all sorts of ideas of the North,* she admitted to her brothers. *If it should ever be your lot to meet with him, try and correct his false views if he has any.*

Whatever suspicions the boys entertained about William's partisanship, they only wanted to help. "Tell Eunice to be sure and write what regiment Bill and Dud. are in and what General they are under and where they are stationed," Henry directed from Ship Island, Mississippi, in 1862. "I have enquired of all the prisoners that have come here and all the deserters that I could find but could get no news." Luther even found an Alabama prisoner who claimed to know William and Dudley, hastening to add, "I did not till him that thay war any relatives of mine." Imagining a Union siege on Mobile, Eunice confessed, *I want it done and yet how I do dread it.*

In the meantime, Claremont felt far distant from mother and sisters, and Eunice wanted Lois to visit from Dracut, Massachusetts, right away. From Lowell (just across the bridge from Dracut), a traveler could take the stagecoach, by way of Manchester and Concord, or spend a bit more to board the rail cars straight to the Claremont depot. The winter roads were impassable, though, and even spring-time would see *such a depth of snow* that the journey would be impossible for quite some time. *Write to me, Mother*, Eunice pleaded in the early months of 1862, for letters kept her *spirits up* and her *courage good*. William's safety, if not his allegiances, daily refreshed the wells of anxiety. *I do not much expect to see William again, since that terriable battle*, Eunice conceded after the bloody northern vic-tory at Shiloh in the spring of 1862, when twenty thousand sol-diers—half on each side—were killed or wounded in two days. From the moment she departed the South, Eunice combined her hopes for reunion with preparations for widowhood. *I have thought that if I live, and my Husband does not get to me, that I shall want a place, a home for sometime*, she concluded.

Home: That was what Eunice wanted more than anything, for it symbolized all the stability and esteem that had eluded her for so long. Poor and working-class women who harbored such wishes were not simply striving to mimic the middle-classes, although Eunice would dearly have loved to join their ranks. But as long as Eunice was poor, a home of her own meant not having to beg for a bed or a meal; it meant a venue of respite from the employer who would soon be ordering her to cook his dinner and refuge from the neighborhood ladies who would soon be gossiping that she didn't wear a proper hat.

IN THE FACE of those bleak early years of the war, Eunice still tried to imagine something brighter. Recalling an old Northfield neighbor's aphorism, *"if it want for hope, the heart would break,"* Eunice reflected, *I did not understand its meaning then, but how fully do I now!* She tried to write brave letters to her brothers, even though it seemed *dreadful hard* when everything looked <u>*all so dark before me*</u>, as she put it. Despair and promise constantly changed places in her thoughts. *I do try to see a <u>silver lining in every dark cloud of adversity</u>,* Eunice wrote one day in 1862, *but when I look on my little ones and think of the uncertainty of their fathers return there is such a swelling up, such a grief in my heart that I almost sink at times, and feel like complaining at my lot, but that I know is wrong so I rally and go on hoping for the best. But what is to become of me and my children if William does not come home again?*

At the autumn holidays (*how unlike former thanksgivings it is with me!*), the Claremont family gathered at Father Stone's, but around the table, Eunice recounted, *there were some choking emotions that could not be controlled.* There was William's most disturbing absence, of course, and Henry and Luther at the front, and the fact that Margaret and Alonzo's son, Albert Russell, had reenlisted with the Ninth Vermont for three years, *and myself with my two children, what my thoughts were I will not tell,* Eunice hinted, for once keeping the worst to herself. When she did tell, she described the *deepest gloom.* Although she had left William behind in the South, it seemed that he had abandoned her first, when he enlisted in the Confederate Army. Like her father, Eunice's husband had deserted his wife and children, in the interim, if not forever.

Deepest gloom: Like everyone else, Eunice searched through the newspapers with trepidation. For her, the war reports conjured vivid images, as she read accounts of battles *being fought in places where I have been.* Sometimes Eunice remarked upon party politics (*most people think it will go Democratic,* she wrote during a local election, but *for me, I hope it will go "<u>right</u>"*) or on Union progress (the death of General Stonewall Jackson was *a good victory on our side, for he was one of our most dangerous enemys*).

But much of the time, Eunice had nothing to say about the causes and consequences of the Civil War. Claremont men fought and died at Fair Oaks in the summer of 1862, at Antietam that autumn, and at Fredericksburg in December. They fell in the peach orchard at Gettysburg in 1863 and the next summer at Cold Harbor, but Eunice had nothing to say about any of that. One day in 1863, a telegram arrived in town announcing the fall of the Confederate capital. Church bells rang and cannons fired before people learned the dispatch was false, but Eunice related none of it in her letters. Even when the Union Navy captured Mobile Bay in the summer of 1864, and Atlanta fell that autumn, Eunice's frequent communications made no mention. For their part, Lois and the sisters carefully followed military affairs, and Eunice's stepsister, Addie Davis, went on about generals and battles in her letters. Eunice had made her politics clear in the decision to move back north, and it was too hard now to sort out her reactions, since each victory for her husband's side was a defeat for her brothers, and each victory for the boys a defeat for William. Sometimes she simply had no more room on the page, and no more time, once she had found an hour of solace in narrating her own daily rounds and troubles.

For Eunice was *jogging around the world so without a home.* When the roads cleared in the summer of 1862, she and the children gave the Claremont kin a rest. Down in Pelham, New Hampshire, just over the border from Dracut, Eunice's sister Ann was having a baby, and Eunice was to serve as caretaker. She and the children stayed five months, though not without discord, since Ann's husband, David McCoy, didn't appreciate adding three more members to his household, and Clarence eventually had to board with his grandmother. *I have a notion that he dislikes me extreamely*, Eunice wrote of Ann's husband—"after working night and day and taking such good care of them," Lois snapped in response, pronouncing David "a regular <u>HOG</u>."

Just before the roads got bad again, Eunice and the children

ASCUTNEY MOUNTAIN FROM BIBLE HILL, SNOW CAPPED.

This view of Claremont, New Hampshire, shows Mount Ascutney from the vantage point of Bible Hill, where William Stone's father lived and where Eunice and her young daughter Clara sometimes boarded during the lean war years.

returned to Claremont. She and Clara moved in with Father Stone up on Bible Hill, while Clarence lived with the Russells down in the village. That way, the boy could earn his room and board by working for his uncle Alonzo, a cooper by trade, and also attend school. *I take comfort with him when he is with me,* Eunice wrote, lamenting their separation once again, compounded by the separation of brother from sister. *Clara was so pleased to see him,* she reported of one visit. *I wish it was so I could keep them together.* To that end, she was trying to *look out for a living right along for three of us.*

Eunice had already begun to work as a servant, but she preferred the job of braiding palm-leaf hats. Ann had taught her the skill (it could be learned within hours), and David started her off with a hundred dollars' worth of leaves, probably in exchange for banishing Clarence. Hat braiding was part of the putting-out system of women's labor in New England's growing market economy (so named because women performed the work at home rather than in factories). Boston merchants imported the palm leaves from the West Indies and sold them to storekeepers, who split the leaves and sold them to laborers, who braided them into hats and sold the finished product back to the storekeepers. The hats were marketed locally or passed back to city merchants to be shipped west and south, worn by farmers or slaves. Unmarried New England farm daughters commonly braided hats when agricultural labor slowed in winter, and sometimes widowed white women took in the work (Ann had learned the craft before remarriage), as did poor black women. Eunice didn't fit into any of those categories exactly, but it was the best employment she could find, especially because she could work at home and care for Clara at the same time. Wages fluctuated with demand and the quality of the leaves, but a single hat could command as much as forty cents, payable in either cash or store credit. When David sent along more material (she would have to pay him back this time), Eunice kept at it any spare moment she could find, which wasn't much, she had to admit. She might braid one hat every few days, with just a few to sell at week's end.

With the new year, everyone wondered when the war would end. As ten-year-old Clarence phrased it early in 1863, "that is more than any body can no." Eunice's most fervent wish beyond William's return was to "go to housekeeping." To do so, she would have to work even harder, *but when I got my day-work done I could have a place to crawl off with my children that would be home*, she reasoned. *Do you suppose I can?* she asked her mother, her incessant calculations attesting to the ongoing contest with poverty. *And can I get enough to eat?—clothes would be all out of the question I know, but I could do without them*, she figured. *It seems as if I could, for the sake of having a place where I could be at home once more in my life time.*

Then again, the plan seemed impossible, for she had *nothing in the world to keep house with*, without the furniture and household items she had given away upon departure for Alabama. Or maybe she could *borrow some of your things you dont use to keep house with*, she schemed to Lois, *any thing from a pewter spoon to an iron candle stick*. If only William would *be spared to come home, and provide for his little family*, she sighed. *Then we shall have a place to call home*. It was an unbidden thought, but those underlined words mixed together two wishes: not only that William would return from the war but also that when he did, he would be able to support her and the children in a way that he had never done, in either Mobile or Manchester.

"Sister Eunice poor child I do pittey her so much," Melissa Stone allowed, ever protective of the wife her own brother had so disappointed. "If there was Enny work she could get to take in so to help her self, if there was Enny way so she could get to keeping house, I think she would have a good deal given to her." Lois, on the other hand, *did not say a single encouraging word*, but Eunice remained determined, directing her mother to send a bed she had once mentioned. When a box arrived from Dracut after all, Eunice was overcome. *Why what a lot of things you sent*, she gushed. *It will give me such a fine start. Why I was perfectly astonished. I would laugh then I would cry when I was looking them over.*

Midsummer 1863: *I am keeping house*, Eunice announced triumphantly to her mother. *I wish you could step in and see me.* It was a Claremont tenement soon to be torn down, and Eunice had no idea where she and the children would go after that, but for now they lived farther up Washington Street from the Russells, and just as Melissa had predicted, many came forward to assist. If the dislocations of an industrializing world seemed to conspire with civil war to break apart family and community, here was proof to Eunice of the survival of kinship and neighborly ties. Her spirits lifted as she gathered Lois's boxful, along with a borrowed stove and chairs, *and came in here and made a begining*, as she put it. One day she *found a bundle on the table* containing *six new Cups & Saucers just as they were done up at the store*; others supplied sheets and pillowcases, a tablecloth and curtains, a towel, a dishrag. Eunice chattered on that Fred Clement put so much wood on his wagon that it broke down two miles from the house, and then neighbors brought the wood in by armfuls, and after that some young men sawed and split and stacked it for her.

Reprieve came too, as Eunice arranged a visit from Lois that autumn. *I think the Money would do me more good to have you use it in coming to see me than any other way*, she decided. Eunice arranged her work schedule, instructed Lois to *make friends with the conductor*, spelled out directions from the depot to Washington Street, then got through her long days on sheer anticipation. The disappointment was so great upon learning of her mother's canceled trip that Eunice got out of bed in the cold September night to set down her feelings. *I thought you would be here when I got home*, she wrote dejectedly, by candlelight. *I gave Clarence directions what to do if Grand Mother comes.* At such moments, New Hampshire seemed no closer than Alabama to her mother and sisters.

By November, Eunice and the children had moved again (that was part of the unsteadiness of renting), this time to yet another Washington Street tenement, divided with the widow Jane Parmelee, roughly halfway between the Russells' home and the center of town, for fifty dollars a year—affordable, though not easily. To be sure, Eunice's Claremont residences were not the notorious kinds of slums found in cities like Boston and New York at midcentury. They were not airless garrets or unlighted cellars, crowded several families to a room with garbage and sewage piling up back and front. More likely, Eunice's quarters were cramped apartments in

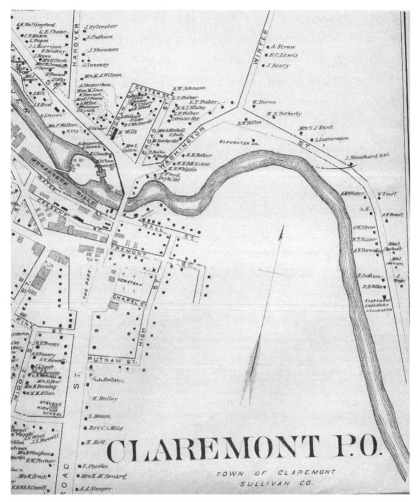

The Washington Street home of Eunice's in-laws Margaret and Alonzo Russell is marked on the far right side of this 1870s map of Claremont, New Hampshire, as are the tenements owned by Leonard Fisher near the corner of Winter and Washington streets where Eunice "went to housekeeping."

one- or two-story wood-frame buildings or former single-family houses, the kitchen in the basement and shared privies in the back-yard. Eunice's new landlord, Leonard Fisher, donated firewood, but this time Eunice did the lion's share of labor herself, *even to the set-*

ting up of my stove which was a great job, for my funnel was too large for the hole in the chiminey, she explained. Then she had to haul the firewood herself, *and it rained quite hard and I had some ways to carry it to get it to the shed, and it was great big four foot wood, and that and moving twice so soon just about used me up.* Without a husband, or at least a husband's Union Army pay, the sweetness of Eunice's foray into housekeeping was considerably diminished.

Now Eunice filled her children's dinner plates with wild blackberries, apples, and dandelions. For poor people, and for women especially, low wages and inflation erased the positive effects of an expanded wartime economy. As prices mounted (flour cost fifteen dollars a barrel, three times what it had before the war), Eunice had little choice but to accept assistance. Father Stone brought her six quarts of applesauce and parts of a slaughtered hog. Margaret brought *a tin of buscits and a pound lump of butter* one day, *a bowl of white Sugar and half a dozen Crackers* on another. Eunice enlisted her stepfather to make shoes and fashioned herself a hood from silk and ribbon donated by Melissa and Margaret. Poor and working-class women did what they could to update older dresses and bonnets into newer styles, but without a sewing machine, it was hard. When Margaret admonished Eunice for going without a hat, Eunice tried to rustle one up. *You gave your old one to Ad, didnt you?* she asked her mother. *Well dont give her that black one even if you dont want it. I will have one out of it another winter if I live.*

EUNICE HAD FIRST entered the ranks of domestic employment when Clara was just six weeks old, working in the home of the elderly Captain James Sperry, a Washington Street neighbor. Sperry soon became Eunice's principal employer, with payment largely in the form of meals, which was *better than to be entirely dependant,* she told herself. Sometimes Father Stone took care of

Clara, and sometimes Clarence stayed home from school to watch his sister, but for the most part Eunice had to take the baby with her, *which makes my work harder and my pay less*, she conceded. Living by herself with both children, she also had her own household to maintain—her own stove to blacken, oatmeal to soak, vegetable garden to tend, chickens to pluck and kill. One week, she worked *three days cleaning house and one day washing besides washing and ironing here*. Another time, she *washed Monday then went to cleaning this house in the afternoon*. After that, she *engaged one day out washing bed cloths*. To work as a servant and washerwoman was far from what Eunice had imagined when she married William Stone at the age of seventeen. It was heartening to blame the interruption of war, but it would have been more heartening by far if her husband had been fighting for the Union.

Eunice did not possess the education or skills that secured Yankee women positions in schoolrooms or behind sales counters. She had once earned extra money sewing frocks, but true dressmaking was a skilled trade. Unskilled northern women preferred the mills to domestic service, since servitude paid less for more demeaning labor ("I think it would be better then so much house work," wrote a cousin of Eunice's about factory labor, noting that she "could stand it much better"), but Eunice couldn't bring Clara along to the factory floor. Alternatively, mothers in need of money could turn their homes into boardinghouses, but with two children, there was no room for that. Next down the ladder was domestic work that provided room and board, but a young child ruled out that option too. *If I could go into the Mill this Summer I could get a long*, Eunice had determined just after Clara was born. *But if my baby lives I cannot do much in the Mill this summer, and I dont know as any one would want me to do house work with so young a child.*

Live-in maids with children of their own had to send their offspring away to board with someone else, so working mothers often settled for live-out housework. Although such positions precluded a boss's constant watchful eye, the cost was high; day wages were no better than those paid to live-ins and did not include shelter. This, however, was precisely the bleak scenario for which Eunice now settled. In Claremont, at thirty years old, she slipped to near the lowest possible status a white woman could know: unskilled, caring for her children in between housecleaning and laundering for hire, vigilantly but barely keeping destitution at arm's length. All in all, it was a lowly and onerous existence. Only prostitution or the poorhouse would have felt more degraded. Only her own tenement served as retreat.

Domestic labor was degrading not least because the work was so hard. It was not simply that middle-class Victorian parlors called for dusting and polishing an abundance of knickknacks, recesses, and moldings but also that cleaning any house included battling the soot from stoves, the grime from fireplaces, and the mud tracked inside from unpaved streets. Preparing a meal meant bending over a smoky open hearth or a wood-burning oven to heave heavy iron skillets. In homes without indoor plumbing, water for cooking and cleaning had to be carried inside (in New England winters that meant cracking and melting ice) and then back outside when dirtied, as many as ten times a day. Chamber pots too had to be emptied, no matter how cold, or how warm, the weather.

Washing was the most frequent request because it was the most burdensome household enterprise; if families could afford only one form of help, they opted for a laundress. The process began with making soap, which involved melting and boiling cooking grease and lard, ashes and lime, for hours over a fire, skimming and stirring until the mixture cooled and hardened, then melting and hardening again. After that, the work entailed hauling water, building a fire to heat the water, soaking soiled articles, boiling and stirring, scrubbing against a washboard, rinsing and wringing out, dipping in starch and wringing out again, then stooping and reaching to hang each item on a clothesline. Instructions for washing blankets began with the warning to "select a warm and long day, and begin at an early hour." The same manual told women to "make suds as hot as the hand can bear." Pressing might be a whole separate day's work. Irons in the nineteenth century were just that: ferrous lumps, with a handle and one flat side, that had to be heated over a fire or atop the stove, then hoisted over wrinkled cottons and linens.

By midcentury, domestic work had earned disdain for another reason: It was the realm in which Irish immigrant and African American women converged (Bridget and Dinah were the respective stereotypical names bestowed upon maids). As early as the 1840s, an observer believed that "fewer and fewer" Yankee girls and women were "willing to hire out as household servants," and in the 1850s a writer found that "menial service" was "left almost exclusively to negroes and the newly-imported Irish." Such commentary filled the pages of middle-class reading, from leisure magazines to advice handbooks. Household expert Catharine Beecher and her sister Harriet Beecher Stowe wrote of the "universal rejection of domestic service in all classes of American-born society," reporting that (white) Yankee girls and women "preferred the factory," preferred even "chances of ruin and starvation." Native-born whites did not take positions as servants, reasoned a gazette editor, "not in the South, because slaves are servants; not in the North, because the Irish are servants." Louisa May Alcott, the author of *Little Women*, discovered that "leaving the paternal roof to wash other people's

BRIDGET.—"Indade, Misthress Smith isn't in the House. She tould me to tell you so, this very minit, when she set her eyes on you."

Native-born white Americans in the nineteenth century believed domestic service suitable only for Irish and African American women. This 1857 cartoon, left, and 1860 advertisement, below, respectively display stereotypical images of "Bridget" and "Dinah."

teacups, nurse other people's ails, and obey other people's orders for hire—this, this was degradation."

Though Claremont's population was almost entirely native-born and white, such long-circulating ideas retained a good deal of power. To families whose husbands provided for their wives and children, to Yankee women who deserted the factories when immigrants arrived, to mistresses who assigned the drudgery of domestic labor to those unlike themselves, Eunice's plebeian occupations crowded her into circumstances resembling those of Irish and black women and so permitted other white people to maintain a sense of superiority over her. As one New Hampshire newspaper put it, "Our native born citizens hate to work by the side of an Irishman," since that aroused "the same feeling which makes it impossible for a respectable white man to labor by the side of slaves at the South." The same could be said about native-born white women, for working the same jobs as Irish and black women made it harder to claim the respectability and dignity meant to accompany white womanhood, and Eunice's share of each was rapidly diminishing in 1863.

Clarence had to earn his keep too, by sawing and stacking wood and haying for Uncle Alonzo, by bringing in wood for a neighbor, and performing chores for Captain Sperry. Sometimes the boy went sledding or ice-skating, once he had *a grand time* at a Universalist festival (the church ladies paid for his ticket), and when a circus came to town, he contrived *every way to earn a quarter*, so he could go. But most of the time, Clarence started early in the morning, labored through dusk, and came home tired enough to head straight for bed. Eunice was proud that her son liked school, but these days he attended only when he had no work. Soon Eunice considered finding him steadier employment, for he was *getting old enough to begin to earn his living* (he was ten years old when she made that consideration). *It grieves me to think of putting him away*, she wrote, meaning that Clarence would live in someone else's household, performing marginal labor in exchange for full support. She and William had once seemed close to creating a better life for their children, first in Manchester, then fleetingly in Mobile; now her son's prospects only made her *anxious and uneasy.*

Sometimes Eunice got sick from working so hard, but keeping busy also staved off depression. *It helps to take up the mind and keep one from thinking so much,* she convinced herself. Still, more days at work inevitably brought more incidents of debasement, and in isolated moments Eunice fought back. One evening, she returned to her tenement to find that the audacious Captain Sperry had stopped in *three times to see if I had got home,* she narrated, and had Clarence fix him a cup of tea. When Eunice arrived, the hateful

Eunice's son, Clarence, was eleven or twelve years old when this photograph was taken. The boy's autograph indicates his full name, William Clarence Stone. No image of Clarence's younger sister Clara survives.

man ordered her to fix him a bowl of porridge, even before she had her shawl off her shoulders.

You have come to a poor place to get porridge made, Mr Sperry—it wasn't her job to feed him in the evenings.

Well I suppose you have been at work, he retorted.

Yes I have been working hard all day, just come in to the house more dead than alive, Eunice shot back. *I think your folks are better able to make your porridge than I be.* With that, the man stormed off. *He had tormented me almost to death with his hateful self for a week,* Eunice finished. When Sperry was arrested for trying to choke his wife, Eunice had to testify against him in court, then (since he wasn't kept in jail) go to work for him the next day. *I dont know what kind of a reception he will give me nor dont care much,* she tossed off, *for I aint afraid of him.* When a Sperry daughter returned from California, though, Eunice lost her job, meaning she also lost meals and wages.

If impertinence momentarily soothed the soul, more lasting solace came in the form of Eunice's renewed access to Universalism, for Claremont had been an early stronghold of that faith, and the church there remained vibrant. The Russell women were active in the Ladies' Samaritan Society, gathering at one another's homes to read, sew, or fund-raise, and Margaret regularly hosted the ladies' meetings. As for Eunice, some Sundays she attended church for half the day, sometimes all day, while Clarence attended Sabbath school or joined his mother at services. *We had a beautiful discourse,* Eunice rhapsodized to her mother one Sunday in June; another week she heard *such a beautiful sermon* that she *could not help hanging upon every word.* Maybe she leafed through the Universalist hymnal, finding consolation in verses about contentment and resignation ("If solid happiness we prize / Within our breasts the jewel lies"). Or, when she wondered when the war would end, perhaps she appealed to God to "bid the human tempest cease / And hush the maddening world to peace." As happiness on earth became an ever more elusive prospect, Eunice kept trying to alleviate her daily concerns with the promise of eternal joy.

Eunice did not, however, accompany Margaret Russell or Albert's wife, Mary Russell, or even her close companion Melissa Stone to the ladies' meetings, just as she did not join Claremont wives and daughters in rolling bandages for Union soldiers. Dues for the wartime sewing circle ran a dollar, and whatever articles Eunice stitched went to her own children. The fee was only twelve cents to socialize with the Universalist ladies, but Eunice's days and evenings were already taken up.

Cash and time aside, however, there was something else to her exclusion. Even the Universalist *Ladies' Repository* wasn't really intended for women like Eunice. An article that asked readers to "remember the poor" counseled that a handout to "these degraded beings" should be "sweetened by a kindly word." That in fact was Eunice's abject place, for Claremont's Universalist church counted her among its charity cases. Her landlord, Leonard Fisher, who gave her firewood, was a prominent Universalist whose wife served as vice-president of Claremont's Auxiliary Sanitary Commission during the war; Fred Clement's family belonged to the church too (he was the one who piled firewood on his wagon when Eunice first went to housekeeping); and one December evening ladies from the Universalist Samaritan Society brought Eunice food and more firewood. Those who received alms could not very well join the social circles of those who provided.

Eunice never had to declare herself a legal pauper or move to Claremont's poor farm, and she never did resort to sending Clarence away. Instead, she managed to maintain her ranking, if just barely, among the working and worthy poor, those whose hardships were

During the war, Eunice found solace at the Universalist church on Broad Street in Claremont, New Hampshire, even as she was excluded from the church ladies' social activities.

understood, at least theoretically, to be the result of misfortune rather than indolence or debauchery. Although her husband's kin readily assisted, Eunice's economic dependence nonetheless banished her just beyond the confines of respectability. That became startlingly clear when sister-in-law Margaret Russell rebuked Eunice for the unladylike act of going about bare-headed. *I said I havent a thing to put on*, Eunice recounted, thinking Margaret was *making fun*. But when Margaret called Eunice *very foolish* and warned her that *every body is wearing hats*, Eunice realized that this wasn't banter. As a poor relation, she had become both an embarrassment and a burden, and a downcast Eunice could only think wistfully about hats much more elegant than the common straw ones she crafted for sale, adding, *so now I wish I had one.*

Trouble was, she earned so little. William could have pocketed a dollar and a half a day at the carpentry trade—enough for a week's rent with some left over for food or fuel—but a woman who took a child to work with her might take in only two dollars for a week's worth of washing, ironing, and sewing for a family of five. Even if the mails could carry money from William to his wife, Confederate bills were worthless up north. Nor was the wife of a Confederate entitled to Claremont's fund for soldiers' families. Once, when Eunice confessed to her mother how poor she was, she asked that the letter be kept *PRIVATE*, but her condition was hard to hide. "She wore her clothes to rags," Lois discovered after Eunice's visit to Dracut. Although sister Ann hired herself a laundress (the Irish Mrs. Murry) and sister Hattie's family owned their own cottage (the ideal residence of the emerging middle classes), wartime inflation meant that neither one could assist Eunice much. One winter, Ann sent a dollar, *which has done me a great deal of good already*, Eunice effused; but Hattie's husband worked in the mill by day and cobbled shoes by night "and has come out spring poor," or so Hattie claimed.

Henry and Luther had always sent most of their soldiers' pay to their mother, but now the boys began to post money directly to Eunice, or sometimes Lois forwarded a portion of hers to Claremont. *I am afraid you make your self short by sending me so much*, Eunice apologized to her mother. *I do not want you to, for I shall live some way.*

ONCE, IN JANUARY 1863, Eunice referred to herself as a widow. Clarence had earned ten cents, and received a gift of seven cents, making him *a rich widows son*, she quipped. What Eunice did not know at the time was that the circumstance she both tried to imagine and constantly pushed away would very shortly come true. The eight forms filed under "Alabama Confederate Service Cards" in the Department of Archives and History in Montgomery indicate that William Stone fell ill and died in an Atlanta hospital on February 11, 1863. Whoever filled in the blanks did not know where he was born or how to reach his wife, but according to hospital records, he suffered from severe weakness following his regiment's participation in the Battle of Stones River. After less than three weeks in a sickbed, William died of chronic diarrhea—an ailment so prevalent among Confederate Army soldiers that it took more lives than enemy gunfire.

Well tomorrow is Williams birth day, Eunice wrote just a few weeks past his death. *O if we could only know if he be living or dead, if we knew he was still among the living we should hope some time to see him. And if we knew him to be dead than we should give up the last hope, and suspense would be at an end.* Precariously balanced, her thoughts were also accompanied by an undeniable sense of foreboding. *When Mobile falls into the hands of our people then I shall know what my fate is,* Eunice wrote to her brothers a few weeks later.

Pushing aside premonition and probability, Eunice wrote explicit directions to Henry and Luther in the event that the Twenty-sixth

Massachusetts should enter the city of Mobile. She told them where Ellen lived and which neighbors they might trust, and she warned them (ignoring, for the moment, her own *many misgivings* about her husband's persuasions) not to *say any thing about William's being a union man or in favor of the North*. She also asked her brothers to write to Ellen: *You might say "dear sister, I am well, please tell me of yourself and family, also of the other friends,"* then just *say Mother and Eunice are well, just to let them know I am alive and at home. But dont say anything about home or the North*. Those directions are preserved on a small square of paper, one end ragged, as if Henry or Luther carried it in a uniform pocket at all times.

Patriotism on the part of northern whites was beginning to wane by 1863, and soon Claremont had to resort to paying bounties or purchasing substitutes to fulfill its draft quotas. Home front forbearance gave way to disillusionment, and faith threatened to desert even the most devout, Eunice included. *It seems to be destined that we should be a broken seperated, and wandering family*, she mourned now, reiterating a theme familiar to the Richardsons, but also to many families during the war. Loneliness remained Eunice's most loyal companion. *It is a pretty day*, she wrote to her mother that September. *I wish you lived so I could see you every day, or every week at least*. Eunice was tired, not just from grinding labor but also from emotional strain. *I know a little what it is to drag around*, she admitted in late 1863, *when you feel more fit to be in bed, than out of it*.

Work became scarcer as 1864 arrived, since families hired fewer servants in hard times. *I do not go washing this winter*, she fretted, *for the reason I do not have any place to go*. Wartime prices continued to mount too. *Prehaps if I had a hundred thousand dollars I should not mind paying five for a cord of green beach wood*, she brooded, as charity again sealed her place on the margins of Claremont society. *I could not begin to live was it not for what is given me*, she admitted plainly. When

Eunice did get work in the lean times of 1864, her near exhaustion made it all the harder. *Last week I went away two days and did my own washing ironing and mending and braided three No. 3 hats besides taking care of Clara which you know is no small thing of its self,* she wrote one February evening, reserving no detail. The humiliation intensified when she received a nighttime call to wash the bedclothes of a man who had died at home, for to clean up after the sick and dead constituted the lowliest domestic work of all. *Do you want to know what I am doing this Spring? working at my trade—washing,* she wrote bitterly that March, sparing no one her emotions. For all her outbursts—*I dont know but I shall work myself to death this Spring*—she regretted complaining. *It will do no good of course, but I like to tell some body once in the will when I feel bad.* As the war continued on, gratefulness mixed with the wretchedness of dependence, and neither love of country nor love of God eased those tensions.

In 1864 too, both brothers reenlisted in the Union Army. *I thought I had become so inured to disapointment,* Eunice wrote to her mother that winter. *And to set down and write my feelings and anticipations and the disapointment would only be making the wound deeper in your own breast.* She earnestly reiterated the formulas of faith and patriotism (*I think I have given them up now into the hands of our Heavenly Father,* and *our Countrys cause demands just such noble true patriotic men*), but neither really helped, for she could only wonder if she would be able to see the boys when they returned north on furlough. "I dont think it would hurt mother to have a little rest," eleven-year-old Clarence put in wisely, and so Eunice decided to forfeit wages (and defy a perturbed mistress) in favor of a visit with Lois and a respite from the drudge of washing dirty clothes in damp weather.

Women who traveled regionally without male escorts (a common enough occurrence, as wives and daughters visited relatives) were treated well on the trains, no matter their social status, and Eunice likely found some relief in relying upon conductors and porters to help her purchase tickets and carry bags. But the cars were not particularly comfortable for a mother with two children: Seats were hard, floors cold, and the dusty compartment air was relieved only by wintry blasts whenever passengers alighted. When Eunice and the children returned from their Massachusetts holiday unwell—the reprieve had allowed Eunice to give in to a bad cold—she again defied her employers. *I had a call for a washing in less than half an hour after I got into the house*, she recounted. *I told them I could not wash for any body at present untill my health was better.* The visit had only aggravated her sense of isolation, and again Eunice made her sorrow plain. *I have thought of you all the time since I left you*, she told Lois, imploring her mother to make a reciprocal journey. *For I am so lonesome*, she confessed. *I want to see you already so soon. I want some of my folks near me.*

Warm weather and greater uncertainty arrived together, with Eunice trying to imagine different ways to support herself. Maybe folks in Nashua paid more for braided hats. Maybe Lois could come up to Claremont for a season to help out. Maybe Eunice could move to Dracut (*if there is any where for me to stay*, she hinted). Maybe she could find a different kind of work there, as a *saleswoman in some Store* or as a seamstress or a dressmaker, so she would *not have to wash and clean and do a work that is so hard.* In the end, Eunice resigned herself, though not without vocal resentment. *There seems to be nothing to do but washing or folks think I can do nothing else*, she cried. Even her own household overwhelmed her. *It is too hard for me to work and earn my living and take care of my house and children*, she went on, alluding to her wish for a husband who could provide, whether as civilian or Union soldier. *You know it comes doubly hard on a woman when they have both to do.*

Small confrontations, like the one with Captain Sperry over his porridge or the run-in with Margaret about the hat, magnified

Eunice's sense of day-to-day abasement. There were other incidents too. *Just as I was finishing up your letter Mrs Parmelees boy came in and turned my ink over into my lap and all over the side of my dress, and spilt a whole bottle of ink,* Eunice seethed one day in 1864. When her tenement mate shrugged off her son's carelessness, telling Eunice, *it aint as if your clothes were nice ones,* that *provoked* her *more than all the rest.* Another time Mrs. Parmelee let slip that a neighbor had spoken ill of Eunice because she refused to send Clarence away. *Some folks think because a person is poor they dont want any thing for comfort,* Eunice bristled. In fact, women who worked as domestic servants risked their very virtue in the supposed coarseness of their daily lives. Catharine Beecher exhorted mistresses to take on "the duties of missionaries," for their "raw, untrained" servants could, with some effort, be molded into "good wives and mothers for the republic." Eunice was selling her labor to earn a living, with no need

My only support—both boys gone to the war. I wonder if they would take me?

Like the woman in this drawing, Eunice undertook the lowly and arduous labor of washing other people's clothes during the Civil War. This laundress, who had two sons at the front and no husband to support her, wondered whether she could join the Union Army herself.

for the maternal guardianship that so often accompanied positions of servitude. While neighbors whispered about her refusal to send her son away, while kin reprimanded her for the rags she wore, Eunice's employers saw her as rough and vulgar, pushing her closer to nativist and racist portraits of Irish and African American women and farther from the ideal of middle-class Yankee womanhood.

You will say I have got the blues, prehaps I have, Eunice wrote to Lois in 1864. She called it *the blues,* but a doctor would have told her she was suffering from "melancholy," defined by the medical literature of the day as despondence resulting from disappointment and grief (and thought to be on a continuum with insanity). Eunice's sense of herself on most days was captured in sentences like *I believe I am about played out,* or *I dont seem to be worth anything,* or *I dont believe I always was such a fool, but some how I cant help it now.* She was, in short, *low spirited* and unused to *giving way to despair quite so much.* That was the gist of the problem, in her own assessment: her inability to invoke Yankee stoicism or Christian sufferance in order to exercise control over her *rather nervous* state.

In the same breath, Eunice anticipated and refuted admonition. *You will say I must not look ahead,* she predicted, adding, *I should like to know where one with a family to take care of will look.* Return mail helped (*I want you should answer evry part of this letter*), and when none came, she cast herself at fault (*Was my last letter one you could not answer or did'nt you want to?*). Any interval of time between correspondence felt like neglect, flaring sadness into anger. *I wondered if you knew how long it had been since you had written to me!* she chided Lois. *What do you suppose I think when you do not write for five or six weeks?* Her verdict: *I know times are only getting worse.* Come cold weather, she might have to move back in with the Russells or Father Stone. Independence Day was meant to be a merry holiday for children, but Clarence was haying that summer, and the Fourth of July found the boy in the field until seven at night, when he snapped a few firecrackers before succumbing to his own exhaustion. All Eunice could think was that *he has got to get used to disapointments in life if he lives.*

Death dwelled with Eunice in 1864, on both sides of the war. It seemed so long until her brothers would return from the army, *if they live.* She continued to hope that Mobile would fall and William escape, *and yet I dread it,* she added, ever uncertain of his survival. And of herself: *I dont know yet what I shall do if I live.* In August, Eunice was already looking toward winter *with dread and anxiety.* Now she sewed stockings at especially pitiable wages. *We get 85 cents for a dosen pairs,* she reported. Water-powered machines formed the tube, which women finished by hand, by knitting heels and toes—mean piecework it was. Wages fell steadily as starving and unskilled women competed in the needle trades, so that a day's toil might yield fifty cents or a quarter. The seamstresses could only console themselves that hand sewing at home was work for white American women, a task seldom given out to blacks or immigrants. Fleeting relief came in the form of a visit to Father Stone or Clara's newest vocabulary, but sometimes even a Sunday at church turned out to be *a rainy lonesome kind of a day.* All Eunice could write about was the unbearable *sence of lonliness,* how everything was *so lonesome and such hard times.*

AFTER THE WAR took Henry and Luther Richardson to Mississippi and Louisiana, it took them to northern Virginia to join General Philip Sheridan's Shenandoah Valley campaign. Sloping downward from south to north, the valuable and contested valley—the fields and orchards between the Allegheny and Blue Ridge mountains kept an army well fed—served as a natural corridor for Confederate encroachment upon Washington. The area had hosted continuous fighting almost from the start of the war, and the autumn of 1864 saw the Third Battle of Winchester, in which Sheridan's Union forces defeated Confederate General Jubal Early.

For the Richardson brothers, it began at three o'clock in the morning, as they set out to march the ten miles from Berryville toward the town of Winchester through a narrow ravine thick with rocks and underbrush, artillery and ammunition wagons. Early's men watched from the bluffs, ready to attack the moment Union troops emerged onto a field, and near noon the Twenty-sixth Massachusetts broke through the woods only to be hit with a volley of fire. "A tremendous and prolonged roar and rattle told us that the battle was on," a Connecticut officer recalled. "Amid the din arose a quick succession of deafening crashes, and shot and shell came singing and howling over us." Away from the front lines, "along every roadway, out of the forests, across the meadows, came ambulances and stretchers," remembered a Massachusetts man, adding, "The dead were horrible dead." The battle continued until sunset, until Sheridan's men drove the Rebels back through town.

Hard Confederate fighting and faulty Union planning aside, the Yankees who triumphed at Third Winchester made memories out of cheering as the enemy fled, General Sheridan riding alongside the lines. The victory would also be recalled as an important turning point in the Civil War, for it helped spur Lincoln's reelection that November. It was "a day of glory but also of sorrow," according to the aforementioned Connecticut man, for the Union losses "told how dearly Sheridan's first great victory was gained." In the brothers' regiment alone, almost forty men died at the Battle of Winchester on September 19, 1864. Luther Richardson Jr. was one among nearly seven hundred Union dead. He was twenty-three years old.

Eunice was apprised of Luther's death on a Sunday morning in early October. Her *first intimation* came while she was taking the newspaper to her in-laws Margaret and Alonzo Russell. Scanning the columns as she walked, her eye caught her brother's name: *I looked at the heading and found why it was there*. In Dracut, Lois had closely watched the news of fighting in Virginia. "O what a blow it was for us all," she mourned. "Luthers name among the killed"— and Henry's among the wounded, for he had lost the tip of a finger—"I canot write my feelings." Meanwhile Eunice's stepsister, Addie Davis, had read the papers in Northfield, Massachusetts, where she was working for Lois's sister. "It said Luther Richardson of company A killed," Addie told Lois. "Is it possible that Luther is dead, there is no middle name given, perhaps there is some misstake."

A letter from Henry arrived for Lois while Hattie and Ira were visiting, and they read along, praying that he would refute the casualty listing. "My Dear Mother," they found instead, "it is with a sad Heart and aching head that I seat myself to Scribble these few lines to you." Henry narrated how the regiment had started out in the morning, "with orders to find the enemy and attack him," before offering the dreaded confirmation: "among one killed was my dear Brother Luther." Henry hadn't been at his side but assured the family that death had come instantly, that Luther never spoke after he was struck. Henry had come upon his older brother "lieing dead upon the field," "stiff and cold upon the field." He buried Luther right there but could say little more, "for it seems like a dream," he recounted.

Echoing the sentimental language that made death bearable to Civil War families, Henry believed that Luther had been "as brave as the best and died the Soldiers death with his face to the foe." One of many popular wartime lyrics imagined the voice of the dead soldier, commanding a survivor to "Bear this gently to my mother," to "Kiss her dear old wrinkled brow / Kiss my sister and my brother / Say 'he is an angel now,'" and that was what Henry tried to accomplish in his letter. Acknowledging Luther's death with all finality, he signed himself "your only and affectionate Son." The stains on the first of Henry's two letters about Luther's death may be Henry's own tears or those of his mother and sister. When Lois wrote back, she signed off "from your affectionate mother Lois Davis to her onely surviving son." When the folks in Dracut brought word to sister Ann, she "controled her feelings better than I was afraid she would," Hattie recorded, "but she was deeply grieved." It would have cost nearly a hundred dollars to have Luther's body disinterred and sent north in a coffin, wholly unaffordable for the Richardsons. The unidentified remains of Union soldiers, many dug up from battlefields on orders from President Lincoln, can be found today in the Winchester National Cemetery in the center of town (the very land where many fell on September 19), Luther Richardson among them in an unmarked grave.

I learned of dear Luthers death Sabbath morning, Eunice wrote to her mother after she saw the newspaper on her way to the Russells. Poverty deprived her of the release of mourning, for even if Henry were permitted a visit home, Eunice couldn't pay for a ticket to Dracut or forsake her wages. *Mr Goss will be after me tomorrow after noon*, she knew, since an employer (as Louisa May Alcott observed) "took no more personal interest in her servants than if they were clocks, to be wound up once a day." Only her own family could *know what I have lost and the depth of my grief*, Eunice wept. *I so much feel the need of comfort myself that I can hardly say any thing to comfort you*, she apologized to Lois. Her heart rebelled at the will of God, and faith danced with doubt, as Eunice grasped at the links between loved ones in heaven and those still on earth. From Universalist theology, she urged her mother, and herself, to *feel that God is <u>love</u> and has <u>taken</u> him to <u>himself</u>*.

Eunice must have prayed in church, in bed, every morning and evening of that terrible autumn and winter. "God does not require that our petition be couched in elegant and beautiful language," a Universalist newspaper counseled, for "the lowliest and poorest soul" could "talk with God, heart to heart." Even the exclusive *Ladies' Repository* made clear that anyone could appeal to God, at dawn or midnight, or in "the evening's quiet hour of sadness." The prayer might be a murmur or a thought, that was enough, and in church Eunice listened to assurances of final happiness for all, as opposed to endless suffering for most. *Mother I am all alone as it were, and I have but one way for comfort*, she tried to convince herself, *through faith alone.* Yet the loss of Luther fed other fears. *If William was with me it seems as if I could bear up better*, she admitted, for there was *no one to go to with my feelings*—perhaps Eunice believed Melissa Stone had already heard enough. Now, with heightened fears about her husband's very survival, crept the shadow of suicide. *I nearly gave up*, Eunice put down cryptically, *but I will try and be strong.* In the meantime, she wanted to know if the family would wear black garments. *In my circumstances*, she lamented, *I can not.*

Eunice scrounged up mourning clothes that winter after all, in the shape of a black bonnet and an old black shawl. Patriotism fortified the others, as it fortified so many families in the face of loss. "I am stronger for the Union than ever now," Hattie asserted, insisting that her brother's blood not be "shed in vein." For Lois, the searing grief was tempered by knowledge of "thousands of Northern mothers weeping, weeping over their loved sons that lay beneath the southern sod."

Not so for Eunice, whose depression numbed all such convictions. *We have a great republican Mass meeting in Claremont expected to be a great affair*, she wrote in October. *Great preparations are being made, but oh dear it seems as though I dont care for any such thing.* "Ann feels the loss but she bears it with christian fortitude," Lois told Henry. "But poor Eunice I am afraid it will overcome her."

Indeed, Eunice made her ever-deepening despair no secret. She was grateful when Henry traveled to New Hampshire to see her on furlough—his letters to their mother constantly betrayed his deep fondness for his sister ("You must help Eunice more," he beseeched Lois. "Take good care of her and do not let her want for anything")—but Eunice couldn't help wishing that Lois would visit too. *You are all to me now, except my children, and they are too young yet for me to go to with trouble*, she pleaded. Now Eunice seriously considered leaving Claremont for good, finally to be closer to mother and sisters in the face of Luther's death.

The very first letter that Eunice had written from Claremont, composed in December 1861, displayed a tentative hopefulness for her family's future. By contrast, the one she wrote exactly three years later conveyed no such glimmers. *It is after I have been off to work as I have now and come home to a cold house and every thing out of fix, that I think I want to go some where or do some way to live different,* she scratched out on a rainy Saturday evening at the end of 1864. Now her sadness felt too intense to preserve in a letter. *Prehaps I shall not send this, for I write you a good many letters that I dont send,* she revealed. *When I feel lonesome and bad as if I must see you, I set down and write, then the next day burn them up.* Three years after her escape from the South, and more than three years into the war, one brother dead and her husband unaccounted for, Eunice, about to turn thirty-three years old, threw away the modest hopes that had accompanied her on the journey back north from Mobile. Alabama had been a great disappointment, not least because the war confounded the Stones' promising sojourn there. As the war raged on, Eunice's beloved New England was proving no better.

In the end, Eunice and the children embarked on a harsh December journey by rail and stagecoach, departing Claremont to go live with Lois in Dracut, and so there are no more letters between

Eunice and her mother during the last months of the war. The men of the Ninth Vermont, including Alonzo and Margaret Russell's son, Albert, entered the Confederate capital at Richmond, Virginia, on April 3, 1865. "Densely packed on either side of the street were thousands upon thousands of blacks, till that moment slaves," wrote one of the regiment's generals. In the words of another, "We knew that our work was done, fully and completely done." By April 9, Union troops had successfully assaulted enough of the surrounding forts that they could have entered the city of Mobile. The same day, at the courthouse in Appomattox, Virginia, Robert E. Lee surrendered to Ulysses S. Grant. At last, the war was over.

IN LOWELL, Massachusetts, church and millyard bells pealed, and cannons boomed. THE MORNING COMETH, announced the headlines. CLOSING VICTORY OF THE WAR. Immediately thereafter arrived the news that John Wilkes Booth had assassinated President Lincoln at Ford's Theater in Washington, D.C. The city of Lowell had planned to dedicate a monument to the Sixth Massachusetts (that was Henry's original regiment), but residents spent the morning draping buildings in black and white bunting instead. "Such unreserved sorrow was never before felt in this land," a Lowell woman recorded in her diary, easily echoing the sentiments of Eunice's family, or at least most of them.

For Eunice, as for so many others on both sides of the war, those mid-April days of national jubilation or trauma were accompanied by everything she had dreaded over the last four years. From Claremont, Margaret Russell posted a letter to Dracut. Margaret had received the tidings from Ellen, who had written to Eunice in care of William's folks. "It is with a sad heart that I write you this eve," Margaret began. "I hope you will pardon me for opening your letter, it came last eve. I felt that I could not let it be. I did not think of death at first but I soon found out that it told of what we have feared would be." Margaret didn't need to say that William was dead, since the enclosed letter from Ellen bore those words. There was a communication from William himself as well, likely written while he was sick in the Confederate hospital in Atlanta, for Margaret knew that the family would "allways remember the last good by." For her part, Margaret realized that her own words were of little help. "If I could write as I can think, I mite say something to comfort you but I am not capable of it," she regretted. "Try and think it is the will of God. I hope there is better days in store for you." As for Ellen, she had proved luckier than her sister once again, for Dudley Merrill survived the war, and now Ellen wished to mend fences with her Union kin. "Eunice, I think your Sister wrote you a beautiful letter," Margaret offered. "It will be a comfort to you all to here from her." Father Stone, she added, had been informed of his son's death.

Mary Russell, Albert's wife, sent a letter to Eunice too. "I feel that I can write nothing to comfort you, in this your hour of suffering," she began. "We have all thought many times that we would give almost any thing if we could learn the Fate of your Husband and probably imagined we were prepared to hear even the sad news of his Death rather than wait longer in terrible suspense." Whatever information the Russells had received, William "did not live to suffer long," as they understood it. "Strength has been given you and I pray God it may be given you now, in your heaviest trial," Mary concluded, adding that she had received word from Albert; "he is all right," she wrote, "encamped in front of Jeff Davis' house." No doubt Melissa Stone wrote to Eunice too, but Eunice probably kept that for herself. Neither Ellen's letter nor William's farewell message has been preserved; Eunice must have kept those for herself too.

Eunice never set down exactly how she felt about her husband's fighting for the South, probably because she was never sure where his sentiments ultimately rested, but no matter his convictions or her own, his death came as a terrible blow. Now, in the summer after the war, she wrote openly about suicide. Perhaps she knew the poem from the *Rose of Sharon* Universalist magazine that went like this:

I would not stay forever here,
In this sad world of care and pain;
I would not have life linger on,
Or give my thoughts to earth again.

I long to close my tearful eyes,
Recline my weary, aching head
Upon the couch where all is peace,
And rest among the early dead.

In her own words, she put it this way: *I believe there comes a time with almost every one when it would be sweet to die.* Once Eunice had nurtured a kernel of optimism, but now, she wrote to Henry, *My star of hope has set, gone down in darkness and despair and left a dark empty void. Where peace and joy should have a home, is nothing, nothing, nothing.*

Well, I have filled up my paper now
I will finish up Mr Connolleys with some
nonsence or other, But it is a busy time.
on board and noise enough on Deck
to break up ten Town meetings, Mr Connoll
and Clara have just been having a dance
and here comes the Steward to make the
the Table ready for supper. I can't give you
much of an idea of what life on board
has been today, But I must finish up
my letter or I shall not get it ashore
tonight for they are going haul off in the
stream, But you and Hattie ____ and
Ira must write some good long letters
and send them on so I will not have
to wait very long after I get out there for
I am wanting to hear from you now so
much that I don't know how to wait, I do
want to know how Harriet is getting along
and how you are. I am afraid you are
sick, I know you have been a dear good
brave little Mother through giving me up
But I could see more anguish in your look

5

FROM WIDOW TO BRIDE

Provincetown, Massachusetts, November 13, 1869

Well, I have filled up my paper now I will finish up Mr Connolly's with some nonsense or other. But it is a buisy time on board and noise enough on Deck to break up ten Town meetings. Mr Connolly and Clara have just been having a dance and here comes the Steward to make the Table ready for supper. I can't give you much of an idea of what life on board has been today. But I must finish up my letter or I shall not get it ashore tonight for they are going to haul off in the stream. But you and Hattie and Ira must write some good long letters and send them on so I will not have to wait very long after I get out there for I am wanting to hear from you now so much that I don't know how to wait. I do want to know how Harriet is getting along and how you are. I am afraid you are sick. I know you have been a dear good brave little Mother through giving me up. But I could see more anguish in your look when I left you than you intended me to. The thought of your pale face as it looked the last time I looked upon it will always make me feel bad. I had many things I waited to say to you and some to Henry & Harriet, but I could not. You all felt bad and my own heart was so full, I found the less I said the better it would be for all of us. For I knew we all needed all the strength we could get. But when I left you __my Mother__ I did not feel as if I went alone with my own strength but I felt as if I was being sustained by unseen powers. What did Father Blood say. Tell him to write me a good Fatherly letter. Tell me what Mrs Wilson said and every body else. I wanted to tell Brother Henry how much I had always loved him and how his treatment had pained me, but it is perhaps better that I did not. What did Clara say to the Shells—and because she did not have a flower? O you must tell me all these little things. Give my love to Ira. I did not leave it for him when I came away for I see how bad sis felt and I could not speak. Let Ann know you have heard from me if you have a chance. I had some thing else here to say but Mr Connolly came and began to play and made me forget what it was. He is afraid my writing will make me down hearted and he is perfectly unhappy himself if he thinks I am not happy. But I wish you could hear him wishing Clara was a Boy, I guess it is as much as the twentieth time. I have not had any letters since I came here. Clarence is going up to the Office to Mail this and may get one. But I must say good by I suppose. Now do not neglect to write to me, give my love to Mrs Van and do not forget me when you see Mr and Mrs Patten. I have a thousand things to say now but must stop and say good by again. So now My dear Mother Sisters Brother and friends Farewell. I feel quite bad to think of the long good by it will be, but do not forget the absent ones, good by good by.

O n Mammoth Road in the town of Dracut, north from today's busy intersection with Lakeview (called River Road in Eunice's day), Lois's home occupied half of a dwelling that still stands, close to the road on the left side. It was here that Eunice and the children arrived when they left Claremont that dismal winter at the end of 1864. A little over a year later, Eunice departed her mother's home to live once again with members of her husband's family, this time in Vermont. In another house that's still standing, this one near an intersection called Morristown Corners, Eunice retreated. The present-day Morristown Corner Store served as the post office in her day, and you can conjure Eunice, bundled in a heavy cloak, making her way through the frigid air and snowdrifts, to dispatch her letters in the equally dismal winter of 1866.

Eunice became gravely ill after the Civil War. In Massachusetts and Vermont, she convalesced and mourned, for with the death of William Stone in the Confederate Army came the complete disintegration of everything she had imagined for herself and her family. In the years just after the war, as Eunice grew strong enough to take up domestic labor again, she resigned herself to an earthly stay of poverty and loneliness, praying only that young Clarence and Clara would find a way out and up.

As it turned out, however, these years marked a crucial turning point, for it was during this time that Eunice made the second unconventional decision of her life. Like the plan to leave Mobile and return north without her husband, this decision was also undertaken in the interest of both family security and personal happiness. Yet the choice she made after the Civil War far surpassed her wartime conduct in its magnitude of nonconformity. Eunice's actions after the war redrew the lines of family conflict, turning attention away from North-South politics and introducing the problem of the black-white color line. Eunice's newfound happiness came tempered by fresh sorrows, even as she remained resolute in the venture she had chosen for herself and her children.

Between December 1864, when Eunice and the children emptied their cramped tenement and bade farewell to relatives in Claremont, and November 1869, when the three of them departed North America for the Caribbean, Eunice wrote very few letters. For some of that time, she was simply too sick. For much of it, she lived with her mother, and close enough to many of the siblings, that daily contact or frequent visits precluded correspondence. Those geographical circumstances, along with missing family papers, shroud some of the details of Eunice's transformation, but the radically altered tone of her letters from the Caribbean attest to how remarkable a transformation it was.

"Mother, write me all of the perticulars about Eunice," sister Ann pleaded after the news of William's death in April 1865, asking Lois to send word up Mammoth Road and across the state border to Pelham, New Hampshire, by way of the milkman. "I am afraid this trouble will be more than she can bear." Ann was right, for Eunice was near collapse at Lois's home in Dracut. Despite the proximity to Lowell's expansive textile mills, Dracut remained a small farming village on the Merrimack River, and Eunice needed just such quiet and isolation to aid her recuperation. Ann took in Clarence, Hattie took in Clara—again the children were separated from their mother and from each other—and Lois nursed Eunice around the clock. Eunice was unable to sit up for more than a few minutes at a time, Lois informed the folks in Claremont, and steadily growing worse. "It was not thought she could live," Lois admitted to Henry, "and in all probability, would have died" if the family had failed to consult a different doctor.

That Lois called three physicians, let alone one, indicates the seriousness of Eunice's condition. Most families in the 1860s, especially among the working classes, cared for the sick themselves. Home nursing was women's work, and traditional remedies mixed from herbs and leaves made for trusted tonics. When families like the Richardsons did seek medical assistance, they could afford only men of lesser education. Diagnoses consisted of naming the patient's symptoms without much regard to cause, and a common prescription was a glass of whiskey. Three different doctors came to Mammoth Road to observe that Eunice was fevered and weak, experiencing "attacks" that made her "helpless," and hallucinating. She "said she felt," Lois related, "as tho she had ben living in Mobile," the place, in her delirious mind, where all her troubles began. The medical men named Eunice's state as one of "universal weakness," attributing the symptoms to her being "so reduced" and to "failing all winter." They ruminated on the lack of "vitality" in her blood, mentioned "southern malaria," the arduous journey from Alabama, and "over exertion" ever since.

Back in Claremont during the war, Eunice had admitted to melancholia, describing herself as *played out* and *low spirited, rather nervous* and unable to surmount a sense of despair. As she lay abed in Dracut, the medical profession stood on the cusp of naming neurasthenia, a disorder understood to be an overwhelming exhaustion of the nerves. Although doctors were quicker to diagnose this condition among the well-to-do, more ordinary folks could also succumb, they believed, if subject to shock and bereavement or fatigue and poor nutrition. Maybe Ann came closest to the root cause of Eunice's affliction when she asked, "Wasnt it sad news for her, Williams death, after liveing in hopes so long?" If that loss hadn't forced Eunice to come to a halt, said Lois, echoing the doctors, "she would probably have kept around a few weeks longer and then gone down never to rise again." That final desertion, William's death, had prompted a breakdown, and Eunice's recovery was long and slow. In the summer heat, progress seemed "scarcely disernable," Lois told the others, and just "one step backward," it seemed, would endanger Eunice's life all over again.

At least Henry's letters, as he waited to be mustered out of the Union Army, cheered her up. Over and over during the war, Henry had reminded his mother to take good care of his unfortunate sister and not to let Eunice "suffer for any thing." *Who ever had such dear, generous, noble hearted Brothers*, Eunice had exclaimed back then. *I never can repay them for their kindness.* Now Luther was dead, and if only her beloved Henry could start home! "Poor thing she wants to say so much to you," Lois told her son, just before the Twenty-sixth Massachusetts was unexpectedly ordered to occupy Savannah, and in the wake of disappointment, old tensions surfaced. "Dear Mother," Henry wrote from Georgia, his mean streak on full display, "thinking that perhaps you had forgotten my address or that you had forgotten that I was alive I enclose you an envelope bearing my address also a sheet of paper and stamps also a pen." Still, Henry's concern for Eunice never waned. "Poor Sister I wish I could be with her," he lamented. "Tell her she must get well before I come home anyway or I shall be lonsome."

That summer, Eunice finally wrote down her own assessment of her condition. *Here I come again after so long a silence, quite a stranger in your tent arent I?* she greeted Henry. But the sprightly tone lasted no further than the salutation. *When I wrote you last (nearly four months ago) I was full of hope and looking forward to a life of joy,* she imparted now, dismissing all previous preparations for William's death. *But it is all gone, past away,* she went on, for she had been *keeping hope alive in my heart and living upon it days, and weeks and months, and years, untill all was gone in an instant as it were, and I seemed slipping off some terriable precipice in the dark.* It was Eunice's daughter, three years old, who pulled her back. *At last I came to look upon it as a terriable dream until darling little Clara put her little arms around my neck,* Eunice recounted, *and says "Dont cry mama, poor child, I will take care of you, mama" and putting her little rosebud mouth to my haggard cheek, brought me back to my self and to life as it was, with all its stearn realities.*

It was at this point that Eunice made her starkest confession of despondence. *I believe there comes a time with almost every one when it would be sweet to die,* she confided to Henry. *But I must live. I hardly knew why for a long time, but I now see I must live for my children, for you, and for all.* Even at that moment of renewed resolve, Eunice nearly abandoned her faith in the benevolent God of Universalism. Her worldly troubles were hers alone, *and I must bear them alone, yes, alone,* she wrote.

THE MATERIAL circumstances of Eunice's life remained deeply discouraging in the summer of 1865. Now she earned only the meager wages of a seamstress, an occupation nearly as lowly as laundering (tolerated, remarked Louisa May Alcott, "if done in the seclusion of home and not mentioned in public"). Mill cities like Lowell were suffering from both economic depression and postwar grief. A dearth of raw cotton from the South made jobs scarce, prompting workers to return to the countryside; shops and businesses closed their doors, and prices rose yet again. Lowell men had fought and died from Baltimore to Antietam, Winchester to Cold Harbor, treating their native city, in the words of a local historian, to a "continual reception of dead bodies and wounded men." As she gained strength little by little and sewed in bed at her mother's house, Eunice's anxieties hardly diminished. She still couldn't "take one step without asistance," Lois reported in August. One morning, Eunice sat in a rocker for less than ten minutes, carried there and back by Hattie's husband. If she dared think ahead in those days, she no doubt ruminated on the practicalities of remarriage, this time to a man who could provide for her and the children, who could once and for all relieve her dependence upon mother, siblings, and in-laws.

Henry came home a second lieutenant at the end of August, and the close of the Civil War also brought home the question of divided loyalties. The Union sentiments of all the New England Richardsons ran deep, even if Ann's husband, David, and Hattie's husband, Ira, had never joined the military. William Stone's death averted the question of his politics, but sister Ellen and her husband, Dudley, had made plain their Confederate zeal. During the war, slaveholding southerners worked hard to create an ideological consensus among whites, a kind of Confederate nationalism that cast slavery as a divinely ordained and uplifting institution for black people and, more to the point, one that benefited white people outside the plantation elite (it was "better for the negro to serve the white man, than for one white man to serve another," went the common wisdom). To the very end, Confederates clung to the religious sanctity of their cause, but now the Merrills had to concede defeat, while the northern kin swallowed their own righteousness.

Moving on, avoiding, deflecting, erasing: These were the strategies by which divided families made peace. "I want to see you as my own precious child," a Yankee mother wrote to her daughter, a Confederate wife, "and all outside turmoil and trouble should be for the time forgotten." Or as a Manchester, New Hampshire, woman wrote to relatives in the Deep South, "I am glad from my heart for you, that your home has not been made desolate." Such conciliatory words were not uncommon in the mail that once again flowed between North and South.

With the Merrills still down south in 1865, the New England family concentrated on stories of Ellen's suffering. "She has been stricken with grief," Margaret Russell wrote, referring to the death of Ellen's young son, Sumner, sometime during the war years. "Poor sister Ellen what a sad story she tells us," Ann chimed in. *I hope she will come home, but probaboly will not if Dudley is living*, Eunice guessed, implying that Ellen's allegiance was more to her husband than to the Confederacy. Ellen's own version of events is missing, but no doubt she mourned the life her family had built in the South, including investments in land, business, a servant, or a slave, all ruined and gone. That fall, Dudley took advantage of the lenient policies of President Andrew Johnson and signed a loyalty oath, swearing, in exchange for amnesty, to "faithfully support, protect and defend the

Constitution of the United States," a Constitution that was to abolish slavery by the end of the year and would soon grant citizenship to all African Americans and the right of suffrage to black men.

When Ellen, Dudley, and their young daughter, Alice, arrived back north in 1866, after nine years of separation, there was a great deal to talk about. Ellen's dashed hopes for a better life made it that much easier for the northern relations to sympathize, and the loss of one man on each side—Luther for the Union, William for the Confederacy—surely aided the process of reconciliation, along with commiseration over the death of Ellen's boy. Comparing wartime deprivations also eased the way. Stationed in Louisiana in 1862, Henry and Luther had heard that Mobilians were "almost starving to death," with flour at forty-five dollars a barrel. Maybe Ellen told stories of the bread riot in 1863, when white women gathered on Spring Hill Road near the Merrills' home and, "armed with knives and hatchets" (as the newspapers reported), "marched down Dauphine street, breaking open the stores" to gather food. Perhaps she told also of the worsening shortages when Mobile Bay fell to the Union in the summer of 1864, and surely she described the declining state of the pretty Gulf Coast city once familiar to Eunice, "laid waste by the military authorities," as a Confederate observer put it. Ann's words—"Poor sister Ellen what a sad story she tells us"—resonated indeed.

In the spirit of North-South reconciliation, perhaps Henry and Dudley traded stories of camp and battlefield. Swept up in sympathy for the defeated, the New Englanders might also have nodded as the Merrills reported with dismay on triumphant black Mobilians welcoming the city's conquerors, how "the sidewalk was filled with them"—black people—"and not one moved to let us pass," as a white Mobilian recalled. As for Ellen's *black girl*, after the war "a negro could not be gotten to work at any price," the same white resident complained. And in the interest of a truce, the Merrills them-

selves likely refrained from mentioning their white compatriots'
intense defamation of Yankees. The "strongest wish of my heart,"
wrote a Mobile woman in 1866, was "to *enjoy* the dire retribution,
the awful Nemesis, which if God reigns in heaven, must descend
upon that *Synagogue of Satan*—New England." Those kinds of hostilities remained potent in the nation for a long time to come, even
as the Richardsons rebuilt their family.

Over the next decades, the Merrills moved back south to Florida,
north again to New Hampshire, then down to Mississippi, and
finally back to Massachusetts, trading off their affection for the
South with the desire to live near kin. Now, however, just after the
war, they boarded with Dudley's father in Manchester, while Dudley
kept on in the sash business, producing frames for windows and
doors. For her part, Ellen was reduced to contributing to her family's income by taking on some of the same jobs as Eunice. She
sewed for wages and worked at the Amoskeag when they were hiring (*How strange to think she is in the Mill to work*, Eunice reflected,
recalling her sister's seeming riches in Mobile). Perhaps the Merrills
found it reassuring that no one in the North had climbed very far
upward either. When Eunice came up short (she was too weak to
enter the mills herself), Ellen parted with two dollars; *I am afraid
she robbed her self to do it*, Eunice sighed gratefully.

In the end, fighting on opposite sides of the Civil War caused no
irreparable rift, for the family shared the loss of Luther and William,
and the New England and Alabama kin alike had suffered so much.
A permanent rupture was to come, for part of the family, only with
the momentous choice that Eunice soon made.

IN THE SUMMER of 1865, Eunice had been too ill to walk without
assistance. Six months later, in the middle of winter and still sick,
she collected the children and left her mother's home to journey far-

ther north. One catalyst was likely her stepfather, Bradley Davis, who regularly threatened to abandon Lois ("You say Davis is bound to leave," Henry wrote from the war. "He may go to that place where they buy brimstone by the wholesale"). Bradley finally made good on his word, and if desertion had felt "tenfold worse than widowed," as Lois grieved when Luther senior departed, she now claimed that preferable status for herself: The Lowell city directory for 1866 listed Lois Davis as a widow, even though Bradley had only gone to live with a brother in Vermont.

In any case, without her husband's shoemaking wages, Lois could no longer care for Eunice. As for staying with Ann, Eunice probably didn't even ask, since Ann had a houseful of children, sent a daughter away to work, and was braiding hats for extra cash herself. Either Hattie refused, or Eunice didn't presume to ask her either. Even Henry was at a loss. Twenty-two years old and working as a machinist in the Lowell mills, he was living at home, with wages enough to support only himself and his mother. But if the Richardsons had little to offer, at least William Stone's sisters had married well. Back in Claremont, Margaret and Alonzo Russell took in thirteen-year-old Clarence, who could work for his uncle again, and William's ever-generous sister Melissa, newly married to Moses Rankin, a farmer and blacksmith in northern Vermont, took in Eunice and four-year-old Clara. Again, the children were separated, and again Clarence had to live apart from his mother and sister.

Morristown, Vermont, was a *little out of the way place* in between the capital of Montpelier and the Canadian border, a village of "charming scenery," "bracing mountain air," and a flourishing Universalist church, to which Melissa Rankin belonged (though her husband remained a Baptist). The flowing waters of the Lamoille River intersected the farmland, powering sawmills to cut lumber and gristmills to grind corn and wheat. Maple sugar production and a starch factory (for surplus potatoes) complemented tanners, wheelwrights, masons, carriage makers, milliners, grocers, and tavern keepers to form a prosperous country town. The hamlet of Morrisville, part of the larger town, had been a stop on the Underground Railroad, which assisted slaves escaping to Canada, and fully half of Morristown's eighty men who fought for the Union had died in the war.

In a place that saw more than a hundred inches of snow a year, the crossroads of Morristown Corners, where the Rankins lived, lay remote even from the center of town a mile or so to the south. Journeying through the February snow and ice by stagecoach (the railroad had yet to reach there) and saying good-bye to Clarence yet again had nothing to do with Eunice's idea of a *life of joy.* "I do hope the poor child will get better soon," Melissa reported to Lois with typical compassion. "We will try and get her cured up." The Rankins were *very kind,* Eunice insisted, and *anxious to have me make my self*

Although Eunice lived several miles from the center of Morristown, Vermont, in 1866, she was surely familiar with the town's Upper Main Street.

at home with them. She sat by the fireplace every morning and evening, Moses brought her oysters, fruit, and whiskey, *and seems,* Eunice marveled once again, *to want to do all he can for me.* Relief, though, came sporadically. *If I feel better one day prehaps the next I will be all down,* she confessed. Simply mending Clara's clothes, Eunice admitted, *takes me pretty much all I do.* Winter entertainment like maple sugaring parties were no diversion, for *I do not dare go and stay out in the woods all the after noon,* she noted with regret.

A rise in spirits surfaced in morsels of humor, as when Eunice laughed about the elderly neighbor who boiled her tea from outdoor slush (*Melissa and I think we shall not take tea with her untill the snow drift is gone*). In these months too, Eunice renewed her interest in national affairs, as the Radical Republicans unveiled plans for black equality. *It rather seems as if Congress were determined to exercise thier prerogative in spite of President Johnson,* she reckoned with a note of admiration—two years later the president narrowly avoided impeachment, as radicals in Congress became increasingly disenchanted with his leniency toward the white South. Still, familiar refrains laced the few letters that Eunice mailed from Vermont: high prices and the resort to charity (*the Ladies of the Universalist Society gave me ten dollars,* no doubt accepted as a way to relieve the Rankins). Familiar shadows too: *Tomorrow is Williams birth day,* Eunice recorded one day in March, as the separation from loved ones brought back the old sense of rootlessness and prompted the usual pleas for correspondence.

The two surviving letters that Eunice wrote from Morristown date from March and April 1866. Her third and last extant letter for that year she composed in December, from Cabot, Vermont, a tiny farming community twenty-five miles away on the Winooski River (until the famous creamery arrived later in the century, the principal industry there was sugaring), where distant Stone relatives resided. *I*

William Stone's sister and brother-in-law Melissa and Moses Rankin welcomed Eunice and Clara to this house in Morristown, Vermont, after Eunice and the children left Dracut, Massachusetts.

was at Azariah's all last week, Eunice wrote from Cabot, referring to an uncle of William's who lived on what is now Ducharme Road, and there was *another cousin* in town as well. Eunice imposed on these extended kin (she had a young child with her, after all), but she was also working again, cleaning and washing for neighbors and probably for her relations too. As for Clarence down in Claremont, he thought of going to work in the mills (boys could serve as weavers or spinners), but Eunice wanted him to stay in school. *Poor folks can only scratch their heads and think what they would like to do*, she wrote with a certain resignation. *I wish I was able to keep house and board*, she added, in another familiar refrain.

THE GREATEST mystery of Eunice's story lies in her transformation from widow to bride. In 1869, four years after the end of the Civil War, Eunice married William Smiley Connolly, a sea captain from the British West Indies and a man of African descent, and moved with her children to his home on Grand Cayman Island. *From the time I first began to be aquainted with him,* Eunice later wrote from Cayman, *I had respect for him, and that grew into love which his gentle affection has increased till I am most devotedly attached to him.* But exactly when and how Eunice *began to be aquainted with* Smiley (as he was called) never received any elaboration, and not one sentence in any known document so much as hints at the circumstances of the couple's meeting or how they came to know each other. The last surviving letter that Eunice wrote from Vermont, dated December 1866 and addressed to Ann, offers some cryptic content. *You think I was feeling blue when I wrote you last!* she exclaimed, promising to *try and do better this time,* but cautioning that *I have so many things I want to say to you I can not say them all so will run try.* In a sentence either straightforward or encoded, she added, *I have heard nothing from any of the Friends yet.* After that, there are no more letters from Eunice or anyone else in the family for nearly three years.

In the most innocent explanation for such a long silence, the family wrote many fewer letters because Eunice and the children came back from their New Hampshire and Vermont sojourns, and everyone visited often enough among Dracut, Pelham, and Manchester. During that time, Henry continued to work in the machine shop for a daily wage, and in 1867, twenty-four years old, he married Clara Pray, the daughter of a Lowell mason whose ancestors had fought in the American Revolution. But the letters that do exist point unmistakably to missing correspondence. *I wrote you after I got to Claremont and Clarence wrote to Henry the day I left Claremont,* Eunice chronicled from Morristown, while the single letter from Cabot made reference to previous communication (*You think I was feeling blue when I wrote you last!*). Eunice also mentioned three letters sent to Ellen and one received in return, and Hattie acknowledged word from Eunice too.

How, when decades of correspondence had been so carefully preserved, could nearly three full years have vanished? Maybe the packets of letters from 1867, 1868, and most of 1869 met the mundane fate of deterioration beneath a leaking attic roof, or maybe they were discarded by an uninterested descendant during a vigorous New England spring cleaning. But it is possible too that someone removed the letters from the family papers and hid them away, knowing that the bundles from those years contained the offending information about an ancestor's taboo romance, for if Eunice's courtship with Smiley Connolly began sometime after 1865, the family correspondence would surely have touched upon—or agonized over—such an astonishing turn of events. Or maybe the letters were purposefully destroyed, the facts and emotions therein deemed best forgotten by someone disgusted by—or fearful of—all they revealed.

As for when and how the lives of Eunice Stone and Smiley Connolly first intersected, one logical chronology would place the meeting in Massachusetts after Eunice had returned from Vermont. Although the city of Lowell lay inland, mariners from the British Caribbean were known to sail for Boston in the nineteenth century. (As a woman born in the Cayman Islands in 1909 remembered, her grandfather had worked on "trading ships" and married a woman "in Maine or Boston . . . somewhere up there.") Eunice may have found her way to Boston after the war, but since sea captains often kept their vessels in port for weeks at a time, loading and unloading goods, it's more probable that Smiley traveled north to Lowell, to purchase cloth directly from the mills or just to see that model industrial city for himself. In this scenario, Eunice and Smiley could have crossed paths in Dracut's Pawtucket Congregational Church, just across the bridge. True, Eunice was a Universalist, but there was no Universalist church in Dracut, the family's roots were Congregationalist, and Lois likely attended the Pawtucket church herself. True too, the Connollys of Grand Cayman were devout Presbyterians, but Smiley might have stopped into the Pawtucket church since a few prominent families of color worshiped alongside the white congregants there. Indeed, the minister who officiated at Eunice and Smiley's wedding served as an interim pastor there in the 1860s.

There is, however, another possibility, and that is that Eunice and Smiley had met years earlier. Mobile, Alabama, served as a frequent port of call for Caymanian ships (more frequent, certainly, than Boston), and for two strangers in a foreign city, church would again have been the most likely meeting place. Mobile's Presbyterians established the Seamen's Bethel Church for transient sailors, but Smiley's light complexion could have permitted him entry into the downtown Government Street Presbyterian Church. Meanwhile, since the pastor there in the early 1860s was a northern man, Eunice could have found sanctuary there too, especially as North-South tensions mounted during the months before the war broke out. The parameters of the couple's camaraderie in Mobile might have been constrained, though not constrained enough to foreclose their remaining in touch after Smiley had completed his business dealings and left the Gulf Port city. Then, if Eunice had written to inform Smiley of her husband's death in the Civil War, Smiley may have begun to court his now-widowed friend, for his own marriage back in Cayman had broken up by then, or would break up soon enough.

If the couple had met during Eunice's year in Mobile, and if Smiley had proposed to Eunice following the news of William Stone's death, then Eunice's journey to Vermont served another purpose besides economic relief for Lois. The rituals of Victorian courtship commonly involved a drama in which the woman tested her future husband's devotion, and the Vermont retreat may have been Eunice's version of that social convention. *When I was trying to see if I could bear to tear myself from him*: Eunice later wrote those words from Grand Cayman Island, albeit without any amplification of the lonely trials to which she had subjected them both. Had she, after all, left her mother's home in Massachusetts, while still recuperating, to travel through the February elements in order to decide whether or not to forsake the man she loved and ultimately in order to measure Smiley Connolly's response to her suspension of their romance? Was Smiley implicated in the reference that sister Ann thought Eunice was *feeling blue* when she last wrote, or in the assertion that *I have so many things I want to say to you I can not say them all so will not try*, or in the comment that *I have heard nothing from any of the Friends yet*—that capitalized and underlined word standing as code for the suitor from whom Eunice awaited word? Had Eunice finally regained her sense of humor and her interest in national politics because mail from the sea captain lifted her spirits?

Indeed, spare hints of a previous acquaintanceship can be found in Eunice's earlier letters. *Miss Clara is the same madcap as ever*, she wrote from Claremont, invoking the common Caymanian manner of address (she was "Miss Eunice," her son "Mr. Clarence"). Had Eunice just received a letter from Smiley, asking after the children, then unwittingly echoed that West Indian turn of phrase in a letter to her mother? *Well Henry*, Eunice wrote in the summer of 1865, adding a few words in the space left over on a letter from Lois, *Mother ran ashore, or aground, I dont know which, before she filled her sheet*. Might that attempted metaphor betray thoughts of the gentleman mariner? In fact, might Eunice's departure from Mobile, leaving her husband in the Confederate Army, also point to her affection for another man? That he was a man of color would only have strengthened Eunice's refusal, based on her Universalist faith, to take up the Confederate cause in support of slavery.

It is also not entirely out of the question that what came to pass

in Mobile was a genuine tryst and that Clara was the daughter, not
of William Stone, but of Smiley Connolly. Indeed, Eunice may have
been unsure of her daughter's paternity, since Clara was conceived
just before William enlisted. That could explain why Eunice rushed
back north, perilously close to childbirth: to avoid facing her husband when the baby came. *It is a Stone baby, with just such a pug nose
as Clarence has got,* Eunice wrote of the newborn, perhaps to deflect
suspicion or just to convince herself of Clara's legitimacy. *She has just
such eyes as William only not so large,* she declared. *She has a very white
fair skin,* Eunice went on, either in relief or to preclude any suggestion
of scandal. (Odd, though, that Claremont neighbors called Clara *little
Secesh Contraband,* a term that referred to black people, those who
freed themselves by joining the Union Army.) This scenario also
explains why Clara proved to be so much happier in the Caribbean
than her brother, if Smiley unwittingly favored his own daughter.
From Grand Cayman Island years later, Eunice wrote, in reference to
Smiley, that Clara *loves her Father much and thinks there never was
another like him.* Perhaps those missing letters also contained rumina-
tions on detected resemblances between Clara and Smiley.

If Eunice attempted to tear herself away from Smiley Connolly
during that Vermont winter of 1866, she discovered instead that he
was, as she later recounted, *firm in his attachment and faithful in his
love for me.* Had Eunice indeed fled to Vermont in the face of such
vexing circumstances, then Smiley passed the test of steadfastness.
In this version of events, Smiley sent letters to Eunice over the
course of several years, while he took his schooners to Jamaica and
Honduras, the Gulf South and New York. Their content isn't hard
to conjecture, for Smiley later told Lois that Eunice looked "more
beautiful to me every day" and described her as "my dear Eunice
which is dear to me as my own life." Mail took a long time, of
course, with every possibility of becoming lost, thus extending the

courtship across time, but when Eunice reached her decision, Smiley combined a New England trading voyage with a reunion. In those years too, Eunice would have recorded her romantic dilemma in letters to her mother, and it would be those pages that were removed from the family collection or destroyed.

Eunice's romantic dilemma of course differed markedly from those of other white women, and her decision to go forward, no matter the intensity of the sea captain's devotion, was truly extraordinary. Smiley Connolly offered Eunice and the children stability for the rest of their lives, but if he could bestow upon her the earthly contentment that had so long eluded her, there was a catch. By marrying him, Eunice would once and for all forfeit the respectability to which she had aspired for so long, as a white woman in her native New England.

"DEAR FATHER, I recieved your very welcome letter," seventeen-year-old Clarence wrote in the autumn of 1869, signing his note to Smiley Connolly with the words "I remain your to be Affectionate son." The wedding hadn't yet taken place, but Clarence, nine years old when he last saw William Stone, now enjoyed a father's attention, and young Clara reveled even more in Smiley's generosity. Around the same time, Smiley sent a letter to Lois from Boston, with the salutation "Dear Mother Davis," conveying that he hoped "to enjoy your sweet presence shortly." By late 1869, engaged to marry Eunice, Smiley had clearly become kin to some of the family. "How do the folks in Lowell feel?" Clarence asked his stepfather-to-be in September, two months before the wedding. He might have been referring to the family's health, but he might also have been asking about Smiley's reception among relatives and neighbors, for not everyone welcomed Eunice's new fiancé so warmly.

Marriage between blacks and whites had remained illegal in Massachusetts until 1843, although authorities rarely enforced the statute. The white abolitionist William Lloyd Garrison had challenged the prohibition in 1831 (the year of Eunice's birth), igniting a twelve-year debate within the state. The most extreme opposition to repeal called such unions unnatural, immoral, and revolting, sermonizing that because black people were inferior, whites must prevent the dilution of purity that resulted from mating with animalistic Negroes. Occasionally these opponents mentioned black women and white men, but mostly they reserved their commentary for "the blue-eyed daughters of the Anglo-Saxon lineage" and "the dark African" man, taking up the refrain that "Every parent would rather follow his daughter to the grave, than to see her married to a black man." On the other side, the most radical proponents of repeal spoke in the name of freedom and equality, claiming "nothing unnatural in the amalgamation of our species." Others believed simply that marriage should not be legislated (for sanction proved "a feeble barrier to the gratification of a depraved taste"), and the most common arguments pronounced the law a relic and a dead letter; couples could readily cross state lines since no other New England state even bothered to address the issue.

Although lawmakers had overturned the ban on black-white marriage a quarter century before Eunice and Smiley's wedding, that action did not imply popular endorsement. After all, many white New Englanders after the Civil War proudly affirmed their role in the destruction of slavery without embracing racial equality. While Eunice had convalesced at her mother's house in 1865, the city of Lowell welcomed the escaped slave and abolitionist Frederick Douglass, and William Lloyd Garrison himself made a sensational appearance there, mounting an auction block retrieved from a southern slave market (he was received "with the strongest demonstrations of applause, prolonged and repeated"). But even as Senator Daniel Clark of New Hampshire argued firmly for the rights of black men ("the rights of man—not of white men, or black men, but all men"), he also made clear that by "negro equality" he meant strictly "political equality, not social." Schools and railroads had been desegregated in Massachusetts by the 1850s, but most whites drew the line precisely at "social equality," otherwise known as full integration in all walks of daily life, with marriage branded as the most repugnant outcome.

In one sense, Eunice's poverty and her romance with Smiley Connolly went hand in hand. The few white women who married black men in the nineteenth-century North tended to be poor— and, for that matter, Irish. When opponents of President Lincoln coined the pejorative term "miscegenation" in 1864 (from the Latin *miscere*, "to mix," and *genus*, "race"), they caricatured such relationships by claiming that "the white Irishwoman loves the black man," despite the fact that the Irish were "a more brutal race and lower in civilization than the negro," and visitors to one of New York City's poorest enclaves were offended by intimacy between Irishwomen and black men, whose marriages can also be documented in census returns. If Eunice's Anglo lineage did not match, her economic circumstances once again placed her close enough to downtrodden Irish immigrant women.

Eunice's sinking class standing—before the war in Manchester, during the war in Claremont, and just after the war in Dracut, Morristown, and Cabot—had already pushed her to the margins of female dignity. In the minds of many New England whites, Eunice's decision to marry across the color line meant that she also surrendered whatever vestiges of honor she had managed to retain as a poor, laboring, husbandless, and at times homeless mother of two children.

To be considered white in the United States meant to be free of the supposed tarnish of African "blood" but for women, the notion of "pure" bloodlines could shade over into another meaning of purity:

the idea of chastity. In tandem came the idea that African ancestry corrupted purity, not only of "blood," but also of virtue. A New Englander writing in 1795 sneered that white women who married black men were "without exception, of the lowest class in society, both for education and morals." The reformer Lydia Maria Child, writing in defense of mixed marriage in 1833, nonetheless believed that "none but those whose condition in life is too low to be much affected by public opinion, will form such alliances," and a legal commentator in 1834 called such unions "revolting" and "an offence against public decorum." William Allen, a man who described himself as of "one-fourth African blood," was violently assaulted by northern whites in the 1850s upon his engagement to a white woman; such a woman, Allen knew, would be "rendering herself an almost total outcast." When Mag Smith, the white woman in Harriet Wilson's 1859 autobiographical novel, *Our Nig*, married the black coal carrier Jim in New England (the name Mag likely denoted Irish ancestry), she "descended another step down the ladder of infamy" in the process. "She was now expelled from companionship with white people," Wilson wrote, "this last step —her union with a black—was the climax of repulsion."

Eunice earned her living the same way the character Mag Smith did, as a washerwoman; she also earned her living the same way as Mag's free black daughter, as a domestic servant and stitcher of palm-leaf hats. If economic proximity to Irish immigrant and African American women contributed to Eunice's social descent in Manchester and Claremont, then marriage across the color line completed her downfall from white womanhood. With certainty in her own mind, Eunice's lineage safely marked her off from African ancestry, but to unsympathetic New Englanders, the decision to marry Smiley Connolly stripped her of any shred of virtue or decency, for she was now no better than Irish—or black—women.

When Eunice dared introduce Smiley Connolly to her family, she must have been surprised to find that the Richardson women treated him well. The ideal reception for a spouse-to-be is captured in Eunice's response to her sister Ann's marriage to David McCoy, in 1860. *We all unite in sending love to our new relative*, Eunice had exulted. *Since it is your choice we give him welcome, and wish you both much joy and happiness.* Addressing David, she continued, *Brother— although we are strangers now I trust we are friends, and may the day come when we shall see and becoming aquainted with each other, form a friend-ship firm and lasting as the hills, untill such times as we shall meet. We shall be most happy to hear from you often, as a member of our Circle.*

Lois and the sisters returned such generous sentiments to Eunice in 1869, indicating that Smiley had earned the respect of his future in-laws, at least in part by way of his genuine concern for Eunice. "I am happy to acknowledge the recept of your kind letter," Smiley wrote to Lois from Boston, revealing a degree of affability between the two. Lois's original letter belongs to the ghostly stack of missing correspondence, but missives to and from the Caribbean disclose the same kind of warmth. *We both want to see you much and Mr Connolly often speaks of you*, Eunice conveyed to her mother from abroad—or, more boldly, *Mr Connolly says I must kiss you for him.*

The sympathy was returned. "Please remember me to brother Conley," Ann later wrote to Eunice in the West Indies. "I have the kindest regard for your husband, hope he will think of me as a sister for as such I esteam him." That particular letter never reached Eunice, but the goodwill of Ann's family ("David often says he should like to go and make you a visit") is confirmed in the regards Smiley sent back to the McCoys. As for Hattie, she soon bestowed a wedding gift of preserved tomatoes upon Eunice, and Smiley later offered his regards to her family as well. Mail was also to arrive in Cayman from Melissa Rankin of Vermont, her love for Eunice

WHAT MISCEGENATION IS!

—AND—

WHAT WE ARE TO EXPECT

Now that Mr. Lincoln is Re-elected.

By L. SEAMAN, LL. D.

WALLER & WILLETTS, Publishers,
NEW YORK.

This Civil War–era northern pamphlet asserted that the reelection of President Abraham Lincoln in 1864 would foster sex between black men and white women. Those who offered such warnings invariably cast the white women as depraved.

undiminished in the face of the new marriage, and Ellen wrote too, undeterred by her former Confederate persuasions.

Such acceptance of course might well reflect garden-variety racism, with a friend set apart from all other, unknown black people and therefore exempt from abstract antipathy. As one nineteenth-century immigrant to Lowell from the British Caribbean put it, "After all the obstacles had been overcome—the obstacles of race and color, paramount objectives in the eyes of prejudice—I became very popular amongst my neighbors." To be sure, African Americans suffered daily indignities in cities like Lowell ("You cannot go in here: we don't allow black men in here," one man was told as he tried to enter a concert hall in the 1860s), and in the face of other people's disdain, Eunice's family likely kept their fondness for Smiley confined to the private sphere, enjoying his presence only at home. As the antislavery activist Charlotte Forten noted of her Salem, Massachusetts, schoolmates, "I have met girls in the schoolroom—they have been thoroughly kind and cordial to me—perhaps the next day met them in the street—they feared to recognize me."

Accommodation by Lois and the sisters almost surely turned too on Smiley's wealth. When Ann married David McCoy in 1860, Eunice had peppered her sister with questions about the groom's economic prospects. *Who is it? his name, business, place of residence, (age) and how did it come about just now?* she queried. *I hope you have bettered your condition, have you Ann?* Of Henry, she inquired, *Have you seen the new Brother in law? . . . how do you like him? is he worth any property? I hope Ann has got, first, a good Husband, second, a good home.* Ann took no offense at this kind of talk. "I am so glad I have got a home and some one to look out for me," she answered, given the "hard times when so meny have no homes." For Eunice and her children, Smiley offered just that: a home and someone to provide for them, and that fact wasn't lost on Lois and the sisters.

Working-class women in the nineteenth century deferred to these practicalities, rendered especially stark for the Richardson women in the wake of lives troubled by absent husbands and fathers. They quickly grasped Smiley's ability to lift the poorest of the siblings out of near destitution and to relieve them of the burden of support. For his part, Smiley made plain his awareness that Eunice was marrying up: When he bought her a pair of earrings in Boston for the exorbitant sum of six dollars and fifty cents, he jested (as Eunice recounted) that she *never should had any if he did not get them for me, for I was too good for nothing*. In fact, because the majority of black people in northern cities were poor, Lois and the sisters may have perceived Smiley, with his light complexion and impressive trade goods, less as a black man and more as a well-to do foreigner with a British accent.

That Smiley came from a family of mixed African and European descent also hastened his welcome into the New England fold. "Black" and "mulatto" were two separate categories in both the United States census and the census of Massachusetts, and the same distinction operated informally. Lighter-skinned African Americans, who suffered comparatively less discrimination, were more likely to be literate, skilled, and better off than their darker neighbors. Moreover, Smiley may have been able to pass for white. The column asking for "color of groom and bride" on the couple's Massachusetts marriage registration remained blank, the same as for the vast majority of those on the roster, indicating that the clerk assumed both parties to be white and that no corrections were offered. The Irish last name probably helped as well.

Indeed, Smiley's skin may have appeared lighter than Eunice's or that of some of his future in-laws. Henry's military records specified a "dark" complexion, and perhaps Eunice made a point of describing newborn Clara's *very white fair skin*, not only because she may have been Smiley's daughter but also because Eunice thought of herself and other family members, regrettably, as dusky. Discussion of newborns' coloring—Eunice wrote that Ellen's daughter had *skin neither too dark or too fair*, whereas Ellen wrote that her son was "fair and white so you know he does not look much like me"—also reveals family concern about complexions. In turn, Smiley's light skin reassured the sisters, especially if they thought about Eunice giving birth to his children. If Eunice believed Smiley Connolly to be a white man when she first encountered him, he never intended to conceal his ancestry, nor did Eunice ask him to do so, for as she stated unequivocally when commenting on Hattie's happy marriage, *I would not change Husbands with her, if hers has got a white skin. I know mine has not.*

Rich, British, mulatto, white: New Englanders might have placed Smiley Connolly in any of those categories, yet his African ancestry also carried enough weight that anyone who knew his lineage could

This photograph of Eunice's sister Ellen Merrill probably dates from after the Civil War. One of Charles Henry's daughters labeled it "Aunt Nellie," using Ellen's nickname. Ellen once lamented that her skin was neither "fair" nor "white," but photographs are often unreliable sources for determining complexion.

place him firmly in the category of "black." As William Allen, the man who described himself as having "one-fourth African blood," observed, even if a man "should be as fair as the fairest Anglo-Saxon, yet, if he have but one drop of the blood of the African flowing in his veins," no white woman was permitted to marry him. The African American writer Frank J. Webb captured this axiom in his 1857 novel *The Garies and Their Friends*, in which he portrayed the virulent enforcement of a one-drop rule in Philadelphia. As one northern character informed the son of a slaveowner and a slave, "if you should settle down here, you'll have to be either one thing or other—white or coloured." Should the man choose to live as a white person in the North, he was advised that "it must never be known that you have a drop of African blood in your veins . . . no matter how fair in complexion or how white you may be." If one day white New Englanders welcomed Smiley Connolly as a British captain conducting important business, another day they could just as swiftly scorn him as a lowly black man scandalizing the neighborhood.

Even Lois, for all her amiability, didn't entirely trust Smiley, for she was wont to joke that the new bridegroom would grow neglectful away from the watchful eyes of his in-laws. *He still pets me, feeds me as he used to do in America,* Eunice later assured Lois from the Caribbean, recalling how her mother *used to laugh about it and say* "*when he got me fast and in his own home he would forget all such things.*" Lois worried too that Smiley would force Eunice falsely to declare contentment. *You made him promise you that I might write you just what treatment I recieved from him,* Eunice later echoed, then added with defiance, *O no, you wronged him there.* To judge from his ongoing affection for his mother-in-law, Smiley took Lois's fears in stride, as the emotions of any parent against a groom who took a daughter so far away.

Lois and the sisters embraced Eunice's husband-to-be, but not all their New England neighbors followed suit. *Tell me what Mrs Wilson said and every body else*, Eunice directed just before she sailed for the West Indies, with no explanation necessary. When she asked from Grand Cayman that her love be offered to *all inquiring friends*, she qualified the request: *those I mean who inquire with an interest*, rather than for the sake of slander. Another time, and in the same vein, Eunice asked to be remembered only to *all who feel friendly*. One neighbor, a woman whose family belonged to the Pawtucket church and whose men had fought in the war with Henry and Luther, caused Eunice particular pain. *And as for Mrs Blood feeling so independant and having no farther use for Mrs Stone*, Eunice wrote, refusing to still her emotions, *how fortunate it is that she can get along without her, for Mrs Stone Connolly feels quite independant of every one but her Husband who is both willing and able to support her himself.* After those pointed references to Smiley's worthiness, Eunice condemned the efforts of this local gossip to malign her. *But if Mrs Blood lived near me I would in rememberance of what she has given me, I would give her some things that I can spare*, she went on, indulging in imagined revenge. And then, the main charge: *I can not quite get over some of her slurs.*

All in all, the local prejudice that Eunice and Smiley faced was considerable, for as Eunice later confided, *I knew I could . . . go from you my Mother easier than I could give him up, even though public opinion was against him and against me on his account.* Then, from the Caribbean, Eunice wrote that Smiley was *in his own home now and feels at liberty to act all the love he feels for me without fear of disturbing any one.*

WHEN EUNICE WONDERED, during the war, why Henry hadn't written to her in Claremont, her brother explained that letters addressed to Lois were fully intended for his sister as well. Eunice "seemed to think that it was something that I had heard that kept me quiet," Henry had written then, referring perhaps to William Stone's traitor status and adding, "It would take more than heresay to turn my mind against one of my Sisters." In those days, Henry couldn't have fathomed the circumstances that led him to spurn that same sister.

Like many New England men, the Richardson brothers experienced their first sustained contact with African Americans during the Civil War. The march through Baltimore with the Sixth Massachusetts had been Henry's initiation, though he never wrote home about how black men came to the aid of white soldiers or how black women offered cloth to bind the white men's wounds. Nor did he write about how the white mob called the Massachusetts men "white niggers" and "nigger thieves," though Baltimore's white residents were mistaken if they believed that men like Henry were fighting for Negro emancipation.

From the start of the war, enslaved men and women escaped to Union lines to seize their freedom, and as the Twenty-sixth Massachusetts moved deeper into the South, the Richardson brothers experienced more substantial encounters with black people. Luther, for instance, wrote from the Mississippi River about the captain's "Nigger" catching fish for the soldiers—no doubt a runaway slave put to work for northern soldiers. In the spring of 1862, the brothers' regiment occupied the fallen city of New Orleans, setting up camp in the customhouse there. Soon the streets were crowded with black men and women fleeing surrounding plantations and accepting work as laborers and laundresses for Union forces. Some fugitive slaves arrived with their backs "shockingly lacerated by whipping" or with the "freshly-burned marks of the branding iron" fully visible, as one Yankee remembered. Others appeared with wrists bound in chains, while masters stopped into the customhouse daily, hoping to reclaim their chattel.

The Emancipation Proclamation, issued by President Lincoln in January 1863, contained a mandate to raise black regiments, and many whites, Henry included, eventually found themselves impressed with African American demonstrations of battlefield bravery. The black men "fought like Blood hounds," he wrote admiringly after their fearless display at the Battle of Port Hudson, Louisiana. But neither the witnessing of slavery's scars and chains nor respect for black men's military courage necessarily erased bigotry, for white northerners were fully capable of espousing noble principles and personal intolerance in concert.

One Massachusetts soldier who called slavery an "enormous crime" also wrote home about "confounded dirty niggers" who were "lazy, filthy, ragged, dishonest & confounded stupid." A Rhode Island sergeant who expressed genuine admiration for black Union soldiers was "not willing to fight shoulder to shoulder with a black dirty nigger." As a Massachusetts man in New Orleans mused, noting his revulsion at shaking hands with a black man, "I can fight for this race more easily than I can eat with them." (In the midst of so many black people, New Englanders also thought of the Irish: "Better such negroes for citizens, aye, for *rulers*, than such foreigners," the same man announced.) Nor were African Americans who fled to Union lines treated especially well. When Luther ganged up on a black teamster in a typical prank—"the more the Nigger aplied the brake the faster he went back in the rong dirrection"—his gloating echoed that of many Yankee soldiers.

The Emancipation Proclamation, Lois noted, was "hailed with joy by nearly all in the free states and probably more in the southern states." Her reference to black people ("probably more" didn't refer to southern whites) illuminates her own abolitionist leanings, but her son Henry didn't agree. Lincoln had presented the proclamation as a military strategy intended to destroy enemy property, for slavery itself was a critical source of wealth and labor for the Confederacy. Lincoln's war tactics did not require any moral opposition to slavery, and abolitionism never became part of Henry's politics. "I think that the Proclamation was a very good thing & in a very good place," he conceded, affirming his Republican loyalties, but, he added, "I do Hate to see these accursed Abolitionists tear this Country to peices." Those who spoke out for Negro rights were, in Henry's estimation, "doing a great deal more hurt than good by their Confounded Howling."

Even when Henry wrote triumphantly of Confederate prisoners with "darkies on guard over them!" the specter of black men watching Confederate prisoners suggested southern white degradation ("wonder how the *Chivalry* like that?") rather than black equality, for Henry also spouted racist convictions with considerable ease. When he came upon a group of escaped slaves building a road for the U.S. Army, he candidly outlined his ideas about black inferiority. "They have just left there Masters and a lazier set of Beings I never saw," he determined. "Sometimes I Pity the poor things and then again I think that they are as well off when slaves as any thing." When the Union Army began to raise a black regiment in Louisiana, Henry considered applying for a commission as lieutenant, though only for the sake of promotion. "The Line officers are to be all white, and I think that I could get a chance if I wanted," he explained, scoffing about a white hospital steward that "there are Niggers hold higher offices than that and I never would consent to have a Nigger over me." When Henry declared in 1864 that he wanted to fight the war "to the bitter, bloody end" for "the cause for which we have fought so long and suffered so much," he referred not at all to black freedom but rather to the preservation of the Union and a world of uncompromised free soil for ambitious white men like himself.

In New Orleans, where the Twenty-sixth Massachusetts lived for more than a year, Henry and Luther discovered the same kind of Creole society that the Stones and Merrills knew in Mobile, though neither brother recorded his opinion of the city's French-speaking, light-skinned, and well-to-do people of color. Occupying New Orleans, the brothers also saw a world in which white men openly took women of color as concubines, and white women of the lower classes formed liaisons with black men. Prostitution too was rampant (local papers reported on the "lewd and abandoned women" who shamelessly greeted Yankee men), and Luther readily told of sex between white soldiers and local women, some of whom no doubt were not white. "There is barely a man in the Regt but what had got a woman here," he divulged, and when the Twenty-sixth finally left town, "it wors a sight to see the wifes lovers and friends a parting." (Perhaps Luther unwittingly conveyed a sexual metaphor when he added that because New Orleans had served as home, "we went in prety deep some times.") Luther even admitted to having an "intermate friend" of his own, "a good respecterble girl," whose name, Emily Hall, he wrote out in careful script. "You say we must be careful and not have children"—he was echoing Lois—"but i gess I shall not be trubled with any." His mother and sisters took Luther's news to mean that he was engaged to Emily, but more realistically his "intermate friend" stood somewhere between wartime companion and prostitute, whether white or black. The more circumspect Henry never bragged about sexual escapades or romance, but Luther disclosed that his younger, more upstanding brother was "as full of the devil as ever."

If Henry admired black troops on some occasions or joined his fellow soldiers in transgressing with women of color, none of that altered his bedrock racism. Stationed in Savannah after Confederate surrender, Henry hired a black man, likely a former slave, then wrote home that he had "a nigger—beg your pardon—a colored citizen of African descent—to black my boots, clean my sword, make my bed." In Henry's vision of emancipation, African Americans were best suited for servitude. Indeed, Henry's open disdain for black people probably made postwar reconciliation with the Confederate Merrills that much swifter.

When the war ended, Henry Richardson had returned to Lowell a twenty-two-year-old officer and a veteran of two regiments, including the celebrated "Old Sixth." Four short years later, he faced the marriage of one of his sisters to a black man—for that was the only way that Henry could think of Smiley. Determined to surpass the station of his own father and to erase from family history Luther senior's disgraceful conduct as a drunkard and an adulterer, Henry cared a great deal about what other people thought. That single-minded focus on personal upward mobility ironically included the attempt to deny Eunice her own climb out of poverty. Even her admission to him of her suicidal grief following William Stone's death and the apparent happiness that Smiley Connolly brought to her and the children couldn't change Henry's mind. In short, he was on his way up in the world, and Eunice's actions threatened his hard-won social reputation. Henry had emphatically not gone to war to fight for the right of black men to marry white women, and that was certainly not what he imagined he would encounter back at home, within his very own family.

Henry no doubt connected his sister's scandalous choice of a groom to her Universalism, a faith that (in his view) permitted deluded sinners to count on guaranteed salvation. Likely he also attempted to talk Eunice out of the marriage, and when that proved futile, he rejected her entirely, thereby also removing himself from the role of loving uncle to Clarence and Clara. When Smiley later sent regards to Eunice's family from the Caribbean, he never included Henry or Henry's wife in the list of names, and Eunice was never able to breach the divide. *This letter must answer for you and Ann & Harriet & Henry and all that want to hear from me*, she wrote from Grand Cayman in a hopeful mention of her brother, only to face disappointment. *Henry never wrote me*, Eunice admitted almost three years later, *in joy or sorrow*. Nor did he ever relent, and after another year passed, Eunice understood that Henry's silence was final. *For Brother Henry and Wife I do not know what to say*, she wrote, *for whenever I have heard from home I have never heard from them, or even heard that they so much as sent to be remembered by me.*

SMILEY CONNOLLY's fortunes mattered a great deal to Eunice, but she also married the sea captain because she loved him. Ideals of romantic love had begun to take hold in American culture by the 1840s, displacing the once-common wisdom that amorous affection paved the way for misfortune or resulted only from the foolishness of youth. By the 1860s, New Englanders were writing voluminously about love as a prerequisite to matrimony, and the working classes were no exception. "When ever you marry I wish there may be a reciprocal attachment found on merited esteem, ripened into *Love*," wrote a father to his daughter in the Amoskeag mills just before the war. In Harriet Wilson's previously mentioned novel, *Our Nig*, the black coal carrier proposed to the white washerwoman with "a tempest gathering in his heart," for he "loved Mag to the last." The sharing of one's soul and self, a love that conquered all obstacles, a companionship unparalleled, a union of spirits: These became the model foundations of Victorian marriage.

In the face of such ideals, the Richardson sisters witnessed not only the abandonment of their mother by their father but also a loveless marriage between their mother and stepfather. *Mother I wish you could live diffrently*, Eunice wrote from Claremont in reference to Lois's troubles with Bradley Davis. *It is just wasting your life.* By contrast, the sisters expressed pride in their own estimable husbands. "Ira is real good to her," Ellen observed of Hattie. "She haves evry thing she wants." For her own part, Ellen called Dudley "a kind afectionate Husband," and when Ann married David, Eunice was glad that her sister had found *some one to go with her, and to care some thing about having her enjoy herself.* And when Eunice wrote that she would never exchange Smiley for a white man, she added, in reference to his color, *But I do not look at that when I look at him, I look for a loving glance of his eye which I always meet.* With Smiley, for the first time, Eunice melded her earthly concerns for security with more transcendent emotions. Although Eunice had occasionally hinted at a certain closeness with William Stone (*without him, she wrote during the war, there was no one to go to with my feelings*), she never invoked the language of romantic devotion until she met Smiley Connolly.

It was Eunice's treasured attachment to Smiley that helped her reach the most momentous decision of her life. Just after the war, white women novelists in the North began to write about love and marriage across the color line as metaphors for national healing. Perhaps Eunice had read the story by Louisa May Alcott, serialized in a Boston newspaper in 1863, in which a white woman fell in love with a man of invisible African descent. When Paul confessed his black "blood" to Claudia, she remained undeterred, even as Paul asked if she could " 'bear to see familiar faces growing strange to you.' " Eunice, reflecting upon the painful gossip in Massachusetts, could have taken Claudia's answer as her own. " 'I do remember that I cannot pay too much for what is priceless; that when I was loveless and alone, there came a friend who never will desert me when all others fail,' " Claudia told Paul, adding, " 'if I cannot bear a few harsh words, a few cold looks, a little pain, for you, of what worth is my love?'" In the end, it may have been Universalism, the faith Henry blamed, that lent Eunice the necessary resolve, for the Universalist tenet of spiritual equality translated also into endorsement of women's greater independence and realization of their own happiness.

Eunice's acceptance of Smiley's marriage proposal entailed not only local ostracism and Henry's rejection but also a separation far greater than any the family had yet endured, for the home that Smiley Connolly offered to Eunice stood on a tiny island in the faraway Caribbean Sea. Indeed, Smiley had little choice but to depart the United States with his new bride, for surely there were days in post–Civil War New England when Captain Connolly was startled that a man such as he should be treated so poorly, especially since that treatment contrasted sharply with his high ranking in the West Indies. In order to maintain that ranking, and therefore in order to bestow comfort and stability upon Eunice and her children, he had to return home. As Paul imparted to Claudia in Louisa May Alcott's story, "'In your world there will be no place for me.'" Or as William Allen's white wife wrote just before she and her husband of African descent left the United States for England, "'gladly and joyfully will I hasten with you to a land where unmolested, we can be happy in the consciousness of the love which we cherish for each other.'" As Eunice prepared to move farther away than any family member had ever ventured, those words too could have been her own.

On a perfect Indian summer Wednesday in November 1869 (Wednesday was the traditional Caymanian day to wed, and not uncommon in nineteenth-century New England either), Eunice Stone married William Smiley Connolly. She was thirty-seven, he was thirty-six. She was a widow with two children, he a once-

When Eunice and her children left Claremont, New Hampshire, just before the war ended, they went to live with Eunice's mother, Lois Davis, in this house on Mammoth Road in Dracut, Massachusetts. It was here that Eunice convalesced after the war and here that she and Smiley Connolly likely married in 1869. Lois probably rented half of the house.

married man with four sons back home. The officiating minister, the Reverend Moses Patten of the forward-thinking Pawtucket Congregational Church in Dracut, was well aware of Smiley's race; *remember me with much love to Mr and Mrs Patten*, Eunice later requested from overseas. The ceremony probably took place in Lois's home on Mammoth Road, quiet and informal to still neighbors' tongues, but also because Richardson women had never indulged in formal weddings. The *Lowell Daily Courier* carried an unadorned notice in its marriage column: "In Dracut, Nov. 3, By Rev. Moses Patten, Mr. Wm. S. Conally of Grand Cayman, West Indies, and Mrs. Eunice L. Stone of Lowell." One week later, the family set sail for Provincetown, at the tip of Cape Cod, where they

DRY   GOODS

CHEAPER THAN EVER AT

H. C. D r e w's,

Under the Universalist Church, Central street.

Splendid Astrachan Beaver, $3.00
Ladies' Waterproofs, only   5.00
Children's   "   "   3.50
Splendid Scotch Plaids,   .50
Extra Fine Alpaca, all colors,   .25
Fine Hill Cotton, only   12 1-2
Unbleached Cottons, yard wide,   12 1-2

And a large lot of new DRESS GOODS just
bought, EXTRA CHEAP.   5

Marriages.

In Dracut, Nov. 3, By Rev. Moses Patten, Mr.
Wm. S. Conally of Grand Cayman, West Indies,
and Mrs. Eunice L. Stone of Lowell.
In this city, Oct. 15, by Rev. Horace James,
Mr. John P. Gregware and Miss Abbie F. Alcott,
both of Lowell.

New Advertisements.

A Card.

The undersigned would thank his friends and
neighbors for calling yesterday and expressing

After Eunice Stone married Smiley Connolly on November 3, 1869, this three-line announcement appeared in the *Lowell Daily Courier*, with Smiley's last name spelled incorrectly.

awaited a boat to the West Indies. They likely spent the days in between visiting with those who cared to bid them farewell.

The tip of the Cape was a whaling port in those days, with impressive captains' houses lining narrow sandy streets. The village already attracted summer vacationers, but in late autumn it was bleak and stormy. Provincetown also contained a Universalist church, and perhaps Eunice visited for one last sermon or prayer. Then, just before the ship set sail, she composed a letter. *My dear sweet Mother,* Eunice wrote, *we will play that I have come to see you and tell you my self.* Invoking a vision of leisure and frolic (Eunice had never written about "playing" before), she imagined the two of them visiting together and described her family's trip from Boston Harbor. It had been cold that night, but they all had stayed up on deck, she narrated, for *I could not bear to go and not take a last look at a place so near you, my Mother.* If only it hadn't yet been dark, so that the children could have seen *what perhaps they never will see again,* but Clara was excited, exclaiming, *O, I can tell grandma all about the Vessels and lights,* and when the little girl became seasick, *Mr Connolly sprang up and took care of her.* Once anchored in Provincetown, Clarence and his new father made an excursion into town. *He is kind to them both,* Eunice assured her mother.

"My dear Mother, I am happy to inform you of our departure," Smiley wrote to Lois two days later. "Mrs. Connolly"—that was what he called Eunice in his letters—was looking "more beautiful to me every day," he expounded. The children were enjoying themselves, Clarence fishing, Clara fascinated with the water. "Only dear Mother, they are so teasing. When you used to tell me about my undertaking to take them home with me I did not realize the truble," he joked easily. "Mrs. Connolly is teasing me for a kiss," he added, avenging Henry just a bit. "I suppose I will have to kiss her when she requestes me." More soberly, Smiley promised to "take all the care of those that is commited to my trust," pledging that "my heart & hand will always be ready to help you all I can." He proffered his regards to Ann and Hattie and their families (Ellen was back in the South by then) and signed his letter "with the greatest respect I am and will ever remain your truly and sinceare Wm. S. Connolly."

Then he passed the paper to Eunice, for there was still room and time enough for her to add some last words. The scene around her, as the boat prepared for departure, was busy and noisy. Smiley was dancing with Clara, the steward readying the table for supper. *I know you have been a dear good brave little Mother through giving me up*, she wrote now. *But I could see more anguish in your look when I left you than you intended me to.* Thinking back to their farewell, attempting to summon words for all the swirling emotions, she just managed *You all felt bad and my own heart was so full.* Moments before the ship set sail, she could draw only upon her faith in God, renewed since her days of spiritual despondence just after the war. *But when I left you my Mother I did not feel as if I went alone with my own strength*, she revealed, *but I felt as if I was being sustained by unseen powers.* Just one weight bore down upon her. *I wanted to tell Brother Henry how much I had always loved him and how his treatment had pained me*, Eunice confessed now, *but it is perhaps better that I did not.* Eunice had offered Henry's wife, Clara, a farewell gift of keepsakes from Cayman that Smiley had brought with him to New England, prompting one further thought on the subject: Was the gift satisfactory, or had Clara Richardson spoken ill of the Connollys? *What did Clara say to the Shells?* Eunice wondered, before she let the matter go.

If emotion threatened to overwhelm her then, Smiley intervened with good cheer, worried that the letter to Lois would *make me down hearted,* Eunice explained, for *he is perfectly unhappy himself if he thinks I am not happy.* As Clarence waited to post the letters onshore, Eunice wrote more hurriedly. *I have a thousand things to say now but must stop and say good by again,* she scratched out, dipping her pen one last time. *So now My dear Mother Sisters Brother and friends Farewell. I feel quite bad to think of the long good by it will be, but do not forget the absent ones, good by good by.*

East End Grand Cayman Dec 15, 71

My ever dear Mother,

A few days ago
I wrote you a long letter by way of
Jamaica. I am trying every way
possible to get a letter to you and see
if I can get just one in return, for
not one word have I ever heard from
any of my family yet, now over two
years. I am writing this in a great
hurry. Mr Connolly sails tomorrow
morning for Ruatan and he will
take this and try to forward it from
there to New Orleans. And you must
write and direct to him in care
of Mr Edward Pillsbury No 52
Carondolet St New Orleans. In
my other letter I wrote you more
particulars than I can do now.

6
THE SEA CAPTAIN'S WIFE

East End, Grand Cayman, December 13 and 14, 1871

My ever dear Mother,

A few days ago I wrote you a long letter by way of Jamaica. I am trying every way possible to get a letter to you and see if I can get <u>just</u> <u>one</u> in return, for not one word have I ever heard from any of my family yet, now over two years. I am writing this in a great hurry. Mr Connolly sails tomorrow morning for Roatan and he will take this and try to forward it from there to New Orleans. And you must write and direct to him in care of Mr Edward Pillsbury No 52 Carondolet St New Orleans. In my other letter I wrote you more particulars than I can do now. We are all well at present. Mr Connolly is going to Roatan with Coffee and Cattle. He does not expect to be from home more than Two weeks, Three at the most. It hurts me much to have him go yet it is some times necessary for a Man to do what does not seem pleasant. He is never from home, much as he promised me he would not be. My little <u>Lou</u> begins to walk. If you get my other letter you will know all about her. She will be a year old the Third day of January 1872. I have lately written to Ellen in Florida with directions how to send me a letter. Do let me hear from some of you at once. Direct as I have already told you or to Mr William Malabre Kingston Jamaica. Clara had a little letter for you before which was carelessly left out of my other letter which I *will send with this one. Clarence is well and wishes to be remembered with much love to you and all the other friends. Christmas will soon be here so I will wish you a Merry Happy one. O, if I could only hear from you and know how it is with you then I would know what to write to you. But Mother I want you to tell me if you want to come out here and live with me. I can not say much now for not having heard any thing from you I do not know how your mind is towards <u>me</u> and <u>mine</u>, so I can not make you much of an offer untill I do hear from you. I can only tell you I have a Happy home and an indulgent loving Husband.*

Mr Connolly is disapointed in sailing today on account of some Cattle which were to be forwarded to him yesterday and have not yet arrived. He will wait for them untill tomorrow and then go with or without them. My little Louie is sleeping in her Hammock. Clara is in School. Remember me to all the Family and all others who feel any way interested about me. You must excuse me for I have written so much to you and so many times that I do not know what to say to you but I expect I should have enough to say if I could but hear from you. Where is Charlie Put.? if no one wants to write to me I should think he would write Clarence, they used to think so much of each other. I often think you could come out here and be as contented as I have been. What a good time we might have. I have a plenty to eat drink & wear and do not have to sit up nights sewing by Lamp light making and trimming dresses to get it better. I must say goodbye. E. L. Connolly

*T*o conjure Grand Cayman Island when Eunice lived there, depart George Town, where the airplanes land and the cruise ships dock, where boutiques and dive shops crowd the capital's small streets, and hotels and condominiums line the famous Seven Mile Beach. On the other side of the island, in the village of East End, a large sand cemetery was once the site of the three-gabled Presbyterian church where the Connolly family worshiped, and gravestones still bear their name. Traveling east, you come to a plot of private seaside land, adjacent to a local bar, that may be the site where Smiley built a house for his new bride; in their day, the property extended across the present-day road, all the way back to the cliffs. Or Eunice and Smiley may have lived a bit farther east still, on land that sits between the Seventh-Day Adventist church and what is now a playing field. Past the public library comes a smaller sand cemetery, the resting place of Thomas Dighton Conolly, Smiley's half brother (all but Smiley spelled the name with one *n* in those days), whom Eunice called *Brother Dighton*.

Eunice's entire world transformed when she crossed boundaries of race and nation to live in a settlement of freed slaves on an island in the remote western Caribbean. On Eunice's Grand Cayman, there was no graveyard by Brother Dighton's house, and no roads, for the land lay unbroken from beach to interior, crossed only by footpaths or bridle tracks. With her husband and children, Eunice traversed these paths, prayed in the church that stood on the sand, sailed on the bay in the evenings, and gazed daily upon the sea. To find a view that she took in, look past East End's convenience store, gas station, and lighthouse (built only in the twentieth century), toward any unobstructed vista of the crystalline jade and turquoise waters, next to a band of fine white sand or the rugged ironshore, that jagged, blackened rock that rings the Cayman coastline.

In the Caribbean, Eunice's marriage to Smiley Connolly meant something quite different from what it had in the eyes of hostile white New Englanders who thought of Eunice as no better than an Irish immigrant or a black woman. For one thing, Smiley was building Eunice a home on land that he owned. Once and for all, Eunice would "go to housekeeping," as she used to say, and live as mistress

This undated postcard of the East End coastline offers the same view that Eunice took in during her years on Grand Cayman Island.

of her own domestic sphere. For another, Eunice no longer needed to hide the love she shared with her new husband. All this meant that Eunice's residence in Cayman—at least at first—marked an interval of years in which she experienced a happiness made sweeter by the hardships that had come before. True, these novel comforts, both material and emotional, came tempered by the pain of separation and unfamiliarity, but women in the nineteenth century routinely parted company with loved ones in order to follow their husbands, just as Eunice herself had done a decade earlier. In certain ways, the decision Eunice made in 1869 was no different from that of any Yankee bride who followed her husband to the prairies, the plains, or the golden hills of California. True too, her newfound happiness was eventually tempered by losses less easy to endure, but for a good long while it seemed to Eunice that she had at last made for herself a life of abiding contentment.

LYING ABOUT five hundred miles south of Miami, in between Cuba and Jamaica, Grand Cayman Island measures a little over twenty miles long and less than a hundred miles square, with sister islands Little Cayman and Cayman Brac nearby. Eunice's ocean voyage from Cape Cod to the West Indies no doubt resembled that of another New Englander tracing a similar route, who found that "with every hour it seemed to grow warmer and brighter, the sea to become a more translucent blue and the atmosphere to take on a softer and more opaline hue." Grand Cayman is so flat that travelers approaching in the darkness of night, before the advent of electricity, were known to mistake the landmass for a reflection of the moon. In 1869, Eunice's port of entry was Gun Bay in the district of East End.

When Eunice left New England after the Civil War, that region stood at the center of industrialization and capitalist expansion, contributing mightily to the creation of a powerful nation on the international stage. The place where Eunice disembarked, by contrast, stood on the margins of world history. Caymanian legend comes steeped in the ghosts of pirates, with Sir Henry Morgan and Blackbeard hiding in coves to plunder unsuspecting merchant ships. Officially, the three islands were encompassed in the treaty drawn up after Oliver Cromwell's troops had captured Jamaica from the Spanish in the seventeenth century. Cayman remained under Jamaican rule long past Eunice's day, peripheral to the British Empire ("What is Grand Cayman?" asked a confused colonial authority in the 1870s, adding dubiously, "I think someone had better go and ask about it"). Accordingly, the indexes of history books skipped from "Cayenne" to

"Ceylon," and enumerations of colonial possessions frequently omitted Cayman. To this day, some maps display the blue ink of oceans where the islands emerge from the water.

Part of this marginal status stemmed from isolation. Trade winds had once forced sailing vessels between Europe and the Caribbean to steer a course alongside Cayman, but the arrival of steamships during the nineteenth century permitted voyagers to bypass the islands. Steamers steered the most direct routes, stopped less frequently, and purposefully avoided Cayman's treacherous surrounding reefs. A Scottish missionary who arrived the same year as Eunice described Grand Cayman, and its perhaps three thousand souls, as a "sequestered isle" and a "lonely" place of "extreme isolation."

Not only was the island "entirely separated from the rest of the world," but the various settlements had little means of communication with one another. Traveling on foot, according to visiting churchmen, meant crossing "an iron shore pointed like the top of a coral reef" or riding on terrain entailing "risk to man and beast; now floundering through a bog, then in danger of breaking the limbs and lacerating the flesh over a solid craggy cliff." Residents of East End "hardly knew what the other end of the island was like," recalled a great-granddaughter of Brother Dighton, speaking of her childhood in the early twentieth century. As for Eunice, "probably she just stayed up there, on that end." It couldn't have been more different from the newly paved roads and ever-multiplying railway lines of post–Civil War New England, for in effect, Eunice hadn't moved so much to the British West Indies, or even to Grand Cayman Island, as to the tiny settlement of East End.

There are no rivers, mountains, or green hillsides on Grand Cayman, yet the island enchanted Eunice, its "rather shabby-looking land" serving as "a foil to the beauty and impressiveness of the deep blue waters," in the words of another newcomer. *O, Mother if I could* *only make you know what handsome, <u>handsome</u> corals I saw in the water you would be nearly crazy to get some of them*, Eunice exclaimed, while little Clara boasted of playing by the bay and finding "such pretty Mosses right in front of our door." Roses, hibiscus, and bougainvillea planted African style in sandy front yards complemented pathways bordered by bright pink conch shell or coral. At home, the family kept *a handsome Parrot* and *a pair of Banana Birds*. Alongside azalea and oleander, honeysuckle and periwinkle, jessamine and camellia, the poinciana trees bloomed orange, red, and yellow all year long, suffusing the island air with soothing tropical fragrances.

How Eunice wanted the family in New England to know of her newfound joy! Mail had always been an uncertain enterprise in her life, but not even wartime Mobile forced such a degree of unpredictability. Caymanians at mid-century asked the Royal Mail Company's steamships to stop by en route between Jamaica and Honduras, but British officials refused, citing "the dangerous navigation of those Islands." Instead, Caymanian mariners and their business associates served as informal (and unreliable) messengers. Over the course of eight years, twelve letters arrived in New England from Eunice and her family in the West Indies. Six were from Eunice, four from Smiley, and two from Clara. Among them, Eunice's six letters bore twelve different dates; in one instance, she began writing in mid-May, added news in early June, and began anew in late August, before a departing ship took her pages off the island. *I hear there is a Vessel going to Jamaica next week*, she announced one summer day in 1870, *so now I will try to write a little more.* That letter left her hands nearly three months later, with no sign-off at all, as if there had been no time to find a well of ink or the nib of a pen with which to close a missive that had been waiting months for pickup.

Once secured in a captain's pocket, the mail embarked on a route circuitous enough to make delivery far from certain. *I sent one in Feb.*

by way of Jamaica, Eunice recounted one day in 1875. *I wrote one last Oct. by way of New Orleans which I supposed you had for a long time, but last week Mr Connolly was at Georgetown and found the man by whom I sent it had not forwarded it, and he took it and gave it to a Mr Brown who was about leaving for a Voyage at Sea, but will be around to the States in the Autumn or first of the Winter. He has two letters for you which if he lives to get there you will be sure to get.* Clearly, the surviving letters from Cayman weren't the only ones that Eunice posted. *My little Lou begins to walk,* she wrote at the end of 1871. *If you get my other letter you will know all about her.* Maybe that *other letter* was passed around too many times to become part of the family papers, but more likely it never reached its destination at all. Down south, Ellen had received word that the baby's full name was Louisa Charlotta and conveyed that news to the New England folks, but no extant letter makes mention of Eunice and Smiley's second daughter, whose presence is proved only in a listing of ship passengers and whose name, Caramiel, can be documented only in island memories.

Unsure if her communications arrived, Eunice kept writing, filling her pages not with anxiety and anger but with descriptions of satisfaction and well-being, for vindicating her decision to cross the Caribbean Sea with a man of color became the main point of the narratives she now composed. *My darling Mother, It is over four months since he took me—or rather* (here Eunice corrected herself to reflect her own agency) *since I went from you to be with him,* she wrote in 1870. Presuming that Lois wanted to know how the couple was getting along, Eunice set out to reassure her. *As for myself I am proud and happy,* she proclaimed, promising that *what I know you to be most anxious about I must be most particular in speaking of, i.e. My Happiness.* Her new husband, she reported, *does every thing for me a man can do and*—now Eunice alluded to her newfound status as a delicate lady—*is very careful of me.* Hinting that Lois might not take her word for it, she added, *I often wish you could see us, and know just how happy he makes me & how much comfort we take together.*

Back in Claremont during the war, Eunice's misery had magnified her sense of distance from mother and sisters (*I want to see you already so soon*, she cried just after a visit from New Hampshire to Massachusetts. *I want some of my folks near me*). In East End, the constant loneliness that Eunice had weathered in those years dissipated. *I have never been home sick for one day*, she wrote several months after arrival, probably permitting herself a slight exaggeration. *And My dear Mother*, she elaborated with a touch of defiance, *so long as we are to each other what we are now, I shall never regret linking my life with his.* Even at that painful moment just before departure, when a *yearning look* in Lois's eyes seemed to want to *pierce the misty future*—to know what would become of the daughter she would most likely never see again—Eunice admitted that she had felt *the cord of love and affection drawing me away from you.* Now, in a place so far away, she could say with equanimity *that much as I love you and cherish the memory of other dear freinds, I could not go from <u>him</u> for the sake of seeing all.*

Eunice's sojourn on earth was turning out, after all, to be more joyful than had seemed possible back in New England or the Deep South, and she wanted her family to know that. She wanted to put them at ease about her decision to marry Smiley Connolly, but she also wanted those scornful New England neighbors—and her brother Henry—to comprehend the details of it all.

Eunice meant everything she wrote, but she didn't impart everything that came to pass. Sometimes it was the rush of a departing ship that stopped her (*I have many more things I want to say to you. But the Captain has gone up to the Vessel and I must haste*). Other times, even now, when it mattered so much, words wouldn't cooperate. *When I go to write you I have so much I want to say and know I cannot say it all*, she confessed another time. Hours and minutes no longer needed to be rationed, and although paper might be in short supply on the island, cost no longer mattered either. Rather, Eunice found it difficult to explain the path she had chosen: to marry across the color line, to forsake her family, to leave her native land probably forever, to live among former slaves and people of African descent. *When I write and find so much to say to you—and think of the great distance that must be traversed before it can reach you*, she reasoned another time, *I see that I must be brief and leave much unsaid that I would like to say.* That *great distance*, Eunice knew, encompassed more than nautical and overland miles.

Hot weather, for instance, was one of the topics to be avoided. Smiley had been wise to introduce his New England bride to the Caribbean in November. "The charms of the land are enhanced by the thought that winter never breaks in upon their beauty," wrote another traveler in the 1870s. "At Christmas the earth is as gay and the sun as bright as in the middle of the year." Summer, on the other hand, offered fewer charms and lasted roughly from April to October. As a great-grandson of Brother Dighton figured it, the pitiless West Indian sun constituted "a dramatic experience" for Eunice.

Those same months also brought rain, when salt marsh mosquitoes buzzed relentlessly, rising in black clouds from the inland mangrove swamps, thickening especially at dusk or following the frequent showers. "Mosquitoes was by the trillion, not millions, trillion of mosquitoes," was how one elderly Caymanian recalled his childhood, before pest control made the islands attractive to tourists in the mid-twentieth century. "Swarming, swarming, swarming!" claimed another. "Smothering," asserted another. "I thought I was going to die!" exclaimed one of Smiley's great-granddaughters from his first marriage who was born in the United States but lived on Grand Cayman as a girl. Though malaria-free, the insects came in choking hordes, deterred only by sisal fans (one in each hand) or swinging smoke pots (buckets of smoldering black mangrove or button-wood). Yet not one of Eunice's surviving letters so much as alludes to the heat or the insects, and if her children thought to describe any discomfort, she instructed them to write about coral and mosses instead.

There were other, more personal subjects to evade too. Although Eunice wrote freely about Smiley's three sons (*He has Gamaliel & Cornelius with him*, she recorded one evening, *while Clarence & Jarrett were making a fire on the Beach*), she never spoke of their mother. When Rachel Partridge Connolly died in 1904 in East End, her son Gamaliel identified her as the "Widow of William Smiley Connolly, a Seaman," either to elevate her status or as an intended erasure of Eunice. Divorce in Cayman was rare; it was also illegal until the 1880s. "Never hardly heard about people divorcing those days," recalled an elderly islander. "Unheard of!" declared Smiley's great-granddaughter, explaining that men would sooner form adulterous liaisons—indeed, others thought it not uncommon "where these men went abroad and married other women and left their wives." Smiley and Rachel may not have been formally married, for a dearth of island ministers made that institution the norm only in the twentieth century, but whatever the circumstances, Eunice stayed mute about any awkward encounters, fresh rounds of gossip, or painful resonances of her father's desertion.

Nor did Eunice ever mention Robert; quite possibly, she didn't even know about him until her arrival in Cayman. Well remembered today by elderly East Enders, everyone knew that Robert was Smiley's son, and half brother to Gamaliel, Cornelius, and Jarrett. No one could recall who was his mother, but Robert was born in 1869, the same year that Smiley brought Eunice to East End. More likely than not, no lost letter from Cayman broached this sensitive issue either. Smiley Connolly by no means presented an unblemished past—not even an unblemished recent past—but Eunice willingly overlooked his transgressions.

On the other side, one of Eunice's favorite subjects was her husband's entrepreneurial spirit. Smiley and his hired carpenters built boats from the island's native hardwoods, both schooners for turtle fishing away from Cayman waters and smaller boats for trade with passing vessels (*Mr Connolly is about fitting another Canoe*). Onshore he had land to cultivate (*he had just come in from the Plantation*—that meant tilled ground) and more property to acquire (*he was after a new Grass peice* and had *cleared the ground and run a stonewall*). In detailing Smiley's enterprise, Eunice kept an eye toward countering Henry's convictions of slothful black people: Smiley was *always driving at something*, was *neither an idle or a lazy man*, and found *plenty to do I'll assure you*, she claimed, while Smiley offered supporting evidence of his own. He was "much engaged in laboring at home to make my family as comfortable as I possiable can," he wrote to New England, "especially my dear Eunice which is dear to me as my own life."

Had Eunice been embellishing her own happiness or her husband's ambitions, she wouldn't have extended repeated invitations to Lois to live out the remainder of her life in East End. Smiley believed, he wrote, in "helping our old Parents when they are Old and are not very able to help themself," and Eunice tried hard to persuade her mother. *What a good time we might have*, she argued, and Smiley even sketched a coconut tree, "that you may see what kind of tree they are, and wish you was here to share the fruits with us." Smiley even considered sailing to Boston to fetch Lois himself. *If I knew you would come back with him I dont know but I would just let him go long enough for that*, Eunice put in. For his part, Smiley promised that should Lois "take our home for your home, our Land for your Land" (echoing the Book of Ruth in the Old Testament), she would find "free access to what we have and shareing our comforts."

Smiley Connolly drew this picture in a letter he wrote to his mother-in-law, Lois Davis, around 1870, accompanied by the words "I have sent you the Sketch of a Cocoanut tree that you may see what kind of tree they are, and wish you was here to share the fruits with us."

Eunice asked her husband to add one more line: "Mrs. Connolly requests me to say to you that you will not find Society & Privileges in Caymans as you have always been used to," he appended, "but think that we can make you comfortable enough in your old age to prevent you from labouring in your old days." That was their way of saying that Lois would never have to work another day in her life, a prospect no son or son-in-law had yet been able to offer her.

As a New Englander whose family became impoverished as their farmland diminished and as someone who moved to a mill town in order to work for meager wages, Eunice found immense gratification in her day-to-day life in East End. "Any lover of the good old times, when machinery was unknown, should pay us a visit," commented the island's Scottish missionary in 1873, and any North American woman used to the amenities of a Victorian household would have found Cayman seriously lacking. With soil too poor to nourish staple crops like sugar and cotton, the three islands could not sustain a plantation economy and thus never sheltered the kind of wealth known to British colonies like Jamaica. Before emancipation, Caymanian slaves grew food crops, worked as domestic laborers, and logged mahogany. Smiley's father may have been among a small number of enslaved men who served as mariners and turtle fishers, and after emancipation in the 1830s, turtle fishing endured as the islands' major industry. After emancipation too, everyone worked hard, with former masters becoming "a plain, hardworking class of men," as another missionary observed, dependent upon "manual labor for their daily bread." Yet the very lack of industrial conveniences likely reminded Eunice of her Northfield girlhood, which—at least in her earliest memories, and compared with her struggles thereafter—represented simpler times.

While Smiley built a home for his new family, Eunice temporarily kept house in a wattle and daub cottage. The walls were framed with ironwood posts, woven with wooden strips, and filled in with lime made from burnt coral mixed with sand; rain stayed on one side of a thatched roof fashioned from palm leaves. Island men carved native mahogany into furniture, while women sewed mattresses and pillows from sail canvas filled with plantain leaves. There were no bright shopwindows crowded with tempting objects; rather, Smiley and his brothers obtained wares from Jamaica, and extras arrived on the island by way of "wrecking" (the liberation of goods from stranded vessels), with islanders and crews dividing the salvaged loot. A Sunday wreck in Eunice's day left East End churches empty, and as one villager explained to a castaway minister, "to tell the truth, sir, our main dependence is on the wrecks, and we all thank God when a ship comes ashore."

Women's labor in Cayman was hardly less strenuous than in New

These East End wattle and daub cottages, photographed in the early twentieth century, were little different from those Eunice knew on Grand Cayman Island in the 1870s. Eunice probably lived in a similar dwelling until Smiley Connolly completed the large "American style" house he was building for his new bride.

England, even without the grime of wood-burning ovens and the chill of laundry on a snowy day. Clothing and linens were washed under shade-trees, with starch made from the pulp of grated cassava. Soapsuds came from native plants, and rocks stood in for washboards. Cooking fires were built on an outdoor caboose, a wooden box on stilts filled with sand, and after weeks of cleaning and sun drying, hollowed-out gourds served as basin, pot, dipper, mixing bowl, and measuring cup. Wood for fires, like heating stones for ironing, had to be hauled from afar in thatch palm baskets. Houses stood by the sea, away from the mosquito-infested inland swamps, but sandy seaside soil meant families kept provision grounds miles away in the interior, entailing long journeys to tend the crops and carry home their yield. East Enders, mostly women, also worked with the tough salt-resistant fronds of the native silver thatch palm and crafted hats (like the ones Eunice once stitched for pitiable wages), along with fans, baskets, and hammocks, and ropes for hoisting sails. Cutting, carrying, drying, pulling, stripping, twisting, and weaving were hard work indeed.

The difference was that Eunice didn't perform most of this labor herself. That was precisely why island life held the deceptive appeal of simplicity for her. *I have always had a woman do my washing and ironing and washing out my house*, she reported. *She does all that and my other work too. Of course I help around the lightest of it*, she admitted. *But I live easy enough I tell you.* When Smiley ordered that his wife *must have a chicken killed and give him some broth*, Eunice added the words *so that is being done now*, having passed the command on to her servant, before going back to writing her letter. As for her own chores, they didn't encompass much beyond mending or leisurely sewing. *I always take my work when he is working at the Bench and go out with him and sit under the Cocoanut trees*, she wrote of her afternoons and evenings with Smiley. Eunice had hired the aforementioned servant for one month *to try her*, she explained, and was considering making *a bargain with her for a year if she will accept my conditions*. Not only had Eunice "gone to housekeeping" in East End, but she now played the part of mistress, in command of domestic help. Where Eunice had once cooked, cleaned, and laundered, both for her own family and for employers, now she only watched and supervised.

As Eunice assumed the role of mistress, she also found that the divide between herself and her servant depended upon ideas about race that were different from what she had known in New England. *She is a good respectable trusty girl*, Eunice wrote of the woman who cleaned her house, then added, *and I think much of her although she is a black girl*. Eunice had once written with a mixture of disdain and envy about the fact that her sister Ellen had a *black girl* in Mobile who did *every thing* for her; now Eunice found herself in the same position that Ellen once occupied. Eunice's Civil War letters never betrayed the kind of racism that came so easily to Henry, but her characterization of her servant as respectable and trustworthy *although she is a black girl* exposed her quickness to echo the attitudes of the West Indian "colored" classes, to which Smiley belonged. Although Eunice's servant and husband both were of African descent, her servant was "black," whereas her husband was "colored"—that expansive Caribbean category in between black and white, African and European—and that made all the difference.

In the British West Indies, Smiley took his place in the middle rank of a three-part hierarchy. An 1855 Cayman census listed "white," "coloured," and "black," just as Jamaica's population tables counted "white," "brown," and "black." Yet even those three official labels proved insufficient in the islands. An observer in Jamaica cataloged "sambos, mulattoes, quadroons, mestecs, and mestiphinoes," and the inventory of an Englishwoman in Antigua included "*mulatto*," "*mustee*," "*fustee*," and "*dustee*." In Cayman, the record of a slave sale described "a Sambo Girl," one Conolly descendant described her mother as "musty," and two Conolly siblings invoked the term "quadroon" to describe their grandmother. Europeans (like North Americans) tended to divide the Caymanian population into "black" and "white," whereas those of African descent described various grades in between.

As Eunice soon discovered, the most significant difference lay in the meaning of those in-between terms. In the United States, a person designated as "mulatto" stood closer to blackness, but in the West Indies, a person designated as "colored" stood closer to whiteness. By the same token, generations of one family in the United States could shift between "black" and "mulatto," whereas generations in the West Indies could shift between "colored" and "white." Reflecting those divisions, missionary census takers on Grand Cayman in 1855 had formulated one category for "black" inhabitants and another, single category for "white and coloured" inhabitants. No doubt unable to sort islanders' descriptions of themselves, the census takers noted that it was "impracticable to distinguish between the white and coloured population." As a *New York Times* correspondent observed in the 1860s, British West Indian society contained a "middle class, composed alike of white and colored mechanics," which stood above "the lower orders, which are the black laborers." In Cayman, black people were buried in segregated cemetery plots, while the white and colored shared a final resting place.

The difference too was that a person's class standing counted in the West Indian order of racial stratification: The higher a person's status, the whiter that person was understood to be. In New England, Smiley's African ancestry ultimately made him a black man, causing him and his new bride the pain of discrimination. In the West Indies, where class and complexion counted openly in racial classification, Smiley's prosperity and light skin shaded him toward the category of "white" (for this reason, Smiley may not have believed himself to be deceiving the marriage clerk back in Massachusetts after all). East End remained the darker and poorer side of Grand Cayman Island, and by the time Eunice arrived, Smiley's extended family counted themselves among that settlement's local elite. The Conolly family "always had a big sway over here," descendants in East End still recall. Educated and literate, they were the "better" ones, "the important people."

Smiley's name does not appear on official lists of Caymanian slaves (nor does Brother Dighton's, although both were born before emancipation in 1834, when the lists were compiled), but the slave registration records do list a "John Connelly" born in 1798, possibly Smiley's father, John Jarrett Conolly. In any case, Conollys were among the earliest settlers of the eastern end of Grand Cayman, where former slaves set up (as one British official put it) a "village for themselves" in order to "live together away from the white people." Resentful former masters called them savage and ungrateful, as these deserters claimed land for themselves—"cut their way up through the bush," in the words of a Conolly descendant. Within the century, Conolly men owned great expanses of property, extending west to Bodden Town and north to Colliers. Smiley and his mariner brothers bought and sold goods in Jamaica, Honduras, Cuba, the Florida keys, New Orleans, Mobile, New York, and Boston (from Kingston, Smiley announced to Lois that he was "Master of the British Schooner Liberty"). When not at sea, the men filled respectable Caymanian occupations like shopkeeping, teaching, and the ministry.

Although Smiley never expounded upon class or color in his letters back to New England, surely he concurred with Eunice's judgment that their servant's blackness cast doubt upon her trustworthiness. In the words of a nineteenth-century observer in the West Indies, "the antagonism between the brown and the black is greater than that of either against the white," and British officials in the Cayman Islands made the same observation after emancipation. In maligning her own *black girl,* Eunice now embraced this kind of hostility between "black" and "colored."

In New England, Smiley was not a white man, but in the West Indies, he was not a black man, and he had likely explained this to Eunice when he proposed to her, for the benefits of his West Indian status were considerable. Clara was *in School constantly,* Eunice reported with pride, and instead of resorting to menial farm labor or millwork, Clarence served as a teacher at the church school in East End. Moreover, while Smiley continued to build a "large House in American style," as he described it, Eunice's domain was shaping up to be more comfortable than any she had ever known. Fancier than the island's common cottages, her home would be an "upstairs house," complete with exterior stairway and timbered second story.

There would be room for Clarence and Clara, Smiley's three boys, Eunice's two Cayman-born daughters, and even space for Lois, should she accept their invitation. Neither rented nor borrowed, never to be shared with a stranger or torn down by a landlord, it would be theirs forever. Descendants still recall that "big house" with its "big veranda," passed down to one of Smiley's sons, then destroyed in a hurricane after Eunice's lifetime.

In New England during the Civil War, Eunice had been *jogging around the world so without a home*, had so wanted William Stone to be *spared to come home, and provide for his little family* in order to *have a place to call home*. Now, as a sea captain's wife, across the waves from her mother and siblings, Eunice found on Grand Cayman a *little "Island Home," a Happy home*, she related, complete with *an indulgent loving Husband*. The idea and daily reality of "home" took on an unfamiliar, though much welcomed, significance for Eunice in these years, as Smiley Connolly, by virtue of local status and hard work, fulfilled the Victorian marriage contract in a way that William Stone had not.

In New England, Eunice had resigned herself to a working-class version of American domesticity, in which a home (when she had one) served as refuge from the day-to-day humiliations of poverty and servile labor. In East End, she enjoyed a distinctly American middle-class incarnation of domesticity, in which her home stood for both security and dignity. To depend upon a husband, unlike imposing upon relatives, made a world of difference, for this was a respectable kind of female dependence. (Whereas Eunice had never referred to her first husband by his surname, she now routinely wrote of *Mr Connolly*, an affectation of the middle classes to which her sisters back in New England didn't feel entitled when naming their own spouses.) *I never go any where only when Mr Connolly and*

I go out to take a walk, and in the evening we go and sit on the beach,
Eunice beamed. *I have no desire to go away from my home*—her
underlining emphasized what mattered most—*I find it there.*

Back in New England, leaving the house had meant going to
work for someone else. In East End, the ability to stay at home all
day represented to Eunice a new form of leisure and privilege that
she had never known as a white woman in North America. One
evening, *after passing a very pleasant day*, Eunice and Smiley sailed
over to Gun Bay; another time Eunice recounted *a pleasant little sail
we have had tonight since dinner*, in which Smiley took the family
out in the Canoe and sailed up and down the Bay with us. Such depar-
tures from home, exploring the beautiful waters around Grand
Cayman Island, couldn't have been more different from the solitary
and anxious trudge to an employer's abode, only to assume the role
of servant to the gentleman or lady who lived there. In Cayman,
Eunice herself became a lady: Smiley headed the family, but Eunice
took charge of the household. *Mr Connolly allows me to do as I think
best about every such thing*, she reported of domestic matters *I
always go to him, but he always says You know what suits you and any
thing you do suits me.* After decades of tenement living and unrelenting toil, Eunice's home in East End came to be the center of her
world and the shelter of her needs.

Smiley offered his new bride the prize of middle-class dignity, but
he also offered her love, and the life that Eunice narrated from East
End conformed nicely to ideals of Victorian companionate marriage
as well. *So while there is a mutual desire and each one takes pleasure in
making the life of the other pleasant and happy, there is nothing to fear*,
Eunice wrote in the spring of 1870, confirming a model of common fulfillment—nothing to fear because Smiley so well met bour-
geois expectations of a husband thoroughly attentive to his wife.
And it is all his kind ways and thoughtful acts prompted by love and

respect which he has for me that makes it so, Eunice spelled out to her mother in earnest. *He told you he would do every thing he could to make me happy. And I may say he devotes himself to that, and I feel sure it is the pleasure of his life to see me enjoy my self.* Smiley probably also offered Eunice an intimacy she hadn't known with her first husband. Clarence wasn't born until three years after Eunice married William Stone, and Clara (if she was even William's child) was born nearly ten years later. With Smiley, on the other hand, Eunice first became pregnant if not during an affair in Mobile, then just a few months after their wedding, close to the age of forty, then again a few years later.

But Eunice had not remarried solely for herself. *He is a <u>good kind tender Husband</u> to me, and a good kind Father to my children,* she informed her mother, for in the realm of fatherhood too, Smiley fulfilled nineteenth-century ideals in a way that William Stone never had. He provided for Clarence and Clara, and passed the skilled craft of boatbuilding on to the boy, with an eye toward making a mariner out of him (*Mr C and Clarence finished the trimming,* Eunice wrote of a canoe they were building, and Clarence worked *when not in School with his Father at the beach*). Smiley also consoled the children when they were ill or unhappy, demonstrated affection and sentiment, and played with them when he returned from his work. *It does my heart good to see it so,* Eunice wrote, gushing about Clara's love for *her Father.* (Once, when Smiley and Clara played at packing Clara's trunk to go back to the United States, the little girl announced that *if she had got to be away from her Father & Mother, she had rather be in the bottom of the sea.*) With Clarence too, Smiley proved *very patient and indulgent,* and little Louisa Charlotta stayed home from church one Sunday when Smiley was busy, Eunice wrote happily, for *she never goes without her Father.*

In the West Indies too, Eunice fulfilled her own aspirations to be *a constant church goer*, with extra time for Bible reading and the religious instruction of her children. Scottish Presbyterians had been evangelizing Grand Cayman for nearly a quarter century when Eunice arrived, and though the single minister rarely made the journey across the island from George Town, East Enders nonetheless built themselves a chapel and took on the work of Sunday services, Sabbath school, and prayer meetings. Like in New England, church life constituted a largely female realm in Cayman, in this case because husbands, fathers, and sons were so often "at sea or in foreign countries," as an island missionary explained. Every Sunday, Eunice took her place among the women of East End (Smiley attended as often as he could) and further assumed the duty of bettering the lives of the less fortunate: *We still continue the School*, she wrote, indicating that she joined Clarence in the work of teaching both literacy and religion. For the first time, Eunice stood as the dispenser of charity rather than its recipient.

Faith itself, however, was one more topic that Eunice evaded in her letters. The Presbyterian church was the only house of worship on Grand Cayman Island in Eunice's day, and Scottish Presbyterians remained rooted in a Calvinism that resisted the tide of liberal Protestantism. Eunice's journey out of impoverishment also entailed a shift toward this more conservative doctrine, and the loss of her cherished Universalist community became another trade-off. Just as Eunice had followed the faith of her first husband's family back in New England, so she now took her place in Smiley's religious fellowship. Such were the compromises of marriage, though more likely than not, Eunice never abandoned Universalist theology, perhaps even sharing that spiritual philosophy with Smiley as part of their *mutual desire* to make each other's lives *pleasant and happy*.

Home and church formed the two axes of Eunice's life in East End, yet her days also included a fair measure of isolation (*I never go*

The Connolly-Conolly family, including Eunice, Smiley, and the children, worshiped at this three-gabled Presbyterian church in East End, destroyed by a hurricane in the early twentieth century.

any where, only when Mr Connolly and I go out). To be sure, some of the new in-laws reached out (*His Mother and Brother Dighton wish to be remembered with their compliments to you*, she conveyed to Lois. *They are all very kind to me*). But others may have shunned her as an intruder who replaced Smiley's Caymanian wife, including Smiley's son Gamaliel, who insisted on thinking of his mother as Smiley's rightful spouse. Certainly it took time for Eunice to converse comfortably in the strongly cadenced English of East Enders, and if she willingly held herself apart from the poorer families around her, that aloofness further cost her the companionship of neighbors. *You know I always have friends when I stay long enough to get aquainted*, she wrote soon after arrival, before confessing, *I dont know whether I shall here or not. I do not get aquainted very fast only as people come to me.*

Ladyhood had its disadvantages within a mostly poor community, but if Eunice had little opportunity to keep company with the majority of East End women—as they made thatch rope and tended their crops out at the provision grounds—that solitude felt liberating compared with what had come before: kin reprimanding her for not wearing a proper hat and intrusive women whispering that she ought to send away her son. Even if Caymanian women circulated gossip about Smiley's first wife or his newborn out-of-wedlock son, Robert, Eunice now had a haven. She could stay at home, or she could leave the house at her husband's side. Even without Smiley—if she took the children to church when he was working—Eunice's community status served as a thick layer of protection.

Eunice's achievements in the West Indies were not so different from those of other nineteenth-century brides who moved far away in order to better their circumstances, and (the same as for those brides) there always loomed the possibility of return. Indeed, even now Eunice revisited her dream of a New England farm, despite the reality of rapidly diminishing land in the industrializing post–Civil War North. *He has often said if he knew what he could do in America to keep along he would go there to live*, she wrote of Smiley. *I think he might live there very well on a Farm but he does not understand Farming there so he feels afraid.* When Eunice thought fleetingly of making a yearlong visit to the United States, she asked Ann's hus-

Catherine Susannah Conolly lived in East End during the same years as Eunice, but Eunice never mentioned her. Catherine Susannah's husband was Thomas Dighton Conolly, whom Eunice called *Brother Dighton* in her letters. The hat and dress in this undated photograph indicate the family's elite status.

band to promise her *one good sleigh ride* and *to learn Mr Connolly to work on the Farm*. Of course Smiley's agricultural inexperience was not the sole reason that he hesitated to make a return journey. He already knew that his status in the West Indies was not transferable to the United States, where he would once again become a black man, at least in the eyes of some. Eunice had followed her new husband to live among people of color in the British Caribbean, in order to find what was impossible to attain, with him, in her native land: the privileges to which she had so long aspired as a white woman hoping to live out a Yankee tale that took its protagonists from poverty to prosperity.

THE IRONIC FACT was that Eunice's Caymanian neighbors may well have assumed that she was a colored woman. Whiteness and African ancestry were not mutually exclusive in the West Indies, and because marriage across shades of color was common, virtually no one (no matter how light-skinned) was thought to be without African "blood." (Ruminating over whether Eunice was the only white person in East End in the 1870s, Brother Dighton's great-grandson mentioned two other families who were "considered white" even though they had "some colored blood," asserting that Eunice wouldn't have stood out.) In Cayman, Eunice lived in a settlement of freed slaves, she was the wife of a colored man of means, and she employed a black servant; any or all of those circumstances could mark her as a colored woman. As for her two Cayman-born daughters, New Englanders who knew the girls' father would have labeled them "black" or "mulatto." Caymanians, on the other hand, might have considered the girls white. Or, if the children appeared dark, Caymanians might have understood that to be the result of Eunice's own "colored blood" (everyone in the islands had some, and, after all, Eunice's nose was not particularly thin or sharp, nor her hair particularly light).

Reflecting upon whether Eunice's Caymanian neighbors thought of her as a colored woman, descendants nearly skipped over the question in an effort to establish that no one would have minded. "I don't think that would have worried them in East End," the great-grandson mused. There was "quite a lot of mixup" at the time, and Eunice would have "fit in to that." Or in the words of another descendant, "Well, I guess in that time they would. . . . I don't think it would make any difference."

That is not to say, exactly, that Eunice "passed" for colored when she lived in East End. The very circumstances of passing depend upon the distinctive post–Civil War U.S. idea that anyone with any African ancestry, no matter how many generations removed, is still "black." Were such a rigid system to function perfectly, no person of African descent could ever pass for white, yet that very same rigidity made it effortless for a person without any African ancestry to be counted as black. (Indeed, in the South just after the Civil War, when a white woman was warned away from living with her black husband, she insisted she was black too; likewise, a black man obtained a license to marry a white woman by claiming that his bride was also black.)

In the United States, to pass for white meant escaping into a world of greater advantage, whereas those who journeyed from "white" to "black" opened themselves only to greater oppression. In Eunice's case, however, the outcome was different. By marrying Smiley Connolly, she sacrificed any claims to respectability, but she also married up. Most starkly, she moved from being a servant in New England to having a servant of her own in the Caribbean, and whereas William Stone was a carpenter, Smiley Connolly hired such men to work under him (*We have Carpenters here now working on her*, Eunice wrote of the canoe Smiley was building). The twist was that Eunice's climb upward depended upon departure from the United States, and in this way, her circumstances mirrored the trials of "passing," for just as African Americans who passed into the white world lost loved ones, so too did Eunice. Most palpably, she sacrificed her brother's love, but she also lost her whole family when she set up a new life so far away.

As for complexion, it is not out of the question that Smiley had taken Eunice, with her dark hair and possibly none too fair skin, to be a colored woman (as he would have put it) when he first encountered her in North America. Then, back in the islands, a hot sun could initially alter any New Englander's skin; in fact, white travelers were known to despair about such transformations. "I am so horribly tanned!" shrieked a Massachusetts native on her trip to the Gulf South in the 1830s. The Caribbean, with its low, strong rays, was particularly troublesome. "It ought to be inculcated on the mind of the newly arrived European," wrote a white doctor in Jamaica, "that he should avoid exposure to the sun." No doubt Eunice did. In fact, in East End she likely paled eventually under the tropical sun— another irony—given her ability to stay indoors (or at least under shade trees) while someone else washed her clothes, tended her garden, and gathered her firewood. If Eunice could not have been described as "fair" in New England, her Caymanian neighbors—who thought of her as "colored"—may have seen her precisely that way, not only because of her now paler skin but also because she was the wife of a well-to-do sea captain.

Almost certainly, Eunice never came to think of herself as a colored woman, for she now lived the life to which she had always aspired as a white woman, far from the realm of Irish and black laborers. Smiley's status in his native country was higher than Eunice's in hers, and the stature that he possessed in East End changed her daily life from everything that had come before: as the daughter of an alcoholic father who deserted his family, as the wife of a man unable to find work in the depressed mill towns of the North or a booming southern city, as a mother compelled to work in a factory and board out her child, as a widow forced to labor as a domestic servant.

As for me I jog along in a quiet easy way, Eunice wrote now from her island home. *I have enough to eat & drink, & wear,* she added, noting that in three months' time she had never twice donned the same dress for Sunday services. So remarkable was all this that she repeated it in another letter. *I have a plenty to eat drink & wear,* Eunice reminded her family, and herself, *and do not have to sit up nights sewing by Lamp light making and trimming dresses to get it better.* In East End, as Eunice stood somewhere in between the blurred West Indian categories of "white" and "colored," she also became a lady with a home of her own who enjoyed a companionate marriage, sent her children to school, directed a dark-skinned maid, and left the house only to attend church or sail the bay with her husband.

By joining her life to Smiley Connolly's, Eunice defied her New England neighbors and especially her brother Henry. As one nineteenth-century North American traveler wrote, prejudices in the Caribbean began to "melt away" in a place "where people of colored blood have attained to such social consideration as to make themselves respected." In the end, though, Eunice's radical choices in North America turned out to be not so radical in the West Indies. When Eunice married Smiley, she sacrificed any claims to honorable white womanhood in New England, but she soon embraced those very same claims in the Cayman Islands, by virtue of membership in a well-off colored family. Eunice didn't expound upon race in her letters—she had said quite enough on the subject through her actions in New England after the Civil War—but she made clear, all the same, that she had found a place, finally, among a local elite, even if that elite constituted the top layer of the poorest and darkest community on an isolated island of limited wealth in the Caribbean Sea.

OVER THE YEARS, Eunice continued to hope that her family in New England would appreciate the degree of happiness she had achieved in the West Indies, and to this end she kept writing letters. The silence that emanated in return made for Eunice's most consistent source of discontent during her Cayman years. More than Smiley's first wife or his son, Robert, by another woman, more than the loss of a Universalist community or the isolation that came with ladyhood, it was the lack of word from her mother and siblings that permitted Eunice to slip back into moments of distress. Six months after arrival, she had *not heard one word from any of those I left behind*, she announced, making it impossible to *know friend or foe*. Three months more, and she began to beg for letters, *good long ones too, for you must remember that I have not heard any thing from one of you since I left America*, she echoed. Three months more again, and

Smiley wrote that he and Eunice remained "much troubled about you and the family not writing," for his wife hadn't received "a single scrach of pen from you or any other sence she left you."

Two years gone, and Eunice was still *trying every way possible to get a letter to you and see if I can get just one in return*, she appealed, *for not one word have I ever heard from any of my family yet*. The old anger, harder to sustain from such a far distance, crept back in. *You must excuse me for I have written so much to you and so many times that I do not know what to say to you*, she recorded with restraint, suggesting that *if no one wants to write to me*, perhaps sister Ann's son Charlie could send a note to Clarence. Lois had always been Eunice's anchor; after Luther senior abandoned the family, after Luther junior died, after William died, after Henry rejected her, Lois's comforting presence had always endured. Now, for the first time, Eunice couldn't be sure of her mother's loyalty. Had Lois given in to the disapproval of Dracut neighbors? Had she come to side, after all, with Henry? Eunice still wanted her mother to come live with them, but, she warned, *not having heard any thing from you, I do not know how your mind is toward me and mine.*

The first letters from New England arrived in Cayman two and a half years after Eunice's departure. Those pages haven't survived, but surely they were filled with recountings of the family's whereabouts, health, and various endeavors, along with news of the New England economy and Reconstruction politics. No doubt the letters reassured Eunice how much everyone (or almost everyone) missed her and the children, and no doubt they contained regards for Smiley and his kin. Then nearly another year passed before any more mail arrived. *When I think of writing I feel my Heart so full that I scarceley know what to say*, Eunice wrote, reliving the joyous moment when a captain stopped by to announce the second round of envelopes for Miss Eunice. How many more letters were "lost in the deep,"

Smiley wondered during the long interval that followed that batch of mail, or had the family once and for all "forgotten or cast us away altogether?" Was Lois even still alive? "After not hearing from you or any of the family for nearly a year we endeavor to drop you these few lines trusting that you are still surviving on this lower world," Smiley communicated one day in 1874. "For often we are almost in dispair thinking you must have left this home for a better one above." But Eunice kept on. *It is going on Three years since I have received any thing from any of you,* she wrote in 1875, *so you will have a great deal to write to make me know all that has transpired with the Family in that time.* Any form of acknowledgment would do. *Try sending me a bundle of papers or some thing,* she begged; *that way, it will make me see that you have not forgotten me, or thrown me away altogether.*

If only Eunice could have known how much some of her New England relatives agonized over mail service. "It does seem so hard that we cannot get a letter to you," Ann wrote as early as 1870. "Mother got a letter from you about a month ago saying you had never herd from home," putting the family at a loss. "Oh dear we have not much curage to write for it seems you do not get any letter that is sent you," she sighed. "Sometimes you come to my bed side and talk with me," Ann revealed further. "It is pleasant to dream of you." A few days later, when Ann picked up her pen again, she cast aside her usual restraint. "Oh my dear Sister don't think your self forgoten because you do not get letters from us," she effused, "for we think of you as a dear sister far from home." For whatever reason, Ann's heartening letter remained unsent; perhaps she didn't know where to post it, or maybe she asked Henry to add a few lines, and he withheld it from the post office.

Still, Eunice's doubts about her family's affections were hardly unfounded. "I have not written to Eunice yet," Hattie tossed off in a letter to Lois in 1872, "dont know as I ever shall get time, hope you have before now." When mail did arrive in Cayman in January 1873, the packet included letters from Lois and Ann (written in October), one from Ellen (written in November), and one from Melissa Rankin. Lois, Ellen, and Melissa probably echoed Ann's encouraging sentiments, but Eunice noted too that *Harriet has not written to me since I wrote her*, and worst of all, *Henry never wrote me*. Whether that muteness resulted from circuitous routes and unreliable ships or from animosity and disdain, Eunice could never be sure, but nine-year-old Clara had plainly grasped the tension; when she wrote to New England asking for letters, she named her grandmothers and aunts but omitted Uncle Henry. Eunice's fears of rejection felt familiar from lonely Claremont days. *I wondered if you knew how long it had been since you had written to me!* she had accused back then. *What do you suppose I think when you do not write for five or six weeks?* The difference was that Eunice could now, with certainty, name a reason why her family had forsaken her.

ALONGSIDE THE lack of letters, Eunice's other consistent source of unhappiness in Cayman was Clarence, and she wrote candidly about her son's troubles from the start. *Miss Clara* was *contented and gets along well*, had *never been homesick at all*, Eunice reported, but not so for the boy. Clarence turned seventeen in the autumn of 1869, but Eunice hadn't wanted him to stay behind in Massachusetts, to *knock about there with no home and no one to care for him*, and he no doubt didn't wish to be separated from mother and sister yet again, this time possibly forever. In East End, even as Smiley tried to treat the boy as his own, Clarence was *a poor home sick child as I ever saw*, who could *think of nothing, speak of nothing, and know nothing but America, continually teasing to go back*, causing *great anxiety both to his Father & myself*, Eunice fretted. That *anxiety*, at least on Eunice's part, was compounded by the trajectory of her son's life, beginning with the departure of William Stone from New England. After that, Clarence had been boarded out, his father died a traitor to the nation, and he repeatedly endured separation from his mother and sister. His mother's emotional breakdown after the war precipitated yet another separation, after which Clarence faced the condemnation that attended his mother's second marriage, including rejection by his much-loved Uncle Henry.

Then, in Cayman, Clarence's eventual fate returned Eunice to the familiar landscape of emotional devastation, forcing her to endure again a depth of desolation she hadn't known since the loss of William Stone. During the last summer of the Civil War, Eunice had written of her son, *He has got to get used to disappointments in life if he lives.* That conviction was easier to embrace when Eunice herself inhabited a realm of dashed hopes. Now, in a place where she had finally found so much happiness, those words came back to haunt her. "We again endeavour to drop you a very few lines informing you that we have not heard from you or any of the other family," Smiley wrote to Lois in October 1872, "since the death of our Dear Clarence." The absence of any explanation points either to a letter unreceived or to one passed around so widely that it never made its way back into the family papers.

Was Clarence among the few cases of smallpox in Cayman in the 1870s, or did he catch typhoid or rheumatic fever or a respiratory disease resulting from those ubiquitous mosquito smoke pots? Did he drown in a boating accident or fall from a tree? Medical treatment in Cayman was limited to salt water and aloe, mint and camphor, periwinkle and almond leaves. Eunice was used to home remedies and folk medicine, but in Cayman there was no doctor to be called even in a dire emergency. Or if Clarence's cumulative traumas had led him to an anguish and despondence equal to his mother's *dark empty void* after the Civil War, and if the boy had inherited a propensity for serious depression, might he have taken advantage of the surrounding sea to end his own life?

Smiley likely fashioned the mahogany coffin himself, while East End women stitched the traditional pillow from scraps of cloth and sewed a sheet to line the casket. Neighbors would have come by to sing funeral hymns through the night, before the burial, intoning "Sleep on, beloved, sleep and take your rest" or "'Round your little grave we linger, 'Til the setting sun is low." The missionary minister, if able to reach East End in time, would have spoken at the Connolly home or out in the cemetery as Clarence's body was lowered into the churchyard on the beach, while the family threw handfuls of sand into the ground. The gravesite (now unmarked in the large sand cemetery where the church once stood) was decorated with hibiscus or orchid blossoms, conch shells or coral edging and later planted with frangipani.

It was a Christian burial, but East Enders also paid attention to African Caribbean folk religion, in which one part of the soul rose to God, while another part lingered on earth. Duppies were spirits of the recent dead who sometimes wandered about at night, troublesome even to those they had loved in life. Manifest in human or animal form, as a bright light or a ball of fire, a noise or a bundle of clothes, a duppy could never be mistaken for a living person playing a white-sheeted ghost. It might demand a drink of water, chase you, argue with you, or strike you, but it could be subdued if you cast rice or peas in the road, for it would always stop to count the grains. Wary of Clarence's dissatisfied spirit, perhaps Eunice pocketed a handful (echoing the New England superstition of throwing rice at weddings in order to distract evil spirits). Eunice's only consolation was that over time Clarence had come to *enjoy him self*, teaching school and working with his stepfather—or so she now told herself and her mother.

After Clarence died, a shattering depression once again descended upon Eunice, and once again her letters omitted few troubled emotions, dwelling now upon her son's *kind thoughtful affectionate ways with me which no earthly one but me knew.* "Mrs. Connolly begs all the family to write often as she needs some comfortable words from some of the family, but especially from you," Smiley implored Lois. Eunice, he continued, "begs you not to forsake her who at this time is very feeble," having "not recovered herself since the great trouble which befell us of our Dear Son." *I think if I could hear some good lively news from you, it would raise my Spirits a little,* Eunice pleaded, but still no letters arrived. "Please write and let aunt Margrett know that you have heard from us and tell them that we have not heard from them since the death of Clarence," eleven-year-old Clara added to the plaintive chorus. For the first time in seven years, Eunice was unable to leave her bed.

I am some what better now, Eunice wrote early in 1873, *able to be up and in pleasant weather I can go out.* Still, *to be candid about it,* she resigned herself, *I never expect to be very healthy or strong.* Now Eunice had returned to a state reminiscent of the weeks and months following the death of her first husband. Her downcast temper lingered; her spirits sank *so low* that her eyes and head often ached to the point of inducing nausea. A subsequent letter from Lois asked for more information, but once again ink proved unable to convey Eunice's despair. She tried one day: *You wish me to write concerning my precious Clarence. Mother you must excuse me this time. If you do not come here nor I come there some future time, I will try to write you about him. But I do not feel equal to it now. For his Grave is still open in my Heart and not a day and night passes me that it is not watered with my tears.* Nor did the company of other mourning parents ease Eunice's grief ("There were many child deaths in these early years," reads a note on a Conolly genealogy chart).

In the face of so much sorrow, Eunice's sense of separation from New England intensified. *I have no Mother no Sister to open my mind to*, she cried. *Mr C is very thoughtful but he fancies it is hurtful for me to talk about him*, she explained, referring to Clarence. After the Civil War, Smiley had nurtured Eunice back from hopelessness, and his desire never to see her less than joyful again (*he is perfectly unhappy himself if he thinks I am not happy*) made him unable to countenance his wife's inconsolability. At the moment of Eunice's most tremendous pain, Smiley couldn't truly comfort her, marring the couple's treasured mutual companionship for the first time.

It was soon after Clarence's death that Eunice contemplated a return trip to New England, conjuring up that *one good sleigh ride*. Yet when Smiley in fact proposed such a voyage, he noted that Eunice was "not willing to leave home at present," for East End was home to Eunice now. *I some times feel since Clarence died and my health has been so poor that I would like to come to America and see you all once more for a few months or a year*, she considered. But Smiley wouldn't be able to join her, *and I do not wish to come without him*, she shrugged. *I do not think I could enjoy myself away from him, even there*. Even when it seemed that Smiley would be able to take her to New England himself, Eunice resisted, for her newfound grief made such a long and difficult journey unthinkable. "I want to take her back to America, but she is afraid that the change of the climate will be too severe," Smiley imparted. Nor could Eunice know what kind of reception to expect, either by herself or as a couple, after so many years and such long silences. Up until the time of Clarence's death, Eunice had barely resorted to the once-familiar refrain, but now she again embraced a melancholy view of life on earth. *The best way for you and Clara to live together is for you to come here and share our Home with us*, Eunice told her mother before appending the caveat *If we all live*.

The last letter from Eunice that rests with the family papers begins with a familiar threat: *After this I am not going to write to you any more untill I hear something from some of you.* Although she was *up and down,* the family was *pretty well.* It was March 1875, and nearly three years since she had heard from anyone, but Eunice still hadn't given up on receiving word. *When you write put one or two Cucumber seeds in your letter, some Tomatoes, and any small seed that you have, vegatables or Flowers,* she directed hopefully. In anticipation, she offered detailed instructions. *You must all write a letter, not all write one letter but each one write one, and so in that way I shall know different things concerning you all.* Of her estranged sibling, she wrote plainly, *For Brother Henry and Wife I do not know what to say for whenever I have heard from home I have never heard from them.*

On a particularly trying winter evening back in New England during the Civil War, Eunice had written to her mother, *It is after I have been off to work as I have now and come home to a cold house and every thing out of fix, that I think I want to go some where or do some way to live different.* That is exactly what Eunice had achieved when she married William Smiley Connolly in 1869 and moved with him to a settlement of freed slaves in East End on Grand Cayman Island in the British West Indies. Her ascent out of poverty and her journey into romantic love came at the cost of permanent separation and irreparable rifts unlike any the protracted and bloody Civil War had imposed upon the Richardson family. *I can not write long letters now untill I hear from some of you,* she reiterated on that late March day, as the weather was beginning to turn hot again in East End, *so with much love I am your faithful E. L. C.* Those are Eunice's last surviving words, though not the last that is known about her.

7 ⮞
HURRICANE

*I*n summer and autumn, the warm surface waters of the Atlantic Ocean, the Caribbean Sea, and the Gulf of Mexico are apt to meet up with humid air and converging winds to create tropical storms. A tempest officially becomes a hurricane when its winds reach seventy-four miles per hour, and Eunice learned firsthand about these seasonal disturbances as the years in Cayman passed.

For seafarers in Eunice's day, there was "no precise rule" to determine the "bearing of the center of a hurricane from the vessel," as an 1872 nautical publication warned. Yet inferences could be drawn, as seamen knew, from how quickly a storm developed, the intensity of the squalls, the roughness of the sea, and the atmospheric pressure. Caymanians salvaged barometers (which measure atmospheric pressure by the height of a column of mercury) from the shipwrecks that came to their shores, but sailors also forecast the weather by looking at the sky and noticing changes in the wind and atmosphere. A crimson and ruby sunset, cirrus clouds overhead the following day, inky nimbus clouds on the horizon, squalls and showers, thunderstorms, ocean swells, gusty breezes, and the telltale falling barometer all pointed to the possibility of danger. Surely Eunice joined native Caymanians in praying that no natural disaster would devastate the island or harm the men who had gone to sea.

Caymanian men had once captured turtles on their own shores (Christopher Columbus called the islands Las Tortugas for their abundance), prizing the green ones for their meat and the rarer hawksbills for their shells. By the nineteenth century, though, the once-rich surrounding waters had been depleted, and the men moved their nets and traps first into Cuban waters, then to the Miskito Cays off the northeast coast of Nicaragua, 350 miles south and west of home. Those voyages took weeks, sometimes months, as the sailors rowed miles out to set their nets at night, then wrestled the next morning with flailing four-hundred-pound reptiles to be released into the schooner's crawls. An expedition typically returned with a catch of hundreds, both to feed islanders and to contribute to a thriving industry. *Tonight he has gone on board a Vessel out in the*

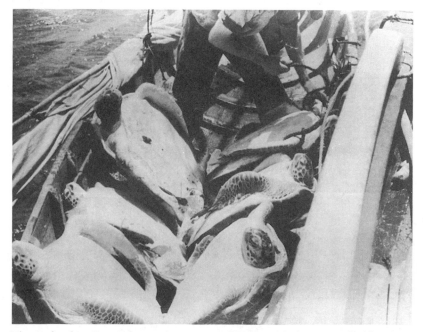

The turtles that Caymanian mariners captured and brought home weighed hundreds of pounds and served both as food and as trade goods.

Sea with a load of Turtle, Eunice wrote of Smiley one spring evening in 1870, for trade with passing ships brought a wealth of goods in return. Meanwhile traditional island songs spun tales of faraway fishermen complemented by weeping wives at home.

That the lives of Caymanian mariners were frequently endangered presented a dilemma for Eunice. After living through the uncertainty of her first husband's fate, followed by the shattering news of his death, she knew that she wouldn't be able to bear the agony of suspense or the shock of widowhood again. When Eunice accepted Smiley Connolly's hand in marriage and agreed to accompany him to the West Indies, she therefore asked in return that he give up long ocean voyages. *He does not expect to be from home more than Two weeks, Three at the most*, Eunice explained when Smiley had pressing business to conduct in the Bay Islands of Honduras. *It hurts me much to have him go*, she admitted freely, careful to make clear that *he is never from home, much as he promised me he would not be*. From Kingston, Smiley concurred. "You must not think that I have broken my promise with Mrs. Connolly about giving up going to sea," he wrote to Lois a year after the couple's departure from New England. "This is the first time that I have left her, and I would not now. But my business call me from her now." At least once, Eunice permitted her husband to make a voyage to the island of Roatán, off mainland Honduras (taking *Coffee and Cattle* with him), but when Smiley finished building his own schooner sometime after 1875, he vowed that Eunice and the children would go with him whenever he sailed.

IN 1876, a devastating hurricane hit Grand Cayman Island. The storm began on a Sabbath morning in mid-October. As islanders tried to secure thatch roofs with thatch ropes, the wind blew furiously, rain fell "like coarse gravel," houses collapsed, and trees came

Master mariners in the Cayman Islands, including Smiley Connolly, built schooners from native hardwoods for extended turtle-fishing voyages far from Cayman waters.

uprooted. Flooding sea waters displaced the fresh water of wells, crops were destroyed, livestock died, schooners smashed on the reefs, and six of Grand Cayman's seven churches fell to pieces, including the one at East End. Remarkably, no lives were lost—and Eunice and Smiley's "big house" remained standing—but missionary John Smith thought "a whole generation must pass away before the circumstances of the people can be quite restored." Had Eunice felt herself relenting a bit, she would now take no more chances on Smiley's traveling without his family. If disaster should strike her husband, Eunice wanted it to strike her and the children too.

In the autumn of 1877, when Smiley joined a turtle-fishing voyage to the Miskito Cays, the whole family climbed aboard his schooner, *The Leader*, packing up all their money and taking it with them, probably as protection against another storm in Cayman. Although Smiley owned the vessel, the captain that fall was a man named Denham Bush from West Bay, a settlement on the other side of Grand Cayman from East End. Smiley's son Jarrett served as captain of another vessel in the same fleet, and Smiley's half brother, Dighton, owned another one of the boats, although he wasn't going along on this particular voyage.

Like other seafaring wives, Eunice no doubt knew boredom and loneliness. The conviction that women brought bad luck to sailors on wooden ships echoed from New England to the West Indies, and the ones who went along were often barred from both camaraderie and labor; even the ship's kitchen remained the domain of men. As the only woman on board, Eunice would have passed the time schooling her three daughters (Clara was fifteen that year, Louisa Charlotta six, Caramiel perhaps four), offering religious instruction to the men, mending clothes and sewing sails, or adding entries to the logbook. Perhaps Smiley taught Eunice and the girls to study the stars or read the sandglasses and compasses, and like other seagoing wives and daughters, Eunice and Clara probably wrote letters and kept journals.

A year after Eunice and her family lived through the hurricane of 1876 on land, they gathered on board Smiley's schooner to face the miserable conditions of a menacing storm at sea. The *New York Maritime Register* for September 26, 1877, recorded "Bad Weather near at Hand." A telegram from Key West warned that a hurricane had passed Puerto Rico at midnight. Kingston, Jamaica, reported an approaching storm. Observers on the southeastern coast of Cuba noticed a drop in the barometer over the course of eight hours. "On such occasions the sea is often lashed to a state of the wildest frenzy," explained a nineteenth-century guidebook. "The waves, upheaved by individual blasts of wind from opposite directions, rush madly against each other, the violence of the collision causing the billows to be piled up mountain high, sending thick volumes of foam far above the tallest masts." The battered pages of surviving logbooks record tattered sails, flooded cabins, and "every thing generally as uncomfortable & miserable as possible."

Those kinds of conditions were the prelude for Eunice and her family. "Our hopes of safety being almost cut off, found we could do nothing better than to cut away the main mast, the main sail, main boom, and fore sail having previously broken away from the masts and impossible to recover them," wrote a sailor on a schooner traveling from Massachusetts to Martinique, suggesting the Connollys' experience. After that, the crew could look only to Divine Providence. A passenger on a schooner sailing between Jamaica and the Miskito Coast saw the water come "like snow, in blinding, drenching sheets." A voyager in a raging storm on the ocean "always thinks of home," this traveler realized, as the past proverbially flashed across his mind.

For Eunice, the images across her mind's eye would have encompassed Northfield, Manchester, Mobile, Claremont, Dracut, and Morristown, her mother, father, sisters, brothers, William, Clarence, the girls, Smiley, and East End, all accompanied by a version of the thoughts recorded by the nineteenth-century seagoing wife of a New England whaleman caught in a storm: "In agony I prayed not for life so much, thinking that was hopeless, but that I might feel an assurance that in eternity all would be well with me." To Caymanian fishermen who survived a hurricane on the Serrana Bank off Colombia, the storm that came upon them "looked like heaven and earth was coming together." Death loomed, one remembered, "so I just say, 'Well, this is death.'" So too for Eunice, as she took comfort in the benevolent God of Universalism.

The United States Weather Bureau later noted that the hurricane lasted from September 21 to October 5, hit the Windward Islands,

THE CARIBBEAN SEA—OFF THE MOSQUITO COAST.

This nineteenth-century engraving portrays a boat caught in a hurricane in the Caribbean Sea, the same waters where Eunice, Smiley, and their children faced a storm in 1877, while sailing in Smiley Connolly's schooner.

passed south of Puerto Rico, then headed west and north, traveling between western Cuba and the Honduran coast. The storm struck Florida, proceeding up the southern seaboard of the United States, with severe rain damaging property and washing out passenger trains, before ending south of Cape Cod and southeast of Cape Breton. "The 25th and few following days in September of this year, ought to be ever memorable," John Smith wrote from Grand Cayman for the February 1878 issue of the Scottish Presbyterian Church newsletter, for a "furious storm" destroyed nine Caymanian schooners on the Miskito Cays. Cayman's "weather-wise people" had noticed the high tides and heavy sea swells and surmised what had come to pass for the fleet of turtle fishers. Eight days into October, a surviving boat returned to Cayman to deliver the tidings of disaster, "throwing the whole community into distress and gloom." Sixty-six lives were taken, including fifty-five Grand Caymanians and "the wife of one of the captains," Smith reported, assuming Smiley to be the captain of the vessel he owned. The loss was particularly profound for Smiley's family. "Denham Bush was drowned in Sept 1877 in the terrible Hurricane that swept the Mosquito Kays," a Bush descendant recorded years later. "He was Capt of the 'LEADER' who was owned by Smiley Connolly of East End. Everyone was drowned as S. Connolly had his family on bord." Among the returning survivors was Smiley's son Jarrett. Some of the other sailors had asked Jarrett "to search around to see if they could find any thing after the storm," the memoirist recalled, "but he said he did not want to find his father dead." Eunice was forty-five years old when the ocean deep closed around her and her beloved family in the Caribbean Sea.

PERHAPS three years later, Ellen Merrill wrote a letter to the postmaster of Grand Cayman Island. The Merrills were then living in Mississippi, in the little town of Moss Point, just across the Alabama border from Mobile, and no one—neither Ellen nor those up in New England—had heard a word from Eunice in a very long time. Ellen told the postmaster that she was writing on behalf of her mother, and in early 1881 she received an answer from a man named John S. Wood, who picked up Ellen's letter at the post office in Kingston, Jamaica. By the second sentence, Ellen had the news. "I beg to say in reply that I knew the late Mr. and Mrs. Connolly also Miss Clara and Master Clarence Stone and also two children that She had while at Cayman." *The late.* "I have to say that Mr. Connolly was a Sea going Captain, he owned a very fine Schooner which he had built under his own eye and after she was Launched He, his wife and family went to sea in her." Ellen knew that she would have to impart word to Lois and the others, so she read on. "I am sorry to say that on her 3d voyage a fishing on the Mosquito Coast S.A. a Hurricane came on, on the evening of the 27 of Sept. 1877 and the vessel foundered during the night and all on board perished, not one escaped to tell the tale." On that particular boat had been "Mr. & Mrs. Connolly, Clara Stone and 2 Miss Connolly's and six seamen, in all 11 souls."

There was more to the letter, and Ellen kept reading. "Mr. Connollys dwelling was at East End Grand Cayman where he always lived. His possession there is now owned by the eldest son of the first wife and I feel sure you are aware of that" (the word "fact" was crossed out) "he" (Ellen could see "was mar" crossed out, as if the writer weren't sure the family knew about Smiley's past) "had been a Married Man before he went to America." After that came more news about Eunice. "Mr. & Mrs. Connolly had accumulated a lot of mony and as far as I can learn they had it on board the vessel when she foundered. You seem to be aware of Mr. Clarence Stones death, he died as near as I can remember in March 1872 or 3. There is no American Minister at Gr. C. but should you wish any further information that I can give I will be most happy to do so. Trusting that the good Lord will strengthen the old lady to bear this shoke which is so severe, I remain yours truly, John S. Wood." Ellen read the letter again, and then again, and then once more, and then once more again.

"My Dear Brother," she wrote to Henry up in Massachusetts, "I have at last succeeded in learning the fate of Mrs. Connolly and family. They were all drowned on the Misquito Coast S. America as you will see by the enclosed letter." It was Henry, then, who would have to deliver the news to Lois. "I think Brother if you will take the letter to Mother in person your presence will somewhat lessen the shock to them all, that is why I send it to you," Ellen directed. "Should you not be able to read it, I can inform you as I have read it all so many times." Ann too would bear the news more easily if she could read the letter herself. "I wish you would write me about her, and after you have seen Mother tell me how they received the sad letter," Ellen requested, hastening to explain that she had written to the postmaster of Grand Cayman, hoping to learn the fate of Clara, perhaps reluctant to admit to Henry that she cared also about Eunice, Smiley, and their two daughters. Then Ellen rushed forward to other topics. She and Dudley were comfortable, the winter had been cold and wet, business was good. After she signed off ("your affectionate Sister from Mississippi Shore"), she thought about hurricanes again. "We had a Storm here last week," she added, "which blowd the tide in and nearly washed us away for three days."

Up in New England, Henry dutifully passed the bad news on to his mother, Ann, and Hattie. News of the hurricane must also have spread through the River Road neighborhood in Dracut in the early 1880s. Maybe the gossipers blamed Eunice for her own demise, casting her fate as retribution for marrying across the color line, or maybe they felt sorry for such a sad ending and how badly they had treated her so many years before.

Lois saved John Wood's letter, along with Ellen's revelation to Henry, placing them with the family correspondence she had been keeping for many years now, correspondence that told of her husband's death, her son's death, William Stone's death, Clarence's death, and now the deaths of Eunice, Smiley, Clara, and two grandchildren she had never met. No doubt a flurry of communication ensued, but whatever Henry reported back to Ellen, whatever expressions of dismay or words of comfort Lois and the other sisters sent to Mississippi and to one another, perhaps even received from Cayman, those pages haven't survived, for Ellen's afterthoughts

about the storm in Moss Point are the last words in the last letter of
the family papers.

LIVING IN THE West Indies, Eunice had never stopped wondering
about her family in New England, and surely she departed for the
Miskito Cays in 1877 wondering still. As it turned out, Hattie and
Ira Harvey eventually came to run a successful business manufacturing and selling overalls, with Hattie later working as an agent for a
sewing machine company in Lowell; she died there in 1886. When
Lois died in 1889, at the age of eighty-three, she had survived four
daughters and one son. Ann was widowed for the second time when
David McCoy died in 1885, but she lived at least until 1912 (a letter she wrote to Henry around that year turned up elsewhere). Over
the years, Ellen and Dudley Merrill moved back and forth between
the Deep South and New England. Their daughter, Alice, died at
the age of fifteen in 1875, and when Dudley died in 1881, Ellen
moved north for the last time. She eventually took up residence in
the Old Ladies' Home in Lowell, where worthy applicants paid the
extravagant entrance fee of two hundred dollars. By that time,
Ellen's Confederate sympathies didn't matter to white northerners,
and when she died in 1914 at the age of seventy-seven, the pastor at
Henry's church conducted the service.

Then there was Henry, the only one of the Richardson siblings
who made a name for himself and the one who became guardian of
the family papers. Three decades' worth of Richardson correspondence came into Henry's hands when Lois passed away, or maybe he
had collected the packets of envelopes after his mother had moved
out of the River Road house a few years earlier. A transfer of family
papers often prompts rereading and sorting, and skimming the letters from earlier years would have been a satisfying endeavor for
Henry. *Are you still in the Machine Shop?* Eunice had queried her

brother when he was seventeen years old, advising him to *stick to it* and *learn your trade if you can.* Stick to it he had, and if Eunice had remained in New England to witness Henry's impressive career, she would have been proud. Indeed, Hattie's obituary in 1886 identified her surviving brother as "our well known fellow citizen, Charles H. Richardson" (Henry used his full name now), just as one of Lois's 1889 death notices identified her as "the mother of Charles H. Richardson."

Henry's Civil War heroism and future successes easily secured him a place in the annals of local history. His first Civil War regiment, the "Old Sixth," gathered for reunions, marched in parades, and listened to orators who regularly equated the veterans with the patriotic heroes of the American Revolution. "The names of Lexington, Concord and Baltimore are indissolubly linked as the initial events in the two great eras of our National history," intoned a Massachusetts mayor on the twenty-fifth anniversary of Henry's dangerous passage through the border state of Maryland. Massachusetts men had fought against oppression, the mayor proclaimed, and their actions had abolished slavery and given black men the vote. If Henry had stood in the crowd that day, his pride might have mixed with anger as he thought of the sister who had married a black man after the war.

When Henry was forty years old, in 1883, survivors of his second Civil War regiment, the Twenty-sixth Massachusetts, joined a reunion of "Sheridan's Veterans" in the Shenandoah Valley. The city of Winchester, Virginia, welcomed Union men, while the northern guests honored the "splendid valor" of their southern hosts, laying wreaths on the graves of Confederate dead. Now blue and gray met as brothers, "all bitterness and hate forever buried." Buried too was the history of black freedom—the reunion's commemorative volume described a scene in which "the darkeys mount the rostrum, and again the great crowd, especially the Northerners, are delighted with plantation antics." Henry would have enjoyed such "antics," but his name doesn't appear on the reunion roster; perhaps he couldn't bear to return to the ground where he had watched his brother, Luther, die. Two years later, however, as president of the Twenty-sixth Massachusetts Regiment Association, Henry attempted to retrieve his regiment's colors, corresponding warmly with a Confederate veteran who had also fought at Winchester. Maybe Henry showed up twenty years later, when a grand reunion of the Society of the Nineteenth Army Corps (that tactical unit included the Twenty-sixth Massachusetts) met at Boston's Parker House Hotel. Or maybe by then, his time was too precious for Civil War gatherings.

By the mid-1870s, Henry had already been promoted to overseer of the Lawrence Mills in Lowell; as he liked to tell the story, he "marched to the counting room in his machinist's working clothes" to apply for the job, then kept moving up, eventually to become assistant superintendent. In 1888, he moved to the Appleton Company, assuming the position of agent, the highest local executive, in charge of production, personnel, and labor. Appleton, which occupied a set of imposing buildings on Lowell's Hamilton and Pawtucket canals, lost less and recovered faster than other mills after the war, and by the early 1890s a thousand employees were producing formidable quantities of cotton cloth. Into the new century, weathering occasional economic downturns, the company continued to modernize machinery and stave off competition from southern manufacturing, and soon Henry moved his wife and children into a large company-owned Italianate-style home in a prestigious neighborhood.

By the late 1890s, when Henry provided biographical informa-

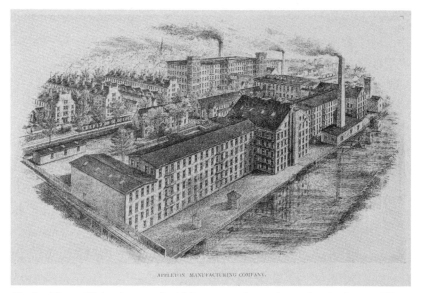

APPLETON MANUFACTURING COMPANY.

Charles Henry Richardson worked his way up the ranks at the Appleton Mills in Lowell, Massachusetts, where he ultimately served as agent, the highest local executive, in charge of production, personnel, and labor.

tion for a volume of local history, he knew exactly how he wanted his family to be remembered. "Mr. Charles H. Richardson, the present Agent of the Appleton Company, is descended from a family of great antiquity," reads the *Illustrated History of Lowell*, published in 1897. The Richardson name could be traced back to before the Norman Conquest, when the family "became masters of a large portion of France in the ninth century, which they called Normandy, and were governed by a succession of Dukes named Richard." After the conquest of England, "several kings of that country bore the name of Richard," and thus Richardson became a common name in England and America. Henry's first known direct ancestor was Thomas Richardson, who arrived in New England in 1636; several generations later came Lot Richardson, a deacon of the Congregational Church. There was less to say about Lot's son, Luther, except

When Charles Henry Richardson served as agent of the Appleton Mills, he and his family lived in this house in Lowell, Massachusetts. It was here that Henry kept the collected family letters.

that he worked as a contractor. Luther's wife, Lois Wright, on the other hand, hailed from a family "noted as famous Indian fighters." Thus did Henry connect his lowly origins to the great bloodlines of Europe and the rugged American frontier, in efforts to produce worthy ancestors on both sides.

When Henry supplied a local historian with this autobiography (he might have paid a genealogist to do the research, then embellished it a bit himself), he stood among a growing number of white Protestants in turn-of-the-century America who were newly concerned with accounting for their British and northern European heritage. As immigrants from eastern and southern Europe, including Catholics and Jews, found their way to New England's manufacturing centers, and as intensified industrialization brought labor unrest in its wake, these native-born white Protestants made a point of tracing their lineage to colonial America and then back to England and

Eunice's brother Charles Henry Richardson, the only member of the family in his generation to achieve prominence, was lauded in late-nineteenth-century local history.

northern Europe. It was a way to establish themselves as the sole authentic Americans in a rapidly expanding nation. Hereditary organizations meanwhile fostered Anglo-Saxon supremacy and exclusivity. The Sons of the American Revolution, Daughters of the American Revolution, Descendants of the Pioneers of America, Society of Mayflower Descendants: These kinds of associations all were founded in the late nineteenth century (the family of Henry's wife, Clara Pray, joined the SAR and the DAR right away), serving as well to nurture nostalgia for a presumably simpler American past.

Accordingly, Henry placed himself squarely in the tradition of the Victorian "self-made man," with a life story crafted to chronicle a climb from poverty to prominence, powered solely by individual virtue and merit—an opportunity, such a story implied, open to anyone yet realized by few. A newspaper article in the 1890s

declared that Henry's successes stood as "a constant protest against
the namby-pamby dilettantism of the modern young man," spinning a fable that opened with his earliest jobs as farmhand and milk
delivery boy. "Mr. Richardson's opportunities for securing an education were extremely limited, and yet were sufficient to develop in
him an intense desire to learn and improve himself," boasted
Henry's biography. His father had died when the boy was just eight
years old, and although young Henry's first employment earned
him only fifty-eight cents a day, that didn't deter his "perseverance,
self-reliance, self-sacrifice, and ambition." In fact, Henry wasn't
eight years old when Luther senior died; rather, he was eight when
his father deserted the family, but Henry had rewritten the facts. A
father's desertion might be humiliating, whereas death was always
tragic, and the loss of one's father in young boyhood made for a
more impressive narrative of a son's achievements.

As Henry grew older, the city of Lowell continued to change
around him. By the 1910s, some forty nationalities were represented
among a population of a hundred thousand, only one-fifth of whom
could be counted as "native-born Americans of native parents."
French and French Canadians mixed with Swedes, Norwegians,
Portuguese, Greeks, Poles, Armenians, Germans, Belgians, Syrians,
Russians, Lithuanians, Austrians, and Chinese, and these newer
arrivals came to replace the Irish as targets of suspicion and prejudice.
The Irish, after all, spoke English and had fought in the Civil War
(Boston even elected its first Irish mayor in the 1880s). To be sure,
many Yankees still thought of the Irish as lazy and alcoholic, but more
recent arrivals proved yet more threatening. The increase in "alien
races," a 1912 report on Lowell noted, "has been most marked," and
"each new alien race has brought a lower standard of living."

Henry surely counted himself among those who longingly
recalled "the happy days" in Lowell, "when life was homogeneous,

and all were one in their loyalty to the new mill town on the Merrimack, when the Yankee girls worked leisurely thirteen hours a day in the mills and wrote poetry at night, when everybody went to church on Sunday, and worshipped God in a common tongue," as one nostalgic portrait had it. Henry had never known those simpler times, of course; it was more that white and native-born New Englanders wanted to shore up a mythical vision that began with unlimited expanses of land, then progressed to antebellum cities free of poverty and oppressive work. The year 1912 saw a massive and successful labor strike in nearby Lawrence, Massachusetts, led by the Industrial Workers of the World, and when Lowell workers struck shortly thereafter, the management of Appleton Mills at first refused to negotiate. Eventually, though, Henry and the other executives had no choice but to concede an increase in wages. Henry Richardson's ambition had always driven him forward; at this juncture he glanced back with a certain wistfulness and ahead with considerable ambivalence.

IF HENRY HAD skimmed through the family letters when he inherited them from Lois, he couldn't have helped noticing how many of them came from Eunice. *My Dear Brother do you not know your Sister better than to think she would be mad at an idolised Brother.* That was on the eve of the Civil War, from Alabama. *Who ever had such dear, generous, noble hearted Brothers. I never can repay them for their kindness.* That was from New Hampshire when Eunice was struggling to feed her children. *I wanted to tell Brother Henry how much I had always loved him and how his treatment had pained me.* That was just before Eunice sailed to the West Indies. Henry didn't discard that particular letter, but maybe it was during the years of his mounting accomplishments and prosperity that he tried to purge from the family papers all references to his sister's shameful marriage. Perhaps the missing letters from 1867, 1868, and most of 1869 included too many details or too much of his own spite and malice, and in the process of trying to weed that out, he ended up disposing of everything from those difficult years. Maybe Ann or Ellen stopped him from destroying Eunice and Smiley's letters from the West Indies, or maybe he simply had no more time in his busy days to pore over the old correspondence and so just stashed it all away.

In those years too, Henry fashioned his own memories of the Civil War. Eunice had died in 1877, the same year that northern troops withdrew from the vanquished South, marking the end of Reconstruction. In the decades after the war, African Americans and their allies celebrated emancipation, while white Americans like Henry made slavery and freedom marginal to the story they told about nation building and collective valor. In this narrative, white northerners fought for the Union, white southerners fought for states' rights, both causes were noble, and both sides suffered.

"I have never had any unkind feelings for those who fought us honestly and bravely," wrote the Confederate veteran who tried unsuccessfully to locate the flag of the Twenty-sixth Massachusetts for Henry, swiftly erasing all bitterness toward the Yankee foe, for "brave enemies can make the best of friends." Henry had even proposed a reunion of the Twenty-sixth Massachusetts and the Twenty-sixth Georgia. "On the ground which absorbed the mingled blood of your Regiment and mine would be a fitting place to renew a brotherhood which should never have been severed," replied Henry's southern countryman twenty years after the Confederate surrender. This version of the Civil War experiences of Henry and Luther Richardson, Dudley Merrill, and William Stone was nicely captured in a poem, composed by an unknown author, about brothers who fought on opposite sides, and later wandered the old battlefields together. "Tho' leaves are gone and limbs are bare / Its heart is true to-day," the verse reads, "As yours was then, tho' fighting blue / To me tho' fighting gray." The voice might have been Dudley's own, the sentiments Henry's as well. If Henry hadn't realized it before, he could see clearly now that the wartime divide between Union and Confederate kin was nearly painless to mend, compared with the line Eunice had crossed after the war was over.

During precisely the same years that Henry moved up the ladder from wage-earning youth to company executive, the post-Reconstruction United States witnessed the triumph of a Jim Crow world. By the last decade of the century, white Americans, both North and South, fortified racial segregation and furthered black disfranchisement. The lynching of black men falsely accused of sexually assaulting white women reached unprecedented heights, and the one-drop rule became yet firmer in white minds; anyone whose ancestry included even the remotest fraction of African "blood" was classified as Negro—European descent, light complexion, and economic status notwithstanding.

Had Eunice, Smiley, and the children lived through the hurricane of 1877, and had they after all made a visit back to New England a decade or so hence, they would have landed in a hostile nation indeed. The federal census of 1890 was the first and only U.S. census to divide people of any African ancestry into four categories: "black," "mulatto," "quadroon," and "octoroon"—categories intended, in their supposed precision, to brand all people of any African descent as inferior. Had the Connolly family arrived in time to be counted that year, Smiley might have told the census taker that he was white, or Eunice might have called herself and Clara quadroon or octoroon in efforts to avoid any trouble. But if the Connollys classified themselves according to the one-drop rule— Eunice and Clara as white, Smiley as fractionally black, and the children of Eunice and Smiley also as fractionally black—then the family would supposedly be contributing to the dilution and contamination of the white race. That was the vision of Eunice's life that haunted Henry as he climbed upward.

While the nation looked to imperial ventures overseas in the name of democracy, white women at home were meant to ensure a noble American future by reproducing the Anglo-Saxon race in the name of white supremacy. In that climate, Eunice's transgressions struck Henry as more deplorable than ever. By the turn of the century, the country's intensifying racism vindicated Henry's immediate antagonism toward his errant sister. Now he knew that he had been right to forsake her after all. For Henry Richardson, a sister who married a black man had no place in his self-fashioned life story. If anyone deliberately consigned those three years' worth of missing letters to the fireplace, it was Henry.

If EUNICE could have glimpsed the contours of her siblings' lives, she might have noticed that the ones who ultimately discarded her were the ones who achieved the greatest upward mobility. Whereas Ann and Ellen reconciled themselves to Eunice's unconventional actions, it wasn't only Henry but also Hattie who cast Eunice away. In the autumn of 1872, around the time that a letter from Smiley arrived in New England pleading that Eunice hadn't heard from anyone since Clarence's death, Hattie and Ira vacationed with Ellen and Dudley in New Hampshire, "rusticating" and having "a jolly time." Now Hattie welcomed her Confederate relatives, even as she found little time to think about her sister abroad. "I have not written to Eunice yet," she admitted to Lois that same autumn, announcing that she couldn't find the time, though Hattie devoted a good many hours to correspondence ("This is the 21st letter I have written this week, dont know how many more I may write"). The gift of tomatoes that Hattie had handed to Eunice just before the Connollys set sail for the Caribbean became her final act of kindness; *Harriet has not written to me since I wrote her,* Eunice mourned in 1873. It had taken Hattie longer than Henry, but she too understood that rising social status could be ruined by association with scandal. Hattie would have been pleased to know that her obituary called her "a very estimable lady." Eunice too had achieved ladyhood, of course, but by means not quite acceptable to her sister.

As for Henry, maybe he was angry that Eunice had chosen to link her life with someone who took her so far away after the terrible losses the family had sustained during the Civil War. Perhaps, then, it was easiest to come to terms with his sense of betrayal through the formulas of racism: His sister had married a "nigger" (that had been the term Henry invoked when writing home from the war), and that was the most logical reason to be angry.

But during the years that Eunice lived in Cayman, it turned out, Henry hadn't banished her entirely from his mind. A single letter, one that remained in the possession of a descendant and therefore never made it into the archives, offers a slim clue. Henry began his personal genealogical quest sometime after the war by canvassing family members. In 1875, he wrote to one of his father's sisters, seeking information, and in her reply Aunt Mary echoed the bits of news that Henry had related to her: "Tell Ann I remember her, and I am sorry her health is so poor." "Your Sister Hattie lives near you." "Ellen is soon going farther off" (the Merrills were returning south). "You lost your dear brother in the late war." Also these words: "Eunice it seems is far from you. I hope you hear from her." Perhaps Henry had conveyed no more than the fact that Eunice had married and gone to live overseas; Mary's "it seems" mirrors a certain vagueness in what Henry had imparted. But if Mary's second sentence ("I hope you hear from her") was also a reiteration, then Henry had noted the passage of a long interval of time without a letter, maybe even expressed a wish to know how Eunice was faring. Aunt Mary's pages arrived in Henry's hands a few months after Eunice's lament, about Henry and his wife, that she had *never heard from them*. Maybe that lament had prompted him to acknowledge her existence after such a long time.

In the end, Henry Richardson recast Eunice's life as one that sullied family history, beginning with her choice of a first husband ("he was always a lucky kind of a fellow," Henry once wrote sarcastically about William Stone, "that is for a man that was always so unfortunate"). Then came Eunice's impoverishment and the way she had to work as a servant and wear her dresses to rags. Even her contemplation of suicide could be recalculated as weak and un-Christian. Disgraceful too was her unrelenting Universalist faith (*Henry before you denounce it so bitterly, I ask you to give it a fair trial*).

Marriage to a black man was only the most ignominious piece of the story, less tolerable than ever by the time Henry was growing old in the racist climate of the new century. Maybe, in his most ungenerous moments, Henry even attributed Eunice's demise at sea to God's punishment. "If our road leads to Heaven, theirs leads to Hell," a Manchester minister had pronounced of Universalists in the 1850s, when Henry hoped Eunice would change her mind. Foes of Universalism preached also about the agony at the infidels' hour of death, spiritual doubts mounting as they found themselves about to sink "in the boiling abyss." Henry named only one of his three sons and four daughters for a sibling. Hattie Florence Richardson was born in 1871. Two years later, Henry named another child for Hattie's daughter, Ella.

Ann had been the one to express her love for Eunice most openly ("Oh my dear Sister don't think your self forgoten because you do not get letters from us, for we think of you as a dear sister far from home"). If Ann found Henry's hostility toward Eunice and

Smiley contemptible, that conflict faded as the decades passed. More than thirty years after Eunice's death, Henry wrote to Ann to ask her assistance in his continuing quest to draw their family tree. "I had a paper with grandfather first wifes name and more perticulars," Ann responded around 1912, adding, "his first wifes name was Eunice, can't think the other name." Maybe that got Ann thinking about old rifts. "I love you, would like to see you so much but dont get out much," she added. "Dont forget your little Sister Ann Mary." Ann was the eldest, of course, but Henry had surpassed them all in his stature.

"Death of Well Known Citizen" proclaimed a headline in the *Lowell Sun* in 1913. Henry's death notices repeated the main contours of his up-by-the-bootstraps plot, describing how he had been "compelled to go to work as a mere boy," how he had once earned fifty-eight cents a day, yet availed himself of "every opportunity for educational advancement." "His Career as Mill Man Here Had Been Long and Honorable," offered the subheadline in the *Lowell Courier-Citizen*, as the lead-in to a story that reiterated the phrase "self made man." Or as the *Lowell Sun* put it, "there was nothing in his character that invited controversy." Henry would have been pleased with his own obituaries, for they proved not only his accomplishments but also his ability to mask the family dishonor that interfered with the image he had carefully constructed. Charles Henry Richardson was seventy years old when he died. Services were held at the city's First Trinitarian Congregational Church. He was buried next to his wife, Clara, in Edson Cemetery, famous today for the grave of Jack Kerouac.

When Henry died, the world of New England mills was dying too. As steam replaced waterpower after the Civil War, the riverbank settings of New England factory towns no longer mattered, and Lowell became an industrial city on the decline. After World War I, the textile companies found themselves challenged again by poorly paid workers, and mills closed or moved south; the Appleton Company eventually left Lowell for South Carolina. Up the Merrimack River, Manchester and its workers struggled too. The Amoskeag had risen to become the largest textile manufacturer in the world, but overexpansion, out-of-date machinery, and southern competition had shut the whole place down by the middle of the Depression, devastating the city that had nurtured Eunice's earliest hopes. The year Henry died also marked the fiftieth anniversary of the Battle of Gettysburg, and the nation's commemoration of that northern victory celebrated the reconciliation of white Union and Confederate veterans, while the emancipation of slaves faded further from the pages of Civil War history. That same year, in response to the uproar over the marriage of black boxer Jack Johnson to a white woman, Massachusetts passed a law forbidding couples to wed if the marriage was illegal in the state where they resided, an unmistakable reference to crossing the color line and specifically to black men and white women.

Henry Richardson cared a great deal about family history—he worked out his family tree for almost forty years—yet his great-grandchildren never so much as heard mention of the sister whose husband fought for the Confederacy, who married a man of color after the Civil War, who went to live in the West Indies, and who drowned in a hurricane.

"SHOULD YOU wish any further information that I can give I will be most happy to do so," John S. Wood had pledged to Ellen, from the West Indies, when he imparted the news of the 1877 storm. Lois and the sisters knew that Eunice had found a brief interlude of happiness with Smiley Connolly in the British Caribbean, and perhaps they wondered how Smiley's family bore up under such a devastating loss. If any of the Richardsons wrote to express condolences or inquire after Smiley's sons (no such correspondence is known to survive), they would have learned something about the fates of their East End in-laws.

John Jarrett Conolly wrote his will soon after his son Smiley drowned at sea, distributing his land and money among his wife and other children. He died in the 1880s, buried in a now-unmarked grave. Smiley's half brother, Dighton, spread his property and money among his wife, children, grandchildren, and the United Presbyterian African Mission Society, with strict instructions that all his inheritors should "work the lands together without division and without Selling." When Dighton died in 1902 at the age of seventy-nine, he was buried in his yard, today a sandy seaside cemetery reserved for his direct descendants. As for Smiley's sons, elderly East End residents could still remember them at the turn of the twenty-first century. Robert, the "outside" child, became a mariner. Jarrett, a seaman as well, also ran a shop where he accepted thatch rope in exchange for flour, corn meal, ginger ale, and cream soda. Gamaliel became a shopkeeper too, taught school, and served as justice of the peace. As the registrar of East End, Gamaliel officially recorded the death of his mother, Rachel Partridge Connolly, naming her as Smiley's widow. Oddly, although Rachel died in 1904, at the age of seventy-six, not one elderly East Ender could produce a single memory of her. Soon after his mother's death, Gamaliel moved to Honduras.

People most vividly remember Smiley's son Cornelius, a master mariner who also kept a shop in East End (one of his granddaughters held on to the old ledgers, which recorded a trade in everything from rice and rum to ladies' shoes and barbed wire). In the summer of 1931, when Cornelius was seventy-five years old, his extended family gathered; CONNOLLY CLAN RE-UNION A BIG CAYMAN EVENT, read the local headline. When Cornelius was a young man, the arti-

John Cornelius Connolly, known as Cornelius, was Smiley Connolly's son by his first wife, a Caymanian woman. Born in 1857, Cornelius was a young boy when Eunice arrived on Grand Cayman. He grew up to be a master mariner, a shopkeeper, and one of East End's largest landholders. Although his face is partly obscured in this portrait, Cornelius's complexion and features appear to indicate his father's partial European ancestry.

cle recounted, "he stayed home to get married while his father with whom he usually sailed rode down in his ship at Mosquito Cay in THE FATEFUL HURRICANE of that memorable year and was lost with all on board." Then, by "sheer grit, indomitable perseverance and sound judgment" (Henry ought to have admired him), Cornelius went on to own six schooners and become the biggest individual landowner in East End. His impressive two-story house, possibly the very same one that Smiley had built for Eunice in the 1870s, stood until the hurricane of 1932.

Today, when you mention the name Smiley Connolly, East Enders think first of Cornelius's son, William Smiley Connolly II, born in 1881. Legendary as a teacher who returned to East End with a degree from Howard University in Washington, D.C. (he was "the first College graduate the island has produced since the beginning of recorded time"), Smiley II was also a crusader against imperial racism, a dentist, a Seventh-Day Adventist preacher, and a musician; photographs show him as headmaster of a George Town school surrounded by pupils or dressed in coat and tails, playing the violin. His much-loved French wife, Rachel—she was "lily white," whereas he was recalled as dark-skinned—died in 1995, at the age of one hundred.

Just as the family passed down Smiley's name, so too did they pass on the names of others. In 1878, Smiley's brother Aaron named a daughter Eunice, and in 1897 one of Smiley's nephews passed the name down again. In 1879, Cornelius named a daughter Lou Carlotha for the lost Louisa Charlotta; the first name was passed down again in 1928 to Cornelius's granddaughter Lou, who was given the middle name Caramiel after Eunice's second Cayman-born daughter. The son of another East End mariner who drowned in the 1877 hurricane named a son Clarence, and in 1884 Cornelius named a son Luther; maybe Eunice had expressed the wish to name a child after her late brother, and Cornelius honored her by doing so after her death.

The names live on, although the Grand Cayman that Eunice knew has disappeared. As steamships navigated more direct routes between Europe and the Caribbean, Caymanians found themselves increasingly isolated in the Atlantic world. By the early twentieth century, declining turtle populations in all waters had forced Caymanian men themselves to become the islands' principal export. They accepted work with Central and North American shipping companies, and by the 1940s the merchant marine had become a major employer. The airstrip built in George Town in the 1950s was intended to facilitate the men's off-island sojourns, but successful mosquito control by the mid-1960s encouraged the earliest tourists too.

In Eunice's day, Cayman's unfertile coastal soil had carried no particular value. Nearly a hundred years later, foreign investors began to buy up waterfront parcels, as new banking and trust laws transformed the islands into an offshore tax haven. Hotel construction began in the 1950s (the turtle-fishing, shipbuilding, and rope-making industries were nearly defunct by then), but the 1970s marked the start of the real boom in tourism. By the 1980s, condominiums and luxury houses were swiftly rising from the sand, accompanied by golf courses, marinas, and upscale shops, and by the end of the century Cayman was catering to cruise ships as well. On Seven Mile Beach in George Town, properties now routinely sell for millions. At the start of the twenty-first century, East End still possesses untouched expanses, but the tourist and real estate glossies are thick with promises of gigantic homes and the next grand hotel. A typical advertisement calls a "reef protected sandy beach front" a "must see for anyone considering a resort community and/or golf course development." If you know where to look in the accompanying satellite photograph, you can find the land where Smiley's brother Moses once lived.

To be sure, new material comforts have eased hardscrabble lives. Telephones, refrigerators, and cars arrived decades after their inventions, and East Enders welcomed electricity only in the 1970s. "The old days was tough days," recalled a Caymanian in the 1980s (he was born at the start of the twentieth century). "Anybody who says it was better then wasn't living then." Still, modernization came at the price of islanders entering a wage-labor market for construction crews, hotel service work, and clerical help, and prime property slipped into the hands of foreigners. Today run-down neighborhoods remain largely hidden from resort guests, scuba divers, and cruise ship shoppers. Among those who first predicted the attendant troubles of too-rapid development was Brother Dighton's great-grandson William Warren Conolly. Warren had traveled the globe in the merchant marine toward the end of World War II and returned to East End to become an attorney, a businessman, and a powerful politician, serving in the Cayman legislature for more than twenty years. His wise vision of controlled growth had largely been superseded by century's end, though his son Burns Conolly, an architect on the island, remains deeply involved in charting Cayman's future course.

In one curious way, Eunice and Smiley's legacy lives on in Cayman's tourism and real estate promotions. "Racial tension is non-existent," reads a representative, if not precisely accurate, description. "Intermarriage between nationalities and races in Cayman has always been acceptable." In the United States after the Civil War, with an increasingly rigid color line, Eunice and Smiley, a white woman and a black man, found themselves outcast objects of derision. In the West Indies, on the other hand, Smiley shaded over into the category of "white," while Eunice's new neighbors could think of her as a "colored" woman, thereby permitting Smiley to *act all the love he feels for me*, as Eunice wrote, *without fear of disturbing any one*.

DEATH FOR THE Puritans of early New England meant divine judgment and the threat of eternal damnation, and bodies were accordingly buried in churchyards or village common corners, with little thought to the tending of gravestones. But the more liberal and optimistic Christian theology of the nineteenth century, coupled with increasingly sentimental attitudes toward nature, meant that overgrown burial grounds gave way to landscaped cemeteries.

Mourners now retreated to pastoral settings, far from the reach of city noise and factory smoke, to commune with loved ones who rested on sunny hillsides or in shady groves. Like Luther Richardson and William Stone before her, however, Eunice Connolly never received a proper funeral. There was a certain "agony," wrote a New

England orator, reflecting upon those never laid to rest, in "the thought, that they are to sleep their last sleep in the land of strangers, or in the unseen depths of the ocean." The lovingly preserved graves of family members were intended as well to foster a "spirit of forgiveness," but neither Henry nor Hattie nor anyone else had such a place to visit. Even Clarence's resting place was too far away to offer the New England family either comfort or reconciliation.

If I live. For all the haunted intimations of death that Eunice expressed over the course of her life, her views of eternal rest were also shaped by Universalism, even as she worshiped alongside Smiley in East End's Presbyterian church. Maybe in those last hours on the sinking schooner off the Miskito Cays, Eunice summoned her old faith and the spiritual ideas that had guided her through the worst years of poverty and widowhood. "It is but a brief voyage, and then the storms of life are all over, and the soul anchors in a peaceful haven," the Universalist *Ladies' Repository* suggested in an essay on disasters at sea. In this vision, there would be "husbands embracing wives, parents caressing children, and friend conversing peacefully with friend" as "the waters engulfed them and the heavens received them." Eunice's sojourn on earth had come to an end, she knew, as the vessel went down, but perhaps she took comfort nonetheless, for as a Universalist she could exult that she was "happy, above all, that I have reached the unshaken conviction that death is but an incident in a life that will never end, and that I shall survive when my body ceases to live."

8
SEARCHING FOR EUNICE

These are only hints and guesses,
Hints followed by guesses
—T. S. Eliot

One late-summer Sunday, as I read about Brooklyn politics in the *New York Times*, I came across a state assembly candidate named James T. Conolly, an immigrant from the Cayman Islands. Yes, James told me when I telephoned, he belonged to the Connolly-Conolly family of East End, Grand Cayman. The family still owned land in East End, and one of his grandmothers was named Eunice. When I visited James in his office at the Human Resources Commission in New York City, he told me how he had come to Brooklyn as a young boy in the late 1950s, when Grand Cayman was a poor island, and the few Caymanians in New York were merchant seamen like his father. James also told me about William Warren Conolly of East End, born in 1920, whom he referred to as the family patriarch. Before traveling to Cayman, I wrote to Warren, who promptly rang me up and told me to call him as soon as I arrived on the island. To my surprise, Erma Eldemire, the proprietor of my George Town guesthouse (she was born in 1911), knew Warren. (Later I identified a young Erma in a photograph of students at the school run by Cornelius's son Smiley Connolly II.) I soon discovered, though, that everyone on Grand Cayman knew Warren. I could ask any bus driver at the George Town depot to take me to Warren Conolly's house, and then everyone on the bus knew him too. He was seventy-eight years old when we first met.

Warren Conolly's spacious East End house stood on land once owned by his great-grandfather Thomas Dighton Conolly—*Brother Dighton*, to Eunice. Sitting on the enclosed veranda, the open door framing turquoise waters down the hill, Warren told me about the three-gabled East End church where Eunice and Smiley worshiped. The structure, rebuilt after the 1876 storm, had gone down again during the hurricane of 1917, but a picture of the pre-1917 building hung in Warren's study. Smiley's father, John Jarrett Conolly, whom Warren called "the Old Man," had two wives; "one, the

William Warren Conolly is the great-grandson of Thomas Dighton Conolly, Smiley's half brother. Warren traveled the world in the merchant marine during World War II, then returned home to work as an attorney and businessman. He also served more than twenty years in the Cayman legislature.

mother of Thomas Dighton Conolly, was black," Warren told me, whereas the mother of Smiley and his brothers Moses, Laban, and Aaron, "was of fair complexion, probably white." The second time I visited Cayman, Warren brought out the family Bible. The genealogy within its pages began with John Jarrett Conolly, and its leaves sheltered a sermon handwritten and preached by Dighton himself. Over several years, Warren also related to me his memories of a George Town with few buildings, and how difficult it had been to return to Cayman in 1948 from his world travels; the biggest shock was the lack of electricity (he couldn't see his feet to put his socks on, he said, laughing). He talked, too, about his experiences in the merchant marine in the Deep South in the 1940s. Once, reprimanded when he refused to "go around the back" of a restaurant ("'Let me tell you something, boy, you went too far'"), Warren had a retort: "That place you sent me there, I'm not going back to that, I'll tell you that now. I don't know how many days we have to go ashore, but I won't go over there."

I found too that members of the family were everywhere in the Cayman Islands National Archive, from the birth, marriage, and death records that commenced in the 1880s to the tapes and transcripts of the Memory Bank project. Still, many historical documents were fragmentary or had not survived. Caymanian slave registration records never included the kind of detailed information found in other British West Indian returns—places of birth, names of parents, descriptions of skin color—and many names on the East End church communicant rolls from the 1870s had been obliterated on decomposed pages, including all the names under the letter C ("exceptionally bad luck," pronounced Dr. Philip Pedley, then head of the archive). Still, the staff was excited to learn of Eunice and Smiley's letters from Cayman, preserved at Duke University, and promptly put me in touch with Jeanne Masters, a white woman from Ohio who had lived in Cayman since the early 1980s. A retired nurse, scuba diver, and local genealogist, Jeanne was seventy-three when we first met and a historian at heart ("I'm about to go crazy with excitement," she wrote to me after locating the will of Smiley's brother Moses). Almost right away, Jeanne confided her own loving relationship with a black man in Cleveland in the 1970s. "My Smiley," she took to calling him. "I still LOVE Eunice's courage," she later wrote to me. "I made the same journey and have never regretted the choice."

During my weeklong summer visits to Cayman across several years, Jeanne took me to the homesites of Smiley's brothers in East End. Moses had lived on land near where the posh Morritt's Tortuga Club resort now stands, and although the hurricane of 1917 had taken the house, remaining behind was a cache of red tiles, originally salvaged from a shipwreck on the nearby reefs. The owners were away when we visited, but they had left me a tile and two shards of pottery dating from the years that Eunice lived in East End. Jeanne also showed me the homesite of Smiley's brothers Aaron and Laban, now a playing field and the site of the island's Pirate's Week celebrations. Laban's son Willie had played with young Clara, collecting beach coral in East End (*You ought to see the Bag of stuff Clara & Willie have got saved up for you*, Eunice wrote to her mother).

The descendants I spoke with in Cayman all mentioned Lou (Connolly) Coleman, who lived near Boston and regularly visited East End. Lou was the daughter of John Cecil Connolly, one of Cornelius's sons. "Mr. William Warren Conolly of East End, Grand Cayman, was so kind as to give me your address," I wrote to her, explaining my research. Did she have any memories of Cornelius? Had she ever heard mention of Eunice and Smiley? "One of their daughters was named Lou," I added. Within days, she called to invite me to visit her in Massachusetts. I had been researching Eunice's life

Lou (Connolly) Coleman, the granddaughter of Cornelius Connolly and the great-granddaughter of Smiley, lives in New England but spent part of her girlhood in East End on Grand Cayman Island.

for about three years when I found myself, in a wholly unpredictable geographical confluence: boarding the Lowell line of the Boston commuter rail to meet Smiley Connolly's great-granddaughter.

It was a rainy March day when Lou Coleman greeted me warmly at the West Medford station, then escorted me to her gracious home, where a portrait of her grandfather Cornelius hung in the stairwell. Lou was born in the United States in 1928 to a Caymanian father and an African American mother but had lived in East End for several years as a girl. Over tea and home-baked Caymanian heavy cake, we read through the ledgers that belonged to Cornelius, discerning the goods that he had sold and traded in his East End shop. Lou also related memories of playing under her grandfather's hammock, though she couldn't recall anyone talking about Cornelius's father, Smiley. Among the family papers spread out across her dining-room table, however, surfaced a page of handwritten notes that Lou had taken while conversing with a relative, in which Smiley's children were listed as Cornelius, Jarrett, Gamaliel, Robert ("1/2 Bro" to the other boys), Lou, and Caramiel. This sheet of paper holds the only record of the name of Eunice's second Cayman-born daughter. Lou's middle name, she told me that afternoon, was Caramiel. "This is so fascinating to me," she exclaimed, as she learned of Henry's hostility to Eunice's marriage. "Fatal attraction!" she laughed in a lighter moment.

That afternoon, Lou and I planned a summer journey to Cayman, and she invited me to attend the family reunion to be held in East End that August. The forty or so guests came from one end of Grand Cayman Island to the other, from Cayman Brac, from the east coast of the United States, and from California, with spouses hailing from Mexico to Italy. Over a buffet lunch of conch stew, jerk chicken, Cayman-style mahimahi, and fried plantains at Morritt's Tortuga Club, each person introduced himself or herself by name and genealogy: Warren, now eighty years old, was the son of Austin Conolly, who was the son of Erskine Conolly, who was the son of Thomas Dighton Conolly; Lou was the daughter of John Cecil Connolly, who was the son of Cornelius Connolly, who was the son of Smiley Connolly. The family talked about the different spellings of the name and commented openly on who was dark and who was fair ("My father looked extremely Italian. You couldn't tell he was a black man at all," Lou announced, adding, "Thank God he married a black woman!").

The family also puzzled over the nationality of Smiley's father, John Jarrett Conolly, understood to be their original ancestor in the Cayman Islands. In one version of family history, "the Old Man" had come to Cayman as one of three brothers from Africa. This story accorded with the Caymanian slave registration records held at the Public Record Office in London, in which "John Connelly" was listed (having been given his master's name) as born in the 1790s;

that birth date also accorded more or less with the one written into Warren's family Bible. Yet widely accepted family lore told a different story: John Jarrett Conolly had come to Cayman not from Africa but from Ireland; he wasn't a slave who had married a fair-skinned woman but rather a white man who had married a woman of African descent. "I heard that so many times," Lou assured me.

In New England in the mid-nineteenth century, Eunice had tried to separate herself from poor Irish immigrants, whose status lay pre cariously close to that of African Americans. Now, almost a century and a half later, Smiley's descendants could not be sure whether their ancestral patriarch was African or Irish. In fact, contradictory family memories probably resulted from the fickle nature of racial classification. When John Jarrett Conolly transformed himself from slave to property owner and then became one of the largest landholders in East End, he might also have transformed himself from African to Irish, capitalizing on the surname once forced upon him by a master. Or maybe he was an immigrant from Ireland who came to be remembered as a former slave when he married an enslaved woman.

Most family members remained convinced by whichever version of John Jarrett's national origins they had heard throughout their lives, and each account proved rewarding in different ways. On one side, the story of a formerly enslaved man seizing and settling empty land that subsequently became enormously valuable held considerable appeal, along with the fact that a former slave had married a fair-skinned woman. On the other side, it seemed particularly important that the original family patriarch had been a free man, even if that cast the original female ancestor as a slave or the descendant of a slave. Like Henry Richardson, the Connolly-Conollys also crafted their own narratives of family history; the difference was that Henry did so unilaterally and in his own interest, whereas Smiley's family remained open to varying interpretations. Although Cleopathra Conolly, born in 1925 in East End, had always heard that John Jarrett Conolly was from Ireland (Galway, she specified), when I showed her a copy of the slave registration record for "John Connelly," she agreed that it could indeed refer to her great-grandfather.

Over the eight years of my visits and research trips to Cayman, I always wondered where Eunice had lived in East End. Warren Conolly believed it was the "big house" eventually inherited by Smiley's son Jarrett and drove me past the land, now occupied by another house. Warren could still remember the mahogany foundation left standing after the hurricane of 1932. But when I mentioned the "large House in American style" (as Smiley had described it) to Lou Coleman, she recalled a piece of property farther west, a dwelling inherited by her grandfather Cornelius but also destroyed in the 1932 storm. Smiley's brother Dighton *lives nearly half a mile from us*, Eunice had written from Cayman. *I can see the Vessel. But can not quite see his House owing to a little curve in the way.* That particular description matches up more closely with Warren's recollections, since the land that Jarrett inherited stands about a half mile from where Dighton's house stood, near what is now East End Lighthouse Park. But since there were no roads in those days, and Eunice traveled by water, either one remains a plausible site.

If the precise location of Eunice's cherished home is uncertain, its contours can be glimpsed in the Cayman Islands National Museum in George Town, a building that served as the courthouse during Eunice's years on the island. The wattle and daub ground floor, outside central stairwell, and timbered second story suggest the house that Smiley so lovingly built for his American bride.

Only a few elderly islanders could recall ever hearing about Smiley and Eunice. The next summer, Lou introduced me to one of them, Bertram Conolly, in East End. Born in 1915 (he was eighty-five years old when we met), Bertram was Smiley's grandson, the son of Smiley's "outside" child, Robert. A mariner like his father and grandfather, Bertram had sailed the sea for over two decades, landing in Boston and Mobile, among other ports. Raised by his uncle Cornelius, he had heard mention of his grandfather and knew that Smiley and his wife had gone down in the hurricane of 1877. The way Bertram had heard it, the crew on Smiley's boat could tell a storm was coming up, but they ultimately decided not to turn back toward Cayman.

When Lou Coleman had sat down with Cleopathra Conolly to compose a family tree several years before I met either of them, Lou had written next to Smiley's name, "lost at sea w/someone who had a child." Cleo had heard the story from her schoolteacher, a man born in 1895. "This woman was Smiley second wife, he told me, and say that he went to Miskito Cays and a hurricane came up," Cleo elaborated to me at Morritt's Tortuga Club, where she had

Bertram Conolly, the son of Robert Conolly and the grandson of Smiley, heard stories about the hurricane of 1877 as a child growing up in East End. Like many other men in the family, Bertram worked as a mariner.

Cleopathra Conolly, the great-granddaughter of Smiley's brother Moses Conolly, also heard stories about the hurricane of 1877 when she was growing up. She worked for many years as head chef at Morritt's Tortuga Club in East End.

worked for forty years, including serving as head chef for more than two decades. The way Cleo heard the tale, Smiley had gone to sea with his wife and son: He "went out to the Cays, him and his wife and this boy, and they all went in the hurricane." Across time, it seemed, memories of Clarence's death in 1872 had become intertwined with the losses suffered in the hurricane that struck five years later. Dorothy McLean Welcome, born in East End in 1917, had also heard stories about Smiley. She was a Conolly on her mother's side, the granddaughter of Smiley's much younger brother Laban, and Jeanne Masters brought me to visit her another summer. "I used to hear them speak about him," she related to us from her modest seaside home in East End. "Smiley, he went to the crawls, the way they used to say, to sea. And they say him and his wife then got drowned there. I heard them say she was an American woman."

IT DIDN'T SEEM possible to conjure my protagonists' lives in the United States as I had been able to do in Grand Cayman. The names—Richardson, Stone—were so common, the family was so lowly during Eunice's lifetime, and the landscape had already been so sweepingly altered. In Manchester, New Hampshire, the closest I came was the discovery of Eunice's signature in an 1860 ledger of Amoskeag employees at the Manchester Historic Association. In Mobile, Alabama, I came a little closer, locating the house at the intersection of Shell Road and Hallett Street where the Stones and Merrills resided just before the Civil War, close to where William and Dudley labored in James Daughdrill's sash factory. In Claremont, New Hampshire, I drove up Bible Hill Road with a seventy-eight-year-old volunteer from the local historical society, who told me about the sugaring parties she had attended there as a girl (*We were all invited up to the old Gentlemans to a sugaring*, Eunice wrote in 1864 about Father Stone's home on Bible Hill).

In Dracut, Massachusetts, I came a little closer when a lifelong resident and local genealogist showed me, from the outside, the house where Lois Davis had lived and where Eunice had likely married Smiley in 1869. Then, at the Center for Lowell History, director Martha Mayo helped me trace Henry Richardson through the city directories, and when we found an address on Highland Street in the 1890s, it turned out that Martha was good friends with the family who lived there. Today the house bears a plaque noting that it once served as the residence of the agent of the Appleton Mills, and Paul Marion (Lowell native, poet, and writer), and Rosemary Noon graciously welcomed us inside. Eunice never knew this dwelling, of course, but its walls had sheltered the family letters that belonged to Henry after Lois's death. Next, in Cabot, Vermont, a historical society volunteer took me to a house on Ducharme Road believed to be the residence of Azariah Stone (*I was at Azariah's all last week*) and helped me locate his gravestone in a nearby cemetery. Eunice's name may yet be discovered within the many boxes of uncataloged material stored in the historical society, in a letter she received from her mother, or a sister, or even Henry, left behind when her Vermont sojourn came to an end.

It was in Morristown, Vermont, that I came closest to conjuring Eunice's presence in New England. On a warm summer day, I proceeded to the Noyes House Museum to meet Bill Lizotte, ninth-generation native and president of the Morristown Historical Society. Bill led me on a tour of the town, including the Universalist church (now a senior center) where Eunice worshiped in 1866. When I unfolded a copy of a nineteenth-century map with the names of residents printed next to each house, Bill showed me the way to where William Stone's sister and brother-in-law Melissa and Moses Rankin had offered Eunice refuge. We gazed from across the road, then found Moses Rankin's gravestone in the cemetery close by.

The next day, I drove up from my Montpelier bed-and-breakfast again. I stopped first at the corner store, housed in the building that once served as the post office where Eunice mailed her letters that dismal Vermont winter and where she may also have picked up envelopes filled with earnest entreaties from her courting sea captain. The young woman behind the counter listened to the story of my research, then encouraged me to knock on the door of the former Rankin home, down the road.

When there was no answer at the front, I walked around to the side (Saturday, a car in the driveway, laundry on the clothesline—someone should have been inside). A woman emerged. "I'm writing a book about a person who lived in this house in 1866," I told her. The woman had never heard the name Rankin, but I sat at her kitchen table while she retrieved the papers from her late husband's search through property records, and in his notes we found the name. The interior of the house had been greatly altered in the intervening 137 years, the woman explained—the center hallway, stairwell, and chimney moved; small rooms opened up—but she pointed out original beams and walls that had known Eunice's presence. She rummaged through a drawer to find her own snapshots of the house in wintertime (how it looked when Eunice lived there, we imagined) and generously gave them to me. The unbroken quilt of snow in the photographs lent a timeless quality to the surroundings, making it easier to envision Eunice's presence at the front door.

By the time I traveled to Vermont that summer, I had retraced Eunice's journeys from New Hampshire and Massachusetts to Alabama and the Cayman Islands. Now I stood within the walls where she had rested by a fire, warmed her insides with whiskey, thought about the politics of Reconstruction, and grieved. In those painful months, perhaps Eunice also pondered a marriage proposal from Smiley Connolly. On Sundays, she walked through the snow or rode a sleigh the two miles from that front door to the Universalist church, to face the *darkness and despair*, the *dark empty void*, in the presence of the benevolent God of Universalism, a faith that foretold a joyful ending to her sojourn on earth.

As I CONTINUED my research, I began to wonder if there was any way to find the descendants of Eunice's New England family. How strange that I had met descendants of Smiley Connolly's family not only in the Caribbean but also in New York and New England yet hadn't located a single living Richardson descendant when in fact,

Eunice had spent most of her life in the northeastern United States, where I too lived.

I began with the letters themselves. The accession record for the Lois Wright Richardson Davis Papers indicated only that Duke University had purchased the collection from an antiquarian book dealer in Massachusetts in 1974; the hundreds of Civil War letters clearly made it an attractive acquisition for the library. William R. Erwin Jr., the now-retired archivist who had prepared and cataloged the Davis Papers at Duke, didn't know any more about their provenance but was "very glad," he wrote to me, that someone was "doing justice to the story of Lois Davis and her family who are my old friends, of which I acquired many during 39 years among the manuscripts." A white Alabamian, he had been particularly intrigued by the "obviously happy interracial marriage (except for Lois' relatives in New England)," as he put it, and it was his handwriting that queried "Eunice Stone? ca. 1863" on one of the photographs in the collection. I contacted the Massachusetts book dealer, but no company records existed from the 1970s, and the man who had purchased the Davis Papers had died. Still, the man's son mentioned a collection from Cape Cod that he thought might have been related, then referred me to another former employee, who also offered a faint recollection of a trunk full of papers in a house on Cape Cod.

Over several winter days, I searched for descendants at the Boston Public Library and the New England Historic Genealogical Society. Such institutions are set up for patrons to trace ancestors backward in time, but this quest took me in the opposite direction, tracing forward. Of Eunice's siblings, I knew it would be harder to track the women. Not only did they change their names upon marriage and remarriage, but they usually merited only the briefest of obituaries. Both of Ellen's children had died young, the brief notices about Hattie named no surviving children, and Ann's death was never even recorded in a newspaper. Luther of course had died unmarried, but the obituaries I found for Henry provided important facts. When Henry died in 1913, two sons and two daughters were still alive. The sons, I again assumed, would yield the most information. George Richardson had worked in a Massachusetts mill, served in the Spanish-American and First World Wars, and died of pneumonia in 1918. City directories listed two sons for decades thereafter, but the trail went cold in the early 1960s. Walter Richardson showed up in Lowell city directories, but his trail ended even earlier, in the 1930s. Turning reluctantly to the women, I found that Henry's daughter Ella proved yet more elusive, just as I had expected. When her husband, John Kelsey, died in 1921, the couple had no children. Of course Ella might have remarried and had children; marriage indexes revealed several Ella Kelseys and Ella Richardsons, but it was impossible to know which, if any, might have been Henry's daughter. My notes by now contained dozens of dead ends: the right name with a completely implausible birth date, for example, as well as lists of what I called wild stabs, inventories of Richardsons with first names like Clarence or Lois.

Henry's other surviving daughter, Ivah Jane Cushman, now emerged as the most promising lead. Massachusetts indexes indicated that she had died in 1952, in the town of Wellfleet on Cape Cod. I found her husband, James Cushman, in Massachusetts city directories, and an obituary in the *Boston Herald* revealed him to have been a graduate of the Massachusetts Institute of Technology, an engineer for the New England Power Company, and a prominent Congregationalist. He had died in 1956, also in Wellfleet. Could this be the connection that would lead to the dimly remembered trunk of letters on Cape Cod?

Going back to older records, I found that the U.S. federal census of 1920 listed Ivah and James Cushman with three children, Clara,

Allerton, and Richard. Clara, I discovered, had died in 1967 with
no children (it seemed fair to assume that she was named, not for
Eunice's daughter, but for Henry's wife). Allerton, also an engineer
with the New England Power Company, appeared in Massachusetts
city directories for the last time in 1960, and the Social Security
death index revealed that he had died in 1999 in Barnstable,
Massachusetts (again the Cape Cod connection). Richard, a shipper
for the New England Power Company, appeared in directories
through 1965, then turned up in driver's license records all the way
up to 1995. I wrote in my notes: "need the children of Allerton and
Richard." I called the book dealer one more time, to ask if the
names Allerton Cushman or Richard Cushman meant anything to
him, but neither did. Back to the archives. Marriage indexes indicated a wedding for Allerton in 1930, and birth indexes revealed
two children: Robert Allerton, born in 1931, and Jane Allerton,
born in 1934. A 1999 obituary in the *Yarmouth Register* finally
yielded the details I needed: Allerton Cushman's only surviving
child was Jane Allerton Cushman of Brewster, another town on
Cape Cod. She was Henry's great-granddaughter.

After so many years of reading the letters that Eunice and her
family had written, it was my turn to compose one of my own.
"Dear Jane Cushman," I began, "I write to you as a professor of
American History at New York University, currently writing a book
about a woman named Eunice (Richardson) Stone Connolly
(1831–1877). Eunice's brother, Charles Henry Richardson, was
your great-grandfather—he was the father of Ivah Jane, your paternal grandmother." Did Jane know about the letters at Duke
University? Did she know the story of Eunice and the Caribbean sea
captain? (Would she, I worried, want anything to do with exposing
her great-great-aunt who had married across the color line and dis-
graced her great-grandfather?) With caution, I inquired: "I wonder

if you heard stories about Eunice, or about your great-grandfather, when you were growing up."

Two days later, a blinking light on my answering machine yielded to a woman's voice. "Good morning," she said. "This message is for Martha Hodes. My name is Jane Cushman. I received your letter yesterday, and it moved me to tears. I sold those letters many years ago when I was first divorced and I needed money, and a gentleman came to my house on a Sunday and paid me $35 for them. I cannot tell you how I wept with joy to know where they are. I would be delighted to talk to you about the family. Ivah was indeed my grandmother. I have wonderful memories of her. I have many things that belonged to Charles Henry, her father. And I remember about the mill that he owned in Lowell, and I'm very, very excited to get your letter. Thank you so very much." My first reaction was surprise that she was thanking me. I was also astonished to realize that of all Eunice's siblings, of all the children of those siblings, and of all their children and grandchildren, the historical records had led me, with concerted, though not extraordinary, effort, to the one great-grandchild who had once been the keeper of what were now called the Lois Wright Richardson Davis Papers.

We spoke for nearly an hour when I called back, Jane's laughter audibly mixed with tears. When Henry died, his daughter Ivah had claimed the family papers, Jane told me, eventually bringing them out to the house at Wellfleet. As Ivah's granddaughter, Jane was next to stake her claim. Jane sold the letters in the late 1960s but instantly regretted the decision. The funny thing was, although the letters had originally been stored in Ivah's house on Cape Cod, Jane had sold them from her home in Bridgewater, just south of Boston; perhaps Jane had told the dealer about the Cape Cod provenance of the letters, and that was what had been recorded and remembered by the collectors with whom I had spoken. Jane had never read through the papers in their entirety and had never once heard Eunice's name mentioned ("I had no idea I had black relatives!" she marveled). It turned out as well that Jane was a sailor herself and that one of her suitors in the early 1950s had been a "man of color," as she put it. She had begged him to marry her, she told me, but he insisted she was too young to take such a risk. Eunice took her place among strong Richardson women, Jane believed, "a long line of beads in a strand." Now Jane would plan a trip to North Carolina to reacquaint herself with the letters. Before we said good-bye, she invited me for a visit.

Upstairs in Jane's brown-shingled house on the Cape, she had laid out all the family material she could find, everything that hadn't

Jane Allerton Cushman, the great-granddaughter of Eunice's brother Charles Henry Richardson, confirmed that her great-great-aunt Eunice was erased from family history. Jane inherited the collection of family letters but never read all the way through them and had never heard of Eunice.

ended up in the hands of the buyer so many years before. She knew about Henry's service in the Sixth and Twenty-sixth Massachusetts regiments (she had always heard him called Charlie), and she remembered that there were letters from New Orleans in the collection. She had heard of "southern relatives," she mused, but hadn't known that Luther senior had deserted his family. And, she reiterated, she had never heard a word about Eunice. Many of the family names had been repeated, Jane realized, but not Eunice, "never, ever Eunice."

We began to look through Jane's papers. An 1852 document from Manchester described a plot of land that Lois had purchased in the public burial ground, probably for her deceased daughter Adelia. Another, from 1895, was labeled "Pappa's poem" and written on stationary marked "Appleton Company Agent's Office." Here was verse upon verse of silly rhyme that Henry had written to his daughter Ivah ("And if you should stub your toes / And in a puddle spoil your clothes / That would be an awful shame / But you wouldn't be to blame"). Jane showed me the handwriting of her grandmother Ivah, which matched the snippets of information recorded in the Davis Papers; on a letter from Alice Merrill to Lois, for instance, someone (now I knew it was Ivah) had written, "Father's sister Nellie's child," invoking the family's nickname for Ellen. When transcribing the letters at Duke, I had written, "This must be the handwriting of someone in the family who was reading the letters; so that would be the child of Henry, perhaps same person who has explained photographs." Indeed, it was Ivah who had misidentified the photograph of Eunice as "Grandmother Davis." Perhaps she hadn't read far enough through the letters and thus assumed the woman in the picture to be Lois, since she knew nothing of Eunice's existence. Or maybe she didn't wish to cross her father, Henry, by acknowledging his disowned sister.

That day in April, Jane also remembered that Henry had been

appointed to a commission to make peace with the Sioux Nation after the Civil War. She had inherited a pair of moccasins and a woven dish that according to family lore, Chief Red Cloud had given to Henry. I subsequently conducted a bit of research on Red Cloud, who had lived in the Dakota Territory and resisted the efforts of the U.S. government to acquire Indian land; although Henry's name didn't appear in the history books, it seemed plausible that he had worked with Senator Henry Dawes of Massachusetts, who intervened to oppose a cession of land in the 1880s. I sent the information along to Jane, wondering if any of those facts echoed family knowledge. When no word came for several weeks, I telephoned, only to find that Jane had just been diagnosed with inoperable cancer.

That summer, when I visited again, we pored over Jane's papers once more. A notice from Washington, D.C., in 1897, granted Henry a patent for "Doubling and Twisting Frames" for the production of multicolored thread. A handwritten list of names bore the headline "Deaths reported since 1908 meeting," indicating that Henry had kept up with the veterans of the Sixth Massachusetts. On a scrap of lined paper dating from about 1912, Ann had written all she could recall about the Richardson family genealogy and sent it to Henry. There were certificates from the Daughters of the American Revolution for Henry's wife and two of his girls. Henry's granddaughter Clara had copied down Emily Dickinson's poem: "I'm Nobody! Who are you? / Are you—Nobody—Too?" And there was the letter from Aunt Mary revealing Henry's thoughts of Eunice ("Eunice it seems is far from you. I hope you hear from her.") "Oh, that's wonderful," Jane breathed when we realized that Henry had decided, if only this once, to name his forsaken sister.

Another letter too struck us as significant. "My darling Ella," Henry began, addressing one of his daughters in 1887. He was sending her Christmas money, and there followed a meditation upon joy and sadness. "If I had the power I would so guard your life that no cloud of trouble or sorrow should ever pass between you and complete happiness," he wrote. "But this is not the lot of human nature. All who live must suffer, and often it is our sufferings and trouble that give us our most valuable experience and bring us the most happiness in the end." What could Henry have meant by that, Jane and I asked each other, after he had disowned his sister, for his words seemed most aptly to describe Eunice's life. "Therefore when trouble and disapointments come, bear them cheerfully as possible," he continued. "We pass this way but once, pluck the roses as you pass and carry them with you to enrich with their fragrance your own and other's lives." Maybe Henry looked back on his treatment of Eunice with regret and wanted his own daughter to live more magnanimously. Maybe, in his more generous moments, Henry saw that Eunice had, after all, borne her troubles admirably and plucked what sweet blossoms she had found along her path.

I thought that would be the last time I saw Jane, but in January she was well enough for another visit; also in attendance were her daughter, her gentleman companion of eighteen years, and one of her dearest and oldest friends, the very person whom Jane had called in dismay the day after she sold the family papers, and with whom she had marched for civil rights in Massachusetts. Beyond all predictions, Jane lived through the winter and spring, but her suffering grew steadily more intense ("She says *after* she dies she's coming down here to see the island!" Jeanne Masters told me, after the two corresponded). From Grand Cayman that August, reading e-mail at an Internet cafe, I learned that Jane had died. Jane's daughter had telephoned, but unable to reach me, she sent a message so I would know about the funeral. Jane's daughter and gentleman companion greeted the mourners as we entered the First Brewster Unitarian Universalist Church of the Sea Captains, founded in 1700. Afterwards people spoke informally at a reception held at Jane's beloved Cape Cod Museum of Natural History, where she had served as a volunteer for many years. Today a plaque there honors her efforts.

As family and friends gathered back at the house, I met Jane's cousin James Cushman, from Washington State, the son of Allerton's brother Richard and Eunice's great-grandnephew. Like Smiley Connolly and his brothers, it turned out, Jim Cushman is a sea captain. He served thirty years in the U.S. Coast Guard and holds the professional license of Unlimited Master Mariner, both U.S. and Bahamian. Jim remembered a framed portrait of Henry hanging in the front stairwell of the Cape Cod house, but he too was unaware of Eunice's existence. He had no doubt, he told me, that she had been struck from family history because of the marriage that had prompted her to leave New England for the Caribbean.

On Sunday, September 12, 2004, and until the next morning, Hurricane Ivan ripped through Grand Cayman Island. Nearly a Category 5 storm, the highest classification, winds blew at 170 miles an hour, the seas reached thirty feet, and islanders saw whitecaps in their backyards. Caymanians described the aftermath as "devastation beyond imagination." People saw houses fall like matchsticks; not even buildings constructed under the islands' strict codes or the most solidly built homes of the wealthiest foreign residents were spared. Posthurricane photographs showed roofless buildings, furniture stranded on the sand, boats smashed against utility poles, cars overturned and submerged, and hotel rooms without walls. The well-remembered hurricane of 1932 had destroyed Cornelius Connolly's home. Now elderly islanders calculated that Ivan had been worse. Cleopathra Conolly, great-granddaughter of Smiley's brother Moses, lost the East End house built by her grandfather, in which she had lived for seventy-two years. Gravestones in Thomas Dighton

Conolly's sand cemetery were torn up and thrown atop one another. A government official noted that "the priority—after helping victims—is to reopen the islands' famous offshore banking industry and reactivate the profitable tourism industry." Curiously, when the *New York Times* reported two days before the storm that forecasters "expected Hurricane Ivan to hit Jamaica early Friday and move on to Cuba," the text and map alike left the Cayman Islands, in between Jamaica and Cuba, unnamed and invisible.

As the island rebuilds once again, Eunice and her family will yet have something of a proper commemoration. At the start of the twenty-first century, a Mariners' Memorial was unveiled in George Town. Standing temporarily across from the Elmslie Memorial Church, near the site of an old fort on Harbour Drive, it will eventually be moved to the new port facility currently under construction. That building has been designed by architect Burns Conolly, the son of Warren Conolly and the great-great-grandson of Eunice and Smiley's *Brother Dighton*. Plans call for the memorial to honor all Caymanians lost at sea, and among them will be Eunice Connolly, Clara Stone, Smiley Connolly, Louisa Charlotta Connolly, and Caramiel Connolly. On Grand Cayman Island, Eunice Richardson Stone Connolly, born white and poor in New England, found an interval of happiness as a member of an elite family of color living in a community of former slaves, and it is there that her name will be engraved in granite.

NOTES

$\mathcal{A}$ ll cited letters to and from Eunice and her family are from the Lois Wright Richardson Davis Papers, held at the Rare Book, Manuscript, and Special Collections Library of Duke University, unless otherwise noted. Documents from the personal papers of James T. Cushman may be added to the Davis Papers in the future. Copies of letters that Eunice and her family wrote from the Caribbean are available at the Cayman Islands National Archive, George Town, Grand Cayman. Copies of some documents from the Public Record Office, London, are also available at the Cayman Islands National Archive.

Names

AD: Addie Davis
AM: Ann McCoy
AP: Ann Putnam
BD: Bradley Davis
CHR: Charles Henry Richardson
CS: Clarence Stone
DDM: Dudley D. Merrill
DM: David McCoy
EC: Eunice Connolly
EM: Ellen Merrill
ER: Eunice Richardson
ES: Eunice Stone
HH: Hattie Harvey
IH: Ira Harvey

JL: Jane Lull
LD: Lois Davis
LLR: Luther L. Richardson Jr.
LR: Lois Richardson
LWRD: Lois Wright Richardson Davis
 Papers, Rare Book, Manuscript, and
 Special Collections Library, Duke
 University, Durham, North Carolina
MJ: Martha Johnson
MR: Melissa Rankin
MS: Melissa Stone
WCS: William C. Stone
WL: Wesley Lull
WSC: William Smiley Connolly

Archives

ADAH: Alabama Department of Archives and History, Montgomery, Ala.

AHL: Andover-Harvard Theological Library, Harvard Divinity School, Cambridge, Mass.

CCL: City Clerk, Lowell, Mass.

CINA: Cayman Islands National Archive, George Town, Grand Cayman, Cayman Islands

CINM: Cayman Islands National Museum, George Town, Grand Cayman, Cayman Islands

CIRG: Cayman Islands Registrar General, George Town, Grand Cayman, Cayman Islands

CLH: Center for Lowell History, University of Massachusetts, Lowell, Mass.

DU: Rare Book, Manuscript, and Special Collections Library, Duke University, Durham, N.C.

LNHP: Lowell National Historical Park Library, Lowell, Mass.

MCPC: Mobile County Probate Court, Mobile, Ala.

MHA: Manchester Historic Association, Manchester, N.H.

MHDC: Mobile Historic Development Commission, Mobile, Ala.

MHS: Massachusetts Historical Society, Boston, Mass.

MMA: Mobile Municipal Archives, Mobile, Ala.

MPL: Mobile Public Library, Mobile, Ala.

MSA: Massachusetts State Archives, Boston, Mass.

NA: National Archives, Washington, D.C.

NHBVR: New Hampshire Bureau of Vital Records, Concord, N.H.

NHDRMA New Hampshire Division of Records Management and Archives, Concord, N.H.

NLS: National Library of Scotland, Edinburgh

NYHS: New-York Historical Society, New York, N.Y.

RAC: Rockefeller Foundation Archives, Rockefeller Archive Center, Sleepy Hollow, N.Y.

RHL: Rhodes House Library, Bodleian Library, Oxford University, Oxford, England

RIHS: Rhode Island Historical Society, Providence, R.I.

SHC: Southern Historical Collection, University of North Carolina, Chapel Hill, N.C.

SPL: Stephen Phillips Library, Peabody Essex Museum, Salem, Mass.

TNA:PRO: The National Archives of the United Kingdom: Public Record Office, London, England

VHS: Vermont Historical Society, Barre, Vt.

Chapter 1. A Story and a History

p. 17: "the late": John S. Wood to EM, Kingston, Jamaica, Feb. 2, 1881.

p. 17: "My Dear": EM to CHR, Moss Point, Miss., Feb. 19, 1881.

p 23: *I cant*: ES to LD, Claremont, N.H., Aug. 3, 1863, continuation of Aug. 2, 1863, letter.

p. 23: "when tomorrow": LD to CHR, Dracut, Mass., June 1, 1865.

p. 23: *and Henry*: ES to LD, Mobile, Ala., March 10, 1861, continuation of March 3, 1861, letter.

p. 23: *seven unanswered*: ES to LD, Claremont, N.H., March 29, 1863.

p. 23: "evry sabbath": LD to CHR, Dracut, Mass., Jan. 3, 1863.

p. 23: *Dont think*: ES to LD, Claremont, N.H., labeled "Autumn 1862?" but likely 1863.

p. 23: "a leaf": CHR to LD, New Orleans, La., Feb. 10, 1863.

p. 23: "well I have": AM to CHR, Pelham, N.H., June 11, 1865.

p. 23: *It is a shame*: ES to LD, Claremont, N.H., Dec. 30, 1863.

p. 24: *find one*: ES to AM, Mobile, Ala., Dec. 23, 1860.

p. 24: "too coarse": CHR to LD, Winchester, Va., Jan. 26, 1865.

p. 24: "one of the boys": LLR and LD, Algiers, La., Sept. 14, 1863, continuation of Sept. 13, 1863, letter.

p. 24: *came in*: ES to LD, Claremont, N.H. Sept. 4, 1864.

p. 24: *It costs*: ES to LD, Claremont, N.H., Feb. 9, 1862.

p. 26: "insipid": LD to CHR and LLR, Dracut, Mass., June 7, 1862; LD to CHR, Dracut, Mass., Jan. 3, 1863.

p. 26: *She writes*: ES to AM and DM, Claremont, N.H., July 3, 1864.

p. 26: "excuse this": AD to LD and BD, Northfield, Mass., Oct. 3, 1864.

p. 26: "do excus": MJ to LD, Northfield, Mass., April 10, 1864.

p. 26: *O Mother*: ES to LD, Claremont, N.H., Oct. 9, 1864.

p. 26: *If I could*: ES to LD, Claremont, N.H., June 12, 1864.

p. 26: "worshing": LLR to LD, "Camp Bisalum," Sept. 26, 1863.

p. 26: "worch": LLR to LD, New Orleans, La., Jan. 19, 1863.

p. 26: "citersons": LLR to LD, Quarantine Station, Mississippi River, June 19, 1862.

p. 26: "polerticks": LLR to LD, Summit Point, Va., Sept. 1, 1864, continuation of Aug. 27, 1864, letter.

p. 27: "Simperthiser": LLR to LD, Algiers, La., Sept. 15, 1863.

p. 27: "wors": LLR to LD, Quarantine Station, Mississippi River, June 19, 1862.

p. 27: *surporting*: ES to CHR and LLR, Claremont, N.H., March 22, 1863.

p. 27: "atall": LLR to LD, New Orleans, La., Feb. 26, 1863.

p. 27: *try afinish*: ES to LD, Claremont, N.H., Aug. 3, 1863, continuation of Aug. 2, 1863, letter.

p. 27: "a Fishing": CS to LD, Claremont, N.H., May 3, 1863.

p. 27: "story papers": CHR to LD, New Orleans, La., June 14, 1863.

p. 27: "A Lonely Hour": HH to LD, Goffstown, N.H., Feb. 4, 1872.

p. 28: "talking," "best white," "blemish," "warm affections," "best, generally" and "a storehouse": D. H. Jacques, *How to Write: A Pocket Manual of Composition and Letter-Writing* (New York: Fowler and Wells, 1857), 36, 9, 18, 65, 37.

p. 28: "objectionable": Arthur Martine, *Martine's Sensible Letter-Writer* (New York: Dick and Fitzgerald, 1866), 18.

p. 29: *I write*: ES to LD, Claremont, N.H., Dec. 3, 1864.

p. 30: *poking over*: ES to LD, Claremont, N.H., May 26, 1864.

p. 30: "This day": Lot Richardson to LR, Royalston, Mass., Dec. 15, 1851.

p. 30: *I have written*: ES to LD, Mobile, Ala., April 29, 1861.

p. 30: "Have you herd": AM to LD, n.p., July 3 [1864?].

p. 30: "Dear Sister": MJ to LD, Northfield, Mass., March 24, 1860.

p. 30: "Another Mail": CHR to LD, Lake End, La., Oct. 14, 1862.

p. 30: "spoiled": HH to LD and AM, Goffstown, N.H., Jan. 26, 1872.

p. 31: "another girl": EM to LLR, Manchester, N.H., May 21, 1856.

p. 31: *All this long*: ES to LD, Mobile, Ala., April 14, 1861.

p. 31: "There never": LLR to LD, Ship Island, Miss., Jan. 23, 1862, continuation of Jan. 22, 1862, letter.

p. 31: "It is provoking": CHR to LD, camp near Morganza, La., June 10, 1864.

p. 31: "How is Mother": AP to CHR, Hudson, N.H., Feb. [no day], 1858.

p. 31: "I would write": CHR to LD, on board U.S. steamship *Cahawba*, May 20, 1864.

p. 32: "we could not": MJ to LD, Northfield, Mass., March 24, 1860.

p. 32: "I knew": AP to LD, n.p., April 16, 1856.

p. 32: "I will write": AP to LD, n.p., Feb. 13, 1859.

p. 32: *recieved a letter*: ES to CHR and LLR, Claremont, N.H., Dec. 7, 1862.

p. 32: *You may send*: ES to LD, Savannah, Ga., Oct. 13, 1860.

p. 32: *must answer*: EC to LD, East End, Grand Cayman, March 7, 1870.

p. 32: *If you see*: ES to LD, Mobile, Ala., April 14, 1861.

p. 32: "and forget": CHR to LD, Winchester, Va., Jan. 26, 1865.

p. 32: "hailed": LD to CHR, Dracut, Mass., Jan. 3, 1863.

p. 32: "accursed": CHR to LD, Lake End, La., Nov. 13, 1862.

p. 32: "a nigger": CHR to LD and ES, Savannah, Ga., July 5, 1865, continuation of June 29, 1865, letter.

p. 33: "It gives": LD to CHR, Dracut, Mass., May 29 [30?], 1861.

p. 33: "What a comfort": MJ to LD, Northfield, Mass., Feb. 13, 1864.

p. 33: *I recieved*: ES to LD, Claremont, N.H., Feb. 9, 1862.

p. 33: *If nothing*: ES to AM and DM, Claremont, N.H., March 13, 1862; ES to AM, Claremont, N.H., April 19, 1863.

p. 34: *I shall*: ES to LD, Claremont, N.H., Dec. 21, 1862.

p. 34: *shall try*: ES to LD, Claremont, N.H., June 24, 1864.

p. 34: *I shall be*: ES to LD, Claremont, N.H., Dec. 18, 1864.

p. 34: *if I live*: ES to LD, Mobile, Ala., March 10, 1861, continuation of March 3, 1861, letter; ES to LD, Claremont, N.H., June 12, 1864.

p. 34: *He has got*: ES to AM and DM, Claremont, N.H., July 3, 1864.

p. 34: *I can spend* and *I dont know*: ES to LD, Claremont, N.H., July 11, 1864.

Chapter 2. A Carpenter's Wife

p. 41: "magnificent": John Hayward, *Gazetteer of New Hampshire* (Boston: John P. Jewett, 1849), 96.

p. 41: 18 Hanover Street: HH to LR, CHR; LLR, Tyngsborough, Mass., July 15, 1854.

p. 42: ER birth and Lois Wright birth: Northfield (Mass.) Town Clerk, "Births, baptisms, marriages, intentions, deaths, 1713–1839, approximately" (manuscript,

Genealogical Society of Utah microfilm, 1972), 106, 155.

p. 42: Luther Richardson birth: Vermont Secretary of State, "General Index to Vital Records of Vermont, Early to 1870" (manuscript, Genealogical Society of Utah microfilm, 1951).

p. 42: Luther Richardson and Lois Wright marriage: *Vital Records of Royalston, Massachusetts, To the End of the Year 1849* (Worcester, Mass.: F. P. Rice, 1906), 140; AM to CHR, n.p., [ca. 1912], personal papers of James T. Cushman.

p. 42: Wright family history: Daniel Wright to LD, Schoolcraft, Mich., Dec. 17, 1864; Mrs. David Wright to LD, "Glover," Jan. 11 and April 30, 1865; Daniel Wright to LD, Schoolcraft, Mich., no date, all in LWRD; Louensa to LD, West Point, May 30, [1850s], personal papers of James T. Cushman.

p. 42: Richardson family history: *Illustrated History of Lowell and Vicinity, Massachusetts* (Lowell, Mass.: Courier-Citizen, 1897), 250–54.

p. 42: Richardson siblings: Northfield Town Clerk, "Births, baptisms, marriages," 106; 1850 Manchester, N.H., federal census, p. 121. Lois wrote of her "nine children," indicating that one died before the 1850s: LD to CHR, Dracut, Mass., May 29 [30?], 1861.

p. 43: Luther Richardson's property: Northfield (Mass.) Town Assessors, Tax Records, 1827–49 (manuscript, Genealogical Society of Utah microfilm, 1972).

p. 44: "you was deprived": LD to CHR [late 1850s?].

p. 44: move to Manchester: CHR pension file, no. C-2498-336, NA.

p. 45: "hard times": Jemima Sanborn to brother and sister, Nashville, N.H., May 14, 1843, in Thomas Dublin, ed., *Farm to Factory: Women's Letters, 1830–1860* (New York: Columbia University Press, 1981), 87.

p. 46: "foamed": Henry D. Thoreau, *A Week on the Concord and Merrimack Rivers* (1849; reprint, Princeton, N.J.: Princeton University Press, 2004), 245.

p. 46: "hardly more": L. Ashton Thorp, *Manchester of Yesterday: A Human Interest Story of Its Past* (Manchester, N.H.: Granite State Press, 1939), 75.

p. 48: "clean": Mary Ann Partridge to family, Manchester, N.H., May 27, 1855, Misc. Personal Papers, Box 8, f. 4, MHA.

p. 48: "prety": Lucy Farington to Emeline (Nancy E. Savage), Manchester, N.H., Nov. 23, 1851, ACC 507, LNHP.

p. 49: "We have to labor": "M." to Editor, *Manchester Operative* 1, no. 23 (June 1844), p. 2, cited in Kimberly Frederick, "The Amoskeag and Its City: Power and Protest in Manchester, New Hampshire, in the 1840s," Brandeis University, unpublished paper, 2000, p. 18.

p. 49: "Corporation Tyranny" and "Slave-driverism": *Voice of Industry* (Oct. 23, 1846).

p. 49: WCS and ER marriage certificate, Manchester, N.H., Oct. 21, 1849, NHBVR. Records regarding William's age are contradictory; see 1850 Manchester, N.H., federal census, p. 121 (age twenty-seven) versus 1860 Mobile, Ala., federal census, 6th ward, p. 604 (age thirty).

p. 49: "Now soon": "The Factory Girl," broadside [United States: 1830–1860?].

p. 50: "Is he industrious?": Luther M. Trussell to Delia Page, New London, N.H., Aug. 24, 1860, in Dublin, *Farm to Factory*, 166.

p. 50: WCS a wheelwright: *Manchester City Directory*, 1852, p. 174.

p. 50: HH marriage: George Plummer Hadley, *History of the Town of Goffstown, 1733–1920* (Goffstown, N.H.: The Town, 1924), 2: 213.

p. 50: JL marriage: LD to JL and WL, Manchester, N.H., July [1851?].

p. 50: EM marriage: DDM and Ellen A. Richardson marriage certificate, Manchester, N.H., Dec. 14, 1855, NHBVR.

p. 51: "young hearts": LR to JL and WL, Manchester, N.H., July [1851?].

p. 51: "We have": Polly Richardson to LR, continuation of Lot Richardson to LR, Royalston, Mass., Jan. 29, 1853, letter.

p. 51: "If I could" and "in a shocking": MJ to LR, Northfield, Mass., April 3, 1855.

p. 52: residences: *Manchester City Directories*, 1850–1858.

p. 52: "beautifull": LR to JL and WL, Manchester, N.H., July [1851?].

p. 52: Ann M. Putnam: thirty-one-year-old "Widow Lady," 1860 Hudson, N.H., federal census, p. 515.

p. 52: "If you": Alexander Moody to LR, Concord, N.H., April 15, 1855.

p. 52: move to Dracut: CHR pension file, no. C-2498-336, NA.

p. 53: "I thought": EM to LD, Manchester, N.H., April 5, 1857.

p. 53: *Ira and Harriet & Ella*: ES to LD, Manchester, N.H., Nov. 1, 1857.

p. 53: *Ira and Harriet rode*: ES to LLR, Manchester, N.H., April 5, 1857.

p. 53: "We are all": HH to LLR, Manchester, N.H., June 19, 1857, continuation of June 14, 1857, letter.

p. 53: "If they knew": EM to LD, Manchester, N.H., Aug. 17, 1856.

p. 54: Adelia Richardson death: Adelia Richardson death certificate, Manchester, N.H., March 6, 1851, NHBVR.

p. 54: *very sorry*: ES to CHR, Manchester, N.H., March 31, 1856.

p. 54: "Mother": AP to LD, n.p., April 16, 1856.

p. 54: *with a heavy heart*: ES to CHR, Manchester, N.H., March 31, 1856.

p. 54: "keeping house": HH to CHR, Manchester, N.H., Feb. 24, 1856.

p. 54: "Dear Mother": JL to LD, Claremont, N.H., April 15, 1855.

p. 54: "has left": EM to LLR, Manchester, N.H., May 21, 1856.

p. 55: "The city": HH to CHR, Manchester, N.H., Feb. 24, 1856.

p. 56: "Anyone": Mary Ann Partridge to family, Manchester, N.H., May 27, 1855, Misc. Personal Papers, Box 8, f. 4, MHA.

p. 56: "brilliantly illuminated": Henry M. Dexter, *The Moral Influence of Manufacturing Towns: Discourse Delivered at the Dedication of the Franklin Street Church in Manchester, N.H., Dec. 22, 1847* (Andover, Mass.: William H. Wardwell, 1848), 13, 14.

p. 58: "commerce and industry": Carl Schurz, "The Doom of Slavery," Aug. 1, 1860, in *Speeches, Correspondence and Political Papers of Carl Schurz*, ed. Frederic Bancroft (New York: G. P. Putnam's Sons, 1913), 1:150, 151.

p. 59: *I dont know*: ES to LLR, Manchester, N.H., April 5, 1857.

p. 59: "Business": HH to LLR, Manchester, N.H., June 19, 1857, continuation of June 14, 1857, letter.

p. 59: *There will*: ES to LLR, Manchester, N.H., Oct. 15, 1857.

p. 59: *a neat*: ES to LLR, Manchester, N.H., April 5, 1857.

p. 59: snowstorms: Sidney Perley, *Historic Storms of New England* (Salem, Mass.: Salem Press, 1891), 323–28.

p. 59: "he never": EM to LD, Manchester, N.H., Sept. 20, 1857.

p. 60: *William does not*: ES to LLR, Manchester, N.H., Oct. 15, 1857.

p. 60: *only hard times*: ES to LLR, Manchester, N.H., Nov. 1, 1857.

p. 60: *I dont know*: ES to CHR, Manchester, N.H., March 29, 1858.

p. 60: *We think*: ES to LLR, Manchester, N.H., Sept. 10, 1858.

p. 60: *country home*: ES to LD, Bradford Springs, N.H., March 15, 1859.

p. 61: "I feel": LD to CHR, Hudson, N.H., April 19, 1860.

p. 61: *Luther*: ES to LLR, Bradford, N.H., Dec. 14, 1859.

p. 62: *I hope you will be*: ES to LLR, Manchester, N.H., Feb. 17, 1858.

p. 62: "Success": HH to CHR, Manchester, N.H., Feb. 24, 1856.

p. 62: "You are both": AP to CHR, Hudson, N.H., Feb. [no day], 1858.

p. 62: "Be prudent": LD to LLR, Dracut, Mass., April 18, 1858.

p. 62: "By all means": HH to LLR, Manchester, N.H., Jan. 25, 1857.

p. 62: *I hope you will try*: ES to LLR, Manchester, N.H., Feb. 14, 1857.

p. 62: *round with*: ES to LD, continuation of ES to LLR, Manchester, N.H., Feb. 17, 1858, letter.

p. 63: "on the cotton": "Sermon by Rev. Edwin M. Wheelock," in James Redpath, *Echoes of Harper's Ferry* (Boston: Thayer and Eldridge, 1860), 180.

p. 63: *I am lonesome*: ES to LLR, Bradford, N.H., Dec. 14, 1859.

p. 63: *Alabama widow*: ES to LLR, Manchester, N.H., April 2, 1860.

p. 63: signature: Employee Register, Amoskeag Manufacturing Company, March 21, 1860, p. 47, MHA.

p. 64: weather: "News of the Day," *Manchester Daily American*, March 31, 1860.

p. 64: address: Employee Register, Amoskeag Manufacturing Company, March 21, 1860, p. 47, MHA.

p. 64: "my little attic": Delia Page to Mary Trussell, Manchester, N.H., April 14, 1861, in Dublin, *Farm to Factory*, 183.

p. 64: "I have had" and food served: Mary Ann Partridge to family, Manchester, N.H., May 27, 1855, Misc. Personal Papers, Box 8, f. 4, MHA.

p. 64: Clarence boarding: 1860 Manchester, N.H., federal census, p. 321; *Manchester City Directory*, 1860, p. 123.

p. 65: eleven workers: Employee Register, Amoskeag Manufacturing Company, March 21, 1860, p. 47, MHA.

p. 65: "When we needed": "Foreign Immigration Formerly and Now," *DeBow's Review* 24 (April 1858), 328.

p. 66: "low class": "Rights and Duties of Mill Girls," *New England Offering* (July 1849), 156.

p. 66: "I think": HH to LD and ES, Manchester, N.H., Aug. 5, 1865 (reading back to 1850s; for similar sentiments, see HH to CHR, Manchester, N.H., Feb. 24, 1856).

p. 67: "disgust": "Memorandum of subjects to be brought to the notice of the Directors of the Salmon Falls Co.," Jan. 18, 1854, Amos A. Lawrence Papers, MHS.

p. 67: "forainers": Arvilla Galusha to Polly Galusha, Lowell, Mass., June 27, 1857, and May 19, no year, Galusha Family Collection, LNHP.

p. 67: "Your Father": LD to CHR and LLR, Hudson, N.H., April 1, 1860.

p. 68: "prehensile" and "wailing": George Templeton Strong, *The Diary of George Templeton Strong*, ed. Allan Nevins and Milton Halsey Thomas (New York: Macmillan, 1952), 1:318; 2:348.

p. 68: "savage": Theodore Parker, "A Sermon of the Dangerous Classes in Society," in *The Collected Works of Theodore Parker*, ed. Frances Power Cobbe (London: Trübner and Company, 1864), 7:64.

p. 69: "offals": *Manchester Daily American*, Jan. 26, 1858, quoted in Peter Haebler, "Nativism, Liquor, and Riots: Manchester Politics, 1858–1859," *Historical New Hampshire* 46 (Summer 1991), 74.

p. 69: Elias Haskall: 1850 Manchester, N.H., federal census, p. 60.

p. 69: "black tint": "A Scene from Irish Life," *Harper's New Monthly Magazine* 3 (Nov. 1851), 833.

p. 69: "next to Slavery": "The Irish in America," *Concord Independent Democrat*, Dec. 28, 1854.

p. 69: "what we call": CHR to LD, "Tanleytown," Washington, D.C., Aug. 9, 1864, continuation of Aug. 6, 1864, letter.

p. 69: black population: 1850 and 1860 Manchester, N.H., federal censuses and Manchester city directories; U.S. Bureau of the Census, *Negro Population, 1790–1915* (Washington, D.C.: Government Printing Office, 1918) indicates that in 1860 about five hundred people of African descent lived in New Hampshire, 0.2 percent of the population (51, 57).

p. 69: "The blacks": Theodore Parker, "A Sermon of Poverty," in *Collected Works*, 7:101–02.

p. 70: "Irish girl": MJ to LR, Northfield, Mass., April 3, 1855.

p. 70: "My colored girl": Charlotte Vance Morrill to Emma J. Page, Augusta, Me., Jan. 27 [1870], Emma Page Correspondence, CLH.

p. 70: "We go": Mary Ann Partridge to family, Manchester, N.H., May 27, 1855, Misc. Personal Papers, Box 8, f. 4, MHA.

p. 71: "thunder": "Letters from Susan," *Lowell Offering* 4 (June 1844), 170.

p. 71: "if I could": Delia Page to Mary Trussell, Manchester, N.H., April 14, 1861, in Dublin, *Farm to Factory*, 183.

p. 71: "not to be absent": "Regulations to be observed by all persons employed by the Amoskeag Manufacturing Company," Employee Register, Amoskeag Manufacturing Company, 1854–1878, MHA.

p. 71: "being a good girl" and "both Health": Eliza S. Trussell to Delia Page, New London, N.H., Dec. 10, 1859; L. M. Trussell to Delia Page, New London, N.H., June 13, 1860, in Dublin, *Farm to Factory*, 143, 157.

p. 71: "better looking": Mary Ann Partridge to family, Manchester, N.H., May 27, 1855, Misc. Personal Papers, Box 8, f. 4, MHA.

p. 71: "uper *crust*": Lucy Farington to Emeline (Nancy E. Savage), Manchester, N.H., Nov. 23, 1851, ACC 507, LNHP.

p. 71: *How many times, I want*, and *Do you know how?* : ES to LLR, Manchester, N.H., May 20, 1860.

p. 72: *I have told* and *black eyed*: ES to LLR, Manchester, N.H., April 15, 1860.

p. 72: *just for fun*: ES to LLR, Manchester, N.H., labeled "summer 1860?," actually spring 1860.

p. 72: 1851 debate: Ellen Stanton to Mary W. Bell, Manchester, N.H., April 6, 1851, Mary W. Bell Personal Papers, MHA.

p. 72: "force of argument": *Manchester Daily American*, March 2, 1860.

p. 73: "to resist": "A Rousing Republican Meeting," ibid.

p. 73: "'the hand'": George Waldo Browne, *The Amoskeag Manufacturing Co. of Manchester, New Hampshire: A History* (Manchester, N.H.: Amoskeag Manufacturing Company, 1915), 157.

p. 73: "I would preserve": "Speech of Mr. D. Wilmot of Pennsylvania," *Congressional Globe*, 29th Cong., 2d sess., Appendix, Feb. 8, 1847, p. 317.

p. 73: "You are": "Voters of Manchester," *Manchester Daily American*, March 10, 1860.

p. 74: "detracts": "Editor's Table," *New England Offering* (June 1848), 71.

p. 74: "diligent": "Our Laborers and Our Drones," *Manchester Daily American*, March 19, 1860.

p. 74: banners: "Republican Jubilee!" *Manchester Dollar Weekly Mirror*, May 26, 1860.

p. 74: antislavery meetings: "Radical Anti-Slavery Meeting Tonight," *Manchester Daily American*, March 20, 1860.

p. 74: "Fourteen black boys": Alexander Crummell, "Eulogium on Henry Highland Garnet," in *Africa and America: Addresses and Discourses* (1891; reprint, New York: Negro Universities Press, 1969), 280.

p. 75: *"colored gentlemen"* and "close intimacy": William Allen Wallace, *The History of Canaan, New Hampshire* (Concord, N.H.: Rumford Press, 1910), 270, 271.

p. 75: "overrun": "Exposition of Affairs Connected with Noyes Academy," *Liberator*, Oct. 3, 1835.

p. 75: destruction of school: "Colored School at Canaan," *Liberator*, Sept. 5, 1835; Crummell, "Eulogium," 280.

p. 75: "amalgamation": N. P. Rogers, "Practical Anti-Slavery," *Liberator*, July 25, 1835.

p. 75: "take up": *Concord Patriot*, Aug. 3, 1835, quoted in Donald B. Cole, *Jacksonian Democracy in New Hampshire, 1800–1851* (Cambridge, Mass.: Harvard University Press, 1970), 178.

p. 75: "brother's sword": *Annals of Congress* 35, 16th Cong., 1st sess., Jan. 1820, p. 175.

p. 75: "sooner risk": James Madison, *Journal of the Federal Convention*, ed. E. H. Scott (Chicago: Scott, Foresman, 1898), 1:583.

p. 75: "If it is debated": John Adams, *The Works of John Adams, Second President of the United States* (Boston: Little, Brown, 1850), 2:498.

p. 76: "crimes": Oswald Garrison Villard, *John Brown, 1800–1859: A Biography Fifty Years After* (Boston: Houghton Mifflin, 1911), illustration opposite p. 554.

p. 76: *doing well*: ES to LLR, Manchester, N.H., April 2, 1860.
p. 77: *I dont see*: ES to LD, Hudson, N.H. [late Sept. 1860?].
p. 77: *I am going*: ES to AP, Hillsborough, N.H., Sept. 14, 1860.

Chapter 3. Yankee in the Deep South

p. 80: "This Creole cottage": *Historic Mobile: An Illustrated Guide* (Mobile, Ala.: Junior League, 1974), 66.
p. 80: residences: 1860 Mobile, Ala., federal census, 6th ward, p. 604; *Mobile City Directory*, 1861, p. 43. "101 N. Hallett St.," Mobile Historic Building Inventory, MHDC.
p. 81: "Old Mobile": Historic Mobile Preservation Society, <www.historicmobile.org/oakleigh.html>.
p. 81: Africatown: <www.loc.gov/bicentennial/propage/prohome.html>.
p. 81: Bienville Square: "Dauphin Street Historic District Walking Tour" (Mobile Convention and Visitors Corporation, no date).
p. 82: *We hear*: ES to LD, Manchester, N.H., Jan. 12, 1858.
p. 82: "We are safe": EM to LD, Mobile, Ala., Nov. 15, 1857.
p. 82: leaves, robins: EM to LD, Mobile, Ala., Jan. 3, 1858.
p. 82: "I have ben": DDM to LLR, Mobile, Ala., Jan. 3, 1858.
p. 82: *Would to God*: ES to LD, Bradford Springs, N.H., March 15, 1859.
p. 82: "You hope": EM to LD, Mobile, Ala., March 14, 1858.
p. 82: "You do not": EM to LLR, continuation of DDM to LLR, Mobile, Ala., Jan. 3, 1858, letter.
p. 83: *keep up*: ES to LD, New York, N.Y., Oct. 9, 1860.
p. 84: "great business": Frederick Law Olmsted, *A Journey in the Seaboard Slave States* (New York: Dix and Edwards, 1856), 567.
p. 84: "small mountains": Matthias H. Welles to Charles and George Welles, Mobile, Ala., Feb. 9, 1845, continuation of Feb. 8, 1845, letter, Misc. Letter 516/59, SHC.
p. 84: "waifs and strays": Charles Mackay, *Life and Liberty in America; or, Sketches of a Tour in the United States and Canada, in 1857–8* (London: Smith, Elder, 1859), 180.
p. 84: "buy cotton": [Hiram Fuller], *Belle Brittan on a Tour, at Newport, and Here and There* (New York: Derby and Jackson, 1858), 112.
p. 84: sash factory: "S. B. Merrill Lease to Sash & Blind Factory," in Sumner B. Merrill estate case; "Final Settlement," Minute Book 13, Aug. 5, 1861, pp. 74–76, both in MCPC.
p. 84: James H. Daughdrill: 1860 Mobile, Ala., federal census, slave schedule, p. 55.
p. 84: *Any one*: ES to LLR, Claremont, N.H., May 5, 1863 no. 2.
p. 85: "Dear me": EM to LD and CHR, Mobile, Ala., Aug. 22, 1858.
p. 85: "Business": DDM to LLR, continuation of EM to LLR, Mobile, Ala., Dec. 4, 1859, letter.
p. 85: *Write all*: ES to LD, Mobile, Ala., Oct. 19, 1860.
p. 85: *Now if* and *It is such*: ES to CHR, Mobile, Ala., Nov. 18, 1860.

p. 85: *Such a sight*: ES to LD, Mobile, Ala., April 14, 1861.

p. 85: "scents": Olmsted, *Journey*, 566.

p. 85: "air": Harriet H. A. Eaton Diaries, Jan. 4, 1854, SHC.

p. 85: "most beautiful": Fredrika Bremer, *The Homes of the New World: Impressions of America* (New York: Harper, 1853), 2:217.

p. 86: "thriving" and "kept by Boston men": Olmsted, *Journey*, 565, 566.

p. 86: neighbors: 1860 Mobile, Ala., federal census, 6th ward, pp. 600–10; ES to LLR, Claremont, N.H., May 5, 1863 (no. 2).

p. 86: summering in Boston: John Oldmixon, *Transatlantic Wanderings; or, A Last Look at the United States* (London: Geo. Routledge, 1855), 156.

p. 86: *not so clean*: ES to LD, Mobile, Ala., Dec. 30, 1860.

p. 86: "dirty": Olmsted, *Journey*, 565.

p. 86: advertisements: *Mobile City Directory*, 1861, pp. 19, 23.

p. 86: elite: Francis and Theresa Pulszky, *White, Red, Black: Sketches of American Society in the United States* (New York: Redfield, 1853), 111.

p. 86: slave: Bremer, *Homes of the New World*, 223.

p. 86: neighborhood: 1860 Mobile, Ala., federal census, 6th ward, pp. 600–610, and p. 363 for the boardinghouse.

p. 87: foreign companies: Confederate States of America Regimental History Files, Mobile County, ADAH.

p. 87: "very queerly": "Virginia and New England," *New England Offering* (Sept. 1848), 139.

p. 87: population percentages: U.S. Bureau of the Census, *Negro Population, 1790–1915* (Washington, D.C.: Government Printing Office, 1918), 51; *Population of the United States in 1860* (Washington D.C.: Government Printing Office, 1864), 9.

p. 88: "crowded": William Howard Russell, *My Diary North and South* (Boston: Burnham, 1863), 191.

p. 88: 1859 laws: *Code of Ordinances of the City of Mobile*, 1859, secs. 128–29, pp. 119–20.

p. 88: Chastang: 1860 Mobile, Ala., federal census, 6th ward, ca. pp. 600–610.

p. 88: "beloved friend": Will Book 2:22–23, 112, Mobile County Records, Mobile County Courthouse, cited in Virginia Meacham Gould, "The Free Creoles of Color of the Antebellum Gulf Ports of Mobile and Pensacola: A Struggle for the Middle Ground," in *Creoles of Color of the Gulf South*, ed. James H. Dormon (Knoxville: University of Tennessee Press, 1996), 31.

p. 89: "poor blacks": Harriet H. A. Eaton Diaries, Jan. 4, 1854, SHC.

p. 89: "Northern mother": ibid., Feb. 17, 1854.

p. 89: "sailors": Mary R. Congdon Diary, aboard clipper *Caroline Tucker*, April 24, 1860, Congdon Family Papers, RIHS.

p. 89: "many more": Horace Howard Justis Diary, Mobile, Ala., Sept. 26, 1859, DU.

p. 89: "negroes": Sarah Jane Girdler Journal, aboard clipper ship *Robert H. Dixey*, Feb. 15, 1857, no. 656 1857/58R, SPL.

p. 89: "stole out": Harriet H. A. Eaton Diaries, March 12, 1854, SHC.

p. 90: *subject*: ES to CHR, Mobile, Ala., Nov. 18, 1860.

p. 90: gradual emancipation: "New Movement for Freedom," *Christian Freeman and Family Visiter*, Sept. 2, 1853.

p. 90: "Prayer for the Slave": J. G. Adams and E. H. Chapin, *Hymns for Christian Devotion: Especially Adapted to the Universalist Denomination* (Boston: Abel Tompkins, 1856), no. 801.

p. 90: "principles of Universalism": "Slavery," *Christian Freeman and Family Visiter*, June 24, 1853.

p. 90: barbarism: "Slavery Alias Barbarism," ibid., Aug. 9, 1861.

p. 90: "in Massachusetts": "Where Are the Abolitionists?" *Montgomery Universalist Herald*, Feb. 17, 1860.

p. 91: "Atheists": "New-Hampshire Patriot Again," *Trumpet and Universalist Magazine* (Jan. 21, 1832).

p. 91: *any one*: ES to CHR, Mobile, Ala., Nov. 18, 1860.

p. 91: "Eat, drink": Samuel C. Bartlett, *Lectures on Modern Universalism: An Exposure of the System* (Manchester, N.H.: Fisk and Gage, 1856), 30.

p. 91: "Calvinistic hell": "The Practical Tendency of Universalism," *Ladies' Repository* 18 (Feb. 1850), 293.

p. 92: "soul": "Love, the Soul of Religion," *Trumpet and Universalist Magazine* (April 19, 1851).

p. 92: "I Love This World": *Ladies' Repository* 19 (July 1850), 9–10.

p. 92: "prove the doctrine": Hosea Ballou, *A Treatise on Atonement* (Portsmouth, N.H.: Charles Peirce, 1812), iii, 43.

p. 92: "happy": Mary A. Livermore, *The Story of My Life; or The Sunshine and Shadow of Seventy Years* (Hartford, Conn.: A. D. Worthington, 1898), 609, 610.

p. 92: *I have*: ES to CHR, Mobile, Ala., Jan. 6, 1861.

p. 92: Universalism in Manchester and Mobile: "Re-opening of the Church at Manchester," *Trumpet and Universalist Magazine* (Feb. 16, 1850); "The Cause Rising in Mobile," *Trumpet and Universalist Magazine* (July 8, 1843). Numbers in Alabama, Massachusetts, and New Hampshire: *Statistics of the United States in 1860* (Washington, D.C.: Government Printing Office, 1866), 354, 409, 427.

p. 92: "all men": Wade H. Richardson, *How I Reached the Union Lines* (Milwaukee, Wis.: Milwaukee Telegraph, 1905), 8.

p. 93: "I wish": EM to LD, Mobile, Ala., Dec. 9, 1857.

p. 93: "niggers": EM to LD, Mobile, Ala., Jan. 3, 1858.

p. 93: "more of a slave": George Fitzhugh, *Cannibals All! or, Slaves without Masters* (Richmond, Va.: A. Morris, 1857), 30.

p. 93: "owne negro": EM to LD, Mobile, Ala., Dec. 9, 1857.

p. 93: "cling": Pulszky, *White, Red, Black*, 112.

p. 94: *commenced* and *Reading*: ES to AM, Mobile, Ala., Dec. 23, 1860.

p. 94: "We are all": EM to LLR, continuation of DDM to LLR, Mobile, Ala., Jan. 3, 1858, letter.

p. 94: *If I keep*: ES to LD, Mobile, Ala., Dec. 30, 1860.

p. 94: *paying*: ES to CHR, Mobile, Ala., Nov. 18, 1860.

p. 94: *O how*: ES to LD, Mobile, Ala., Dec. 30, 1860.

p. 94: *but William*: ES to AM, Mobile, Ala., Dec. 23, 1860.

p. 94: *Poor folks*: ES to LD, Mobile, Ala., Dec. 30, 1860.

p. 95: "advertise": Frances Anne Kemble, *Journal of a Residence on a Georgian Plantation in 1838–1839* (New York: Harper and Brothers, 1863), 70.

p. 95: "Southerners": J. H. Ingraham, ed., *The Sunny South: or, The Southerner at Home* (Philadelphia: G. G. Evans, 1860), 504.

p. 95: " 'you is turned' ": Frederick Law Olmsted, *The Cotton Kingdom: A Traveller's Observations on Cotton and Slavery in the American Slave States* (1861; reprint, New York: Alfred A. Knopf, 1962), 231.

p. 95: "as a sort" and "almost as degraded": Kemble, *Journal*, 94, 70.

p. 95: "commonest": Olmsted, *Cotton Kingdom*, 98.

p. 95: "should be waited": J. Milton Mackie, *From Cape Cod to Dixie and the Tropics* (New York: G. P. Putnam, 1864), 138.

p. 95: "one of those": "Municipal Court," *Mobile Daily Register*, April 13, 1859.

p. 95: "insolence": Kemble, *Journal*, 70.

p. 96: *How I should*: ES to LD, Mobile, Ala., Dec. 30, 1860.

p. 96: *He dont try*: ES to CHR, Mobile, Ala., Nov. 18, 1860.

p. 96: "John Brown excitement": DDM to LLR, continuation of EM to LLR, Mobile, Ala., Dec. 4, 1859, letter.

p. 96: "Down with": *Mobile Register*, Nov. 30, 1859, quoted in Ralph Brown Draughon, Jr., " 'Sir, This Is Not the End of It': The Mobile *Register* Interviews John Brown," *Alabama Review* 27 (April 1974), 154.

p. 97: *Now henry*: ES to CHR, Mobile, Ala., Nov. 18, 1860.

p. 97: *I suppose*: ES to LD, Mobile, Ala., Jan. 1, 1861.

p. 97: "city was": Kate Cumming, *Gleanings from Southland* (Birmingham, Ala.: Roberts and Son, 1895), 20–21.

p. 98: *How is it*: ES to CHR, Mobile, Ala., Jan. 6, 1861.

p. 98: "our late associates": Jefferson Davis inaugural address, Montgomery, Ala., Feb. 18, 1861, in *The Alabama Confederate Reader*, ed. Malcolm C. McMillan (1963; reprint, Tuscaloosa: University of Alabama Press, 1992), 59, 61.

p. 98: "amalgamation": S. F. Hale to B. Magoffin, Frankfort, Ky., Dec. 27, 1860, in *War of the Rebellion: A Compilation of the Official Records of the Union and Confederate Armies*, ser. 4, vol. 1, pp. 9, 8.

p. 98: *I hardly think*: ES to LD, Mobile, Ala., March 3, 1861.

p. 99: *So Henry*: ES to LD, Mobile, Ala., March 10, 1861, continuation of March 3, 1861, letter.

p. 99: *sick spells*: ES to LD, Mobile, Ala., March 3, 1861.

p. 99: *I was homesick*: ES to LD, Mobile, Ala., March 10, 1861, continuation of March 3, 1861, letter.

p. 99: *And the brave*: ES to LD, Mobile, Ala., April 14, 1861.

p. 100: "The men": CHR to LD, New York, N.Y., April 18, 1861.

p. 100: *at home* and *Times*: ES to AM and DM, Mobile, Ala., April 18, 1861.

p. 100: *poor spells*: ES to LD, Mobile, Ala., April 14, 1861.

p. 100: *not very well*: ES to AM and DM, Mobile, Ala., April 18, 1861.

p. 101: *Put yourselves*: ES to LD, Mobile, Ala., April 14, 1861.

p. 101: *Prehaps*: ES to AM and DM, Mobile, Ala., April 18, 1861.

p. 101: *I am with*: ES to LD, Mobile, Ala., April 29, 1861.

p. 101: "separation": William Proctor Gould Diary, Sept. 1861, p. 16, ADAH.

p. 101: "not one": Russell, *My Diary*, 193.

p. 102: street names: Minutes of the Board of Aldermen, City of Mobile, Jan. 19 and Aug. 8, 1861, MPL.

p. 102: "Party feeling": Samuel Eichold, "Edward Bloch's Memoirs: The Early Years," *Gulf Coast Historical Review* 7 (Fall 1991), 57.

p. 102: "socially ostracized": Richardson, *Union Lines*, 9.

p. 102: arrest: Harriet E. Amos, "Trials of a Unionist: Gustavus Horton, Military Mayor of Mobile during Reconstruction," *Gulf Coast Historical Review* 4 (Spring 1989), 134–51.

p. 102: "An Exile from Alabama": *The New Reign of Terror in the Slaveholding States* (New York: American Anti-Slavery Society, 1860), 42–44.

p. 102: "mob law": "Outrage on a Massachusetts Man," in *A Fresh Catalogue of Southern Outrages upon Northern Citizens* (New York: American Anti-Slavery Society, 1860), 10, 12.

p. 102: "'to shovel Boston'": Livermore, *Story of My Life*, 274.

p. 102: "Secessionists": George Adams Fisher, *The Yankee Conscript; or, Eighteen Months in Dixie* (Philadelphia: J. W. Daughaday, 1864), 68.

p. 103: *foreign land*: ES to LD, Mobile, Ala., May 7, 1861.

p. 103: "Everything": LD to CHR, Dracut, Mass., May 29 [28?], 1861.

p. 103: "There is nothing": LD to CHR, Dracut, Mass., May 12, 1861.

p. 103: "we eate": LD to CHR, Dracut, Mass., June 6, 1861.

p. 103: "there is little": Luther M. Trussell to Delia Page, New London, N.H., Dec. 21, 1860, in Thomas Dublin, ed., *Farm to Factory: Women's Letters, 1830–1860* (New York: Columbia University Press, 1981), 178.

p. 103: "Evry one": LD to CHR, Dracut, Mass., June 17, 1861, continuation of June 16, 1861, letter.

p. 103: "Business dead": LD to CHR, Dracut, Mass., May 29 [30?], 1861.

p. 103: "I suppose": LD to CHR, Dracut, Mass., June 23, 1861.

p. 103: "Ann Eunice": LD to CHR, Dracut, Mass., July 7, 1861.

p. 104: David McCoy: forty-four-year-old farmer, worth over two thousand dollars, with six children; 1860 Manchester, N.H., federal census, p. 524.

p. 104: "You know": LD to CHR, Dracut, Mass., June 23, 1861.

p. 104: "emotion I felt" and "glorious cause": LD to CHR, Dracut, Mass., April 27, 1861.

p. 104: "succede": LD to CHR, Dracut, Mass., May 12, 1861.

p. 105: "I hope": HH and IH to LLR, Bradford, N.H., June 11, 1861.

p. 105: "I know": AM to CHR, Pelham, N.H., June 2, 1861.

p. 105: *small chance*: ES to AM and DM, Mobile, Ala., April 18, 1861.

p. 105: "I prey": LD to CHR, Dracut, Mass., labeled "April 4," actually May 1861.

p. 105: "Now Henry": LD to CHR, Dracut, Mass., June 6, 1861.

p. 105: "give an account": HH to CHR, Bradford, N.H., June 18, 1861.

p. 105: "with a request": LD to CHR, Dracut, Mass., April 27, 1861.

p. 106: "white niggers": John W. Hanson, *Historical Sketch of the Old Sixth Regiment of Massachusetts Volunteers, during Its Three Campaigns* (Boston: Lee and Shepard, 1866), 40, 45.

p. 106: "preserve": "Speech of Mr. D. Wilmot of Pennsylvania," *Congressional Globe*, 29th Cong., 2d sess., Appendix, Feb. 8, 1847, p. 317.

p. 107: "We did not": LD to CHR, Dracut, Mass., April 27, 1861.

p. 107: "Dear and never": LLR to CHR, Tyngsborough, Mass., May [no day], 1861.

p. 107: "It gives": LD to CHR, Dracut, Mass., May 29 [30?], 1861.

p. 107: "You dont know": LD to CHR, Dracut, Mass. May 29 [28?], 1861.

p. 107: "be the last": LD to CHR, Dracut, Mass., June 6, 1861.

p. 107: "I do not": CHR to AM, "Camp near Relay House," June 17, 1861, continuation of June 16, 1861, letter.

p. 107: "ready": CHR to LLR, "Camp near Relay House," May 28, 1861.

p. 107: "calculate" and "fight for": LD to CHR, Dracut, Mass., labeled "April 4," actually May 1861.

p. 108: "It was not": CHR to LD, "Relay House," July 24, 1861.

p. 108: "It makes me": CHR to LLR, "Camp near Relay House," June 8, 1861.

p. 108: "We are used": ibid.

p. 108: "I wish," "It dont appear," and "in extasy": LD to CHR, Dracut, Mass., July 25, 1861.

p. 109: "Can we spare": HH to LD, Bradford, N.H., Oct. 13, 1861.

p. 110: Confederate service: DDM and WCS Compiled Service Records of Confederate Soldiers, Alabama, ADAH and NA; *Brief Historical Sketches of Military Organizations Raised in Alabama during the Civil War* (Montgomery: ADAH, 1966), 627–28.

p. 110: "with his heart": James G. Terry, comp., "Record of the Alabama State Artillery," *Alabama Historical Quarterly* 20 (Summer 1958), 310.

p. 110: "I feel": EM to LD, Mobile, Ala., May [no day], 1861.

p. 111: "forced in": LD to CHR, Dracut, Mass., May 29 [30?], 1861.

p. 111: "help them" and "I regret": LD to CHR, Dracut, Mass., June 6, 1861.

p. 111: "I suppose": HH and IH to LLR, Bradford, N.H., June 11, 1861.

p. 111: "I dont know": HH to CHR, Bradford, N.H., June 18, 1861.

p. 111: "It is sad": IH and HH to LLR, Bradford, N.H., June 11, 1861.

p. 111: "I was sorry": CHR to AM, "Camp near Relay House," June 17, 1861, continuation of June 16, 1861, letter.

p. 112: "folly": Charles Atwood to A. L. Alexander, Boston, Mass., Dec. 5, 1860, Alexander and Hillhouse Family Papers, SHC.

p. 112: "tenderness": Lucy Warren to Fred Warren, Brattleboro, Vt., March 31, 1863, Edward Jenner Warren Papers, SHC.

p. 112: "I don't much": William S. Townsend to parents, Benton's Ferry, Livingston Parish, La., May 29, 1861, William Townsend Family Letters, VHS.

p. 112: "I boast": Sarah Morgan, *Sarah Morgan: The Civil War Diary of a Southern Woman*, ed. Charles East (Athens: University of Georgia Press, 1991), 411.

p. 112: "What a remarkable": Katherine H. Cumming, *A Northern Daughter and a Southern Wife: The Civil War Reminiscences and Letters of Katharine H. Cumming, 1860–1865*, ed. W. Kirk Wood (Augusta, Ga.: Richmond County Historical Society, 1976), 33.

p. 112: "If I should": Harold A. Dwinell, "Vermonter in Gray: The Story of Melvin Dwinell," *Vermont History* 30 (July 1962), 227.

p. 112: "long letter": LD to CHR, Dracut, Mass., May 29 [28?], 1861.

p. 112: "I was an alien": Cumming, *Northern Daughter*, 3, 8.

p. 113: *To be plain*: ES to LD, Mobile, Ala., April 29, 1861.

p. 113: "real secession letter": HH and IH to LLR, Bradford, N.H., June 11, 1861.

p. 113: Merrill property in Mobile: Deed Book 15, July 21, 1860, pp. 270–71; Mortgage Book 7, July 21, 1860, pp. 510–11; Deed Book 16, Nov. 18, 1861, pp. 392–93, all in MCPC.

p. 113: *You will think*: ES to LD, Mobile, Ala., March 3, 1861.

p. 114: "owne negro": EM to LD, Mobile, Ala., Dec. 9, 1857.

p. 114: "Could you" and "We have": Henry M. Ellis to Leander Ellis, Marion, Ark., Jan. 15, 1860, and April 25, 1861, typescript, Henry M. Ellis Letters, VHS.

p. 114: "meshes": William G. Stevenson, *Thirteen Months in the Rebel Army* (1862; reprint, New York: A. S. Barnes, 1959), 33.

p. 114: "forced into": Fisher, *Yankee Conscript*, 3, 54.

p. 115: "whole tenor": W. B. Spoor to Austin Spoor, Fort Delaware, Del., July 19, 1863, Misc. File Add., VHS.

p. 115: *She has*: ES to AM, Mobile, Ala., Dec. 23, 1860.

p. 115: "communication": LD to CHR, Dracut, Mass., May 29 [30?], 1861.

p. 116: suspension of mail: John A. Dix to Richard A. Dana, Jr., Fort Monroe, Va., Oct. 5, 1862, in *Official Records,* ser. 2, vol. 4, p. 599.

p. 116: *I do so much*: ES to LD, Mobile, Ala., April 29, 1861.

p. 116: *absent*: ES to LD, Mobile, Ala., May 7, 1861.

p. 116: "dark suspence": MJ to LD, Northfield, Mass., Dec. 8, 1861.

p. 117: "dreadful": Cumming, *Northern Daughter*, 11.

p. 117: "veary glad": LLR to LD, Ship Island, Miss., Jan. 23, 1862, continuation of Jan. 22, 1862, letter.

Chapter 4. Servant and Washerwoman

p. 121: "enchanting": Journal of Louisa C. Richards, Aug. 17, 1859, Richards Family Papers II, MHS.

p. 121: Stone and Russell families in Claremont: Charles Byron Spofford, *Grave Stone Records: From the Ancient Cemeteries in the Town of Claremont, New Hampshire* (Claremont, N.H.: G. I. Putnam, 1896), 37–38; Records of the First Universalist Church, Claremont, N.H., 1853–57, AHL, including Records of the Sullivan County Association of Universalists and Records of the Ladies' Samaritan Society.

p. 121: map: 1860 map of Sullivan County, NHDRMA.

p. 121: Albert Russell: Otis F. R. Waite, *Claremont War History: April, 1861, to April, 1865* (Concord, N.H.: McFarland and Jenks, 1868), 256.

p. 122: *the offer*: ES to LD, Claremont, N.H., Dec. 29, 1861.

p. 122: *Margarett says*: ibid.

p. 122: "so thankfull": MS to LD, Claremont, N.H., Feb. 25, 1862.

p. 122: *a rest*: ES to LD, Claremont, N.H., Dec. 29, 1861.

p. 122: *If it was*: ibid.

p. 123: *cried*: ES to LD, Claremont, N.H., March 6, 1862.

p. 123: "Eunis says": MS to LD, Claremont, N.H., Feb. 25, 1862.

p. 123: *I believe*: ES to LD, Claremont, N.H., March 20, 1862, continuation of March 19, 1862, letter.

p. 123: *every day*: ES to LD, Claremont, N.H., Dec. 21, 1862.

p. 123: *How many times*: ES to CHR and LLR, Claremont, N.H., Dec. 7, 1862.

p. 123: *So many times*: ibid.

p. 124: *little Secesh*: ES to AM and DM, Claremont, N.H., March 13, 1862.

p. 124: "one vital question": quoted in Otis F. R. Waite, *History of the Town of Claremont, New Hampshire for a Period of One Hundred and Thirty Years from 1764 to 1894* (Manchester, N.H.: John B. Clarke, 1895), 250.

p. 124: lecture: "Slavery," *Claremont Northern Advocate*, April 16, 1861.

p. 124: "interests": "The Shame of the Nation," *Claremont National Eagle*, June 5, 1862.

p. 124: "harsh sound": Lemuel Hitchcock to John Hitchcock, Claremont, N.H., Sept. 15, 1856, Hitchcock Family Papers, MHS.

p. 124: "unreasoning hatred": "The Shame of the Nation," *Claremont National Eagle*, June 5, 1862.

p. 124: "dirty": *Dover Gazette*, March 2, 1861, quoted in Lex Renda, *Running on the Record: Civil War–Era Politics in New Hampshire* (Charlottesville: University Press of Virginia, 1997), 98.

p. 125: *I do hope*: ES to LD, Claremont, N.H., Feb. 9, 1862.

p. 125: "I do hope": MS to LD, Claremont, N.H., Feb. 25, 1862.

p. 125: *many misgivings*: ES to LD, Claremont, N.H., Feb. 9, 1862.

p. 125: *I feel*: ES to CHR and LLR, Claremont, N.H., Dec. 7, 1862.

p. 125: "Tell Eunice": CHR to LD, Ship Island, Miss., Feb. 21, 1862, continuation of Feb. 20, 1862, letter.

p. 125: "I have enquired": CHR to ES, New Orleans, La., Sept. 16, 1862.

p. 125: "I did not": LLR to [ES?], n.p., April 21, [1863?].

p. 125: *I want*: ES to CHR and LLR, Claremont, N.H., Dec. 7, 1862.

p. 126: *such a depth*: ES to LD, Claremont, N.H., April 6, 1862.

p. 126: *Write to me*: ES to LD, Claremont, N.H., Feb. 9, 1862 .

p. 126: *spirits up*: ES to AM and DM, Claremont, N.H., March 13, 1862.

p. 126: *I do not*: ES to LD, Claremont, N.H., April 27, 1862.

p. 126: *I have thought*: ES to LD, Claremont, N.H., Dec. 29, 1861.

p. 126: *"if it want"*: ES to LD, Claremont, N.H., April 6, 1862.

p. 126: *dreadful hard* and *I do try*: ES to AM and DM, Claremont, N.H., March 13, 1862.

p. 127: *how unlike*: ES to LD, Claremont, N.H., Nov. 23, 1862.

p. 127: *there were* and *and myself*: ES to LD, Claremont, N.H., Nov. 30, 1862.

p. 127: *deepest gloom*: ES to LD, Claremont, N.H., April 6, 1862.

p. 127: *being fought*: ES to LD, Claremont, N.H., April 27, 1862.

p. 127: *most people*: ES to LD, Claremont, N.H., March 8, 1863.

p. 127: *good victory*: ES to LD, Claremont, N.H., May 22, 1863.

p. 128: *jogging*: ES to AM, Claremont, N.H., April 19, 1863.

p. 128: *I have*: CS and ES to LD, Claremont, N.H., Jan. 7, 1863.

p. 128: "after working": LD to LLR and CHR, Dracut, Mass., Feb. 1, 1863.

p. 128: Alonzo Russell: forty-eight-year-old cooper, 1860 Claremont, N.H., federal census, p. 1265.

p. 129: *I take*: CS and ES to CHR, Claremont, N.H., March 22, 1863.

p. 129: *Clara was*: ES to LD, Claremont, N.H., Feb. 8, 1863.

p. 129: *I wish*: ES to CHR and LLR, Claremont, N.H., Dec. 7, 1862.

p. 129: *look out*: ES to LD, Claremont, N.H., April 27, 1862.

p. 130: "that is more": CS to LD, Claremont, N.H., Feb. 1, 1863.

p. 130: *but when*: ES to LD Claremont, N.H., April 30, 1863.

p. 130: *Do you suppose*: ES to LD, Claremont, N.H., Jan. 25, 1863.

p. 130: *nothing*: ES to LD, Claremont, N.H., March 20, 1862, continuation of March 19, 1862, letter.

p. 131: *borrow*: ES to LD, Claremont, N.H., March 8, 1863.

p. 131: *any thing*: ES to LD, Claremont, N.H., March 29, 1863.

p. 131: *be spared*: ES to LD, Claremont, N.H., April 6, 1862.

p. 131: "Sister Eunice": MS to LD, continuation of CS to LD, Claremont, N.H., May 3, 1863, letter.

p. 131: *did not say*: ES to LD, Claremont, N.H., April 30, 1863.

p. 131: *Why what a lot*: ES to LD, Claremont, N.H., June 7, 1863.

p. 131: *I am keeping house, came in here*, and *found a bundle*: ES to LD, Claremont, N.H., July 12, 1863.

p. 132: *I think* and *make friends*: ES to LD, Claremont, N.H., Sept. 6, 1863.

p. 132: *I thought*: ES to LD, Claremont, N.H., Sept. 17, 1863.

p. 133: *even to* and *and it rained*: ES to LD, Claremont, N.H., Nov. 8, 1863.

p. 134: *a tin*: ES to LD, Claremont, N.H., May 26, 1864.

p. 134: *a bowl*: CS and ES to LD, Claremont, N.H., May 29, 1864.

p. 134: *You gave*: ES to LD, Claremont, N.H., June 12, 1864.

p. 134: James Sperry: seventy-one-year-old farmer, worth over three thousand dollars: 1860 Claremont, N.H., federal census, p. 1265.

p. 134: *better than*: ES to LD, Claremont, N.H., April 6, 1862.

p. 135: *which makes*: ES to AM, Claremont, N.H., April 19, 1863.

p. 135: *three days*: ES to LD, Claremont, N.H., April 30, 1863.

p. 135: dressmaking: HH to LLR, Manchester, N.H., June 19, 1857, continuation of June 14, 1857, letter.

p. 135: "I think": Mattie M. Harvey to CHR, West Salisbury, Vt., Feb. 18, 1866.

p. 135: *If I could*: ES to LD, Claremont, N.H., March 20, 1862, continuation of March 19, 1862, letter.

p. 137: "select" and "make suds": Catharine E. Beecher, *A Treatise on Domestic Economy, for the Use of Young Ladies at Home* (Boston: Marsh, Capen, 1841), 312, 311.

p. 137: "fewer and fewer": "Our Yankee Girls," *New York Tribune*, Dec. 26, 1846.

p. 137: "menial service": Charles Mackay, *Life and Liberty in America; or, Sketches of a Tour in the United States and Canada, in 1857–8* (London: Smith, Elder, 1859), 1:42.

p. 137: "universal rejection" and "preferred the factory": Catharine E. Beecher and Harriet Beecher Stowe, *The American Woman's Home or, Principles of Domestic Science* (1869; reprint, Hartford, Conn.: Stowe-Day Foundation, 1987), 319, 320, 322.

p. 137: "not in the South": "Domestic Servants," *North American and United States Gazette*, May 23, 1857.

p. 137: "leaving": Louisa M. Alcott, "How I Went Out to Service," *New York Independent*, June 4, 1874.

p. 139: Claremont population: The city counted seventeen people of color out of four thousand in 1860; *Population of the United States in 1860* (Washington, D.C.: Government Printing Office, 1864), 309. In the 1860 Claremont, N.H., federal census, the very few women of color were either servants or had no occupation. Twelve native-born women were servants, compared with eleven Irishwomen. That meant that a much larger percentage of native-born women worked as servants than did Irish immigrant women.

p. 139: "Our native born": "The Irish in America," *Concord Independent Democrat*, Dec. 28, 1854.

p. 139: *grand time*: ES to LD, Claremont, N.H. [Jan. 1863?].

p. 139: *every way*: ES to LD, Claremont, N.H., Aug. 25, 1864.

p. 139: *getting old enough* and *It grieves*: ES to AM and DM, Claremont, N.H., March 13, 1862.

p. 140: *anxious*: ES to LD, Claremont, N.H., March 20, 1862, continuation of March 19, 1862, letter.

p. 140: *It helps*: ES to LD, Claremont, N.H., Feb. 8, 1863.

p. 140: *three times*: ES to LD, Claremont, N.H., Nov. 8, 1863.

p. 141: *You have come*: ibid.

p. 141: *I dont know*: ibid.

p. 141: *We had*: ES to LD, Claremont, N.H., June 7, 1863.

p. 141: *such a beautiful*: ES to LD, Claremont, N.H., Nov. 27, 1864.

p. 141: "If solid happiness" and "bid the human": J. G. Adams and E. H. Chapin, *Hymns for Christian Devotion: Especially Adapted to the Universalist Denomination* (Boston: Abel Tompkins, 1856), no. 625, no. 875.

p. 142: "remember the poor": "Remember the Poor," *Ladies' Repository* 26 (Feb. 1858), 289–90.

p. 144: *I said*: ES to LD, Claremont, N.H., June 12, 1864.

p. 144: *PRIVATE*: ES to LD, Claremont, N.H., labeled "Autumn 1862?" but likely 1863.

p. 144: "She wore": LD to LLR and CHR, Dracut, Mass., Feb. 1, 1863.

p. 144: Mrs. Murry: ES to AM and DM, Claremont, N.H., July 3, 1864.

p. 144: *which has done*: ES to LD, Claremont, N.H., Feb. 9, 1862.

p. 144: "and has come out": HH to CHR and LLR, East Washington, N.H., April 29, 1864.

p. 145: *I am afraid*: ES to LD, Claremont, N.H., Oct. 9, 1864.

p. 145: *rich widows son*: ES to LD, Claremont, N.H. [Jan. 1863?].

p. 145: WCS: Alabama Confederate Service Cards, Compiled Service Records of Confederate Soldiers, ADAH and NA. Jack D Welsh, *Two Confederate Hospitals and Their Patients: Atlanta to Opelika* (Macon, Ga.: Mercer University Press, 2005), Appendix C, Hospital Patients: Fairgrounds Hospital No. 1, on accompanying CD-ROM.

p. 145: *Well tomorrow*: ES to LD, Claremont, N.H., March 8, 1863.

p. 145: *When Mobile*: ES to CHR and LLR, Claremont, N.H., March 22, 1863.

p. 146: *many misgivings*: ES to LD, Claremont, N.H., Feb. 9, 1862.

p. 146: *say any thing*: ES to LLR, Claremont, N.H., May 5, 1863.

p. 146: *It seems*: ES to LD, Claremont, N.H., Aug. 2, 1863.

p. 146: *It is a pretty day* and *I know a little*: ES to LD, Claremont, N.H., Sept. 6, 1863.

p. 146: *I do not, Prehaps if I had*, and *I could not*: ES to AM and DM, Claremont, N.H., Jan. 3, 1864.

p. 147: *Last week*: ES to LD, Claremont, N.H., Feb. 7, 1864.

p. 147: *Do you* and *I dont know*: ES to LD, Claremont, N.H., March 29, 1864.

p. 147: *I thought* and *I think*: ES to LD, Claremont, N.H., Feb. 7, 1864.

p. 147: "I dont think": CS to LD, Claremont, N.H., March 2, 1864.

p. 148: *I had a call* and *I have thought*: ES to LD, Claremont, N.H., May 26, 1864.

p. 148: *I want*: CS and ES to LD, Claremont, N.H., May 29, 1864.

p. 148: *if there is*: ibid.

p. 148: *saleswoman*: ES to LD, Claremont, N.H., June 1, 1864.

p. 148: *There seems*: ES to LD, Claremont, N.H., June 24, 1864.

p. 148: *It is too hard*: ES to LD, Claremont, N.H., June 12, 1864.

p. 149: *Just as I* and *it aint as if*: ES to LD, Claremont, N.H. Sept. 4, 1864.

p. 149: *Some folks*: CS and ES to LD, Claremont, N.H., May 29, 1864.

p. 149: "duties": Beecher and Stowe, *American Woman's Home*, 327.

p. 150: *You will say*: CS and ES to LD, Claremont, N.H., May 29, 1864.

p. 150: *I believe* and *I dont seem*: ES to LD, Claremont, N.H., May 26, 1864.

p. 150: *I dont believe, low spirited*, and *giving way*: ES to LD, Claremont, N.H., June 1, 1864.

p. 150: *rather nervous*: ES to LD, Claremont, N.H., March 29, 1864.

p. 150: *You will say*: ES to LD, Claremont, N.H., June 24, 1864.

p. 150: *I want* and *Was my last*: ES to LD, Claremont, N.H., June 12, 1864.

p. 150: *I wondered*: ES to LD, Claremont, N.H., Aug. 18, 1864.

p. 150: *What do you suppose*: ES to LD, Claremont, N.H., Aug. 25, 1864.

p. 150: *I know times*: ES to LD, Claremont, N.H., June 24, 1864.

p. 151: *he has got*: ES to AM and DM, Claremont, N.H., July 3, 1864.

p. 151: *if they live*: ES to LD, Claremont, N.H., July 11, 1864.

p. 151: *and yet I dread*: ES to LD, Claremont, N.H., Aug. 18, 1864.

p. 151: *I dont know yet*: ES to LD, Claremont, N.H., July 11, 1864.

p. 151: *with dread* and *We get*: ES to LD, Claremont, N.H., Aug. 18, 1864.

p. 151: *rainy*: ES to LD, Claremont, N.H. Sept. 4, 1864.

p. 151: *sence of lonliness*: ES to LD, Claremont, N.H., July 11, 1864.

p. 151: *so lonesome*: ES to LD, Claremont, N.H., Aug. 18, 1864.

p. 152: "tremendous": Homer B. Sprague, *Lights and Shadows in Confederate Prisons: A Personal Experience, 1864–5* (New York: G. P. Putnam's Sons, 1915), 13.

p. 152: "along every roadway": Frank M. Flinn, *Campaigning with Banks in Louisiana, '63 and '64, and with Sheridan in the Shenandoah Valley in '64 and '65* (Boston: W. B. Clarke, 1889), 189.

p. 152: "day of glory": Sprague, *Lights and Shadows*, 3.

p. 152: LLR death: "To the Heirs of Luther Richardson" from War Claim Agency, Boston, Mass., Oct. 1, 1864, in folder labeled "Legal and Financial Papers," LWRD.

p. 152: *first intimation* and *I looked*: ES to LD, Claremont, N.H., Oct. 6, 1864

p. 153: "O what a blow": LD to CHR, Dracut, Mass., Oct. 2, 1864.

p. 153: "It said": AD to LD and BD, Northfield, Mass., Oct. 3, 1864.

p. 153: "My Dear Mother": CHR to LD, Winchester, Va., Sept. 21, 1864.

p. 153: "stiff and cold" and "for it seems": CHR to LD, Nicetown, Pa., Sept. [28?], 1864.

p. 153: "as brave": ibid.

p. 153: "Bear this gently": Thomas Manahan and Geo. A. Russell, "Bear This Gently to My Mother" (New York: Horace Waters, 1864), Historic American Sheet Music Collection, DU.

p. 154: "your only": CHR to LD, Winchester, Va., Sept. 21, 1864.

p. 154: "from your": LD to CHR, Dracut, Mass., Oct. 2, 1864.

p. 154: "controled": HH to CHR, East Washington, N.H., Oct. 6, 1864.

p. 154: *I learned*: ES to LD, Claremont, N.H., Oct. 6, 1864.

p. 154: *Mr Goss*: ES to LD, Claremont, N.H., Oct. 9, 1864.

p. 154: "took no more": Louisa M. Alcott, *Work: A Story of Experience* (Boston: Roberts Brothers, 1873), 25.

p. 154: *know what, I so much*, and *feel that God*: ES to LD, Claremont, N.H., Oct. 9, 1864.

p. 154: "God does not": "A Word about Prayer," *Christian Freeman and Family Visiter*, Aug. 17, 1860.

p. 155: "evening's quiet hour": "Prayer," *Ladies' Repository* 32 (Aug. 1863), 95.

p. 155: *Mother I am, If William*, and *I nearly*: ES to LD, Claremont, N.H., Oct. 9, 1864.

p. 155: "I am stronger": HH to LD, East Washington, N.H., Oct. 19, 1864.

p. 155: "thousands": LD to CHR, Dracut, Mass., Oct. 17, 1864.

p. 155: *We have*: ES to LD, Claremont, N.H., Oct. 20, 1864.

p. 155: "Ann feels": LD to CHR, Dracut, Mass., Oct. 2, 1864.

p. 156: "You must": CHR to LD, New Orleans, La., Feb. 7, 1863, continuation of Feb. 16, 1863, letter.

p. 156: "Take good care": CHR and LLR to LD, Quarantine Station, Mississippi River, June 24, 1862.

p. 156: *You are all*: ES to LD, Claremont, N.H., Nov. 18, 1864.

p. 156: *It is after* and *Prehaps I shall*: ES to LD, Claremont, N.H., Dec. 3, 1864.

p. 157: "Densely packed" and "We knew": G. G. Benedict, *Vermont in the Civil War: A History* (Burlington, Vt.: Free Press, 1888), 2:267, 264.

p. 157: MORNING COMETH: Frederick W. Coburn, *History of Lowell and Its People* (New York: Lewis Historical Pub. Co., 1920), 1:337.

p. 157: bunting and "Such unreserved sorrow": Martha Fisher Anderson Diaries, April 19, 16, 1865, MHS.

p. 157: "It is with": Margaret Russell to ES, Claremont, N.H., April 19, 1865.

p. 158: "I feel": Mary Russell to ES, Claremont, N.H., April 16, 1865.

p. 159: "I would not stay": "The Broken-Hearted," *Rose of Sharon: A Religious Souvenir* 1 (1840), 225.

p. 159: *I believe*: ES to CHR, Dracut, Mass., July 23, 1865.

Chapter 5. From Widow to Bride

p. 162: LD residence: *Lowell City Directory*, 1866, p. 84.

p. 164: "Mother": AM to LD, Pelham, N.H. [early May 1865?]

p. 164: "It was not": LD to CHR, Dracut, Mass., May 15, 1865.

p. 164: "attacks": LD to CHR, Dracut, Mass., May 15, 1865.

p. 164: "said she felt": LD to Margaret or Mary Russell, Dracut, Mass., May 3, 1865.

p. 165: "universal weakness": LD to CHR, Dracut, Mass., June 5, 1865.

p. 165: "vitality": LD to CHR, Dracut, Mass., June 1, 1865.

p. 165: "southern malaria": LD to CHR, Dracut, Mass., June 21, 1865.

p. 165: *played out*: ES to LD, Claremont, N.H., May 26, 1864.

p. 165: *low spirited*: ES to LD, Claremont, N.H., June 1, 1864.

p. 165: *rather nervous*: ES to LD, Claremont, N.H., March 29, 1864.

p. 165: "Wasnt it sad": AM to CHR, Pelham, N.H., June 11, 1865.

p. 165: "she would probably": LD to CHR, Dracut, Mass., June 5, 1865.

p. 165: "scarcely": LD to CHR, Dracut, Mass., June 21, 1865.

p. 165: "one step": LD to CHR, Dracut, Mass., June 5, 1865.

p. 165: "suffer": CHR to LD, Philadelphia, Pa., Nov. 19, 1864.

p. 165: *Who ever*: ES to LD, Claremont, N.H., March 8, 1863.

p. 165: "Poor thing": LD to CHR, Dracut, Mass., June 11, 1865, continuation of June 5, 1865, letter.

p. 166: "Dear Mother": CHR to LD, Savannah, Ga., Aug. 10, 1865.

p. 166: "Poor Sister": CHR to LD, near Washington D.C., May 7, 1865.

p. 166: *Here I come*: ES to CHR, Dracut, Mass., July 23, 1865.

p. 166: *I believe*: ibid.

p. 167: "if done:" Louisa M. Alcott, "How I Went Out to Service," *New York Independent*, June 4, 1874.

p. 167: "continual reception": Frederick W. Coburn, *History of Lowell and Its People* (New York: Lewis Historical Pub. Co., 1920), 1:327.

p. 167: "take one step": LD to CHR, Dracut, Mass., Aug. 3, 1865.

p. 167: CHR as 2nd lieutenant: "Oath of Office," CHR [no day], 1865, personal papers of James T. Cushman.

p. 168: "better for": (Turnwold, Ga.) *Countryman*, Feb. 7, 1865, cited in Drew Gilpin Faust, *The Creation of Confederate Nationalism: Ideology and Identity in the Civil War South* (Baton Rouge: Louisiana State University Press, 1988), 72.

p. 168: "I want": Katherine H. Cumming, *A Northern Daughter and a Southern Wife: The Civil War Reminiscences and Letters of Katharine H. Cumming, 1860–1865*, ed. W. Kirk Wood (Augusta, Ga.: Richmond County Historical Society, 1976), 58.

p. 168: "I am glad": Georgeanna B. Ray to Mrs. Henry Richmond Slack, Manchester, N.H., June 14, 1866, Slack Family Papers, SHC.

p. 168: "she has been": Margaret Russell to ES, Claremont, N.H., April 19, 1865.

p. 168: "Poor sister": AM to LD, Pelham, N.H. [early May 1865?].

p. 168: *I hope*: ES to CHR, part of LD to CHR, Dracut, Mass., Aug. 3, 1865.

p. 168: "faithfully support": DDM loyalty oath, Commissioner's Office, USA, Middle District of Alabama, Selma, Ala., Sept. 20, 1865, in folder labeled "Legal and Financial Papers," LWRD.

p. 169: "almost starving": CHR to LD, Lake End, La., Nov. 3, 1862, continuation of Oct. 31, 1862, letter.

p. 169: "armed": Frank Moore, ed., *The Rebellion Record: A Diary of American Events* (New York: D. Van Nostrand, 1864), 7:48.

p. 169: "laid waste": Kate Cumming, *Kate: The Journal of a Confederate Nurse*, ed. Richard Barksdale Harwell (Baton Rouge: Louisiana State University Press, 1959), 249.

p. 169: "sidewalk": Kate Cumming, *Gleanings from Southland* (Birmingham, Ala.: Roberts and Son, 1895), 259.

p. 169: *black girl*: ES to LD, Mobile, Ala., March 3, 1861.

p. 169: "negro could not": Cumming, *Gleanings from Southland*, 257.

p. 170: "strongest wish": Augusta J. Evans to Mrs. J. H. Chrisman, Mobile, Ala., Feb. 3, 1866, Augusta Evans Wilson Letters, ADAH.

p. 170: Merrill residence: *Manchester City Directory*, 1866, p. 100.

p. 170: *How strange*: ES to AM, Cabot, Vt., Dec. 24, 1866.

p. 170: *I am afraid*: ES to LD, Morristown, Vt., April 11, 1866.

p. 171: "You say Davis": CHR to LD, Winchester, Va., Feb. 17, 1865.

p. 171: "tenfold": LR to JL and WL, Manchester, N.H., July [1851?].

p. 171: LD a widow: *Lowell City Directory*, 1866, p. 84.

p. 171: CHR occupation and residence: ibid., p. 215.

p. 171: Rankins: 1870 Morristown, Vt., federal census, p. 148; land records in the Town Clerk's Office, Morristown, Vt., ca. 1825–75, record many transactions of Moses Rankin, including purchase of a blacksmith shop in 1865 (Book 14, p. 206).

p. 171: *little out of the way*: ES to LD, Morristown, Vt., April 11, 1866.

p. 171: "charming": William H. Jeffrey, *Successful Vermonters: A Modern Gazetteer of Lamoille, Franklin and Grand Isle Counties* (East Burke, Vt.: Historical Pub. Co., 1907), 45.

p. 172: *life of joy*: ES to LD, Dracut, Mass., July 23, 1865.

p. 172: "I do hope": MR to LD, Morristown, Vt., Feb. 25, 1866.

p. 172: *very kind*: ES to LD and CHR, Morristown, Vt., March 8, 1866.

p. 173: *If I feel*: ES to LD, Morristown, Vt., April 11, 1866.

p. 173: *Melissa and I* and *It rather seems*: ES to LD, Morristown, Vt., April 11, 1866.

p. 173: *Ladies* and *Tomorrow*: ES to LD and CHR, Morristown, Vt., March 8, 1866.

p. 174: *I was at, another cousin*, and *Poor folks*: ES to AM, Cabot, Vt., Dec. 24, 1866.

p. 174: Azariah Stone: sixty-seven-year-old farmer worth forty-three hundred dollars, 1860 Cabot, Vt., federal census, p. 11.

p. 175: *From the time*: EC to LD, East End, Grand Cayman, March 7, 1870.

p. 175: *You think*: ES to AM, Cabot, Vt., Dec. 24, 1866.

p. 175: CHR's marriage: CHR and Clara A. Pray, Massachusetts Vital Records, Marriages, Lowell, Jan. 3, 1867, vol. 200, p. 211, MSA.

p. 175: John J. Pray: 1855 Massachusetts state census, Dracut, 1st sec., household no. 116; and Tom Pray to author, e-mail message, Nov. 17, 2004.

p. 175: *I wrote*: ES to LD and CHR, Morristown, Vt., March 8, 1866.

p. 175: *You think*: ES to AM, Cabot, Vt., Dec. 24, 1866.

p. 176: "trading ships": Alma Catherine Foster (b. 1909), interview no. 1, by Heather McLaughlin, Cayman Brac, Cayman Islands, Feb. 25, 1992, p. 11, Memory Bank, CINA.

p. 177: minister: WSC and ES, Massachusetts Vital Records, Marriages, Dracut, Nov. 3, 1869, vol. 218, p. 166, MSA.

p. 177: *When I was trying*: EC to LD, East End, Grand Cayman, March 7, 1870.

p. 178: *feeling blue, I have so many*, and *I have heard*: ES to AM, Cabot, Vt., Dec. 24, 1866.

p. 178: *Miss Clara*: ES to LD, Claremont, N.H., Aug. 18, 1864.

p. 178: *Well Henry*: ES to LD, part of LD to CHR, Dracut, Mass., Aug. 3, 1865.

p. 179: *It is a Stone*: ES to AM and DM, Claremont, N.H., March 13, 1862.

p. 179: *She has just*: ES to CHR and LLR, Claremont, N.H., Dec. 7, 1862.

p. 179: *little Secesh*: ES to AM and DM, Claremont, N.H., March 13, 1862.

p. 179: *loves her Father*: EC to LD, East End, Grand Cayman, March 7, 1870.

p. 179: *firm*: EC to LD, East End, Grand Cayman, March 7, 1870.

p. 179: "more beautiful": WSC to LD, Provincetown, Mass., Nov. 13, 1869.

p. 179: "my dear": WSC to LD, East End, Grand Cayman [1870?].

p. 180: "Dear Father": CS to WSC, Claremont, N.H., Sept. 27, 1869.

p. 180: "Dear Mother Davis": WSC to LD, Boston, Mass., Oct. 6, 1869.

p. 180: "How do the folks": CS to WSC, Claremont, N.H., Sept. 27, 1869.

p. 180: marriage law: *Acts and Resolves Passed by the Legislature of Massachusetts* (Boston, 1843), 4.

p. 181: "blue-eyed," "Every parent," "nothing unnatural," "feeble barrier": *Liberator*, March 15, 1839, Feb. 25, 1842, May 7, 1831, April 30, 1831.

p. 181: "with the strongest": William Lloyd Garrison to Jacob Horton, Boston, Mass., March 17, 1865, in *The Letters of William Lloyd Garrison*, vol. 5, *Let the Oppressed Go Free, 1861–1867*, ed. Walter M. Merrill (Cambridge, Mass.: Harvard University Press, 1979), 262–63.

p. 182: "rights of man": Daniel Clark, *Suffrage of Loyal Black Men, Both a Duty and Necessity* (Washington, D.C.: H. Polkinhorn, 1866), 4, 8.

p. 182: "white Irishwoman": David Goodman Croly, *Miscegenation: The Theory of the Blending of the Races, Applied to the American White Man and Negro* (New York: H. Dexter Hamilton, 1864), 30.

p. 183: "without exception": "Queries Respecting the Slavery and Emancipation of Negroes in Massachusetts," *Collections of the Massachusetts Historical Society*, 1st ser., vol. 4 (Boston: Samuel Hall, 1795), 209.

p. 183: "none but those": Lydia Maria Child, *An Appeal in Favor of That Class of Americans Called Africans* (New York: John S. Taylor, 1836), 196.

p. 183: "revolting": *Crandall v. Connecticut*, 10 Conn. 339 (1834), 346.

p. 183: "one-fourth" and "rendering": William G. Allen, *The American Prejudice against Color: An Authentic Narrative* (London: W. and F. G. Cash, 1853), 3, 7.

p. 183: "descended": Harriet E. Wilson, *Our Nig; or, Sketches from the Life of a Free Black* (1859; reprint, New York: Random House, 1983), 13, 15.

p. 184: *We all unite*: ES to AM, Mobile, Ala., Dec. 23, 1860.

p. 184: "I am happy": WSC to LD, Boston, Mass., Oct. 6, 1869.

p. 184: *We both*: EC to LD, East End, Grand Cayman, March 7, 1870.

p. 184: *Mr Connolly says*: EC to LD, East End, Grand Cayman [1869 or 1870?].

p. 184: "Please remember" and "David often": AM to EC, Dracut, Mass., Feb. 20, 1870, continuation of Feb. 16, 1870, letter.

p. 186: "After all": *The Life and Adventures of John Levy*, ed. Rachel Frances Levy (Lawrence, Mass.: Robert Bower, 1871), 73.

p. 186: "You cannot". *Alexander Burton v. John C. Scherpf*, 83 Mass. 133 (1861), 133.

p. 186: "I have met": Charlotte Forten, *The Journals of Charlotte Forten Grimké*, ed. Brenda Stevenson (New York: Oxford University Press, 1988), 140.

p. 186: *Who is it?*: ES to AM, Mobile, Ala., Dec. 23, 1860.

p. 186: *Have you seen*: ES to CHR, Mobile, Ala., Jan. 6, 1861.

p. 186: "I am so glad": AM to CHR, Pelham, N.H., June 2, 1861.

p. 187: *never should*: EC to LD, Provincetown, Mass., Nov. 11, 1869.

p. 187: "color of groom and bride": WSC and ES, Massachusetts Vital Records, Marriages, Dracut, Nov. 3, 1869, vol. 218, p. 166, MSA.

p. 187: "dark": CHR Oath of Identity, Certificate of Discharge, 26th Massachusetts Battalion, Aug. 26, 1865, personal papers of James T. Cushman; CHR pension file, no. C-2498-336, NA.

p. 187: *very white*: ES to CHR and LLR, Claremont, N.H., Dec. 7, 1862.

p. 188: *skin neither*: ES to LD, Mobile, Ala., March 3, 1861.

p. 188: "fair and white": EM to LD, Manchester, N.H., Jan. 30. 1857.

p. 188: *I would not*: EC to LD, East End, Grand Cayman, March 7, 1870.

p. 189: "should be": Allen, *American Prejudice*, 7.

p. 189: "if you should": Frank J. Webb, *The Garies and Their Friends* (1857; reprint, Baltimore: Johns Hopkins University Press, 1997), 44.

p. 189: *He still* and *You made*: EC to LD, East End, Grand Cayman, March 7, 1870.

p. 190: *Tell me*: ES to LD, continuation of WSC to LD, Provincetown, Mass., Nov. 13, 1869, letter.

p. 190: *all inquiring*: EC to LD, East End, Grand Cayman [1869 or 1870?].

p. 190: *all who feel* and *And as for*: EC to LD, East End, Grand Cayman, March 7, 1870.

p. 190: Blood family: *Lowell City Directory*, 1864–65, p. 19; *Lowell City Directory*, 1866, p. 45; A. C. Varnum, *History of Pawtucket Church and Society* (Lowell, Mass.: Morning Mail, 1888), 101.

p. 190: *I knew* and *in his own home*: EC to LD, East End, Grand Cayman, March 7, 1870.

p. 190: "seemed to think": CHR to LD, New Orleans, La., Aug. 19, 1862.

p. 191: "white niggers": John W. Hanson, *Historical Sketch of the Old Sixth Regiment of Massachusetts Volunteers, during Its Three Campaigns* (Boston: Lee and Shepard, 1866), 40, 45.

p. 191: "Nigger": LLR to LD, Quarantine Station, Mississippi River, June 19, 1862.

p. 191: "shockingly" and reclaiming: Homer B. Sprague, *History of the 13th Infantry Regiment of Connecticut Volunteers during the Great Rebellion* (Hartford: Case, Lockwood, 1867), 63–65.

p. 192: "fought": CHR to LD, New Orleans, La., May 27, 1863.

p. 192: "enormous crime" and "not willing": William Augustus Walker, New Bern, N.C., July 11, 1862; George M. Turner to "aunt Susan," Jacksonville, Fla., May 2, 1864, both quoted in Nina Silber and Mary Beth Sievens, eds., *Yankee Correspondence: Civil War Letters between New England Soldiers and the Home Front* (Charlottesville: University Press of Virginia, 1996), 62, 61, 87.

p. 192: "I can fight" and "Better such": Henry T. Johns, *Life with the Forty-ninth Massachusetts Volunteers* (Washington, D.C.: Ramsey and Bisbee, 1890), 171, 386.

p. 192: "the more": LLR to LD, New Orleans, La., Aug. 26, 1863.

p. 192: "hailed": LD to CHR, Dracut, Mass., Jan 3, 1863.

p. 193: "I think": CHR to LD, Lake End, La., Nov. 13, 1862.

p. 193: "darkies": CHR to LD, Winchester, Va., April 8, 1865.

p. 193: "They have": CHR to LD, Lake End, La., Oct. 14, 1862.

p. 193: "The Line officers": CHR to LD, New Orleans, La., Jan. 23, 1863.

p. 193: "to the bitter": CHR to LD, Summit Point, Va., Sept. 2, 1864.

p. 194: "lewd": "Lewd and Abandoned Women," *New Orleans Daily Picayune*, May 9, 1862.

p. 194: "There is barely": LLR to LD, New Orleans, La., Aug. 21, 1863.

p. 194: "it wors": LLR to LD, Baton Rouge, La., Sept. 1, 1863.

p. 194: "an intermate": LLR to LD, Algiers, La., Sept. 14, 1863, continuation of Sept. 13, 1863, letter.

p. 194: "a good": LLR to LD, near Berwick City, La., Sept. 18, 1863.

p. 194: Emily Hall and "You say": LLR to LD, near Berwick Bay, La., Sept. 20, 1863.

p. 194: "as full": LLR to LD, Baton Rouge, La., Sept. 1, 1863.

p. 195: "nigger": CHR to LD and ES, Savannah, Ga., July 5, 1865, continuation of June 29, 1865, letter.

p. 196: *This letter*: EC to LD, East End, Grand Cayman, March 7, 1870.

p. 196: *Henry never*: EC to LD, East End, Grand Cayman, Jan. 5, 1873, continuation of Jan. 2, 1873, letter.

p. 196: *For Brother*: EC to LD, East End, Grand Cayman, March 29, 1875.

p. 196: "When ever": Luther M. Trussell to Delia Page, New London, N.H., Aug. 31, 1860, in Thomas Dublin, ed., *Farm to Factory: Women's Letters, 1830–1860* (New York: Columbia University Press, 1981), 168.

p. 196: "tempest": Wilson, *Our Nig*, 11, 15.

p. 196: *Mother I wish*: CS and ES to LD, Claremont, N.H., May 29, 1864.

p. 197: "Ira": EM to LLR, Manchester, N.H., Aug. 17, 1856.

p. 197: "kind": EM to LD, Mobile, Ala., March 14, 1858.

p. 197: *some one*: ES to CHR, Mobile, Ala., Feb. 9, 1862.

p. 197: *But I do not*: EC to LD, East End, Grand Cayman, March 7, 1870.

p. 197: *no one*: ES to LD, Claremont, N.H., Oct. 9, 1864.

p. 197: " 'bear to see' " and " 'I do remember' ": Louisa M. Alcott, "M.L.," *Boston Commonwealth*, Jan. 24–Feb. 21, 1863, in Lorenzo Dow Turner, *Anti-Slavery Sentiment in American Literature prior to 1865* (Washington, D.C.: Association for the Study of Negro Life and History, 1929), 146, 149.

p. 198: " 'In your world' ": ibid., 147.

p. 198: " 'gladly' ": Allen, *American Prejudice*, 102.

p. 198: wedding: "The Weather" and "Marriages": *Lowell Daily Courier*, Nov. 6, 1869; also "Intentions of Marriage," *Lowell Daily Citizen and News*, Nov. 8, 1869; WSC and ES, Massachusetts Vital Records, Marriages, Dracut, Nov. 3, 1869, vol. 218, p. 166, MSA.

p. 198: Wednesday: Will Jackson, *Up from the Deep: The Beginnings of the Cayman Islands* (St. Petersburg, Fla.: Lithofilms, 1996), 19.

p. 199: *remember me*: EC to LD, East End, Grand Cayman, March 7, 1870.

p. 201: *My dear*: EC to LD, Provincetown, Mass., Nov. 11, 1869.

p. 201: "My dear Mother": WSC to LD, Provincetown, Mass., Nov. 13, 1869.

p. 202: *I know*: ES to LD, continuation of WSC to LD, Provincetown, Mass., Nov. 13, 1869, letter.

p. 202: *make me*: ibid.

Chapter 6. The Sea Captain's Wife

p. 209: "with every hour": Alfred M. Williams, *Under the Trade Winds* (Providence, R.I.: Preston and Rounds, 1898), 36.

p. 209: moon: Charles Roberts, *Observations on the Gulf Passage, or, The Passage from Jamaica through the Gulf of Florida by the Grand Cayman and Cape St. Antonio and of the Bahama Islands* (London: W. Faden, 1795), 4.

p. 209: "What is Grand Cayman?": Correspondence regarding the wreck of the *Iphegenia* of Cardiff, May 23, 1874, TNA:PRO: MT 9/93/M13437/74.

p. 209: "Cayenne" to "Ceylon": C. P. Lucas, *Introduction to a Historical Geography of the British Colonies* (Oxford, U.K.: Clarendon Press, 1887), 139.

p. 210: "sequestered," "lonely," "extreme isolation," "entirely separated," "iron shore," "risk to man": *Missionary Record of the United Presbyterian Church*, June 2, 1873, p. 530; May 1, 1872, p. 149; June 2, 1879, p. 537; June 1, 1874, p. 168; Nov. 1847, p. 181, Nov. 1852, p. 186.

p. 210: "hardly knew": author's conversation with Theoline (Conolly) McCoy (b. 1919), Bodden Town, Grand Cayman, July 13, 1999.

p. 210: "rather shabby": T. H. MacDermot, "The Cayman Corner of the Empire," *United Empire* 18 (Nov. 1927), 598.

p. 210: *O, Mother*: EC to LD, East End, Grand Cayman, May 20, 1870, continuation of May 16, 1870, letter.

p. 211: "such pretty": Clara Stone to LD, East End, Grand Cayman, Nov. 28, 1871.

p. 211: *handsome*: EC to LD, East End, Grand Cayman, March 7, 1870.

p. 211: "dangerous": Admiralty to Governor of Jamaica, April 18, 1854, TNA:PRO: CO 137/325/14.

p. 211: *I hear*: EC to LD, East End, Grand Cayman, June 3, 1870, continuation of May 16, 1870, letter.

p. 211: *I sent one*: EC to LD, East End, Grand Cayman, March 29, 1875.

p. 212: *My little Lou*: EC to LD, East End, Grand Cayman, Dec. 13, 1871.

p. 212: Louisa Charlotta: HH to LD and AM, Goffstown, N.H., Jan. 26, 1872 (about Ellen's letter).

p. 212: second daughter: John S. Wood to EM, Kingston, Jamaica, Feb. 2, 1881; notes by Lou (Connolly) Coleman, ca. 1996–97, photocopy in possession of the author.

p. 212: *My darling Mother* and *As for myself*: EC to LD, East End, Grand Cayman, March 7, 1870.

p. 212: *does every thing*: EC to LD, East End, Grand Cayman, Aug. 25, 1870, continuation of May 16, 1870, letter.

p. 213: *I often wish*: EC to LD, East End, Grand Cayman, March 7, 1870.

p. 213: *I want*: CS and ES to LD, Claremont, N.H., May 29, 1864.

p. 213: *I have never* and *yearning look*: EC to LD, East End, Grand Cayman, Aug. 25, 1870, continuation of May 16, 1870, letter.

p. 213: *And My dear*: EC to LD, East End, Grand Cayman, March 7, 1870.

p. 213: *I have many*: EC to LD, East End, Grand Cayman [1869 or 1870?].

p. 213: *When I go*: EC to LD, East End, Grand Cayman, June 3, 1870, continuation of May 16, 1870, letter.

p. 214: *When I write*: EC to LD, East End, Grand Cayman, March 7, 1870.

p. 214: "charms": Jabez Marrat, *In the Tropics; or, Scenes and Incidents of West Indian Life* (London: Wesleyan Conference Office, 1876), 2–3.

p. 214: "dramatic": author's conversation with William Warren Conolly (b. 1920), East End, Grand Cayman, July 22, 1998.

p. 214: "Mosquitoes": E. Leonard Bodden (b. 1930), interview, by Heather McLaughlin, George Town, Grand Cayman, Dec. 18, 1996, p. 4, Memory Bank, CINA.

p. 214: "Swarming": James Earlie Whittaker (b. 1912), interview no. 1, by Heather McLaughlin, East End, Grand Cayman, Nov. 27, 1990, p. 12, Memory Bank, CINA.

p. 214: "Smothering": author's conversation with Theoline (Conolly) McCoy, Bodden Town, Grand Cayman, July 13, 1999.

p. 214: "I thought": author's conversation with Lou (Connolly) Coleman (b. 1928), West Medford, Mass., March 11, 2000.

p. 215: *He has*: EC to LD, East End, Grand Cayman, May 16, 1870.

p. 215: "Widow": Death certificate of Rachel Partridge Conolly, East End, Grand Cayman, Sept. 29, 1904, XH/203/2 #H02, CINA.

p. 215: 1881 divorce law: "Turks, Caicos, & Cayman Islands Divorce Law," Jan. 21, 1882, TNA:PRO: CO 137/504/101–03.

p. 215: "Never": Leila Rose Bodden (b. 1932), interview no. 2, by Leonard Bodden, Cayman Brac, Cayman Islands, June 20, 1993, p. 3, Memory Bank, CINA.

p. 215: "Unheard": author's conversation with Lou (Connolly) Coleman, West Medford, Mass., March 11, 2000.

p. 215: "where these men": author's conversation with Theoline (Conolly) McCoy, Bodden Town, Grand Cayman, July 13, 1999.

p. 215: Robert: marriage certificate of Robert Conolly and Eviluna Watler, East End, Grand Cayman, Jan. 19, 1898, no. 69, Book 40, XH/723/1, CINA; WSC is listed as the father, but the mother's name is not requested.

p. 216: *Mr Connolly* and *he had just*: EC to LD, East End, Grand Cayman, May 16, 1870.

p. 216: *he was after*: EC to LD, East End, Grand Cayman, Aug. 25, 1870, continuation of May 16, 1870, letter.

p. 216: *always driving*: EC to LD, East End, Grand Cayman, March 7, 1870.

p. 216: "much engaged": WSC to LD, East End, Grand Cayman [1870?].

p. 216: "helping": WSC to LD, East End, Grand Cayman, Feb. 2, 1874.

p. 216: *What a good*: EC to LD, East End, Grand Cayman, Dec. 14, 1871, continuation of Dec. 13, 1871, letter.

p. 216: "that you may": WSC to LD, East End, Grand Cayman [1870?].

p. 216: *If I knew*: EC to LD, East End, Grand Cayman, June 3, 1870, continuation of May 16, 1870, letter.

p. 216: "take our home": WSC to LD, East End, Grand Cayman, Oct. 16, 1872.

p. 217: "Any lover": *Missionary Record*, Jan. 1, 1873, p. 375.

p. 218: "plain": E. A. Wallbridge to Mico Charity, Kingston, Jamaica, Sept. 13, 1839, Section E1/1, Mss. Brit. Emp. s. 16–24, Anti-Slavery Society Papers, RHL.

p. 218: Sunday wreck: *Missionary Record*, Sept. 1, 1874, p. 264.

p. 218: "to tell": Hope Masterton Waddell, *Twenty-nine Years in the West Indies and Central Africa: A Review of Missionary Work and Adventure, 1829–1858* (London: T. Nelson, 1863), 216.

p. 220: *I have always* and *must have*: EC to LD, East End, Grand Cayman, Aug. 25, 1870, continuation of May 16, 1870, letter.

p. 220: *I always*: EC to LD, East End, Grand Cayman, March 7, 1870.

p. 220: *to try her*: EC to LD, East End, Grand Cayman, Aug. 25, 1870, continuation of May 16, 1870, letter.

p. 220: *She is*: ibid.

p. 220: *black girl*: ES to LD, Mobile, Ala., March 3, 1861.

p. 221: census: *Missionary Record*, Nov. 1, 1855, p. 190; *Blue Book*, Jamaica, 1868, p. R11, TNA:PRO: CO 142/83.

p. 221: "sambos": James M. Phillippo, *Jamaica: Its Past and Present State* (London: Dawsons, 1843), 144.

p. 221: *"mulatto"*: [Mrs. Flannigan and Mrs. Lanaghan], *Antigua and the Antiguans: A Full Account of the Colony and Its Inhabitants* (London: Saunders and Otley, 1844), 2:165.

p. 221: "Sambo Girl": Public Recorder's Records, Nov. 18, 1829, XH/5/2, p. 59, CINA.

p. 221: "musty": Aurellia Conolly (b. 1903), interview, by Heather McLaughlin, East End, Grand Cayman, Feb. 12, 1990, p. 8, Memory Bank, CINA.

p. 221: "quadroon": author's conversations with William Warren Conolly, East End, Grand Cayman, July 22, 1998, and Theoline (Conolly) McCoy, Bodden Town, Grand Cayman, July 13, 1999.

p. 222: "impracticable": *Missionary Record*, Nov. 1, 1855, p. 190.

p. 222: "middle class": William G. Sewell, *The Ordeal of Free Labor in the British West Indies* (New York: Harper and Brothers, 1861), 37.

p. 222: segregated cemeteries: "A Wesleyan Missionary in Grand Cayman, 1837," Cayman Islands National Library Collection, Acc. no. 177, CINA.

p. 222: "always had": Cleopathra Conolly to author, East End, Grand Cayman, Aug. 9, 2001.

p. 222: "better" and "important": Cecily Pierson (b. 1916), interview no. 2, by Heather McLaughlin, George Town, Grand Cayman, April 3, 1991, pp. 6, 7, Memory Bank, CINA.

p. 222: "John Connelly": Return of Alexander Watler, Cayman slave registration records, 1834, TNA:PRO: T 71/243/119.

p. 222: Cayman slaves: In 1834 there were 116 slaveowners and 985 slaves in Cayman, in a population of about 1,500; Cayman slave registration records, 1834: TNA:PRO: T 71/243; "An Account of the Number of Slaves," British Sessional Papers, House of Commons, vol. 51 (1835), 289.

p. 222: "village" and "live together": Report of Governor, June 27, 1835, TNA:PRO: CO 137/199/274 and 286.

p. 223: land settlement by former slaves: Report of Governor, May 14, 1835, TNA:PRO: CO 137/198/382-95; Report of Governor, received June 6, 1836, TNA:PRO: CO 137/210/394-403; "East End: History in the Making," *Newstar* (Jan.–Feb. 1989), 64.

p. 223: "cut their way": Aurellia Conolly interview, p. 3.

p. 223: Connolly-Conolly property: Will of John Jarrett Conolly, March 21, 1878, Public Recorder's Records, pp. 187–89, XH/5/5, CINA, transcribed by Jeanne Masters; Will of Thomas Dighton Conolly, Sept. 28, 1906 (orig. Jan. 17, 1894), Public Recorder's Records, pp. 12–18, XH/121/1, CINA.

p. 223: "Master": WSC to LD, Kingston, Jamaica, Nov. 23, 1870.

p. 223: occupations of Connolly-Conolly men: traced on death certificates and children's birth certificates, CINA.

p. 223: "antagonism": Edward Bean Underhill, *The West Indies: Their Social and Religious Condition* (London: Jackson, Walford, 1862), 225.

p. 223: *black girl*: EC to LD, East End, Grand Cayman, Aug. 25, 1870, continuation of May 16, 1870, letter.

p. 223: *in School*: EC to LD, East End, Grand Cayman, March 7, 1870.

p. 223: "large House:" WSC to LD, East End, Grand Cayman, Oct. 16, 1872.

p. 224: "big house": author's conversation with Theoline (Conolly) McCoy, Bodden Town, Grand Cayman, July 13, 1999.

p. 224: *jogging*: ES to AM, Claremont, N.H., April 19, 1863.

p. 224: *spared*: ES to LD, Claremont, N.H., April 6, 1862.

p. 224: *little "Island Home"*: EC to LD, East End, Grand Cayman, May 16, 1870.

p. 224: *Happy home*: EC to LD, East End, Grand Cayman, Dec. 13, 1871.

p. 224: *I never*: EC to LD, East End, Grand Cayman, March 7, 1870.

p. 225: *after passing*: EC to LD, East End, Grand Cayman, May 16, 1870.

p. 225: *pleasant*: EC to LD, East End, Grand Cayman, May 20, 1870, continuation of May 16, 1870, letter.

p. 225: *Mr Connolly allows*: EC to LD, East End, Grand Cayman, Aug. 25, 1870, continuation of May 16, 1870, letter.

p. 225: *So while* and *And it is*: EC to LD, East End, Grand Cayman, March 7, 1870.

p. 226: *He is*: ibid.

p. 226: *Mr C*: EC to LD, East End, Grand Cayman, May 16, 1870.

p. 226: *when not*: EC to LD, East End, Grand Cayman, June 3, 1870, continuation of May 16, 1870, letter.

p. 226: *It does my heart, if she had*, and *very patient*: EC to LD, East End, Grand Cayman, March 7, 1870.

p. 226: *she never*: EC to LD, East End, Grand Cayman, Jan 5, 1873, continuation of Jan. 2, 1873, letter.

p. 227: *constant*: EC to LD, East End, Grand Cayman, March 7, 1870.

p. 227: "at sea": *Missionary Record*, June 1, 1872, p. 176.

p. 227: *We still*: EC to LD, East End, Grand Cayman, June 3, 1870, continuation of May 16, 1870, letter.

p. 227: *mutual desire*: EC to LD, East End, Grand Cayman, March 7, 1870.

p. 227: *I never, His Mother*, and *You know*: ibid.

p. 229: *He has often*: EC to LD, East End, Grand Cayman, Jan. 2, 1873.

p. 230: *one good sleigh*: EC to LD, East End, Grand Cayman, Jan. 5, 1873, continuation of Jan. 2, 1873, letter.

p. 231: "considered white": author's conversation with William Warren Conolly, East End, Grand Cayman, July 22, 1998.

p. 231: "I don't think": author's conversation with William Warren Conolly, East End, Grand Cayman, July 13, 1999.

p. 231: "Well, I guess": author's conversation with Dorothy McLean Welcome (b. 1917), East End, Grand Cayman, July 15, 1999.

p. 232: warned away: J. T. Trowbridge, *The South: A Tour of Its Battle-Fields and Ruined Cities* (Hartford, Conn.: L. Stebbins, 1866), 343.

p. 232: obtained a license: *Richmond Daily Dispatch*, Feb. 3, 1873.

p. 232: *We have*: EC to LD, East End, Grand Cayman, Aug. 25, 1870, continuation of May 16, 1870, letter.

p. 232: "I am so horribly": Melissa P. Russell Diary, Nov. 1, 1835, ADAH.

p. 232: "It ought to be": John Williamson, *Medical and Miscellaneous Observations Relative to the West India Islands* (Edinburgh: Alex. Smellie, 1817), 1:42.

p. 233: *As for me*: EC to LD, East End, Grand Cayman, Aug. 25, 1870, continuation of May 16, 1870 letter.

p. 233: *I have enough*: EC to LD, East End, Grand Cayman, March 7, 1870.

p. 233: *I have a plenty*: EC to LD, East End, Grand Cayman, Dec. 14, 1871, continuation of Dec. 13, 1871, letter.

p. 234: "melt away": Benjamin S. Hunt, *Remarks on Hayti as a Place of Settlement for Afric-Americans; and on the Mulatto as a Race for the Tropics* (Philadelphia, T. B. Pugh, 1860), 28.

p. 234: *not heard*: EC to LD, East End, Grand Cayman, May 16, 1870.

p. 234: *know friend*: EC to LD, East End, Grand Cayman, June 3, 1870, continuation of May 16, 1870, letter.

p. 234: *good long*: EC to LD, East End, Grand Cayman, Aug. 25, 1870, continuation of May 16, 1870, letter.

p. 235: "much troubled": WSC to LD, Kingston Jamaica, Nov. 23, 1870.

p. 235: *trying*: EC to LD, East End, Grand Cayman, Dec. 13, 1871.

p. 235: *You must*: EC to LD, East End, Grand Cayman, Dec. 14, 1871, continuation of Dec. 13, 1871, letter.

p. 235: *not having heard*: EC to LD, East End, Grand Cayman, Dec. 13, 1871.

p. 235: *When I think*: EC to LD, East End, Grand Cayman, Jan. 2, 1873.

p. 235: "lost" and "After not": WSC to LD, East End, Grand Cayman, Feb. 2, 1874.

p. 236: *It is going*: EC to LD, East End, Grand Cayman, March, 29, 1875.

p. 236: "It does seem": AM to EC, Dracut, Mass., Feb. 16, 1870.

p. 236: "Oh dear" and "Oh my dear": AM to EC, Dracut, Mass., Feb. 20, 1870, continuation of Feb. 16, 1870, letter.

p. 236: "I have not": HH to LD, Goffstown, N.H., Oct. 11, 1872.

p. 237: *Harriet* and *Henry*: EC to LD, East End, Grand Cayman, Jan. 5, 1873, continuation of Jan. 2, 1873, letter.

p. 237: Clara: Clare Stone to LD, East End, Grand Cayman, Nov. 28, 1871.

p. 237: *I wondered*: ES to LD, Claremont, N.H., Aug. 25, 1864.

p. 237: *Miss Clara*: EC to LD, East End, Grand Cayman [1869 or 1870?].

p. 237: *never been, knock about*, and *a poor*: EC to LD, East End, Grand Cayman, March 7, 1870.

p. 238: *He has got*: ES to AM and DM, Claremont, N.H., July 3, 1864.

p. 238: "We again": WSC to LD, East End, Grand Cayman, Oct. 16, 1872.

p. 238: *dark empty void*: ES to CHR, Dracut, Mass., July 23, 1865.

p. 238: "Sleep on" and " 'Round your little grave": Cecily Pierson interview no. 2, p. 33.

p. 238: *enjoy*: EC to LD, East End, Grand Cayman, May 16, 1870.

p. 240: *kind*: EC to LD, East End, Grand Cayman, Jan. 5, 1873, continuation of Jan. 2, 1873, letter.

p. 240: "Mrs. Connolly": WSC to LD, East End, Grand Cayman, Oct. 16, 1872.

p. 240: *I think*: EC to LD, East End, Grand Cayman, March 29, 1875.

p. 240: "Please write": Clara Stone to LD, continuation of WSC to LD, East End, Grand Cayman, Oct. 16, 1872, letter.

p. 240: *I am some what*: EC to LD, East End, Grand Cayman, Jan 2, 1873.

p. 240: *so low*: EC to LD, East End, Grand Cayman, March 29, 1875.

p. 240: *You wish*: EC to LD, East End, Grand Cayman, Jan. 5, 1873, continuation of Jan. 2, 1873, letter.

p. 240: "There were many:" Family Group Sheet for Thomas Dighton Conolly, by Jeanne Masters, Jan. 1 1999.

p. 241: *I have no*: EC to LD, East End, Grand Cayman, Jan. 5, 1873, continuation of Jan. 2, 1873, letter.

p. 241: *he is perfectly*: EC to LD, Provincetown, Mass., Nov. 13, 1869.

p. 241: *one good sleigh*: EC to LD, East End, Grand Cayman, Jan. 5, 1873, continuation of Jan. 2, 1873, letter.

p. 241: "not willing": WSC to LD, East End, Grand Cayman, Oct. 16, 1872.

p. 241: *I some times*: EC to LD, East End, Grand Cayman, Jan. 5, 1873, continuation of Jan. 2, 1873, letter.

p. 241: "I want to": WSC to LD, East End, Grand Cayman, Feb. 2, 1874.

p. 241: *the best way*: EC to LD, East End, Grand Cayman, Jan. 5, 1873, continuation of Jan. 2, 1873, letter.

p. 242: *After this*: EC to LD, East End, Grand Cayman, March 29, 1875.

p. 242: *It is after*: ES to LD, Claremont, N.H., Dec. 3, 1864.

p. 242: *I can not*: EC to LD, East End, Grand Cayman, March 29, 1875.

Chapter 7. Hurricane

p. 243: "no precise rule": U.S. Hydrographic Office, *Hurricanes; with Nautical Directions for Avoiding and Maneuvering in Them* (Washington, D.C.: Government Printing Office, 1872), 7–8.

p. 244: *Tonight*: EC to LD, East End, Grand Cayman, May 16, 1870.

p. 245: *He does not*: EC to LD, East End, Grand Cayman, Dec. 13, 1871.

p. 245: "You must not": WSC to LD, Kingston, Jamaica, Nov. 23, 1870.

p. 245: *Coffee*: EC to LD, East End, Grand Cayman, Dec. 13, 1871.

p. 245: "like coarse gravel" and "whole generation": *Missionary Record of the United Presbyterian Church*, Jan. 1, 1877, p. 348.

p. 246: *The Leader*: Brent Bush, "History of my Fathers," no date, Cayman Islands National Library Collection (vertical file), folder labeled "Genealogy, A–E," CINA.

p. 247: "Bad Weather": *New York Maritime Register*, Sept. 26, 1877.

p. 247: "On such occasions": H. W. Bates, *Central America, the West Indies, and South America* (London: Edward Stanford, 1882), 145.

p. 248: "every thing generally": "Ben" to ?, aboard *Hydra* on voyage to Mauritius, May 7, 1860, Mss. 0.561, SPL.

p. 248: "Our hopes": Dispatch Packet (Schooner) Logbook, Jan. 8, 1821, M656, 1820D, typescript, SPL.

p. 248: "like snow": Samuel A. Bard [Ephraim George Squier], *Waikna; or, Adventures on the Mosquito Shore* (New York: Harper and Brothers, 1855), 33, 30.

p. 248: "In agony": Susan M. Norton to "the dear Home Circle," "At Sea," Oct. 31, 1858, quoted in Emma Mayhew Whiting and Henry Beetle Hough, *Whaling Wives* (Edgartown, Mass.: Dukes County Historical Society, 1965), 85.

p. 248: "looked like heaven": Heather R. McLaughlin, comp. and ed., *The '32 Storm: Eye-witness Accounts and Official Reports of the Worst Natural Disaster in the History of the Cayman Islands* (George Town: Cayman Islands National Archive, 1994), 53, 55.

p. 248: 1877 hurricane: War Department, Office of the Chief Signal Officer, *Monthly Weather Review* (Oct. 1877), 3–4.

p. 249: "The 25th": *Missionary Record*, Feb. 1, 1878, p. 33.

p. 250: "Denham Bush": Bush, "History of my Fathers."

p. 250: "I beg": John S. Wood to EM, Kingston, Jamaica, Feb. 2, 1881.

p. 251: "Mr Connollys dwelling": ibid.

p. 251: "My Dear Brother": EM to CHR, Moss Point, Miss., Feb. 19, 1881.

p. 253: overall manufacturing business: HH to LD and AM, Goffstown, N.H., Jan. 26, 1872.

p. 253: HH death: Hattie L. Harvey death certificate, Lowell, Mass., July 15, 1886, CCL; *Lowell Morning Mail*, July 17, 1886.

p. 253: LD death: Massachusetts Vital Records, Deaths, June 6, 1889, vol. 401, p. 135, MSA.

p. 253: DM death: David McCoy death certificate, Lowell, Mass., July 29, 1885, CCL.

p. 253: AM death: AM to CHR, n.p., ca. 1912, personal papers of James T. Cushman.

p. 253: Alice Merrill death: *Manchester Daily Union*, May 10, 1875.

p. 253: DDM death: ibid., April 29, 1881.

p. 253: two hundred dollars: George F. Kenngott, *The Record of a City: A Social Survey of Lowell, Massachusetts* (New York: Macmillan, 1912), 179.

p. 253: EM death: Ellen A. Merrill death certificate, Lowell, Mass., Nov. 28, 1914, CCL and *Lowell Sun*, Dec. 1, 1914.

p. 253: *Are you still*: ES to CHR, Mobile, Ala., Nov. 18, 1860.

p. 254: "our well known": *Lowell Morning Mail*, July 17, 1886.

p. 254: "mother of": ibid., June 8, 1889.

p. 254: "names of Lexington": Benjamin F. Watson, *Addresses, Reviews and Episodes Chiefly Concerning the "Old Sixth" Massachusetts Regiment* (New York: no publisher, 1901), 8.

p. 254: "splendid valor," "all bitterness," and "darkeys": Francis Henry Buffum, *Sheridan's Veterans: A Souvenir of Their Two Campaigns in the Shenandoah Valley* (Boston: no publisher, 1883), 62, 75.

p. 255: corresponding warmly: James S. Blain to CHR, Brunswick, Ga., Jan. 19, 1885, personal papers of James T. Cushman.

p. 255: grand reunion: Society of the Nineteenth Army Corps, collection of printed material, 1894–1906, NYHS.

p. 255: "marched": "Copy of an article from the (LOWELL)? newspaper dated Sept. 4, 1894, relative to the life of Mr. Charles Henry Richardson, a successful manufacturer and then Agent of the Appleton Mills, Lowell, Mass.," typescript, personal papers of James T. Cushman.

p. 255: CHR's work history: Lowell city directories, 1870s–1900; *Illustrated History of Lowell and Vicinity, Massachusetts* (Lowell: Courier-Citizen Company, 1897), 250–54; "Death of Well Known Citizen," *Lowell Sun*, Feb. 25, 1913.

p. 256: "Mr. Charles H. Richardson": *Illustrated History of Lowell*, 250–54.

p. 258: SAR and DAR: Tom Pray to James T. Cushman, e-mail, Nov. 4, 2004, forwarded to author.

p. 258: "self-made man" and "constant protest": "Copy of an article."

p. 258: "Mr. Richardson's opportunities": *Illustrated History of Lowell*, 254; Henry was seventeen years old when Lois wrote, "Your Father has ben dead nearly 2 years" (LD to CHR and LLR, Hudson, N.H., April 1, 1860).

p. 259: "native born," "alien races," and "each new alien": Kenngott, *Record of a City*, 28, 77, 102.

p. 259: "happy days": ibid., 225.

p. 260: *My Dear Brother*: ES to LD, Mobile, Ala., March 10, 1861, continuation of March 3, 1861, letter.

p. 260: *Who ever*: ES to LD, Claremont, N.H., March 8, 1863.

p. 260: *I wanted*: EC to LD, continuation of WSC to LD, Provincetown, Mass., Nov. 13, 1869, letter.

p. 261: "I have never": James S. Blain to CHR, Brunswick, Ga., Jan. 19, 1885, personal papers of James T. Cushman.

p. 261: "Tho' leaves": G. W. Nichols, *A Soldier's Story of His Regiment (61st Georgia)* (Jessup, Ga.: no publisher, 1898), 227.

p. 263: "rusticating" and "I have not": HH to LD, Goffstown, N.H., Oct. 11, 1872.

p. 263: "This is": HH to LD and AM, Goffstown, N.H., Jan. 26, 1872.

p. 264: *Harriet has not*: EC to LD, East End, Grand Cayman, Jan. 5, 1873, continuation of Jan. 2, 1873, letter.

p. 264: "very estimable": *Lowell Saturday Vox Populi*, July 17, 1886.

p. 264: "Tell Ann": "Aunt Mary" to CHR, Royalston, Mass., Nov. 1, 1875, personal papers of James T. Cushman.

p. 265: *never heard*: EC to LD, East End, Grand Cayman, March 29, 1875.

p. 265: "he was always": CHR to LD, Winchester, Va., Jan. 26, 1865.

p. 265: *Henry before*: ES to CHR, Mobile, Ala., Nov. 18, 1860.

p. 265: "If our road" and "in the boiling": Samuel C. Bartlett, *Lectures on Modern Universalism: An Exposure of the System* (Manchester, N.H.: Fisk and Gage, 1856), 37, 61.

p. 265: CHR's children: *Illustrated History of Lowell*, 254.

p. 265: "Oh my dear": AM to EC, Dracut, Mass., Feb. 20, 1870, continuation of Feb. 16, 1870, letter.

p. 266: "I had": AM to CHR, n.p., ca. 1912, personal papers of James T. Cushman.

p. 266: "Death of Well Known Citizen": *Lowell Sun*, Feb. 25, 1913.

p. 266: "His Career": "County Commissioner Charles H. Richardson Dies at His Home," *Lowell Courier-Citizen*, Feb. 25, 1918.

p. 266: "there was nothing": "Death of Well Known Citizen," *Lowell Sun*, Feb. 25, 1913.

p. 266: CHR death information: Charles H. Richardson death certificate, Lowell, Mass., Feb. 24, 1913, CCL.

p. 266: Clara Richardson death: Clara Adelaide Richardson death certificate, Jan. 18, 1908, Lowell, Mass., CCL.

p. 267: 1913 marriage law: "An Act to Make Uniform the Law Relating to Marriages," *Acts and Resolves Passed by the General Court of Massachusetts, 1913* (Boston: Wright and Potter, 1913), 302.

p. 267: "Should you wish": John S. Wood to EM, Kingston, Jamaica, Feb. 2, 1881.

p. 268: will: Will of John Jarrett Conolly, March 21, 1878, Public Recorder's Records, pp. 187–89, XH/5/5, CINA, transcribed by Jeanne Masters.

p. 268: "work the lands": Will of Thomas Dighton Conolly, Sept. 28, 1906 (orig. Jan. 17, 1894), Public Recorder's Records, pp. 12–18, XH/121/1, CINA.

p. 268: WSC widow: Death certificate of Rachel Partridge Conolly, East End, Grand Cayman, Sept. 29. 1904, XH/203/2 #H02, CINA.

p. 268: ledgers: Lou Connolly Coleman Collection, no. 386, Acc. no. 736, MSD 277, CINA.

p. 268: CONNOLLY CLAN RE-UNION: unnamed, undated newspaper clipping, copy given to author by Lou (Connolly) Coleman.

p. 270: "first College graduate": William Smiley Connolly II to Colonial Secretary, London, May 15, 1919, TNA:PRO: CO 137/736.

p. 270: career of William Smiley Connolly II: Scholastic Record of WSC II, Office of the Registrar, Howard University, Washington, D.C. (thanks to Lou [Connolly] Coleman for permission to release these records); WSC II correspondence, TNA:PRO: CO 137/736; WSC II to Commissioner, Washington, D.C., March 17, 1913, Custos Correspondence, AA/1/19–20, XH/793/2, C02–04, CINA; Letter no. 196 and no. 246 in Commissioner Correspondence, Transfer no. 49, Box 3, CINA.

p. 270: photographs of William Smiley Connolly II: Heather R. McLaughlin, *Cayman Yesterdays: An Album of Childhood Memories* (George Town: Cayman Islands National Archive, 1991), 22; Lou Connolly Coleman Collection, XG/CN/315/BS/C5, CINA.

p. 270: "lily white": family discussion at Connolly-Conolly family reunion, Morritt's Tortuga Club, East End, Grand Cayman, Aug. 27, 2000.

p. 270: Eunice: death certificate of Eunice Mahilda Conolly, East End, Grand Cayman, Jan. 1, 1958, age seventy-nine, CIRG; birth certificate of Eunice Victoria Dixon, Cayman Brac, Cayman Islands, Dec. 24, 1897, XH/12/3 #N2, CINA.

p. 270: Lou: "Family Record as in the Family Bible," copy of typescript given to author by Lou (Connolly) Coleman.

p. 270: Clarence: Family Group Sheet of William Joshua McCoy, by Jeanne Masters, June 27, 1997.

p. 270: Luther: "Family Record as in the Family Bible," copy of typescript given to author by Lou (Connolly) Coleman.

p. 271: "reef protected": "Colliers Resort Assembly," MLS no. 032621, *Cayman Islands Real Estate*, Fall 2005, p. 36.

p. 271: "old days": Dave Martins, "Ironwood," *Cayman Horizons* 3 (May–June 1986), 18.

p. 272: William Warren Conolly: *The Wall of Honour: Quincentennial Celebration Year 2003* (Cayman Islands: Quincentennial Celebrations Office, 2004), 24; Michael Craton, *Founded upon the Seas: A History of the Cayman Islands and Their People* (Kingston: Ian Randle, 2003), 315–16, 348–49, 409. "Mr. Warren—Where Is He Now?" *Cayman Net News*, Aug. 1, 2002.

p. 272: Burns Conolly: "Burns Conolly: The President with a Vision—A New Hope for Cayman's Businesses," *Cayman Net News*, Jan. 2002.

p. 272: "Racial tension": J. C. Calhoun, "Time to Buy?," *Destination Cayman* (1999), 86.

p. 272: *act all the love*: EC to LD, East End, Grand Cayman, March 7, 1870.

p. 272: "agony" and "spirit": Joseph Story, *An Address Delivered on the Dedication of the Cemetery at Mount Auburn, September 24, 1831* (Boston: Joseph and Edwin Buckingham, 1831), 6, 20.

p. 273: "It is but": "Our Disasters at Sea," *Ladies' Repository* 35 (May 1866), 301, 302.

p. 273: "happy, above all": Mary A. Livermore, *The Story of My Life; or The Sunshine and Shadow of Seventy Years* (Hartford, Conn.: A. D. Worthington, 1897), 610.

Chapter 8. Searching for Eunice

p. 275: James T. Conolly: Somini Sengupta, "A Candidate Cites His Race as Credential," *New York Times*, Aug. 18, 1996, City Section, p. 8

p. 275: photograph of William Smiley Connolly II's school: photocopy given to author by Heather McLaughlin, no citation, CINA.

p. 276: "Old Man": author's conversation with William Warren Conolly (b. 1920), East End, Grand Cayman, July 22, 1998.

p. 276: "one, the mother": William Warren Conolly to author, East End, Grand Cayman, Jan. 18, 2000.

p. 277: "go around the back": author's conversation with William Warren Conolly, East End, Grand Cayman, July 13, 1999.

p. 277: obliterated names: Communicants Roll, East End, 1870–1910, United Church in Jamaica and the Cayman Islands, Coll. no. 87, Acc. no. 350, MSC 57, CINA.

p. 277: "exceptionally": author's conversation with Philip Pedley, CINA, Aug. 27, 1998.

p. 278: "I'm about": Jeanne Masters to author, North Side, Grand Cayman, Aug. 2, 1998.

p. 278: "I still LOVE": Jeanne Masters to author, North Side, Grand Cayman, April 24, 2001.

p. 278: *You ought*: EC to LD, East End, Grand Cayman, March 7, 1870.

p. 278: "Mr. William Warren Conolly": author to Lou (Connolly) Coleman, New York, N.Y., Feb. 9, 2000.

p. 280: "1/2 Bro": notes by Lou (Connolly) Coleman, ca. 1996–97, photocopy in possession of the author.

p. 280: "This is so fascinating": author's conversation with Lou (Connolly) Coleman (b. 1928), West Medford, Mass., March 11, 2000.

p. 280: "My father": Lou (Connolly) Coleman speaking at Connolly-Conolly family reunion, Morritt's Tortuga Club, East End, Grand Cayman, Aug. 27, 2000 (written notes), and cassette tape marked "Warren GC Aug 2000," copy in possession of the author.

p. 280: "John Connelly": Return of Alexander Watler, Cayman slave registration records, 1834, TNA:PRO: T 71/243/119.

p. 281: Ireland: author's conversation with Cleopathra Conolly (b. 1925), Morritt's Tortuga Club, East End, Grand Cayman, June 30, 2001; the name Conelly appears in the Galway area (western Ireland) in William Petty's census of Ireland (see Petty Papers, Add 72876, Census [1659], British Library, London) (thanks to Joe Lee; thanks to Jenny Shaw for the citation).

p. 281: "I heard": author's conversation with Lou (Connolly) Coleman, West Medford, Mass., March 11, 2000.

p. 282: "big house": author's conversation with William Warren Conolly, East End, Grand Cayman, July 22, 1998.

p. 282: "large House": WSC to LD, East End, Grand Cayman, Oct. 16, 1872.

p. 282: *lives nearly*: EC to LD, East End, Grand Cayman, Jan. 5, 1873, continuation of Jan. 2, 1873, letter.

p. 282: museum building: William L. Tennent, "Treasure Chest," *Destination Cayman* (Winter–Summer Millennium Edition, 1999–2000), 24.

p. 282: memory of WSC: author's conversation with Bertram Conolly (b. 1915), East End, Grand Cayman, July 1, 2001.

p. 283: "lost at sea": notes taken by Lou (Connolly) Coleman in conversation with Cleopathra Conolly, East End, Grand Cayman, March 2000, photocopy in possession of the author.

p. 283: "This woman": author's conversation with Cleopathra Conolly, Morritt's Tortuga Club, East End, Grand Cayman, Aug. 27, 2000.

p. 283: Cleopathra Conolly: *Wall of Honour*, 22 (here spelled "Cleopatra"); Fiona Pimentel, "East End's beloved 'Miss Cleo' Conolly: A Bold Cancer Survivor Looks Back," *Cayman Net News*, Sept. 26–28, 2003, p. 13.

p. 284: "I used to hear": author's conversation with Dorothy McLean Welcome (b. 1917), East End, Grand Cayman, July 15, 1999.

p. 285: Eunice's signature: Employee Register, Amoskeag Manufacturing Company, March 21, 1860, p. 47, MHA.

p. 285: *We were all*: ES to LD, Claremont, N.H., March 29, 1864.

p. 286: *I was at*: ES to AM, Cabot, Vt., Dec. 24, 1866.

p. 287: *darkness and despair*: ES to CHR, Dracut, Mass., July 23, 1865.

p. 288: "very glad": William R. Erwin Jr., to author, e-mail, Nov. 29, 2000; a letter in the Davis Papers to "Dear Bill," dated 1978, is to William Erwin and has no connection to the family (Edward and Renee Cross to William R. Erwin Jr., Maidencombe, Torquay, Devon, England, Dec. 3, 1978).

p. 289: George Richardson: "Aboard the U.S.S. Huron: Lt. George E. Richardson of Lancaster, Is a Victim of Influenza," *Clinton Courant*, Nov. 1, 1918; obituary, *Clinton Courant*, Nov. 22, 1918.

p. 289: John H. Kelsey: obituary, *Lowell Courier-Citizen*, March 14, 1921.

p. 289: James A. Cushman: obituary, *Boston Herald*, March 4, 1956.

p. 289: Ivah and James A. Cushman: 1920 Montague, Mass., federal census, vol. 40, ed. 120, sheet 21, line 18.

p. 290: Allerton R. Cushman: obituary, *Yarmouthport Register*, May 6, 1999.

p. 290: "Dear Jane Cushman": author to Jane Allerton Cushman (b. 1938), New York, N.Y., March 21, 2001.

p. 291: "Good morning": telephone message from Jane Allerton Cushman, Brewster, Mass., March 23, 2001.

p. 292: "I had no idea": author's telephone conversation with Jane Allerton Cushman, Brewster, Mass., March 26, 2001.

p. 292: "man of color": author's conversation with Jane Allerton Cushman, Brewster, Mass., April 21, 2001.

p. 292: "long line": author's telephone conversation with Jane Allerton Cushman, Brewster, Mass., March 29, 2001.

p. 293: "southern relatives" and "never, ever Eunice": author's conversation with Jane Allerton Cushman, Brewster, Mass., April 21, 2001.

p. 293: "Pappa's poem": read into tape recorder by Jane Allerton Cushman, Brewster, Mass., April 21, 2001.

p. 293: "Father's sister": Alice Merrill to LD, Baghdad, Fla., Feb. 10, 1871.

p. 294: "Doubling and Twisting"; "Deaths reported"; AM to CHR, n.p., ca. 1912; DAR certificates; "I'm Nobody!": personal papers of James T. Cushman and personal papers of Heidi Jacobe.

p. 294: "Eunice it seems": "Aunt Mary" to CHR, Royalston, Mass., Nov. 1, 1875, personal papers of James T. Cushman.

p. 294: "Oh, that's wonderful": author's conversation with Jane Allerton Cushman, Brewster, Mass., July 30, 2001.

p. 294: "My darling Ella": CHR to Ella Richardson, Lowell, Mass., Dec. 22, 1887, personal papers of James T. Cushman.

p. 295: "She says": Jeanne Masters to author, North Side, Grand Cayman, Jan. 14, 2002.

p. 295: Jane Allerton Cushman death: "Jane A. Cushman, 67, Former advertising director; sales rep; museum volunteer," *Cape Cod Times*, Aug. 19, 2002.

p. 296: "devastation": "Grand Cayman: 'Devastation beyond Imagination,'" *Cayman Net News*, Sept. 13, 2004.

p. 297: "priority": Alfonso Chardy, "Reports from the Cayman Islands," *Miami Herald*, www.miami.com/mld/miamiherald, Sept. 13, 2004.

p. 297: "expected": Joseph B. Treaster, "After Devastating Grenada, Hurricane Bears Down on Jamaica," *New York Times*, Sept. 10, 2004, p. A22.

p. 297: Mariner's Memorial: e-mail correspondence with JoEllen Rae-Smith and Suzy Soto, Grand Cayman, 2002–6. "The Cayman Islands: Walking Tour. Take Time to Stroll through Historic Georgetown," <www.caribbean-on-line.com/cy/>; "Port Proceeds," *Cayman Net News*, Jan. 19, 2004.

ESSAY ON SOURCES

Abbreviations for archives can be found on page 300.

Chapter 1. A Story and a History

On the year 1831, see Louis P. Masur, *1831: Year of Eclipse* (New York: Hill and Wang, 2001).

On letter writing, see Nigel Hall, "The Materiality of Letter Writing: A Nineteenth Century Perspective," in *Letter Writing as a Social Practice*, ed. David Barton and Nigel Hall (Philadelphia: John Benjamins, 2000), 83–108; Rebecca Earle, ed., *Epistolary Selves: Letters and Letter-Writers, 1600–1945* (Aldershot, U.K.: Ashgate, 1999); and William Merrill Decker, *Epistolary Practices: Letter Writing in America Before Telecommunications* (Chapel Hill: University of North Carolina Press, 1998). On letter writing during the Civil War, see James M. McPherson, *For Cause and Comrades: Why Men Fought in the Civil War* (New York: Oxford University Press, 1997); Nina Silber and Mary Beth Sievens, eds., *Yankee Correspondence: Civil War Letters between New England Soldiers and the Home Front* (Charlottesville: University Press of Virginia, 1996); and Bell Irvin Wiley, *The Life of Billy Yank: The Common Soldier of the Union* (New York: Bobbs-Merrill, 1952). For letter-writing manuals, see Harry B. Weiss, *American Letter-Writers, 1698–1943* (New York: New York Public Library, 1945).

On reading among the working classes, see Ronald J. Zboray and Mary Saracino Zboray, "Cannonballs and Books: Reading and the Disruption of Social Ties on the New England Home Front," in *The War Was You and Me: Civilians in the American Civil War*, ed. Joan E. Cashin (Princeton, N.J.: Princeton University Press, 2002), 237–61, including a discussion of letter writing; Ronald J. Zboray, *A Fictive People: Antebellum Economic Development and the American Reading Public* (New York: Oxford University Press, 1993), including a chapter on letter writing; and Michael Denning, *Mechanic Accents: Dime Novels and Working-Class Culture in America* (New York: Verso, 1987).

On the workings of the U.S. mail, see Wayne E. Fuller, *The American Mail: Enlarger of the Common Life* (Chicago: University of Chicago Press, 1972) and Gerald Cullinan, *The Post Office Department* (New York: Frederick A. Praeger, 1968).

On photography, see Floyd Rinhart, Marion Rinhart, and Robert W. Wagner, *The American Tintype* (Columbus: Ohio State University Press, 1999) and Joan L. Severa, *Dressed for the Photographer: Ordinary Americans and Fashion, 1840–1900* (Kent, Ohio: Kent State University Press, 1995).

On history and storytelling, see for example Anrew R. L. Cayton, "*In*sufficient Woe: Sense and Sensibility in Writing Nineteenth-Century History," *Reviews in American History* 31 (Sept. 2003), 331–41; James Goodman, "For the Love of Stories," *Reviews in American History* 26 (March 1998), 255–74; Brook Thomas, "Ineluctable Though Uneven: On Experimental Historical Narratives," *Common Knowledge* 5 (Winter 1996), 163–88; William Cronon, "A Place for Stories: Nature, History, and Narrative," *Journal of American History* 78 (March 1992), 1347–76; and Elsa Barkley Brown, "Polyrhythms and Improvization: Lessons for Women's History," *History Workshop Journal* 31 (Spring 1991), 85–90.

Chapter 2. A Carpenter's Wife

On Royalston, Massachusetts, including the family of Eunice's father, Lot Richardson, see Lilley B. Caswell, *The History of the Town of Royalston, Massachusetts* (Royalston: Town of Royalston, 1917). On Northfield, Massachusetts, including the family of Eunice's mother, Lois Wright, see Herbert Collins Parsons, *A Puritan Outpost: A History of the Town and People of Northfield, Massachusetts* (New York: Macmillan, 1937); Joel Munsell, *Reminiscences of Men and Things in Northfield as I Knew Them from 1812 to 1825* (Albany, N.Y.: Joel Munsell, 1876); and J. H. Temple and George Sheldon, *A History of the Town of Northfield, Massachusetts for 150 Years* (Albany, N.Y.: Joel Munsell, 1875).

On Manchester, New Hampshire, and the Amoskeag Manufacturing Company, see John Coolidge, *Mill and Mansion: Architecture and Society in Lowell, Massachusetts, 1820–1865* (1942; reprint, Amherst: University of Massachusetts Press, 1993), which includes valuable information on Manchester; Elizabeth Durfee Hengen, "Corporation Housing at Amoskeag Manufacturing Company," *Historical New Hampshire* 45 (Summer 1990), 117–35; Tamara K. Hareven, *Family Time and Industrial Time: The Relationship between the Family and Work in a New England Industrial Community* (New York: Cambridge University Press, 1982); James P. Hanlan, *The Working Population of Manchester, New Hampshire, 1840–1886* (Ann Arbor: University of Michigan Research Press, 1981); Tamara K. Hareven and Randolph Langenbach, *Amoskeag: Life and Work in an American Factory-City* (New York: Pantheon, 1978); Grace Holbrook Blood, *Manchester on the Merrimack: The Story of a City* (Manchester, N.H.: Manchester Historic Association, 1975); L. Ashton Thorp, *Manchester of Yesterday: A Human Interest Story of Its Past* (Manchester, N.H.: Granite State Press, 1939); George Waldo Browne, *The Amoskeag Manufacturing Co. of Manchester, New Hampshire: A History* (Manchester, N.H.: Amoskeag Manufacturing Co., 1915); "The Mills of Manchester," *Manchester Historic Association Collections* 4, part 1 (1908), 149–57; [Maurice D. Clarke], *Manchester: A Brief*

Record of Its Past and a Picture of Its Present (Manchester, N.H.: John B. Clarke, 1875); "Statistics of Manchester, N.H., Manufactures, 1860, compiled from authentic sources" (flyer, Manchester, N.H.: C. F. Livingston, 1860); and Kimberly Frederick, "The Amoskeag and Its City: Power and Protest in Manchester, New Hampshire, in the 1840s," Brandeis University, unpublished paper, 2000. Important unpublished sources at MHA include the National Register of Historic Places Inventory, Nomination Form, National Park Service, U.S. Department of the Interior, in "Research File: National Register of Historic Places, Properties—Amoskeag Manufacturing Company Housing" and "Research File, 18–52 Hanover St., Harrington and Smith."

On the fate of the Amoskeag and urban renewal in Manchester, see Manchester Housing Authority, *The Amoskeag Millyard Urban Renewal Project Summary Report* (Manchester, N.H.: no publisher, 1982); Randolph Langenbach, "A City No One Knew," *Architectural Forum* 130 (January–February 1969), 84–91; and Randolph Langenbach, "An Epic in Urban Design," *Harvard Alumni Bulletin* 70 (April 13, 1968), 18–28. For the Millyard Museum, see <www.manchesterhistoric.org/mill.htm>.

For sentimental popular poetry, see Thomas Buchanan Read, *The Female Poets of America* (Philadelphia: E. H. Butler, 1857) and Caroline May, *The American Female Poets* (Philadelphia: Lindsay and Blakiston, 1848).

On rural family life, including reputation and gossip, see Karen V. Hansen, *A Very Social Time: Crafting Community in Antebellum New England* (Berkeley: University of California Press, 1994). On the institution of marriage, see Nancy F. Cott, *Public Vows: A History of Marriage and the Nation* (Cambridge, Mass.: Harvard University Press, 2000) and Hendrik Hartog, *Man and Wife in America: A History* (Cambridge, Mass.: Harvard University Press, 2000). On the idea of "housekeeping," see Laurel Thatcher Ulrich, *A Midwife's Tale: The Life of Martha Ballard, Based on Her Diary, 1785–1812* (New York: Alfred A. Knopf, 1990). On desertion, see Roderick Phillips, *Putting Asunder: A History of Divorce in Western Society* (New York: Cambridge University Press, 1988).

On the transition to a capitalist economy, including industrialization and attendant changes in landownership, labor, markets, and family, see Scott C. Martin, ed., *Cultural Change and the Market Revolution in America, 1789–1860* (Lanham, Md.: Rowman and Littlefield, 2005); Melvyn Stokes and Stephen Conway, *The Market Revolution in America: Social, Political, and Religious Expressions, 1800–1880* (Charlottesville: University Press of Virginia, 1996); Jeanne Boydston, "The Woman Who Wasn't There: Women's Market Labor and the Transition to Capitalism in the United States," *Journal of the Early Republic* 16 (Summer 1996), 183–206; Allan Kulikoff, *The Agrarian Origins of American Capitalism* (Charlottesville: University Press of Virginia, 1992); Jeanne Boydston, *Home and Work: Housework, Wages, and the Ideology of Labor in the Early Republic* (New York: Oxford University Press, 1990); Christopher Clark, *The Roots of Rural Capitalism: Western Massachusetts, 1780–1860* (Ithaca, N.Y.: Cornell University Press, 1990); Stephanie Coontz, *The Social Origins of Private Life: A History of American Families, 1600–1900* (New York: Verso, 1988); and Paul E. Johnson, "The Modernization of Mayo Greenleaf Patch: Land, Family, and Marginality in New England, 1766–1818," *New England Quarterly* 55 (December 1982), 488–516. On shoemaking in particular, see Paul G. Faler, *Mechanics and Manufacturers in the Early Industrial Revolution: Lynn, Massachusetts, 1780–1860* (Albany: State University of New York Press, 1981) and Alan Dawley, *Class and Community: The Industrial Revolution in Lynn* (Cambridge, Mass.: Harvard University Press, 1976). For Thomas Jefferson's vision of a nation of farmers, see "Query XIX," in Thomas Jefferson, *Notes on the State of Virginia* (Philadelphia: Prichard and Hall, 1788), 174–75.

On the meaning and significance of timekeeping, see Michael O'Malley, *Keeping Watch: A History of American Time* (New York: Viking, 1990) and the classic, E. P. Thompson, "Time, Work-Discipline, and Industrial Capitalism," *Past and Present* 38 (December 1967), 56–97. On the railroads, see John H. White, Jr., *American Locomotives: An Engineering History, 1830–1880* (Baltimore: Johns Hopkins University Press, 1968).

On the New England textile industry, including industrialization, labor conditions and relations, living conditions, and the contours of the workforce, see William Moran, *The Belles of New England: The Women of the Textile Mills and the Families Whose Wealth They Wove* (New York: St. Martin's Press, 2002); Thomas Dublin, *Transforming Women's Work: New England Lives in the Industrial Revolution* (Ithaca, N.Y.: Cornell University Press, 1994); Thomas Dublin, *Women at Work: The Transformation of Work and Community in Lowell, Massachusetts, 1826–1860* (New York: Columbia University Press, 1979); and Caroline F. Ware, *The Early New England Cotton Manufacture: A Study in Industrial Beginnings* (Boston: Houghton Mifflin, 1931).

On women's efforts to reform men, see Elaine Frantz Parsons, *Manhood Lost: Fallen Drunkards and Redeeming Women in the Nineteenth-Century United States* (Baltimore: Johns Hopkins University Press, 2003); Bruce Dorsey, *Reforming Men and Women: Gender in the Antebellum City* (Ithaca, N.Y.: Cornell University Press, 2002); and Ruth M. Alexander, " 'We Are Engaged as a Band of Sisters': Class and Domesticity in the Washingtonian Temperance Movement, 1840–1850," *Journal of American History* 75 (December 1988), 763–85. On the work ethic, see Daniel T. Rodgers, *The Work Ethic in Industrial America, 1850–1920* (Chicago: University of Chicago Press, 1978).

On antebellum political parties and the ideology of free labor, see Sean Wilentz, *The Rise of American Democracy: Jefferson to Lincoln* (New York: W. W. Norton, 2005); John Ashworth, *Slavery, Capitalism, and Politics in the Antebellum Republic*, vol. 1, *Commerce and Compromise, 1820–1850* (New York: Cambridge University Press, 1995); Tyler Anbinder, *Nativism and Slavery: The Northern Know Nothings and the Politics of the 1850s* (New York: Oxford University Press, 1992); John Ashworth, *"Agrarians" and "Aristocrats": Party Political Ideology in the United States, 1837–1846* (London: Royal Historical Society, 1983); Eric Foner, *Politics and Ideology in the Age of the Civil War* (New York: Oxford University Press, 1980); and Eric Foner, *Free Soil, Free Labor, Free Men: The Ideology of the Republican Party before the Civil War* (New York: Oxford University Press, 1970).

On New Hampshire politics, see Lex Renda, *Running on the Record: Civil War–Era Politics in New Hampshire* (Charlottesville: University Press of Virginia, 1997); Peter Haebler, "Nativism, Liquor, and Riots: Manchester Politics, 1858–1859," *Historical New Hampshire* 46 (Summer 1991), 66–91; Peter Haebler, "Nativist Riots in Manchester: An Episode of Know-Nothingism in New Hampshire," *Historical New Hampshire* 39 (Fall–Winter 1984), 122–38; Thomas R. Bright, "The Anti-Nebraska Coalition and the Emergence of the Republican Party in New Hampshire, 1853–1857," *Historical New Hampshire* 27 (Summer 1972), 57–88; Donald B. Cole, *Jacksonian Democracy in New Hampshire, 1800–1851* (Cambridge, Mass.: Harvard University Press, 1970); and Lucy Lowden, "The Granite State for Lincoln: New Hampshire's Role in the Nomination of Abraham Lincoln at the Republican National Convention, 1860," *Historical New Hampshire* 25 (Spring 1970), 1–26.

On Irish immigrants and the question of whiteness, see Matthew Frye Jacobson, *Whiteness of a Different Color: European Immigrants and the Alchemy of Race* (Cambridge, Mass.: Harvard University Press, 1998) and David R. Roediger, *The Wages of Whiteness: Race and the Making of the American Working Class* (New York: Verso, 1991). Also see Noel Ignatiev, *How the Irish Became White* (New York: Routledge, 1995); Theodore W. Allen, *The Invention of the White Race* (New York: Verso, 1994); and Dale T. Knobel, *Paddy and the Republic: Ethnicity and Nationality in Antebellum America* (Middletown, Conn.: Wesleyan University Press, 1986). On the intersection of Irish and African American lives, see Graham Hodges, "'Desirable Companions and Lovers': Irish and African Americans in the Sixth Ward, 1830–1870," in *The New York Irish*, ed. Ronald H. Bayor and Timothy J. Meagher (Baltimore: Johns Hopkins University Press, 1996), 107–24. For important assessments of the literature, see Peter Kolchin, "Whiteness Studies: The New History of Race in America," *Journal of American History* 89 (June 2002), 154–73, and Eric Arnesen et al., "Scholarly Controversy: Whiteness and the Historians' Imagination," *International Labor and Working-Class History* 60 (Fall 2001), 3–92. On domestic labor in the North, see the sources listed for Chapter 4, below.

On African Americans in New England and the North, see Joanne Pope Melish, *Disowning Slavery: Gradual Emancipation and "Race" in New England, 1780–1860* (Ithaca, N.Y.: Cornell University Press, 1998) and James Oliver Horton and Lois E. Horton, *In Hope of Liberty: Culture, Community and Protest among Northern Free Blacks, 1700–1860* (New York: Oxford University Press, 1997); see also Ronald Bailey, " 'Those Valuable People, the Africans': The Economic Impact of the Slave(ry) Trade on Textile Industrialization in New England," in *The Meaning of Slavery in the North*, ed. David Roediger and Martin H. Blatt (New York: Garland, 1998), 3–31. On the niche of barbering, see Douglas Bristol, Jr., "From Outposts to Enclaves: A Social History of Black Barbers from 1750 to 1915," *Enterprise and Society* 5 (December 2004), 594–606.

On antislavery activism in New Hampshire, see John L. Myers, "The Beginning of

Antislavery Agencies in New Hampshire, 1832–1835" and "The Major Effort of Anti-slavery Agents in New Hampshire, 1835–1837," *Historical New Hampshire* 25 (Fall 1970), 2–25, and 26 (Fall 1971), 3–27. On the John Brown affair, see David S. Reynolds, *John Brown, Abolitionist: The Man Who Killed Slavery, Sparked the Civil War, and Seeded Civil Rights* (New York: Alfred A. Knopf, 2005).

Chapter 3. Yankee in the Deep South

On the westward migration of antebellum Americans, see Joan E. Cashin, *A Family Venture: Men and Women on the Southern Frontier* (New York: Oxford University Press, 1991) and John Mack Faragher, *Women and Men on the Overland Trail* (New Haven, Conn.: Yale University Press, 1979).

On antebellum Mobile, Alabama, including population, economics, labor, slavery, and politics, see David T. Gleeson, *The Irish in the South, 1815–1877* (Chapel Hill: University of North Carolina Press, 2001); Elizabeth Barrett Gould, *From Fort to Port: An Architectural History of Mobile, Alabama, 1711–1918* (Tuscaloosa: University of Alabama Press, 1988); Harriet E. Amos, *Cotton City: Urban Development in Antebellum Mobile* (University: University of Alabama Press, 1985); Randall M. Miller, "The Enemy Within: Some Effects of Foreign Immigrants on Antebellum Southern Cities," *Southern Studies* 24 (Spring 1985), 30–53; Harriet E. Amos, " 'Birds of Passage' in a Cotton Port: Northerners and Foreigners among the Urban Leaders of Mobile, 1820–1860," in *Class, Conflict, and Consensus: Antebellum Southern Community Studies,* ed. Orville Vernon Burton and Robert C. McMath Jr. (Westport, Conn.: Greenwood Press, 1982), 232–60; Alan S. Thompson, "Southern Rights and Nativism as Issues in Mobile Politics, 1850–1861," *Alabama Review* 35 (April 1982), 127–41; Harriet E. Amos, " 'City Belles': Images and Realities of the Lives of White Women in Antebellum Mobile," *Alabama Review* 34 (January 1981), 3–19; Alan Smith Thompson, "Mobile, Alabama, 1850–1861: Economic, Political, Physical, and Population Characteristics," Ph.D. dissertation, University of Alabama, 1979; Richard C. Wade, *Slavery in the Cities: The South, 1820–1860* (New York: Oxford University Press, 1964); James Benson Sellers, *Slavery in Alabama* (University: University of Alabama Press, 1950); Herbert Weaver, "Foreigners in Ante-bellum Towns of the Lower South," *Journal of Southern History* 13 (February 1947), 62–73; Ella Lonn, *Foreigners in the Confederacy* (Chapel Hill: University of North Carolina Press, 1940); and City of Mobile Sexton's Reports, 1860, and "An Indexed-Catalogue of Minute Entries Concerning Naturalization in the Courts of Mobile County, Alabama," both in MMA.

On Josiah Nott's ideas about race, see Reginald Horsman, *Josiah Nott of Mobile: Southerner, Physician, and Racial Theorist* (Baton Rouge: Louisiana State University Press, 1987).

On free people of color in the Gulf South, see Virginia Meacham Gould, " 'A Chaos of Iniquity and Discord': Slave and Free Women of Color in the Spanish Ports of New Orleans, Mobile, and Pensacola," in *The Devil's Lane: Sex and Race in the Early*

South, ed. Catherine Clinton and Michele Gillespie (New York: Oxford University Press, 1997), 232–46; Virginia Meacham Gould, "The Free Creoles of Color of the Antebellum Gulf Ports of Mobile and Pensacola: A Struggle for the Middle Ground," in *Creoles of Color of the Gulf South*, ed. James H. Dormon (Knoxville: University of Tennessee Press, 1996), 28–50; Virginia R. Domínguez, *White by Definition: Social Classification in Creole Louisiana* (New Brunswick, N.J.: Rutgers University Press, 1986); and Ira Berlin, *Slaves without Masters: The Free Negro in the Antebellum South* (New York: Pantheon, 1974). On the practice of slaves for hire, see Jonathan D. Martin, *Divided Mastery: Slave Hiring in the American South* (Cambridge, Mass.: Harvard University Press, 2004).

For background and context on the Civil War, see James M. McPherson, *Ordeal by Fire: The Civil War and Reconstruction* (1982; reprint, New York: McGraw-Hill, 2001); James M. McPherson, *Battle Cry of Freedom: The Civil War Era* (New York: Oxford University Press, 1988); and E. B. Long and Barbara Long, *The Civil War Day by Day: An Almanac, 1861–1865* (Garden City, N.Y.: Doubleday, 1971). On secession, see Charles B. Dew, *Apostles of Disunion: Southern Secession Commissioners and the Causes of the Civil War* (Charlottesville: University Press of Virginia, 2001), and for Alabama in particular, see Sutton S. Scott, "Recollections of the Alabama Democratic State Convention of 1860," *Transactions of the Alabama Historical Society* 4 (1899–1903), reprint no. 15, pp. 313–20.

On Mobile, Alabama, during the Civil War, see Michael W. Fitzgerald, *Urban Emancipation: Popular Politics in Reconstruction Mobile, 1860–1890* (Baton Rouge: Louisiana State University Press, 2002); Arthur W. Bergeron Jr., *Confederate Mobile* (Jackson: University Press of Mississippi, 1991); Harriet E. Amos, "From Old to New South Trade in Mobile, 1850–1900," *Gulf Coast Historical Review* 5 (Spring 1990), 114–27; "Minutes of the Executive Committee of the Committee of Safety of Mobile in 1862–1863," *Bulletin of the New York Public Library* 8 (December 1904), 596–621; and "Mayor Asks for Material Aid for the Destitute and Sick of City," Minutes of the Aldermen of the City of Mobile, September 2, 1861, typescript, MMA.

On Lowell, Massachusetts, during the Civil War, see Frederick W. Coburn, *History of Lowell and Its People*, vol. 1 (New York: Lewis Historical Publishing Co., 1920); *Illustrated History of Lowell and Vicinity, Massachusetts* (Lowell, Mass.: Courier-Citizen, 1897); Charles Cowley, *Illustrated History of Lowell* (Boston: Lee and Shepard, 1868); and the following unpublished papers available at CLH: John W. Bassett, "Recruiting and Conscription in the City of Lowell during the American Civil War (1861–1865)," 1973; William T. Koczarski, "A Study of the Lowell Mills (1858–1866)," 1973; and Ronald A. Marcouillier, "The Economic Effect of the Civil War on Lowell, Massachusetts," no date.

On the Sixth Massachusetts Regiment, including the Baltimore riot of 1861, see Stephen M. Klugewicz, " 'The First Martyrs': The Sixth Massachusetts and the Baltimore Riot of 1861," *Southern Historian* 20 (Spring 1999), 5–24; Frank Towers, " 'A Vociferous Army of Howling Wolves': Baltimore's Civil War Riot of April 19, 1861,"

Maryland Historian 23 (Fall–Winter 1992), 1–27; Benjamin F. Watson, *Addresses, Reviews and Episodes Chiefly concerning the "Old Sixth" Massachusetts Regiment* (New York: no publisher, 1901); Charles Winslow Hall, ed., *Regiments and Armories of Massachusetts: An Historical Narration of the Massachusetts Volunteer Militia* (Boston: W. W. Potter, 1899); "Riot in Baltimore, Md.," U. S. War Department, *The War of the Rebellion: A Compilation of the Official Records of the Union and Confederate Armies* (Washington, D.C.: Government Printing Office, 1880–1901), ser. I, 2:7–21; and John W. Hanson, *Historical Sketch of the Old Sixth Regiment of Massachusetts Volunteers during Its Three Campaigns* (Boston: Lee and Shepard, 1866).

On soldiers' experiences and ideology in the Civil War, see James M. McPherson, *For Cause and Comrades: Why Men Fought in the Civil War* (New York: Oxford University Press, 1997) and Reid Mitchell, *Civil War Soldiers* (New York: Viking, 1988). On Union soldiers in particular, see Bell Irvin Wiley, *The Life of Billy Yank: The Common Soldier of the Union* (New York: Bobbs-Merrill, 1952).

On Confederate identity and nationalism, see Drew Gilpin Faust, *The Creation of Confederate Nationalism: Ideology and Identity in the Civil War South* (Baton Rouge: Louisiana State University Press, 1988).

On northern white women during the Civil War, see Nina Silber, *Daughters of the Union: Northern Women Fight the Civil War* (Cambridge, Mass.: Harvard University Press, 2005) and Lyde Cullen Sizer, *The Political Work of Northern Women Writers and the Civil War, 1850–1872* (Chapel Hill: University of North Carolina Press, 2000).

On divided families during the Civil War, see Amy Murrell Taylor, *The Divided Family in Civil War America* (Chapel Hill: University of North Carolina Press, 2005).

On Unionism in the South, see Margaret M. Storey, *Loyalty and Loss: Alabama's Unionists in the Civil War and Reconstruction* (Baton Rouge: Louisiana State University Press, 2004); John C. Inscoe and Robert C. Kenzer, eds., *Enemies of the Country: New Perspectives on Unionists in the Civil War South* (Athens: University of Georgia Press, 2001); and Thomas G. Dyer, *Secret Yankees: The Union Circle in Confederate Atlanta* (Baltimore: Johns Hopkins University Press, 1999).

On the history of Universalism, see Ann Lee Bressler, *The Universalist Movement in America, 1770–1880* (New York: Oxford University Press, 2001) and Russell E. Miller, *The Larger Hope: The First Century of the Universalist Church in America, 1770–1870* (Boston: Unitarian Universalist Association, 1979). See also G. Wayman McCarty, "A History of the Universalist Church in the Mid-South," M.A. thesis, Mississippi State University, 1964. For the context of Universalist theology, see Nathan O. Hatch, *The Democratization of American Christianity* (New Haven, Conn.: Yale University Press, 1989). For Universalist theology about happiness, see *The Correspondence and Discussion of the Question of Endless Misery, between Miss L. A. Prouty, Orthodox, and E. S. Foster, Universalist* (Claremont, N.H.: Claremont Manufacturing Co., 1870) and Thomas Baldwin Thayer, *Theology of Universalism: Being an Exposition of Its Doctrines and Teachings* (Boston: Tompkins and Co., 1863).

On religion during the Civil War, see Steven E. Woodworth, *While God Is Marching On: The Religious World of Civil War Soldiers* (Lawrence: University Press of Kansas, 2001) and Philip Shaw Paludan, *"A People's Contest": The Union and Civil War, 1861–1865* (New York: Harper and Row, 1988).

Chapter 4. Servant and Washerwoman

On Claremont, New Hampshire, see Thomas R. Kemp, "Community and War: The Civil War Experience of Two New Hampshire Towns," in *Toward a Social History of the American Civil War: Exploratory Essays*, ed. Maris A. Vinovskis (New York: Cambridge University Press, 1990), 31–77; Otis F. R. Waite, *History of the Town of Claremont, New Hampshire for a Period of One Hundred and Thirty Years from 1764 to 1894* (Manchester, N.H.: John B. Clarke, 1895); *Dedication of a Soldiers' Monument, at Claremont, N.H.* (Claremont, N.H.: Claremont Manufacturing Co., 1869); and Otis F. R. Waite, *Claremont War History: April, 1861, to April, 1865* (Concord, N.H.: McFarland and Jenks, 1868).

On Claremont's efforts at preservation, see Richard Candee, "Claremont Multiple Resources: Lower Village Historic District, National Register Nomination Information" (Portsmouth, N.H.: 1977) and Bryant F. Tolles Jr., "Monadnock Mills, National Register Nomination Information" (Concord, N.H.: 1974), both available online from the Connecticut River Joint Commissions, <www.crjc.org/heritage>.

On the Universalist Church in Claremont, see *First Universalist Church of Claremont, N.H., Organized 1834* (Claremont, N.H.: National Eagle, 1885) and Asa Mayo Bradley, "Notes on Societies in New Hampshire" (typescript, no date, AHI.

On working-class family life, see Steven Mintz and Susan Kellogg, *Domestic Revolutions: A Social History of American Family Life* (New York: Free Press, 1988). On working-class domesticity, including housing, see Stephanie Coontz, *The Social Origins of Private Life: A History of American Families, 1600–1900* (New York: Verso, 1988); Christine Stansell, *City of Women: Sex and Class in New York, 1789–1860* (New York: Alfred A. Knopf, 1986); and Gwendolyn Wright, *Building the Dream: A Social History of Housing in America* (New York: Pantheon, 1981). On working-class fashion, see Joan L. Severa, *Dressed for the Photographer: Ordinary Americans and Fashion, 1840–1900* (Kent, Ohio: Kent State University Press, 1995). On poverty, see Bruce Dorsey, *Reforming Men and Women: Gender in the Antebellum City* (Ithaca, N.Y.: Cornell University Press, 2002) and Michael B. Katz, *In the Shadow of the Poorhouse: A Social History of Welfare in America* (New York: Basic Books, 1986).

On train travel, see Amy G. Richter, *Home on the Rails: Women, the Railroad, and the Rise of Public Domesticity* (Chapel Hill: University of North Carolina Press, 2005) and August Mencken, *The Railroad Passenger Car: An Illustrated History of the First Hundred Years* (1957; reprint, Baltimore: Johns Hopkins University Press, 2000).

On the contours of women's labor, see Alice Kessler-Harris, *Out to Work: A History of Wage-Earning Women in the United States* (1982; reprint, New York: Oxford University Press, 2003) and Jacqueline Jones, *American Work: Four Centuries of Black and White Labor* (New York: W. W. Norton, 1998). On options for women's wagework outside the home, see Virginia Penny, *The Employments of Women: A Cyclopaedia of Woman's Work* (Boston: Walker, Wise, 1863). On child labor and the lives of working-class children, see Steven Mintz, *Huck's Raft: A History of American Childhood* (Cambridge, Mass.: Harvard University Press, 2004) and Joseph F. Kett, *Rites of Passage: Adolescence in America, 1790 to the Present* (New York: Basic Books, 1977).

For wages and prices in the nineteenth century, see Helen L. Sumner, *History of Women in Industry in the United States* (1910; reprint, New York: Arno Press, 1974); Edgar W. Martin, *The Standard of Living in 1860: American Consumption Levels on the Eve of the Civil War* (Chicago: University of Chicago Press, 1942); Arthur Harrison Cole, *Wholesale Commodity Prices in the United States, 1700–1861: Statistical Supplement, Actual Wholesale Prices of Various Commodities* (Cambridge, Mass.: Harvard University Press, 1938); and Emerson David Fite, *Social and Industrial Conditions in the North during the Civil War* (New York: Peter Smith, 1930).

On domestic labor in the North, see Catherine E. Kelly, *In the New England Fashion: Reshaping Women's Lives in the Nineteenth Century* (Ithaca, N.Y.: Cornell University Press, 1999); Thomas Dublin, *Transforming Women's Work: New England Lives in the Industrial Revolution* (Ithaca, N.Y.: Cornell University Press, 1994); Jeanne Boydston, *Home and Work: Housework, Wages, and the Ideology of Labor in the Early Republic* (New York: Oxford University Press, 1990); Carol Lasser, "The Domestic Balance of Power: Relations between Mistress and Maid in Nineteenth-Century New England," *Labor History* 28 (Winter 1987): 5–22; Christine Stansell, *City of Women: Sex and Class in New York, 1789–1860* (New York: Alfred A. Knopf, 1986); Hasia R. Diner, *Erin's Daughters in America: Irish Immigrant Women in the Nineteenth Century* (Baltimore: Johns Hopkins University Press, 1983); Faye E. Dudden, *Serving Women: Household Service in Nineteenth-Century America* (Middletown, Conn.: Wesleyan University Press, 1983); Daniel E. Sutherland, *Americans and Their Servants: Domestic Service in the United States from 1800 to 1920* (Baton Rouge: Louisiana State University Press, 1981); and David M. Katzman, *Seven Days a Week: Women and Domestic Service in Industrializing America* (New York: Oxford University Press, 1978).

On the contours of housework, see Priscilla J. Brewer, *From Fireplace to Cookstove: Technology and the Domestic Ideal in America* (Syracuse, N.Y.: Syracuse University Press, 2000); Jeanne Boydston, *Home and Work: Housework, Wages, and the Ideology of Labor in the Early Republic* (New York: Oxford University Press, 1990); Ruth Schwartz Cowan, *More Work for Mother: The Ironies of Household Technology from the Open Hearth to the Microwave* (New York: Basic Books, 1983); and especially Susan Strasser, *Never Done: A History of American Housework* (New York: Pantheon, 1982).

On braiding palm-leaf hats, see Thomas Dublin, *Transforming Women's Work: New England Lives in the Industrial Revolution* (Ithaca, N.Y.: Cornell University Press, 1994) and Thomas Dublin, "Women and Outwork in a Nineteenth-Century New England

Town: Fitzwilliam, New Hampshire, 1830–1850," in *The Countryside in the Age of Capitalist Transformation: Essays in the Social History of Rural America*, ed. Steven Hahn and Jonathan Prude (Chapel Hill: University of North Carolina Press, 1985), 51–69. On sewing, see Jeremy Farrell, *Socks and Stockings* (London: B. T. Batsford, 1992).

On the northern home front during the Civil War, see J. Matthew Gallman, *The North Fights the Civil War: The Home Front* (Chicago: Ivan R. Dee, 1994). On northern women's responses to the Civil War, see Nina Silber, *Daughters of the Union: Northern Women Fight the Civil War* (Cambridge, Mass.: Harvard University Press, 2005) and Lyde Cullen Sizer, *The Political Work of Northern Women Writers and the Civil War, 1850–1872* (Chapel Hill: University of North Carolina Press, 2000). On New Hampshire politics, see Lex Renda, *Running on the Record: Civil War–Era Politics in New Hampshire* (Charlottesville: University Press of Virginia, 1997).

On the Twenty-sixth Massachusetts Regiment, see *Massachusetts Soldiers, Sailors, and Marines in the Civil War* (Norwood, Mass.: Adjutant General's Office, 1931), vol. 3; Frederick H. Dyer Publishing Co., *A Compendium of the War of the Rebellion* (Des Moines, Iowa: Dyer, 1908); and Richard B. Irwin, *History of the Nineteenth Army Corps* (New York: G. P. Putnam's Sons, 1892).

On the Third Battle of Winchester in particular, see Gary W. Gallagher, ed., *The Shenandoah Valley Campaign of 1864* (Chapel Hill: University of North Carolina Press, 2006); Brandon H. Beck and Charles S. Grunder, *The Three Battles of Winchester: A History and Guided Tour* (Berryville, Va.: Civil War Foundation, 1997); Gary W. Gallagher, ed., *Struggle for the Shenandoah: Essays on the 1864 Valley Campaign* (Kent, Ohio: Kent State University Press, 1991); and Jeffry D. Wert, *From Winchester to Cedar Creek: The Shenandoah Campaign of 1864* (New York: Simon and Schuster, 1987). On Winchester cemetery today, see Adrian O'Connor, "The Stories of National Cemetery," *Winchester Star*, March 30, 2002.

On the Twenty-fourth Alabama Regiment, see Arthur Middleton Manigault, *A Carolinian Goes to War: The Civil War Narrative of Arthur Middleton Manigault*, ed. R. Lockwood Tower (Columbia: University of South Carolina Press, 1983) and Alexander F. Stevenson, *The Battle of Stone's River near Murfreesboro, Tenn., December 30, 1862, to January 3, 1863* (1884; reprint, Dayton, Ohio: Morningside Bookshop, 1983). For an overview of the Twenty-fourth Alabama and Gage's Battery, see Clement A. Evans, *Confederate Military History: A Library of Confederate States History*, vol. 7 (Atlanta: Confederate Publishing Co., 1899).

On coping with death, see Drew Gilpin Faust, "'The Dread Void of Uncertainty': Naming the Dead in the American Civil War," *Southern Cultures* 11 (Summer 2005), 7–32; Drew Gilpin Faust, "The Civil War Soldier and the Art of Dying," *Journal of Southern History* 67 (February 2001), 3–38; and Steven E. Woodworth, *While God Is Marching On: The Religious World of Civil War Soldiers* (Lawrence: University Press of Kansas, 2001). On the sentimental language invoked to describe soldiers' deaths, see Alice Fahs, *The Imagined Civil War: Popular Literature of the North and South,*

1861–1865 (Chapel Hill: University of North Carolina Press, 2001). On causes of death in the Confederate Army, see H. H. Cunningham, *Doctors in Gray: The Confederate Medical Service* (Baton Rouge: Louisiana State University Press, 1958). On depression, see the sources listed for Chapter 5, below. On Universalist theology, see the sources listed for Chapter 3, above. On Lowell, Massachusetts, at the end of the Civil War, see the sources listed for Chapter 3, above.

Chapter 5. From Widow to Bride

On Dracut, Massachusetts, see Alan Manoian, *Pawtucketville: A 325-Year-Old Neighborhood* (Lowell, Mass.: Patrick J. Mogan Cultural Center, 1993); Edwin P. Conklin, *Middlesex County and Its People: A History* (New York: Lewis Historical Publishing Co., 1927), vol. 2; Silas R. Coburn, *History of Dracut, Massachusetts* (Lowell, Mass.: Courier-Citizen, 1922); and Samuel Adams Drake, *History of Middlesex County, Massachusetts* (Boston: Estes and Lauriat, 1880).

On Morristown, Vermont, including the Universalist Church there, see Bill Lizotte, "From the President," *Morristown Historical Society Newsletter* 2 (Winter–Spring 2003), 2; W. K. Sanders, *A Brief History of the Town of Morristown, Vermont* (Morrisville, Vt.: Morrisville Women's Club, 1974); Henry G. Fairbanks, "Slavery and the Vermont Clergy," *Vermont History* 27 (October 1959), 305–12; Wilbur H. Siebert, *Vermont's Anti-Slavery and Underground Railroad Record* (Columbus, Ohio: Spahr and Glenn, 1937); Anna L. Mower, *History of Morristown, Vermont* (Morrisville, Vt.: Messenger-Sentinel Co., 1935); Lou F. Rand, "A Bit of History and a Glimpse of Morrisville, Vt., Today," *Inter-State Journal: An Illustrated Monthly of Vermont and New Hampshire* 9 (October 1904), no pagination; "Morristown Celebrates Its Centennial Anniversary," *Rutland Herald*, July 5, 1890; F. W. Beers, *Atlas of the Counties of Lamoille and Orleans, Vermont* (New York: F. W. Beers, 1878); and "Morristown," in Abby Maria Hemenway, comp., *The Vermont Historical Gazetteer* (Burlington, Vt.: A. M. Hemenway, 1871), 680–92.

On Universalism in Vermont, see Zadock Thompson, *History of Vermont, Natural, Civil, and Statistical* (Burlington: Chauncy Goodrich, 1842), vol. 2, and Edith Fox MacDonald, *Rebellion in the Mountains: The Story of Universalism and Unitarianism in Vermont* (Concord, N.H.: New Hampshire–Vermont Unitarian-Universalist Association, no date).

On Cabot, Vermont, see Jane Brown, Barbara Carpenter, Amanda Legare, and Caleb Pitkin, *Cabot, Vermont: A Collection of Memories from the Century Past* (Cabot, Vt.: Cabot Oral History Committee, 1999); *Our Town: Cabot Past and Present* (Cabot, Vt.: Cabot High School, 1977); Abby Maria Hemenway, *Vermont Historical Gazetteer: A Local History of All the Towns in the State* (Montpelier: Vermont Watchman, 1882), vol. 4; Abby Maria Hemenway, *The History of Washington County in the Vermont Historical Gazetteer* (Montpelier: Vermont Watchman, 1882); and F. W. Beers, *County Atlas of Washington, Vermont, from Actual Surveys* (New York: F. W. Beers, 1873).

On depression, "neurasthenia," and medical care just after the Civil War, see Jennifer

Radden, ed., *The Nature of Melancholy: From Aristotle to Kristeva* (New York: Oxford University Press, 2000); Nancy Tomes, *The Gospel of Germs: Men, Women, and the Microbe in American Life* (Cambridge, Mass.: Harvard University Press, 1998); Simon Wessely, "Neurasthenia and Fatigue Syndromes," in *A History of Clinical Psychiatry: The Origin and History of Psychiatric Disorders*, ed. German E. Berrios and Roy Porter (New York: New York University Press, 1995), 509–44; Susan E. Cayleff, "'Prisoners of Their Own Feebleness': Women, Nerves and Western Medicine—A Historical Overview," *Social Science and Medicine* 26, no. 12 (1988), 1199–1208; F. G. Gosling, *Before Freud: Neurasthenia and the American Medical Community, 1870–1910* (Urbana: University of Illinois Press, 1987); Stanley W. Jackson, *Melancholia and Depression from Hippocratic Times to Modern Times* (New Haven, Conn.: Yale University Press, 1986), Edward Shorter, *Bedside Manners: The Troubled History of Doctors and Patients* (New York: Simon and Schuster, 1985); Paul Starr, *The Social Transformation of American Medicine* (New York: Basic Books, 1982); and Ann Douglas Wood, "'The Fashionable Diseases': Women's Complaints and Their Treatment in Nineteenth-Century America," *Journal of Interdisciplinary History* 4 (Summer 1973), 25–52. See also Joshua Wolf Shenk, *Lincoln's Melancholy: How Depression Challenged a President and Fueled His Greatness* (Boston: Houghton Mifflin, 2005). For contemporary sources, see George Beard, "Neurasthenia, or Nervous Exhaustion," *Boston Medical and Surgical Journal* 3 (April 29, 1869), 217–21, and E. H. Van Deusen, "Observations on a Form of Nervous Prostration, (Neurasthenia,) Culminating in Insanity," *American Journal of Insanity* 25 (April 1869), 445–61.

On women's wagework just after the Civil War, see the sources listed for Chapter 4, above.

On responses to the war's conclusion, see Steven E. Woodworth, *While God Is Marching On: The Religious World of Civil War Soldiers* (Lawrence: University Press of Kansas, 2001). On the surrender of Mobile, Alabama, see Sean Michael O'Brien, *Mobile, 1865: Last Stand of the Confederacy* (Westport, Conn.: Praeger, 2001) and Joe A. Mobley, "The Siege of Mobile, August, 1864–April, 1965," *Alabama Historical Quarterly* 38 (Winter 1976), 250–70. On immediate postwar Mobile, see Michael W. Fitzgerald, *Urban Emancipation: Popular Politics in Reconstruction Mobile, 1860–1890* (Baton Rouge: Louisiana State University Press, 2002).

On the era of Reconstruction, see Steven Hahn, *A Nation under Our Feet: Black Political Struggles in the Rural South from Slavery to the Great Migration* (Cambridge: Mass.: Harvard University Press, 2003) and Eric Foner, *Reconstruction: America's Unfinished Revolution, 1863–1877* (New York: Harper and Row, 1988). On reconciliation between white northerners and white southerners, see David W. Blight, *Race and Reunion: The Civil War in American Memory* (Cambridge, Mass.: Harvard University Press, 2001) and Nina Silber, *The Romance of Reunion: Northerners and the South, 1865–1900* (Chapel Hill: University of North Carolina Press, 1993). On the post–Civil War reconciliation of divided families, see Amy Murrell Taylor, *The Divided Family in Civil War America* (Chapel Hill: University of North Carolina Press, 2005).

On courtship and romantic love, see Catherine E. Kelly, *In the New England Fashion: Reshaping Women's Lives in the Nineteenth Century* (Ithaca, N.Y.: Cornell University Press, 1999); Steven Seidman, *Romantic Longings: Love in America, 1830–1980* (New York: Routledge, 1991); Karen Lystra, *Searching the Heart: Women, Men, and Romantic Love in Nineteenth-Century America* (New York: Oxford University Press, 1989); and Ellen K. Rothman, *Hands and Hearts: A History of Courtship in America* (Cambridge, Mass.: Harvard University Press, 1987).

On the Dracut church, see A. C. Varnum, *History of Pawtucket Church and Society* (Lowell, Mass.: Morning Mail, 1888). On the Mobile church, see "Presbyterian Churches, Mobile, Mobile County," typescript, Alabama Church Records, ADAH.

On attitudes and laws about race and marriage in the North, see Elise Lemire, *"Miscegenation": Making Race in America* (Philadelphia: University of Pennsylvania Press, 2002); Leslie M. Harris, "From Abolitionist Amalgamators to 'Rulers of the Five Points': The Discourse of Interracial Sex and Reform in Antebellum New York City" and Lyde Cullen Sizer, "Still Waiting: Intermarriage in White Women's Civil War Novels," both in *Sex, Love, Race: Crossing Boundaries in North American History*, ed. Martha Hodes (New York: New York University Press, 1999); Graham Hodges, "'Desirable Companions and Lovers': Irish and African Americans in the Sixth Ward, 1830–1870," in *The New York Irish*, ed. Ronald H. Bayor and Timothy J. Meagher (Baltimore: Johns Hopkins University Press, 1996), 107–24; and Louis Ruchames, "Race, Marriage, and Abolition in Massachusetts," *Journal of Negro History* 40 (July 1955), 250–73.

On ideas about white women and purity, see Martha Hodes, *White Women, Black Men: Illicit Sex in the Nineteenth-Century South* (New Haven, Conn.: Yale University Press, 1997); Evelyn Brooks Higginbotham, "African-American Women's History and the Metalanguage of Race," *Signs* 17 (Winter 1992), 251–74; and Nancy F. Cott, "Passionlessness: An Interpretation of Victorian Sexual Ideology, 1790–1850," in *A Heritage of Her Own: Toward a New Social History of American Women*, ed. Nancy F. Cott and Elizabeth H. Pleck (New York: Simon and Schuster, 1979), 162–81.

On the treatment of people of African descent in the North, see James Oliver Horton and Lois E. Horton, *Black Bostonians: Family Life and Community Struggle in the Antebellum North* (New York: Holmes and Meier, 1999); Joanne Pope Melish, *Disowning Slavery: Gradual Emancipation and "Race" in New England, 1780–1860* (Ithaca, N.Y.: Cornell University Press, 1998); and Leon F. Litwack, *North of Slavery: The Negro in the Free States, 1790–1860* (Chicago: University of Chicago Press, 1961). On discrimination based on complexion, see James Oliver Horton, *Free People of Color: Inside the African American Community* (Washington, D.C.: Smithsonian Institution Press, 1993) and Willard B. Gatewood, *Aristocrats of Color: The Black Elite, 1880–1920* (Bloomington: Indiana University Press, 1990). On foreigners of African descent in the United States, see Marilyn Halter, *Between Race and Ethnicity: Cape Verdean American Immigrants, 1860–1965* (Urbana: University of Illinois Press, 1993).

For further explorations of mutable racial classification, see Martha Hodes, "The

Mercurial Nature and Abiding Power of Race: A Transnational Family Story," *American Historical Review* 108 (February 2003), 84–118.

On African Americans in Lowell, Massachusetts, see Martha Mayo, *Profiles in Courage: African-Americans in Lowell* (Lowell, Mass.: Patrick J. Mogan Cultural Center, 1993); Brad Parker, *Black and Antislavery History of Early Lowell* (Lowell, Mass.: Landmark Printing Co., 1986); and Loretta Ryan, "African Americans in Lowell, Massachusetts (1826–1880): A Research Report," unpublished paper, 1980, CLH.

On racism among northern white soldiers, see James M. McPherson, *For Cause and Comrades: Why Men Fought in the Civil War* (New York: Oxford University Press, 1997),

On New Orleans and Creole society, see Judith Kelleher Schafer, *Becoming Free, Remaining Free: Manumission and Enslavement in New Orleans, 1846–1862* (Baton Rouge: Louisiana State University Press, 2003); Sybil Kein, ed., *Creole: The History and Legacy of Louisiana's Free People of Color* (Baton Rouge: Louisiana State University Press, 2000); Walter Johnson, *Soul by Soul: Life Inside the Antebellum Slave Market* (Cambridge, Mass.: Harvard University Press, 1999); Arnold R. Hirsch and Joseph Logsdon, eds., *Creole New Orleans: Race and Americanization* (Baton Rouge: Louisiana State University Press, 1992); and John W. Blassingame, *Black New Orleans, 1860–1880* (Chicago: University of Chicago Press, 1973).

On Provincetown, Massachusetts, see Karen Christel Krahulik, *Provincetown: From Pilgrim Landing to Gay Resort* (New York: New York University Press, 2005).

Chapter 6. The Sea Captain's Wife

On the Cayman Islands, including East End, see Michael Craton, *Founded upon the Seas: A History of the Cayman Islands and Their People* (Kingston, Jamaica: Ian Randle, 2003); Roger C. Smith, *The Maritime Heritage of the Cayman Islands* (Gainesville: University Press of Florida, 2000); Neville Williams, *A History of the Cayman Islands* (1970; reprint, Grand Cayman: Government of the Cayman Islands, 1998); Doren Miller, "Upon the Seas: A Study of the Cayman Islands," Cayman Film Associates, 1975; I. R. Buchler, "Caymanian Folk Racial Categories," *Man: A Monthly Record of Anthropological Science* 62 (December 1962), 185–86; Edwin Beale Doran, Jr., "A Physical and Cultural Geography of the Cayman Islands," Ph.D. dissertation, University of California–Berkeley, 1953; and George S. S. Hirst, *Notes on the History of the Cayman Islands* (Kingston, Jamaica: P. A. Benjamin, 1910).

On daily life on Grand Cayman and in East End, see interviews conducted by the Cayman Islands Memory Bank, CINA; "The People of the Cayman Islands," permanent exhibition, CINM; Richard Westmacott, *Gardens, Yards, Pieces, and Grounds: The Domestic Places and Spaces of the Cayman Islands* (Grand Cayman: Cayman Islands National Museum, 1999); "Caymanian Gardens and Yards," *Horizons* (May–June 1998), 107; "Our Islands' Daughters," exhibition, CINM (viewed 1998); Will Jackson, *Smoke-Pot Days* (Grand Cayman: Cayman National Cultural Foundation, 1997);

Aarona Booker Kohlman, *Under Tin Roofs: Cayman in the 1920s* (Grand Cayman: Cayman Islands National Museum, 1993); Elizabeth Ebanks, "Bodden Town Report: Miss Netie Looks Back in Time," *Nor'wester* (August 1981), 8–9; "Stories Our Grandparents Told," in *Our Islands' Treasure* (Cayman Islands: Pirates' Week Committee, 1980), vol. 1; E. F. Aguilar and P. T. Saunders, *The Cayman Islands: Their Postal History, Postage Stamps, and Postmarks* (Folkestone, U.K.: F. J. Parsons, 1962); William T. Eden and E. Noel McLaughlin, *The Island of Grand Cayman at the Jamaica Exhibition* (Jamaica: DeCordova and Co., 1891); "Traditional Uses of the Silver Thatch Palm," CINM film, no date; Aarona Booker Kohlman, *Wotcha Say: An Introduction to Colloquial Caymanian* (Grand Cayman: Cayman ArtVentures, no date); and Governor's Reports at TNA:PRO, dating from Eunice Connolly's years on the island.

On the Scottish-Presbyterian church in particular, see Harwell M. McCoy, *Journey to Partnership: A History of the Presbyterian (United) Church in Grand Cayman* (Surrey, U.K.: Optichrome, 1997); *United Presbyterian Missionary Record*, the church newsletter, published in Edinburgh, Scotland, 1846–1900; United Presbyterian Church Mission Board, Church of Scotland, Overseas Council, Deposit 298, and United Presbyterian Church, Letter-books of the Secretaries of the Foreign Mission Committee, Mss. 7638–48, both in Department of Special Collections, NLS; and John M'Kerrow, *History of the Foreign Missions of the Secession and United Presbyterian Church* (Edinburgh: Andrew Elliot, 1867).

On duppies in particular, see Anita Ebanks, "All about Duppies . . . " *Newstar* (December 1988), 80; Richard Goldberg, "The Way We Were or Duppies: A Caribbean Phenomenon," *Journal of Psychological Anthropology* 2 (Spring 1979), 197–212; Robert S. Fuller, *Duppies Is* (Grand Cayman: Cayman ArtVentures, 1967); and MacEdward Leach, "Jamaican Duppy Lore," *Journal of American Folklore* 74 (July–September 1961), 207–15.

On illness and medical care in particular, see "Remedies," *Horizons* (July–August 2002), 31; "Report of Medical Aid Afforded to the Inhabitants of Grand Cayman," November 20, 1878, TNA:PRO: CO 137/492/2–15; "Reporting on the Health of Grand Cayman," March 1877, TNA:PRO: CO 137/483/400–405; and records relating to the Cayman Islands in the International Health Board, Division Records, RG5, Rockefeller Foundation Archives, RAC.

On slavery in particular, see Cayman slave registration records, TNA:PRO: T 71/243; Roy James Murray, "'The Man That Says Slaves Be Quite Happy in Slavery . . . Is Either Ignorant or a Lying Person . . .': An Account of Slavery in the Marginal Colonies of the British West Indies," Ph.D. dissertation, University of Glasgow, 2001; Roy Murray, "'Slavery Be Dead . . . We Be Free!': An Account of Slavery and Emancipation in the Cayman Islands," M.A. Heritage Studies Research Project, 1995, unpublished paper, CINA; and B. W. Higman, *Slave Populations of the British Caribbean, 1807–1834* (Baltimore: Johns Hopkins University Press, 1984).

On Caribbean racial systems, see Hilary McD Beckles, "White Women and Freedom," in *Centering Woman: Gender Discourses in Caribbean Slave Society* (Kingston, Jamaica: Ian Randle, 1999), 60–72; Stanley L. Engerman and B. W. Higman, "The Demographic Structure of the Caribbean Slave Societies in the Eighteenth and Nineteenth Centuries" and Gad Heuman, "The Social Structure of the Slave Societies in the Caribbean," both in *The Slave Societies of the Caribbean*, ed. Franklin W. Knight (London: UNESCO, 1997), 45–103, 138–68; Kevin D. Smith, "A Fragmented Freedom: The Historiography of Emancipation and Its Aftermath in the British West Indies," *Slavery and Abolition* 16 (April 1995), 101–30; Patrick Bryan, "The Black Middle Class in Nineteenth Century Jamaica," in *Caribbean Freedom: Economy and Society from Emancipation to the Present*, ed. Hilary Beckles and Verene Shepherd (Princeton, N.J.: Markus Weiner, 1993), 284–95; Michel-Rolph Trouillot, "The Inconvenience of Freedom: Free People of Color and the Political Aftermath of Slavery in Dominica and Saint-Domingue/Haiti," in *The Meaning of Freedom: Economics, Politics, and Culture after Slavery*, ed. Frank McGlynn and Seymour Drescher (Pittsburgh: University of Pittsburgh Press, 1992), 147–82; Patrick Bryan, *The Jamaican People, 1880–1902* (London: Macmillan Caribbean, 1991); Arnold A. Sio, "Marginality and Free Coloured Identity in Caribbean Slave Society," *Slavery and Abolition* 8 (September 1987), 166–82; Gad J. Heuman, "White over Brown over Black: The Free Coloureds in Jamaican Society during Slavery and after Emancipation," *Journal of Caribbean History* 14 (May 1981), 46–69; B. W. Higman, *Slave Population and Economy in Jamaica, 1807–1834* (Cambridge, U.K.: Cambridge University Press, 1976); and Douglas Hall, "Jamaica," in *Neither Slave nor Free: The Freedman of African Descent in the Slave Societies of the New World*, ed. David W. Cohen and Jack P. Greene (Baltimore: Johns Hopkins University Press, 1972), 193–213. On British West Indian race and politics, see Thomas C. Holt, *The Problem of Freedom: Race, Labor, and Politics in Jamaica and Britain, 1832–1938* (Baltimore: Johns Hopkins University Press, 1992).

On the United States versus British Caribbean racial systems, see Martha Hodes, "The Mercurial Nature and Abiding Power of Race: A Transnational Family Story," *American Historical Review* 108 (February 2003), 84–118; Werner Sollors, *Neither Black nor White yet Both: Thematic Explorations of Interracial Literature* (New York: Oxford University Press, 1997); Stephen Small, "Racial Group Boundaries and Identities: People of 'Mixed-Race' in Slavery across the Americas," *Slavery and Abolition* 15 (December 1994), 17–37; and Winthrop D. Jordan, "American Chiaroscuro: The Status and Definition of Mulattoes in the British Colonies," *William and Mary Quarterly* 19 (April 1962), 183–200. Also see Rebecca J. Scott, *Degrees of Freedom: Louisiana and Cuba after Slavery* (Cambridge, Mass.: Harvard University Press, 2005). On the United States one-drop rule, see F. James Davis, *Who Is Black? One Nation's Definition* (University Park: Pennsylvania State University Press, 1991) and Joel Williamson, *New People: Miscegenation and Mulattoes in the United States* (New York: Free Press, 1980).

On white people "passing" for black, see Martha Hodes, "The Mercurial Nature and Abiding Power of Race: A Transnational Family Story," *American Historical Review* 108

(February 2003), 84–118. On people of African descent understood as white, see Adrian Piper, "Passing for White, Passing for Black," in *Passing and the Fictions of Identity*, ed. Elaine K. Ginsberg (Durham, N.C.: Duke University Press, 1996), 234–69, and Virginia R. Domínguez, *White by Definition: Social Classification in Creole Louisiana* (New Brunswick, N.J.: Rutgers University Press, 1986). The best-known literary renderings are Mark Twain, *The Tragedy of Pudd'nhead Wilson* (Hartford, Conn.: American Publishing Co., 1894) and Edna Ferber, *Show Boat* (Garden City, N.Y.: Doubleday, Page, 1926). For a brilliant treatment, see Langston Hughes, "Who's Passing for Who?" in Hughes, *Laughing to Keep from Crying* (New York: Henry Holt, 1952), 1–7.

On the idea of "home" representing a middle-class ideal of domesticity, see Christine Stansell, *City of Women: Sex and Class in New York, 1789–1860* (New York: Alfred A. Knopf, 1986) and Kathryn Kish Sklar, *Catharine Beecher: A Study in American Domesticity* (New Haven, Conn.: Yale University Press, 1973). On the ideal home in the nineteenth century, see Louise L. Stevenson, *The Victorian Home Front: American Thought and Culture, 1860–1880* (Ithaca, N.Y.: Cornell University Press, 1991) and Colleen McDannell, *The Christian Home in Victorian America, 1840–1900* (Bloomington: Indiana University Press, 1986).

On companionate marriage, see Karen Lystra, *Searching the Heart: Women, Men, and Romantic Love in Nineteenth-Century America* (New York: Oxford University Press, 1989). On ideals of fatherhood, see Stephen M. Frank, *Life with Father: Parenthood and Masculinity in the Nineteenth-Century American North* (Baltimore: Johns Hopkins University Press, 1998) and E. Anthony Rotundo, *American Manhood: Transformations in Masculinity from the Revolution to the Modern Era* (New York: Basic Books, 1993).

Chapter 7. Hurricane

On turtling in the Cayman Islands, see the general sources listed for the Cayman Islands for Chapter 6, above, as well as Archie F. Carr, *The Windward Road: Adventures of a Naturalist on Remote Caribbean Shores* (New York: Alfred A. Knopf, 1956); David D. Duncan, "Capturing Giant Turtles in the Caribbean," *National Geographic* 84 (August 1943), 177–90; and Glanville Smith, "Turtles and Postage Stamps," *Atlantic Monthly* 160 (September 1937), 347–50. For the songs of mariners' wives, see "Traditional Songs from the Cayman Islands," in *Our Islands' Past: Historical Documents about Cayman from the Cayman Islands National Archive*, vol. 3 (George Town: Cayman Islands National Archive and Cayman Free Press, 1996).

On all aspects of sailing, see Peter Kemp, ed., *The Oxford Companion to Ships and the Sea* (New York: Oxford University Press, 1988); see also David R. MacGregor, *Schooners in Four Centuries* (Annapolis, Md.: Naval Institute Press, 1982).

On seafaring wives, see Lisa Norling, *Captain Ahab Had a Wife: New England Women and the Whalefishery, 1720–1820* (Chapel Hill: University of North Carolina Press, 2000); Joan Druett, *Hen Frigates: Passion and Peril, Nineteenth-Century Women at Sea* (New York: Simon and Schuster, 1998); Haskell Springer, "The Captain's Wife at Sea," in *Iron Men, Wooden Women: Gender and Seafaring in the Atlantic World, 1700–1920,* ed. Margaret S. Creighton and Lisa Norling (Baltimore: Johns Hopkins University Press, 1996), 92–117; Joan Druett, "Those Female Journals," *The Log of Mystic Seaport* 40 (Winter 1989), 115–25; Margaret S. Creighton, *Dogwatch and Liberty Days: Seafaring Life in the Nineteenth Century* (Salem, Mass.: Peabody Museum, 1982); and Julia C. Bonham, "Feminist and Victorian: The Paradox of the American Seafaring Woman of the Nineteenth Century," *American Neptune* 37 (July 1977), 203 18.

On hurricanes, see Patrick J. Fitzpatrick, *Natural Disasters: Hurricanes, A Reference Handbook* (Santa Barbara, Calif.: ABC-CLIO, 1999); Peter Kemp, ed., *The Oxford Companion to Ships and the Sea* (New York: Oxford University Press, 1988); Ivan Ray Tannehill, *Hurricanes: Their Nature and History, Particularly Those of the West Indies and the Southern Coasts of the United States* (Princeton, N.J.: Princeton University Press, 1950); Oliver L. Fassig, *Hurricanes of the West Indies* (Washington, D.C.: Weather Bureau Bulletin X, Government Printing Office, 1913); and Edward B. Garriott, *Weather Folk-Lore and Local Weather Signs* (Washington, D.C.: Weather Bureau, Government Printing Office, 1903). For a contemporary source, see Henry Piddington, *The Sailor's Horn-Book for the Law of Storms* (London: Smith, Elder, 1851).

On hurricanes relevant to the Cayman Islands, see the general sources listed for the Cayman Islands for Chapter 6, above, as well as Heather R. McLaughlin, comp. and ed., *The '32 Storm: Eye-witness Accounts and Official Reports of the Worst Natural Disaster in the History of the Cayman Islands* (George Town: Cayman Islands National Archive, 1994). On the 1876 hurricane in Grand Cayman, see "Hurricane in the Grand Cayman," *Missionary Record of the United Presbyterian Church,* Jan. 1, 1877, pp. 348–49; "Proceedings of H.M.S. 'Plover' at the Cayman Islands, Sept. 29, 1877, TNA:PRO: CO 137/485/181–86; "Present condition and prospects of the distressed people in Grand Cayman," Feb. 5, 1877, TNA:PRO: CO 137/483/86–94; "Report of Inquiry into the condition of the Inhabitants of the Cayman Islands," 1877, TNA:PRO: CO 137/483/391–95; and "Visit of the H.M.S. 'Bullfinch' to the Cayman Islands," March 1877, TNA:PRO: CO 137/483/398–403.

On the 1877 hurricane on the Miskito Cays, see Ivan Ray Tannehill, *Hurricanes: Their Nature and History, Particularly Those of the West Indies and the Southern Coasts of the United States* (Princeton, N.J.: Princeton University Press, 1950); E. B. Garriott, *West Indian Hurricanes* (Washington, D.C.: Weather Bureau Bulletin H, Government Printing Office, 1900); War Department, Office of the Chief Signal Officer, *Monthly Weather Review,* September 1877 and October 1877; and "1877 Hurricane/Tropical Data for Atlantic," <weather.unisys .com/hurricane/atlantic/1877>.

On middle-class ideas and experiences of achievement and success, see Scott A. Sandage, *Born Losers: A History of Failure in America* (Cambridge, Mass.: Harvard University Press, 2005); Anne C. Rose, *Victorian America and the Civil War* (New York: Cambridge University Press, 1992). On the idea of the self-made man in particular, see

Michael Kimmel, "The Birth of the Self-Made Man," in *The Masculinity Studies Reader*, ed. Rachel Adams and David Savran (Malden, Mass.: Blackwell, 2002); John G. Cawelti, *Apostles of the Self-Made Man* (Chicago: University of Chicago Press, 1965); and Irvin G. Wyllie, *The Self-Made Man in America: The Myth of Rags to Riches* (New Brunswick, N.J.: Rutgers University Press, 1954).

On the post–Civil War New England textile industry, see Mary B. Rose, *Firms, Networks and Business Values: The British and American Cotton Industries since 1750* (New York: Cambridge University Press, 2000); Fidelia O. Brown, "Decline and Fall: The End of the Dream," in *Cotton Was King: A History of Lowell, Massachusetts*, ed. Arthur L. Eno, Jr. (Somersworth: New Hampshire Publishing Co., 1976), 141–58; and Margaret Terrell Parker; *Lowell: A Study of Industrial Development* (New York: Macmillan, 1940). On the Appleton Mills in Lowell, Massachusetts, see Shepley Bulfinch Richardson and Abbott, *Lowell National Historical Park and Preservation District, Cultural Resources Inventory Report* (Boston: SBRA, 1980).

On the closing of the Amoskeag Manufacturing Company, see Daniel Creamer and Charles W. Coulter, *Labor and the Shut-Down of the Amoskeag Textile Mills* (Philadelphia: Work Projects Administration, National Research Project, Report no. L-5, 1939); "New Hampshire Collapse," *Time* (August 3, 1936), 46, 48; "Taps for Amoskeag," *Business Week* (July 25, 1936), 36; and Louis Adamic, "Tragic Towns of New England," *Harper's Magazine* 162 (May 1931), 748–60.

On Lowell, Massachusetts, in the late nineteenth and early twentieth centuries, see William Moran, *The Belles of New England: The Women of the Textile Mills and the Families Whose Wealth They Wove* (New York: St. Martin's Press, 2002); Thomas Dublin, "Beginnings of Industrial America," in *Lowell, The Story of an Industrial City: A Guide to Lowell National Historical Park* (Washington, D.C.: National Park Service, 1992), 13–92; Peter F. Blewett, "The New People: An Introduction to the Ethnic History of Lowell," in *Cotton Was King: A History of Lowell, Massachusetts*, ed. Arthur L. Eno, Jr. (Somersworth: New Hampshire Publishing Co., 1976), 190–217; and George F. Kenngott, *The Record of a City: A Social Survey of Lowell, Massachusetts* (New York: Macmillan, 1912).

On native-born Americans' attitudes toward immigrants, see John Higham, *Strangers in the Land: Patterns of American Nativism, 1860–1925* (New Brunswick, N.J.: Rutgers University Press, 2002) and Barbara Miller Solomon, *Ancestors and Immigrants: A Changing New England Tradition* (1956; reprint, Boston: Northeastern University Press, 1989).

On the rise of genealogy and nostalgia among white Protestants, see Francois Weil, *Family Trees: A Cultural History of Genealogy in America* (Cambridge, Mass.: Harvard University Press, forthcoming); Joseph A. Conforti, *Imagining New England: Explorations of Regional Identity from the Pilgrims to the Mid-Twentieth Century* (Chapel Hill: University of North Carolina Press, 2001); Shawn Michelle Smith, *American Archives: Gender,*

Race, and Class in Visual Culture (Princeton, N.J.: Princeton University Press, 1999); Michael Kammen, *Mystic Chords of Memory: The Transformation of Tradition in American Culture* (New York: Alfred A. Knopf, 1991); Wallace Evan Davies, *Patriotism on Parade: The Story of Veterans' and Hereditary Organizations in America, 1783–1900* (Cambridge, Mass.: Harvard University Press, 1955); and Eugene Zieber, *Ancestry: The Objects of the Hereditary Societies and the Military and Naval Orders of the United States and the Requirements for Membership Therein* (Philadelphia: Department of Heraldry, 1895).

On race relations in the post-Reconstruction United States, see Steven Hahn, *A Nation under Our Feet: Black Political Struggles in the Rural South from Slavery to the Great Migration* (Cambridge: Mass.: Harvard University Press, 2003); David W. Blight, *Race and Reunion: The Civil War in American Memory* (Cambridge, Mass.: Harvard University Press, 2001), including the erasure of slavery from Civil War memories; Leon F. Litwack, *Trouble in Mind: Black Southerners in the Age of Jim Crow* (New York: Alfred A. Knopf, 1998); and Nell Irvin Painter, *Standing at Armageddon: The United States, 1877–1919* (New York: W. W. Norton, 1987). On lynching, see Philip Dray, *At the Hands of Persons Unknown: The Lynching of Black America* (New York: Random House, 2002); Martha Hodes, *White Women, Black Men: Illicit Sex in the Nineteenth-Century South* (New Haven, Conn.: Yale University Press, 1997); and Ida B. Wells-Barnett, *Southern Horrors and Other Writings: The Anti-Lynching Campaign of Ida B. Wells, 1892–1900*, ed. Jacqueline Jones Royster (Boston: Bedford Books, 1997).

On the Cayman Islands in the twentieth century, in addition to the general sources on Cayman listed for Chapter 6, above, see John Connell, "The Cayman Islands: Economic Growth and Immigration in a British Colony," *Caribbean Geography* 5 (March 1994), 51–66; J. E. Davies, "Mosquitoes of the Cayman Islands," in *The Cayman Islands: Natural History and Biogeography*, ed. M. A. Brunt and J. E. Davies (Dordrecht, Netherlands: Kluwer Academic Publishers, 1994), 357–76; Peter Benchley, "Fair Skies for the Cayman Islands," *National Geographic* 167 (June 1985), 798–824; Mina Davis Caulfield, "Taxes, Tourists and Turtlemen: Island Dependency and the Tax-Haven Business," in *The World as a Company Town: Multinational Corporations and Social Change*, ed. Ahamed Idris-Soven, Elizabeth Idris-Soven, Mary K. Vaughan (The Hague: Mouton Publishers, 1978); Richard Steven Goldberg, "East End: A Caribbean Community under Stress," Ph.D. dissertation, University of Texas-Austin, 1976; and Morris D. Rosenberg, "The Cayman Islands: One of Caribbean's Big Success Stories," *Philadelphia Inquirer*, February 16, 1975, p. 8H.

On changing ideas about death, see Gary Laderman, *The Sacred Remains: American Attitudes toward Death, 1799–1883* (New Haven, Conn.: Yale University Press, 1996); David Charles Sloane, *The Last Great Necessity: Cemeteries in American History* (Baltimore: Johns Hopkins University Press, 1991); James J. Farrell, *Inventing the American Way of Death, 1830–1920* (Philadelphia: Temple University Press, 1980); David E. Stannard, *The Puritan Way of Death: A Study in Religion, Culture, and Social Change*

(New York: Oxford University Press, 1977); and Thomas Bender, "The 'Rural' Cemetery Movement: Urban Travail and the Appeal of Nature," *New England Quarterly* 47 (June 1974), 196–211.

Chapter 8. Searching for Eunice

For more sustained speculation, stemming from my visit to where Eunice Stone lived in Morristown, Vermont, see Martha Hodes, "Four Episodes in Re-Creating a Life," *Rethinking History: The Journal of Theory and Practice* 10 (June 2006): 277–90. For more sustained analysis on Eunice and Smiley Connolly in relation to the United States census of 1890, see Martha Hodes, "Fractions and Fictions in the United States Census of 1890," in *Haunted by Empire: Race and Colonial Intimacies in North American History*, ed. Ann Laura Stoler (Durham, N.C.: Duke University Press, 2006). I also engaged in more sustained analysis about varying memories of racial categories in "Memory, Storytelling, and Racial Classification across Borders," a paper presented to the Southern Intellectual History Circle at Radcliffe College in 2006; "Archives of Complexion: Race, Memory, and Storytelling across Borders," a paper presented to the Faculty Forum at New York University in 2005; and "Race and Memory across Borders," a paper presented to the Johns Hopkins University History Department Seminar in 2004.

On Hurricane Ivan's consequences for the Cayman Islands, see Terri Merren, ed., *Hurricane Ivan Survival Stories: as Told by the People of the Cayman Islands* (Kingston, Jamaica: Mill Press, 2005) and Sheree Ebanks and Karie Bergstrom, *Spirit of Cayman: The Aftermath of Ivan* (Grand Cayman and United States: Our Secret Agency Ltd., 2004).

ACKNOWLEDGMENTS

*M*y first expression of gratitude is reserved for the descendants of my protagonists, whose knowledge and generosity are narrated in the last chapter of this book. The late Jane Allerton Cushman welcomed me into her life (and gave permission to quote from the family letters). Heidi Jacobe and Captain James T. Cushman have kept Jane's generosity alive, and Jim sent me a veritable trove of family documents, including much that Jane had given to him before she died. William Warren Conolly and Islay Conolly welcomed me every summer, as Warren graciously shared both memory and history on his lovely veranda. Lou (Connolly) Coleman invited me to her home and to the Connolly-Conolly family reunion and, along with her husband, Al, took me visiting in East End. Cleopathra Conolly took time during the family reunion to share memories and wrote me letters when she thought of more family history. Harwell McCoy and the late Theoline (Conolly) McCoy, Dorothy McLean Welcome, Bertram Conolly, and the late East End neighbor Phoebe Watler Spence all opened their homes and took time to speak with me. James T. Conolly gave his time in New York, as did the late Ken Watler; very special thanks to James for putting me in touch with Warren.

Many other people connected to the places where Eunice and her family once lived have earned my gratitude. On Grand Cayman, the indomitable Jeanne Masters created genealogical charts, took me visiting and snorkeling, helped me search for gravestones, and kept me supplied with mangoes from her yard. JoEllen Rae-Smith made sure that Eunice and her family will be remembered in the Mariner's Memorial, and Suzy and Bob Soto continue to dedicate themselves to realizing the memorial. In New England, I thank Amanda Legare, Bill Lizotte, Paul Marion and Rosemary Noon, Lois McGee (who also crocheted me a beautiful set of coasters), and Hazel Fortin Pomiecko.

At Duke University, where this book began, I thank Linda McCurdy and Janie C. Morris, as well as William R. Erwin Jr., who cataloged the Davis Papers so beautifully. At the Cayman Islands National Archive, I benefited from the invaluable assistance of Philip Pedley, Roger Craig, Charisse Morrison, Isobel Taylor, and especially Jan Liebaers and Tamara Selzer. At the Cayman Islands National Museum, Margaret Leshikar-Denton showed me shards of pottery from Eunice's years on the island. I also received invaluable assistance from Martha Mayo at the Center for Lowell History, Lowell genealogist Arthur Paquin, Eileen O'Brien at the Manchester Historic Association, David Smolen at the New Hampshire Historical Society, Donna Gilbreth at the New Hampshire State Library, Jill Reichenbach at the New-York Historical Society, Ken Rose at the Rockefeller Archive Center, and Louise Yeoman at the National Library of Scotland. As well, I thank the staffs of all the other libraries and archives, from New England to the Deep South to Great Britain, where I pieced together Eunice's life.

Three very generous friends read a draft of the entire manuscript. James M. McPherson, my esteemed professor at Princeton University, taught me profound respect for narrative history and offered his unparalleled knowledge of the Civil War era. Susan B. Whitlock, poet and editor, brought her expert eye and beautiful literary sensibility to every shading of meaning in Eunice's story. Ben Yagoda, author of *The Sound on the Page: Style and Voice in Writing*, both read the manuscript with amazing rigor and served as ally and mentor during an important year of writing. One person read many drafts: Bruce Dorsey sagely counseled me on everything from historical context and interpretation to the placement of punctuation (and kept me laughing with his Vicki Lawrence imitations). Copyeditor Pearl Hanig read with great care and indulged my fondness for commas. Before, during, and after these gracious readers, Amy Cherry believed in this book and completely fulfilled my idealized expectations of the perfect editor. She has also become a friend, and for this I am grateful too.

For important friendship and conversation all along the way, I thank Sharon Achinstein, Ada Ferrer, James Goodman and Jennifer McFeeley, Jody Goodman and Marc Fisher, Mary Marissen and Michael Marissen, Sharon Ullman, and Bathsheba Veghte. Heartfelt thanks as well to Brigitte Bedos-Rezak, Thomas Bender, Julie Berebitsky, Jane Burbank, Fred Cooper, Sarah Cornell, Konstantin Dierks, Hasia Diner, Allison Dorsey, Nicole Eustace, Michel Gobat, Linda Gordon, Laura Gotkowitz, Adam Green, James Green, Fiona Griffiths, Leslie Harris, Walter Johnson, Sarah Knott, Paul Kramer, Barbara Krauthamer, Karen Kupperman, Rachel Mattson, Molly Nolan, Woody Register, Sarah Schulman, Bryant Simon, Moshe Sluhovsky, Christine Stansell, Ann Laura Stoler, Lisa Tessler, and Barbara Walker.

For ongoing and ever-generous support of my work, I thank Edward L. Ayers, Drew Gilpin Faust, Glenda Gilmore, James M. McPherson, Nell Irvin Painter, and Christine Stansell. David Norbrook helped me settle into research at Oxford University. Marsha Rich and Steve Camerino made me feel at home in New Hampshire. Roger Minnick at Winchester National Cemetery explained Civil War cemeteries to me. Tal Ben-David helped me compose my first letter to Jane Cushman. Robert Rosenstone inspired me in the use of italics with his pioneering work *Mirror in the Shrine: American Encounters with Meiji Japan.* I am also deeply indebted to my fellow Scholars-in-Residence at the Schomburg Center, Carolyn Brown, Leslie Harris, Debra Walker King, Jeffrey Stewart, Margaret Vendryes, and Craig Wilder, along with Colin Palmer, Zita Nunes, and Diana Lachatanere for their leadership there.

For financial assistance that permitted concentrated research, I thank the Schomburg Center for Research in Black Culture of the New York Public Library, the Gilder Lehrman Institute of American History, the Rockefeller Archive Center, the Library Company of Philadelphia, and New York University.

At New York University, I am also indebted to Thomas Bender and the conference on Internationalizing American History, cosponsored by the Organization of American Historians; the Atlantic History Workshop; the Black Cultures and Testimonies Faculty Seminar; and the Tamiment Library. Special thanks to Nancy Regalado and Evelyn B. Vitz for our NYU Humanities Council yearlong workshop on storytelling, and extra-special thanks to the talented undergraduates in my Experimental History Workshops. Michael Gomez served as a superb department chair and Ali Salamey as a superb graduate administrator, while I was serving as director of graduate studies at the same time that I was finishing this book.

For important commentary, I thank audiences at American University, Binghamton University, Bowdoin College, Brandeis University, Clark University, the College of William and Mary, Columbia University, Davidson College, Emory University, Hunter College High School, Johns Hopkins University, Princeton University, Rutgers University, Stanford University, Tulane University, the University of Chicago, the University of Michigan, the University of Richmond, Yale University, the Amistad Research Center, the Library of Congress, the American Historical Association, the Berkshire Conference on the History of Women, the British Association for American Studies, the German Association for American Studies, the New York Metropolitan American Studies Association, the Organization of American Historians, and the World History Association.

Most important, I thank my sisters Ryn Hodes and Tal Ben-David and the other members of my family who brightened my days of writing: Matthew Choi, Timothy Dorsey, Quinn Brady, Stuart Hodes, Linda Hodes, Danielle Abrams, Kevin Brady, Stephen Margolies, Dalen Cole, Julietta Cole, and the late Steve Cole. For my final expression of gratitude, reserved for Bruce Dorsey, it seems fitting to borrow Eunice's words. *From the time I first began to be aquainted with him* thirteen years ago, *I had respect for him, and that grew into love.* It is *all his kind ways and thoughtful acts prompted by love and respect which he has for me that makes it so,* and *I shall never regret linking my life with his.* There is much more but, like Eunice, *I see that I must be brief and leave much unsaid that I would like to say.*

New York, N.Y.
Swarthmore, Pa.

PERMISSIONS AND
ILLUSTRATION CREDITS

*P*ortions of this book were previously published, in a different form, in "The Mercurial Nature and Abiding Power of Race: A Transnational Family Story," *American Historical Review* 108 (February 2003), 84–118, reprinted in *American Dreaming, Global Realities: Rethinking U.S. Immigration History*, ed. Donna R. Gabaccia and Vicki L. Ruiz (Urbana: University of Illinois Press, 2006), and in "Four Episodes in Re-Creating a Life," *Rethinking History: The Journal of Theory and Practice* 10 (June 2006), 277–90.

Excerpt from "The Dry Savages" in *Four Quartets*, copyright 1941 by T. S. Eliot and renewed 1969 by Esme Valerie Eliot, reprinted by permission of Harcourt, Inc. and Faber and Faber, Ltd.

Illustrations

p. 25 Lois Wright Richardson Davis Papers. Courtesy of the Rare Book, Manuscript, and Special Collections Library, Duke University.

p. 29 *Appleton's Complete Letter Writer* (New York: D. Appleton, 1854). Courtesy of the General Research Division, The New York Public Library, Astor, Lenox and Tilden Foundations.

p. 35 Lois Wright Richardson Davis Papers. Courtesy of the Rare Book, Manuscript, and Special Collections Library, Duke University.

p. 47 George Waldo Browne, *The Amoskeag Manufacturing Co. of Manchester, New Hampshire: A History* (Manchester, N.H.: Amoskeag Manufacturing Company, 1915).

p. 55 Courtesy of the Manchester (N.H.) Visual History Collection.

p. 64   George Waldo Browne, *The Amoskeag Manufacturing Co. of Manchester, New Hampshire: A History* (Manchester, N.H.: Amoskeag Manufacturing Company, 1915).

p. 65   Courtesy of the Manchester (N.H.) Historic Association.

p. 81   Photograph by the author.

p. 106   *Regiments and Armories of Massachusetts: An Historical Narration of the Massachusetts Volunteer Militia* (Boston: W. W. Potter, 1899). Courtesy of the General Research Division, The New York Public Library, Astor, Lenox and Tilden Foundations.

p. 109   Courtesy of Heidi Jacobe.

p. 109   Courtesy of Heidi Jacobe.

p. 129   Josiah Gove, *Glimpses in and around Claremont, N.H.* (Claremont, N.H.: n.d.). Courtesy of the New Hampshire State Library.

p. 133   F. W. Beers map of Claremont, N.H., 1870s.

p. 138   *Harper's New Monthly Magazine* 14 (January 1857). Courtesy of the Fales Library and Special Collections, New York University.

p. 138   Edward Chamberlin and Co.'s Concentrated Leaven or Bread Powders. LC-USZ62-4628. Courtesy of the Library of Congress, Prints and Photographs Division.

p. 140   Lois Wright Richardson Davis Papers. Courtesy of the Rare Book, Manuscript, and Special Collections Library, Duke University.

p. 143   Otis F. R. Waite, *History of the Town of Claremont, New Hampshire for a Period of One Hundred and Thirty Years from 1764 to 1894* (Manchester, N.H.: John B. Clarke, 1895). Courtesy of the Milstein Division of United States History, Local History and Genealogy, The New York Public Library, Astor, Lenox and Tilden Foundations.

p. 149   No. F4291. Courtesy of the New Hampshire Historical Society.

p. 172   Anna L. Mower, *History of Morristown, Vermont* (Morrisville, Vt.: Messenger-Sentinel Co., 1935). Courtesy of the Milstein Division of United States History, Local History and Genealogy, The New York Public Library, Astor, Lenox and Tilden Foundations.

p. 174   Photograph by the author.

p. 185   L. Seaman, *What Miscegenation Is! What We Are to Expect Now that Mr. Lincoln Is Re-elected* (New York: Waller and Willetts, 1864). AC905 Box.S4386 W4. Courtesy of the Collection of The New-York Historical Society.

p. 188   Courtesy of Heidi Jacobe.

p. 199   Photograph by the author.

p. 200   Courtesy of the Boston Public Library.

p. 208   #XG DI 6492. Courtesy of the Cayman Islands National Archive.

p. 217   Lois Wright Richardson Davis Papers. Courtesy of the Rare Book, Manuscript, and Special Collections Library, Duke University.

p. 219   Courtesy of the Rockefeller Archive Center.

p. 228   Courtesy of William Warren Conolly, OBE JP and Burns Conolly, AIA.

p. 230 Doris Wood Levy Collection, XG/CN/290/BS/E4. Courtesy of the Cayman Islands National Archive.

p. 244 #XG DI 4707. Courtesy of the Cayman Islands National Archive.

p. 246 #XG DI 6924. Courtesy of the Cayman Islands National Archive.

p. 249 *Harper's Weekly* (Dec. 17, 1859). Courtesy of the Fales Library and Special Collections, New York University.

p. 256 James Bayles, *Lowell, Chelmsford, Graniteville, Forge Village, Dracut, Collinsville of To-day* (Lowell, Mass.: Lowell Daily Citizen, 1893). Neg. no. 78186d. Courtesy of the Collection of The New-York Historical Society.

p. 257 Photograph by the author.

p. 258 *Illustrated History of Lowell and Vicinity, Massachusetts* (Lowell, Mass.: Courier-Citizen, 1897). Neg. no. 78187d. Courtesy of the Collection of The New-York Historical Society.

p. 269 Lou Connolly Coleman Collection no. 386, Acc. no. 736, MSD277, XG/CN/315/BS/F1. Courtesy of the Cayman Islands National Archive.

p. 276 Photograph by the author. Courtesy of William Warren Conolly.

p. 279 Photograph by Alfonso H. Coleman. Courtesy of Lou (Connolly) Coleman.

p. 283 Photograph by the author. Courtesy of Bertram Conolly.

p. 284 Photograph by the author. Courtesy of Cleopathra Conolly.

p. 292 Photograph by the author. Courtesy of Heidi Jacobe.

INDEX

Page numbers in *italics* refer to illustrations.